THE ARCHITECTURE
OF REASON

RSA

Library

THE ARCHITECTURE
OF REASON

The Structure
and Substance
of Rationality

Robert Audi

OXFORD
UNIVERSITY PRESS

2001

OXFORD
UNIVERSITY PRESS

Oxford   New York

Athens   Auckland   Bangkok   Bogotá   Buenos Aires   Calcutta
Cape Town   Chennai   Dar es Salaam   Delhi   Florence   Hong Kong   Istanbul
Karachi   Kuala Lumpur   Madrid   Melbourne   Mexico City   Mumbai
Nairobi   Paris   São Paulo   Shanghai   Singapore   Taipei   Tokyo   Toronto   Warsaw

and associated companies in
Berlin   Ibadan

Copyright © 2001 by Robert Audi

Published by Oxford University Press, Inc.
198 Madison Avenue, New York, New York 10016

Oxford is a registered trademark of Oxford University Press.

Library of Congress Cataloging-in-Publication Data
Audi, Robert
The architecture of reason : the structure and substance
of rationality / by Robert Audi.
p.   cm.
Includes bibliographical references and index.
ISBN 0-19-514112-1
1. Reason.   I. Title.
BC177 .A83 2000
128'.33—dc21   00-034687

1 3 5 7 9 8 6 4 2

Printed in the United State of America
on acid-free paper

[16149]

To my colleagues,
near and far

PREFACE

This book is intended to develop and defend the core of a comprehensive, full-scale theory of rationality, applicable to practical as well as theoretical reason. Most of the philosophical literature on rationality is addressed to one or the other of these two major dimensions of reason. There is, moreover, a certain asymmetry in the treatment of the two. Theoretical rationality is addressed mainly in epistemological works; practical rationality is treated mainly in ethical works and also too infrequently as a general topic that includes not only the moral dimensions of action but also the entire realm of practical reason. Very few writers on practical reason have addressed the overall territory of reasons for action, encompassing both moral and non-moral conduct.

Even when the exploration of practical or theoretical reason is not piecemeal, it is often focused on just one major element in the domain, for instance on rational belief in the case of epistemology and on morally justified action in the case of ethics. Philosophers commonly assume that in both cases the justified and the rational are equivalent. I believe this is a mistake. If it is, then the task of understanding rationality is even more complex and challenging than it appears. Epistemology must connect rationality with justification and knowledge; the theory of practical reason must not only account for the rationality of desires, intentions, and actions but must also incorporate a distinction between the rational and the justified and between each of these and the reasonable.

Even if we have an adequate theory of rationality for theoretical and practical reason taken separately, there is a need to integrate them and ascertain their similarities and differences. And if we succeed in that, there remains the large question of what constitutes the overall rationality of persons—global rationality. This book seeks to understand theoretical and practical reason in their integrity, to articulate their parallels while taking due account of their differences, and to bring the theory that achieves this to bear in clarifying global rationality.

As compared with other philosophical approaches to rationality, particularly in the domain of action and desire, mine is informed both by a wide-ranging epistemological theory (developed particularly in my books *The Structure of Justification*, 1993, *Epistemology*, 1998, and *Moral Knowledge and Ethical Character*, 1997) and extensive previous work in action theory and moral psychology (in, for instance, my *Action, Intention, and Reason*, 1993). There are many points at which it is illuminating to view practical reason in comparison with theoretical reason epistemologically conceived, for instance to examine the basis of rational desire in relation to that of justified belief. But there is another good reason to seek an epistemologically informed conception of practical reason. If there is the degree of parity that I find between theoretical and practical reason, then some of the same problems—and resolutions—that arise in epistemology may bear on practical rationality. If, for instance, there is such parity between rational belief and rational desire, then relative to skepticism about their status, we can perhaps view the latter as no worse off than the former.

There are three further respects in which the theory of rationality set forth here differs from others proposed in the past half century. All of them affect my treatment not only of rationality but also of the closely related concepts of justification and reasonableness.

First, despite the welcome emphasis among philosophers on taking account of psychological findings in constructing philosophical theories, too few are adequately realistic in the psychology they presuppose in accounting for rationality. One error here is inferentialism: the tendency to posit far more inferences than we actually make or—unless inference is reduced to a mere brain process as opposed to a mental operation—even *can* make in the rational conduct of our lives. Another error is overascription of beliefs and other propositional attitudes, including intentions and desires, particularly in ascribing them where there is only a disposition to form them. My own theory is designed to avoid positing inferences, beliefs, and other mental elements beyond necessity.

The second respect in which my approach differs from most others in accounting for rationality is in its unabashed use of (moderate) foundationalist assumptions. As I have argued in detail elsewhere (for instance in *The Structure of Justification* and *Epistemology*), foundationalism is not widely understood and is often simplistically stereotyped; and although such well-known versions as Descartes's are certainly too strong, in some forms the position is highly plausible. We are perhaps seeing increasing recognition of this, in part because of contributions to the contemporary literature but perhaps also in part because philosophers as different as Aristotle, Aquinas, Hume, Reid, Kant, Moore, and (in my judgment) Wittgenstein and Quine hold plausible and, in some cases, enduringly resilient versions of the view.

My third point concerns an even broader philosophical matter: the contrast between rationalism and empiricism. Like foundationalism, rationalism has been largely out of favor, at least in the Anglo-American world, since the middle of the twentieth century. But it, too, will not go away and in some versions is surely plausible. Although little in this book entirely depends on rationalist assumptions, a number of my views are best understood on such assumptions. My overall position, however, has at least one major affinity to empiricism: the position is experientialist in the sense that it attributes an indispensable and indeed enormous role to experience in grounding rationality. The role I ascribe to reason in our lives is inseparable from the part played by experience, and on my view their normative authority is both shared and mutually integrated.

To argue directly and in detail for even the kinds of moderate, post-Cartesian foundationalist or rationalist principles that figure in my theory would require so much space that this would have to be a very different book—and a long one. However, where I cannot argue for something controversial, I often refer in a note to a place where I do or to other philosophical work that may help. My hope is that the overall plausibility of the position I defend will provide a context in which some of my views that may not be plausible in isolation will appear compelling, and that even those who do not accept the overall view will be able to endorse many theses argued along the way and to use many of the raw materials I provide as a basis for constructing an account of rationality from any reasonable alternative point of view.

I have sought to set out my position in a non-technical way and with sufficient clarity to reach both students of philosophy and general readers interested in rationality or related topics. For many readers, moreover, Parts II and III will be quite adequately comprehensible even apart from a close reading of the more epistemologically oriented Part I. Parts I and II taken together are in a certain way theoretically self-sufficient, but both their content and their significance are more clearly and far more widely intelligible in the light of Part III.

ACKNOWLEDGMENTS

This book has been in development for many years. Far more people than I can name have helped me in thinking about the questions it addresses. I am deeply grateful for what I have learned from them. I had a number of the basic ideas as early as 1980 when I planned my first National Endowment for the Humanities Seminar (on Reasons, Justification, and Knowledge). Participants and visiting philosophers in that and in the later NEH seminars and institutes I directed have been of incalculable help. My debt to colleagues and students, not only at the University of Nebraska, Lincoln, but at Dartmouth, Notre Dame, Santa Clara University, and elsewhere in and outside the United States, is also great. Among the philosophers with whom I have for many years beneficially discussed a number of the issues treated in this book are William Alston, Bernard Gert, Hugh McCann, Alfred Mele, Joseph Mendola, Paul Moser, Bruce Russell, Walter Sinnott-Armstrong, Ernest Sosa, and Mark van Roojen. Less frequently, but also very fruitfully, I have discussed some of the issues—and sometimes received valuable comments on my work concerning them—from Laurence BonJour, Panayot Butchvarov, John Deigh, Michael DePaul, Gilbert Harman, Brad Hooker, Christine Korsgaard, Thomas Nagel, Derek Parfit, Thomas Scanlon, Eleonore Stump, Judith Thomson, Raimo Tuomela, and Linda Zagzebski. I regret being unable to address their important work in detail (the various references to some recent works by Butchvarov, Harman, Korsgaard, Nagel, Parfit, Scanlon, and Thomson indicate only a representative portion of the writings that I would have liked to discuss).

On one or another topic of the book I have benefited from discussions or exchanges of papers (often both) with Robert Adams, Lynne Baker, John Bender, Hilary Bok, Sissela Bok, Michael Bratman, Ruth Chang, Earl Conee, David Copp, Dan Crawford, Roger Crisp, Jonathan Dancy, Stephen Darwall, Wayne Davis, Fred Dretske, Julia Driver, Robert Fogelin, Richard Foley, Elizabeth Fricker, Berys Gaut, Joshua Gert, Douglas Geivett, Allan Gibbard, Alvin Goldman, Irwin Goldstein, James Griffin, John Heil, Terence Horgan, Donald Hubin, Philip Kain, Robert Kane, Tomis Kapitan, Jaegwon Kim, Hilary Kornblith, Christopher Kulp, Jonathan Kvanvig, Keith Lehrer, Noah Lemos, Alasdair MacIntyre, John McDowell, Brian McLaughlin, Richard Miller, Elijah Millgram, James Montmarquet, James Moor, James Murphy, Onora O'Neill, George Pappas, John Perry, Paul Pines, Louis Pojman, John Post, William Prior, Elizabeth Radcliffe, Peter Railton, Amelie Rorty, David-Hillel Ruben, Geoffrey Sayre-McCord, Stefan Sencerz, Thomas Senor, Michael Smith, David Sosa, Matthias Steup, Nicholas Sturgeon, Richard Swinburne, William Throop, Mark Timmons,

William Tolhurst, Jonathan Vogel, Jay Wallace, Ralph Wedgwood, and Nicholas Wolterstorff.

A number of people have generously commented on drafts of at least part of the book: Panayot Butchvarov, Bernard Gert, John Greco, David Alan Johnson, John Longeway, Hugh McCann, Alfred Mele, Joseph Mendola, Michael Meyer, Derek Parfit, Bruce Russell, Mark Timmons, and Michael Zimmerman. I am grateful to all of them. Butchvarov, Gert, Johnson, McCann, Russell, and Timmons were exceptionally thorough-going, and their critical remarks led to many additions and improvements. Johnson, Parfit, and Russell provided numerous comments on a recent draft, and I wish time had permitted a better response to their judicious critical remarks. I have tried to respond to essentially all of the comments from readers, but the range of issues is so wide that it has been impossible to do full justice to all who have responded to earlier versions of the ideas published here.

Assistance from Oxford University Press has been extensive. I especially want to thank Peter Ohlin for editorial help and advice at several stages. His assistant, Julia Balestracci, and Jennifer Rozgonyi, from the production department, also assisted me in numerous essential tasks, and Peter Momtchiloff provided helpful information on a number of aspects of layout and production.

Although this book contains no previously published paper or chapter of mine, it does build on previous work. The first two parts in a way descend from my American Philosophical Association Presidential Address given in the spring of 1988 and appearing in the APA's *Proceedings* in the fall of that year (vol. 62, no. 1). I hope the book clarifies the main points made there and justifies some that were argued too briefly or insufficiently defended. Even here, it has been impossible to argue in the detail that would be appropriate if space were not a major constraint, or to discuss the related work of many philosophers who have helped me in the reflections that underlie this book. Limitations of time and space have permitted reference to far fewer than there are. The references and acknowledgments in the papers and books of mine that I cite express my gratitude to some of these friends and colleagues and authors, but not nearly all of them.

June 2000   R. A.
Lincoln, Nebraska

CONTENTS

Introduction: Experience and Reason   3

I   THEORETICAL REASON

    1   Groundwork   13

        1. Sources and Grounds of Justification   13
        2. Defeasibility and Prima Facie Justification   20
        3. Epistemic Autonomy   21
        4. Coherence   24
        5. Relativity and the Contextual Element in Justification   28
        6. Contextualized Foundations   29

    2   Superstructure   32

        1. Spontaneous Inference   32
        2. Inferential Belief   34
        3. Inferential Grounds   35
        4. The Transmission of Justification   38
        5. Defeasibility and the Cartesian Response to It   40
        6. Principles of Generation, Transmission, and Defeasibility   43

7. The Role of Coherence in Inferential Justification   46
8. Internal Accessibility   48
9. Justification, Rationality, and Reasons   49
10. Rationality Viewed as a Virtue Concept   55

II   PRACTICAL REASON

3   Action, Belief, and Desire   61

1. A Structural Analogy between Belief and Action   62
2. Cognitive and Behavioral Hierarchies   63
3. Inferential Belief and Intentional Action   65
4. Some Rationality Constraints on Desires   68
5. The Possibility of Rationality for Intrinsic Desire   71
6. Desires, Intentions, and Values   74
7. Foundationalist, Coherentist, and Functionalist
   Conceptions of Practical Rationality   76
8. A Procedural Instrumentalism   79

4   The Sources of Practical Reasons   81

1. The Phenomenology of Intrinsic Desire   81
2. Pleasure as an Object of Intrinsic Desire   83
3. Elemental Desires   86
4. Agent-Centered Aspects of Desire   89
5. Three Kinds of Desire   91
6. Pleasure, Pain, and the Good   94
7. Experience as a Locus of Value   98
8. Intrinsic Value and Inherent Value   99
9. A Cognitive Analogue of Basic Rational Desires   101
10. Practical Skepticism and the Egocentric
    Point of View   104
11. Desire and Valuation   106

5   Desires, Intentions, and Reasons for Action   108

1. Desire and Intention   108
2. Rational Desire and Reasons for Action   112

3. *The Authority of the Theoretical over the Practical* 114
4. *Instrumentally Rational Action* 116
5. *Beliefs as Underlying Elements in*
   Rational Actions 117
6. *Some Major Kinds of Reasons for Action* 119
7. *The Normative Power of Desire* 122
8. *Difficulties for Instrumentalism* 123
9. *Hedonic Value, Desire, and Reasons for Action* 127
10. *The Internal Grounds of Rational Action* 129
11. *The Mutual Irreducibility of Practical*
    and Theoretical Reason 131

6   Others as Ends   135

1. *Rationality from the Inside Out* 136
2. *Altruism as a Rational Disposition* 139
3. *The Limited Priority of the Near at Hand* 145
4. *Toward a Reasonable Altruism* 148
5. *Obstacles to Recognizing the Rationality of*
   Altruistic Desires 153
6. *Altruism as a Basis for Moral Dispositions* 155
7. *Altruism as a Pathway to Moral Principles* 157
8. *The Status of Moral Reasons* 162
9. *Practical Reason and the Epistemic Autonomy*
   of Ethics 165
10. *Cognitivism and Objectivity* 166

III   RATIONALITY AND RELATIVITY

7   Relativity, Plurality, and Culture   171

1. *Rationality and the Space of Relativity* 172
2. *Relativity to Grounds* 173
3. *Genetic Relativity* 176
4. *Relativity of Rational Content* 178
5. *Conceptual Relativity* 179
6. *Doxastic Relativity* 180
7. *Relativity of Normative Status* 182

8. *The Permissiveness of Rationality*   185
9. *The Practice Conception of Rationality*   188
10. *Objectivity and Realism in the Theory of Rationality*   191

8   Global Rationality   195

1. *The Range of Criteria for Global Rationality*   196
2. *Desire, Belief, and Will*   199
3. *The Rationality of Attitudes and Emotions*   202
4. *Structural Features of Global Rationality*   204
5. *Integration and Coherence*   207
6. *Voluntariness and Autonomy*   211
7. *Substantive Elements in Rationality*   213
8. *The Substantive Latitude of the Concept of Happiness*   215
9. *The Place of Other-Regarding Desire in Global Rationality*   218
10. *Reason and Morality*   221
11. *Rationality, Reasonableness, and Irrationality*   222
12. *The Internal Constitution of Rationality*   223

Conclusion   227

Notes   235

Index   277

THE ARCHITECTURE
OF REASON

INTRODUCTION
Experience and Reason

Listening to a fine performance of Beethoven's "Appassionata" from the eighth row just left of center, I am flooded with sounds, fascinated by the sight of the pianist's moving fingers, and conscious of the integration between the two. I hear melodic statement and restatement, the harmony of chords, the grace of delicate arpeggios, the resonance of the bass. I see the sweep of the arms, the intricate work of the fingers, and the spaces appearing and disappearing as the white keys are played. The piano forms the immediate background of what I see as I watch the artist, but I also see the surrounding stage in the distance and, nearer by, the audience sitting in front of me. This experience is utterly dominating. Sound and sight occupy my consciousness completely.

Even thinking about the musical experience itself can detract from the enjoyment of it. A soft overtone is easily missed by divided attention. Yet it can be rewarding to think about such experiences, and philosophers must sometimes do so. My musical experience, as a perceptual response to what I hear and see, is a source of knowledge; and, as an enjoyable response to those sounds and sights, it is a source of value and a ground of rational desire for more of the same. From what I hear and see, there is a great deal that I can know and much that I can appreciate. The sights and sounds provide grounds for a multitude of beliefs about them and for valuing the performance that yields them. On the basis of what I see and hear, I have a great quantity of information—about the colors and shapes of things, the number of people present, the acoustics, the restiveness of someone to my right—far more information than I need. My experience also yields grounds for valuing the performance: it comes

3

through to me as expressive and moving, vigorous yet delicate, technically polished but not mechanical.

I need not have thought of these qualities of the performance in order to be moved by them. The basis of my appreciation need not be articulated in my thinking. It may indeed resist formulation even when I recall the performance vividly. Our experience provides grounds for knowing and valuing its objects, but it does not label those grounds as such, and they can evoke many kinds of responses in us without being conceptualized. We may need to have learned the difference between musical excellence and technical virtuosity in order to be fully moved by the former and properly cool to the latter. But musical appreciation does not require conceiving what we hear under any such description, and the effort to label a feature of our experience can easily obscure or falsify what our words are meant to capture.

It is no accident that I begin with an experience that is at once perceptual and rewarding. My interest is in how experience is connected with reason, both theoretical and practical. A rewarding perceptual experience such as we can have in hearing beautiful music provides grounds, and thereby in a sense reasons—normative reasons—in both the theoretical and the practical domains. If we think of theoretical reasons as reasons to believe, and of practical reasons as reasons to act, we can see how the aesthetic experience I have described provides both. It is obvious (to non-skeptics, at least) that its perceptual elements yield good grounds and, at least indirectly, good reasons, for beliefs. Surely its rewarding qualities, those in virtue of which we enjoy it, provide reasons for action: that rare integration of melody, harmony, and crescendo gives us a reason for continuing to listen, for attending a similar performance in the future, and for commending the program to others who may reap comparable rewards from hearing it next week.

Both kinds of reasons, theoretical and practical, have explanatory as well as justificatory roles. I can at once explain and justify my belief that the piano was a concert grand because I distinctly recall its length and know that only the concert size is that long. I can both explain and justify my judging the performance to be a good one by describing the basis on which I appreciate it: its emotional power, its delicacy, its exquisite integration of technique and expressiveness. It is possible, however, for something to explain a belief or an action without justifying it. Depression might explain, without in the least justifying, a belief that one is incompetent. The connection between explanation and justification is a major concern of the theory of rationality, and I will explore it at several points.

Philosophers have written a great deal on theoretical reason; it is roughly the topic of epistemology. There is also a large philosophical literature on

4

practical reason, though it is small by comparison with the more volumi-nous works in epistemology, and it is often focused on practical reason in relation to morality rather than—as in this book—in its full generality as concerning reasons for action and desire. There is only a much more lim-ited literature on rationality conceived as encompassing both the theoreti-cal and the practical domains. This is in part because there may be a wide-spread sense that a unified comprehensive theory of rationality is beyond reach. After all, neither actions nor the motivating elements underlying them, such as desires and intentions, are even true or false. This indicates a profound difference between these practical elements and the central theoretical attitudes, such as belief, which are true or false. Moreover, the practical elements seem to be subjective or, as regards their rationality, "relative," in a way beliefs apparently are not. How, then, can a unified theory account for both practical and theoretical rationality?

There is another source of resistance to the idea that a unified compre-hensive theory of rationality can be achieved. It is the powerful influence of the instrumentalist tradition, epitomized in the history of philosophy by David Hume. For pure instrumentalism about practical reason, its func-tion is to serve desire: our basic desires—by which I mean simply those not based on further desires—are not in general open to evaluation as ration-al or irrational; those categories of assessment apply, in the practical sphere, chiefly to actions and to instrumental desires, desires for things as a means (in some sense) to something further. The counterpart view for basic beliefs—roughly, those not based on further beliefs—is not plausible. Beliefs based on perception, for instance, surely are appraisable as ration-al or (in principle) not rational. What we (normal people) believe on the basis of sight or hearing is typically rational, whereas refusing to believe what one's senses indicate is not rational except in special cases, as where we know the lighting distorts perspective.

The influence of instrumentalism about practical reason, then, tends to leave theoretical reason unaffected. But the theory has convinced many that basic desires, the most important motivators of action, cannot be con-sidered rational or irrational. In the minds of many philosophers and psy-chologists, the plausibility of the theory has dimmed the prospects for a unified account of rationality; for many of them, whatever rationality ulti-mate grounds of action may have lies on the theoretical side.

If, contrary to instrumentalism, experience may provide normative rea-sons for both belief and desire, then it may presumably be a basis of both theoretical and practical rationality. The theoretical reasons can ground justified (and hence rational) beliefs; the practical reasons can ground rational desire. There are differences as well as similarities between the basis of rational belief and that of rational desire, as will be apparent in much of this book. The central question is whether these similarities and differences can be integrated in a way that permits an illuminating general account of rationality. I believe that they can be.

In arguing for this, I start (in Chapter 1) with a brief account of theoretical reason, particularly its basis. What are the sources of justified beliefs? How are such beliefs grounded? How does their justification vary from one context to another? How may their justification be defeated by, say, counter-evidence? What is the role of coherence or incoherence in this grounding or defeat? And is such defeat itself based on the same kinds of grounds as the justification it vanquishes?

Assuming we have justified beliefs, how can other beliefs be justified on the basis of them? This is a central question pursued in Chapter 2, which explores how justification is transmitted from one belief to another, as where one acquires justification for believing a proposition by inferring it from something else that one already justifiedly believes. An account of theoretical reason must also consider knowledge. Knowledge is not merely justified true belief, and its relation both to theoretical justification and to practical rationality is quite complicated.

In discussions of theoretical reason it has been standard to take knowledge and justification as the fundamental notions to be accounted for, and I do this. But in both Chapters 1 and 2 I consider the relation between justification and rationality. I do so not only because my aim is to understand rationality in relation to kindred notions but also because rationality has been more fundamental than knowledge, and even justification, in discussions of practical reason, which encompasses both moral justification and any other kind of rational consideration—say, prudential, altruistic, or aesthetic—that supports action. All three—rationality, justification, and knowledge—are based on reasons, and Chapter 2 distinguishes several kinds of reasons we must understand in order to see how they are so based.

There is still another reason to clarify the relation between justification and rationality: a major aim of a general theory of rationality should be to provide an understanding of the overall rationality of persons. Here the notion of justification must be recognized as an element in that rationality. But (I argue) it differs in application: the notion of justification as applied to persons is narrower than that of rationality applicable to them, and not precisely parallel. Justification applies to people, as opposed to their actions and attitudes, only with respect to specific matters, such as actions and beliefs; their rationality is a global property. Persons are justified only in a relative sense: in believing something or other, or in doing one or another deed. We are rational (or not) overall.

Once we develop an account of theoretical reason (the task of Part I), we can assess the prospects for a parallel conception of practical reason (the task of Part II). That there should be at least some significant parallels might be expected from the applicability, in both domains, of many of the same terms of description and appraisal: 'rationality' and 'irrationality', 'justified' and 'unjustified', 'groundless' and 'well-grounded', 'basic', 'reflective', 'reasoned', and others. The parallels between the theoretical and the practical are extensive. I first (in Chapter 3) consider the structural ones, such as the analogy between, on the one hand, inferential beliefs and the beliefs they are based on and, on the other hand, instrumental desires (desires for things as means) and the basic desires to which they are subordinate. Beliefs of conclusions we infer from certain premises can be justified by our beliefs of those premises. Desires with certain contents can be justified by further desires, above all when the former are desires to take means toward satisfying the latter, "premise" desires. Chapter 3 will also explicate some major substantive parallels between theoretical and practical reason. Can there be rational intrinsic ("basic") desires, as there apparently can be rational non-inferential (and in that sense basic) beliefs? And is there in the theory of practical reason a contrast between foundationalist and coherentist theories, as in the theoretical case?

When the main structural parallels between theoretical and practical reason have been described, we can fruitfully consider (in Chapter 4) basic practical reasons. A central issue here, which is discussed extensively in Chapter 5 as well, is whether practical reason is substantive or only instrumental. Are basic practical reasons, as instrumentalism says, determined simply by our non-instrumental desires, above all by what we want for its own sake? This would not entail egoism but yields a form of it on the assumption that our basic desires are self-interested. Egoism, in a normative form, is critically examined in this chapter. So is hedonism, for which pleasure and pain are the fundamental sources of practical reasons.

Chapter 4 also considers what metaphysical commitments a theory of practical rationality must make if it embraces some apparently irreducible normative notion, such as that of intrinsic value. Must a theory of practical reason take normative properties, such as the injustice of a deed, to have causal power in determining behavior, so that they may take their place among the properties of chief interest to empirical science? Or can it treat normative properties as non-causal and take normative terms as sui generis, whether because of what they describe or because, as noncognitivists hold, normative vocabulary is not primarily descriptive at all but functions chiefly to express moral and other evaluative attitudes?

With practical reason, as with theoretical reason, there is an important difference between reasons that are in some sense basic and those based on further reasons. Beliefs, actions, and desires can all be rational on the basis of rational elements that "transmit" rationality to them. There are, for instance, beliefs justified by and hence rational on the basis of inference from premises, and there are desires rational because their fulfillment is believed to be necessary for realizing further desires. It may be quite rational to want to swim even when one is tired and dreads the prospect, because it can be quite clear that swimming will contribute to maintaining good health, which one quite rationally desires. By contrast, just as I may believe that there is, say, white paper here on the basis on my visual experience, rather than on the basis of some further belief, I may want good health on a basis other than a desire for something further, to which I take good health to be a means. What sorts of relationships hold between desires that are, for the agent, basic, as a desire to maintain good health might be, and desires based on those, such as the desire to swim? And how might desires, taken together with beliefs, justify actions? These are among the central questions explored in Chapter 5.

Such questions quickly lead us to the matter of defeasibility: a prima facie rational desire may turn out, because of the perceived unpleasant consequences of satisfying it, not to be rational on balance. It may initially be rational to want surgery, but it may cease to be so when one discovers a less risky treatment. The same holds for the action of requesting such surgery. These are cases of the defeat of the rationality of the want or the instrumentally subordinate action. There are parallels for beliefs, as where the discovery of distorting reflections defeats the justification of an incautiously formed belief about the color of a fabric. We must try to understand not only what produces rationality but also what defeats it and how the two are related.

Much of what we want, such as food and entertainment and good company, we want for our own consumption or enjoyment; but we can also want those same sorts of things for other people. Indeed, if we love other people, we must want certain kinds of things not only *for them*, but *for their sake*. If parents want success for their children only in order to bring credit on themselves, this desire, despite being directed at the children's well-being, does not bespeak love. Does love, so conceived, imply a measure of irrationality? Can we, as egoists hold, rationally want something for others only so far as it will lead to something we want for ourselves? I think not. But it is a further question whether, given an ordinary knowledge of how others are like us, a kind of altruism is rationally demanded of us. If it is, then practical reason provides at least a limited foundation for ethics, in the sense that a rational person will, under certain conditions, have adequate reason to treat others in accordance with some basic moral principles. This is a major issue pursued in Chapter 6 once the general account of rationality is articulated.

It is obvious that rational persons disagree about some important matters and that even a high degree of rationality in persons is consistent with great diversity among them. Is there a kind of relativity built into the notion of rationality, or at least consistent with it, say, relativity to one's own experience or culture? This is a central question in Chapter 7. If many kinds of grounds may sustain rational elements in persons, there should be a plurality of rational ideals. But there are also constant elements that play a prominent role in the make-up of rational persons, least controversially a measure of simple logicality. An adequate theory of rationality must do justice both to the variability that marks different ranges of experience and diverse cultural settings and to the constancies that, because of important elements in our humanity, can be expected as recurring elements, at least in any civilized society.

As conceived in this book, rationality is not just a critical tool or a minimal standard for belief, desire, valuation, and action. It also represents an ideal to which we can aspire for our lives as a whole. If theoretical and practical rationality are the two basic kinds, we should expect a rational person to be rational in both respects, even if sometimes more in one than the other. This is surely how it is. If we have a unified, comprehensive account of rationality for both domains, we should have much of the theoretical material needed to understand the notion of a rational person. One of my aims is to provide such an understanding (this is the project of Chapter 8). But the matter is complicated. There are tradeoffs; for instance, a high degree of theoretical rationality might counterbalance some degree of practical irrationality, and no rational person need exhibit rationality all of the time. Some irrational actions, and even isolated moments of a wider irrationality, are compatible with the overall rationality of a person. Indeed, if some things, such as certain emotions, may fail to be rational without being *ir*rational, then it is entirely consistent with being a rational person that one cultivate certain non-rational elements in oneself and allow them to play a significant role in one's life.

The notion of a rational person has many dimensions, and the account we need will not simply fall in place when the other work is done. Even if we understand rational belief, rational desire, and all the other concepts of rationality that apply to aspects of persons or their conduct, we must still integrate our results in a way that provides an overall view of what constitutes a rational person. We need such a view, as well as a better understanding of rationality for belief, desire, action, and other notions central in characterizing persons. A major problem of our age is how to develop and express compelling ideals of rationality that respect human differences yet can also unify us in many of the endeavors common to us as civilized people. As individuals, moreover, we need standards for self-appraisal and self-improvement. The theory of rational persons to be offered here is intended as a contribution toward these ends.

PART I

THEORETICAL REASON

GROUNDWORK

The architecture that surrounds us is quite varied. There are differences in shape, height, composition, and style. But every building has some foundation, even if it is as shifting as planks on a sandy beach. It also has a superstructure rising from that foundation, even if it is just a single story. The metaphor of foundations and superstructure has, at least since Aristotle, seemed to many philosophers to apply to our beliefs.[1] It is one thing, of course, to take it to apply to the psychology of belief: to maintain, for instance, that our beliefs are ultimately based on experience in some causal way and that they divide into the experiential in the foundations and the inferential in the superstructure. It is quite another to apply this architectural metaphor to normative notions: to hold, for example, that what ultimately justifies those of our beliefs that are justified is some aspect of experience. Similar questions arise for rationality. It is essential that we both distinguish and connect the psychological and epistemic aspects of the metaphor. I will, then, consider the architectural picture in both the psychology and the epistemology of cognition, particularly in relation to the development and structure of belief on the psychological side and, on the epistemological side, in relation to justification and knowledge.

1. SOURCES AND GROUNDS OF JUSTIFICATION

When I look directly at the piano keyboard before me in the full light of the concert stage, I plainly see its ebony and ivory, the fallboard behind the keys, and the raised top. This visual experience is a ground both *of* beliefs I have and *for* a multitude of beliefs I could have but do not form. The experience is thus both a causal and a normative ground. I take note of the prominence of the maker's name in gold letters, and I believe that the letters are in a gothic font. I also see the spaces between the keys; but these I do not attend to, and I form no belief about them. Seeing them clearly, however, I have in that very experience a justification for believing that they are not two inches wide. That is obvious from what I see, and my justification for believing it is so good that I not only may rationally believe it, in the sense that my believing it would be consonant with reason, but should believe it if (as is unlikely) the proposition occurs to me: it would be unreasonable not to believe it. Granted, if I happened to be asked if the spaces were that wide, I would readily say that they are not, and would believe what I said. But it does not follow that I had formed this belief before there was any occasion to do so, and it is doubtful that I did.[2] Our justification for believing something may precede the belief itself, and some grounds for justification never issue in belief at all.

I am of course taking the notion of justification to be applicable to belief, even if its more common employment is in connection with action.[3] There is no question that one may *justify* a belief by arguing for it. This is roughly a process of providing one or more premises that support the proposition believed. The justifiedness of belief may be understood on this basis: it is the property a belief possesses in virtue of being based on grounds of a kind that a successful justification of it would provide. These grounds might be either premises for the proposition believed or something experiential, such as a perceptual basis for holding the belief. The notion of justified belief, then, is no less clear than that of a belief based on justifying grounds citable in meeting a challenge of the belief. That notion is both clear enough for the work it will do here and epistemologically indispensable.

There are countless things that a single experience justifies one in believing. This is the point to be stressed here. It matters less whether one holds that the propositions in question are in some implicit way believed: the ground for believing them is there, whether or not it produces all the beliefs it can justify. In my view, nature does not build, or incline us to build, unnecessarily; but everyday experience does give us materials to build as the need arises. Nature is at once psychologically economical and normatively generous. Perception underdetermines belief, producing far fewer beliefs than it can support; but it overdetermines justification, providing justifying grounds for far more beliefs than we normally form and yielding far more justification than we need as warrant for many beliefs we do form.

14

Hearing is quite like seeing in all this. There is the auditory experience of the music, there are certain beliefs evoked by it, and there are multitudinous dispositions to form beliefs should appropriate questions or needs arise. I hear a rolling melody in the left hand; I notice the rich tones and form the belief that the piano has a good bass. I acquire justification for believing, but need not in fact believe—or disbelieve—the musically unimportant proposition that some of the melody is above middle C.

As different as the senses are from one another in quality, they all have the capacity to ground belief and its justification as I have illustrated. But the senses are not our only sources of belief and justification. Looking inward in a self-conscious moment, I am aware of my musical experience. This awareness provides a ground for justified introspective beliefs whether I form them or not. It has this much in common with sensory experience, though in other ways introspection and sensory experience are quite different.[4]

Memory should also be recognized as a source of justifying grounds and, in that sense, a source of justification. Suppose that after the concert I am asked whether the pianist was wearing a long sleeveless dress. I may have noticed that she was and simply remember this; or I may have retained a sufficiently definite image of her which I as it were consult, forming the belief that she wore a long sleeveless dress only on the basis of that image; or, quite apart from imagery, it may simply seem to me, as I consider the question, that she was wearing a long dress. (That in this third case I am remembering and not merely imagining might be confirmed by my recognizing the dress when I see it later.) In each case, I may be memorially justified in believing that she wore a long dress. In the first case, memory can preserve both my belief and its justification; in the second, it preserves the basis of that justification: my image. In the third, something we might call the sense of remembering is what both yields and justifies my belief.

Memory is different from perception and introspection, the other common experiential sources of justification, in at least three respects. First, memory is preservative in a way introspection is not. The latter, unlike the former, occurs contemporaneously with its object and dies with its disappearance. Memory often preserves a non-propositional memorial ground of justification, as in the case of the retained image of the pianist. Second, even where memory is a source of justification, it is apparently not by itself a source of belief: for instance, it is perception that produces the belief that the pianist is wearing a long dress; memory retains this belief. Third, memory is not, in the same basic way as perception, a source of knowledge. I may know something *from* memory, but not unless I came to know it in some other way, as by seeing that it is so. Knowledge from memory is more like a book from a library than like fruit from a tree. For knowledge, memory is preservative, not generative.[5]

Perception, introspection, and memory have been conceived as experiential sources of justification: each provides, in the distinctive elements it brings to consciousness, justificatory grounds. It is chiefly these grounds that philosophers have had in mind in contrasting experience with reason as a source of belief and justification. Compare, for instance, justification based on what one hears and justification based on elementary logical intuition, as in an awareness that if some bears are pets, then some pets are bears. There is ample warrant to contrast experience and reason, particularly if the kinds of justification acquired in each case are importantly different. But the contrast can mislead. The *use* of reason requires having an experience of some kind, and, often, having an experience implies the use of reason.[6] Nonetheless, even if the use of reason requires having an experience, say one of considering some proposition, it does not follow that this experience is what justifies every belief arrived at through that use of reason.

For some purposes we may want an overall rubric for the four standard sources of belief and justification—perception, introspection (consciousness, in one sense), memory, and reason. To frame it we can simply distinguish between intuitive, or, in one sense, reflective, experience and the other kinds just described: sensory, introspective, and memorial. We may then construe all basic justification as broadly experiential. Consider, for example, the question whether a desire must have an object, that is, be *for* something. Just from reflecting on the concepts that figure in the question, we can be justified in believing that this is so; and if I believe this on the basis of sufficient reflection about the question, I am justified in believing it.

If we regard reflection as a kind of experience, then the justification here is experiential; if we restrict the notion of experience to objects in the empirical world and construe the relevant reflection as concerning abstract objects, or at least as different from, and not evidentially dependent on, perceptual or introspective experience, then the justification should not be considered experiential. The clearest terminology preserves the distinction between experiential and reflective (intuitive) justification, whatever theory one holds about their nature. But it is important to see that a kind of experience, in the sense of mental activity or conscious awareness, occurs in both cases and, in each, supplies grounds for many more beliefs than we need to form.

Each of the four sources of belief and justification, then, may be said both to *provide* justification *for* believing and to *confer* justification *on* beliefs: on

16

actual beliefs appropriately based on those sources.[7] This terminology is common and not inappropriate, but strictly speaking the sources provide, in the sense that their operation gives us, *grounds* of justification, and it is these that confer justification. Our perceptual capacities, for instance, enable us to see things, and the visual experiences we thereby have are grounds of visually justified beliefs. It is quite similar with the other three sources, and in speaking of sources of justification and of their conferring justification, or as simply justifying beliefs, this is the idea we should keep in mind.

Some philosophers may here think of a dilemma put forward by Wilfrid Sellars: if experiences are non-conceptual, they do not stand in need of justification but have none to give; and if they are conceptual (e.g., entailing belief), they may provide justification but also stand in need of it and hence cannot play a foundational role.[8] This argument may be buttressed by the idea that only propositions stand in logical relations to the propositional objects of beliefs, and non-conceptual experiences can at best stand in causal relations to the beliefs in question. The commonest response to accepting the argument is to claim that only a coherence theory of justification can succeed. This argument and related ones have been discussed at length by many philosophers, and there is no need here to deal with it in detail.[9] Several points, however, may be made briefly.

First, the argument depends for much of its plausibility on the idea that justification, like money, can be received only from what has it. To assume this without argument is to beg the question against the intuitive, common-sense view that perceptual grounds can confer justification, as opposed to transmitting it. Granted, in justifying a claim that it is densely foggy by saying (e.g.) 'I see dense fog', one expresses a belief whose content is "conceptualized." But that the *expression* or indication of one's ground is conceptual does not necessarily mean that one's ground itself is. Citing a ground in this justificatory way is intrinsically conceptual. Citing it in this way, however, constitutes giving it as a *reason* in defense of the claim being supported or explained; the reason, though it indicates the source of one's ground (vision), is not itself that ground (visual experience). The *fact* that I see it is my reason—and a good one—because it identifies my ground.

Second, suppose the ground itself *is* conceptual, as with seeing a green arrow as such. This may require conceptualizing what one experiences in terms of the concept of an arrow. It does not follow that the grounding visual *experience* needs or even admits of justification, and neither seems to be the case. The conceptual, as opposed to the doxastic (the belief-constituted) need not admit of justification.

Third, an experience may have *qualities*, such as the visual sense of the dense grey of fog, that—quite apart from whether they are believed to

17

belong to it—*can* stand in "logical" relations to the content of the proposition believed. The phenomenal property of my having a visual impression of grey is in a certain way appropriate to the property of being grey: the internal instantiation of the former is at least arguably best explained by causation by the external instantiation of the latter.

A fourth point here concerns the very notion at issue. The justification relation is epistemic, not logical. Conferral of justification, then, need not (at least on that count) be inferential. This point is easily missed because 'justification' has a process sense as well as a status sense, and plainly the process *is* conceptual.[10] The two senses are related in the way I described in arguing that the notion of justification applies to beliefs: roughly, they possess the property (justifiedness) provided that the process as directed toward them would succeed. Nothing about the notion of justification entails that justifiedness can never be experientially rather than inferentially grounded. A ground that confers it, moreover, may stand in a broadly causal relation to the belief justified by it (as well as in other sorts of relations).

None of this is to suggest that coherence has no place in understanding justification. It will soon be shown to have an important role in this quite consistent with the conception of justification (and rationality) being developed. It should be stressed, however, that coherence itself does not admit of justification and hence must be viewed as, like experiential grounds, conferring it rather than transmitting it. Once certain facts are seen in perspective, what is plausible in the Sellarsian dilemma can be accommodated without accepting its conclusion.

I have spoken of four basic sources of justification. I doubt that any general argument shows that there can be no other basic sources, i.e., sources whose justificatory power is non-derivative, in the sense that it does not come from further sources. But it is not clear that there are other basic sources, particularly considering how broad the notion of perception is.[11] Perception is not necessarily tied to the five senses. It could occur through some other causally sensitive modality associated with the right sorts of experiential responses.[12] I will, then, sometimes refer to these four sources of justification as the standard sources, but I leave open the possibility of other basic sources.

The theory I am developing can also provide for a variety of non-derivative sources of justification and knowledge. This need not require radical changes in the theory, as opposed, say, to broadening the range of experiential qualities relevant to justifying beliefs. There is, however, no reason to think that any other sources play the same role in the notion of justification that operates in the standard descriptive and critical practices of

18

normal adults.[13] It appears that the four standard sources of justification are the only sources of it which do not need to earn their justificational credentials, as extrasensory perception presumably would, by correlation with one or another kind of ground already taken to generate justification. The visual impression of rain, for instance, unquestionably provides a measure of justification to believe that it is raining. Consider, by contrast, a bodily sensation that I take to indicate that it is raining. If it can provide justification, it must first be seen to do so, as where it is traced to an arthritic joint that reliably reacts to the weather.

How is the justification we have been exploring to be conceived? The notion is too basic to admit of analysis in terms of a set of notions that are at once simple and significantly less problematic. We might say that a justified belief is one that there is adequate reason for the believer to think true; but, as suggestive as this is, it transfers the burden of analysis to the relevant notion of adequate reason. We can say that a justified belief is one that is rationally acceptable, which, in turn, might be taken to mean that one does not deserve criticism, from the point of view of rationality, for holding it.[14] But does being beyond rational criticism imply justification? I think not. I could escape such criticism for holding an unjustified belief if it has been ineradicably implanted in me by brain manipulation. In any case, this kind of analysis invites assimilation of justification to rationality, which will shortly be shown to be significantly different and is surely also no easier to understand. One might say that justified beliefs are those that are reliably produced or sustained.[15] One might also say that a justified belief is one that appropriately expresses epistemic virtue.[16] These views each have something to recommend them. I cannot discuss them here, but the account I offer will capture many of their plausible features.

On my view, and in broad terms that will be clarified in this chapter and the next, justification, for any kind of element, is *well-groundedness* of a rather full-blooded sort, ample well-groundedness, we might say; and *a* justification is roughly an adequate ground. For beliefs, one kind of adequate grounding is the sort that commonly goes with a belief's directly (non-inferentially) resting on one or more of the standard sources I have described. Another, to be described in Chapter 2, is (adequate) *indirect* grounding—roughly, inferential grounding—in those same sources. It seems to me that it is because a justified belief is well-grounded that it has most of the properties, such as permissibility, reasonableness, and appropriateness to epistemic virtue, that other accounts stress. What a theory of justification should do is provide a good indication of how justification arises, how it is transmitted and communicated, how it may be strengthened or overridden, what sorts of things have it, and how they are con-

nected with other things that have it and with the wider notion of rationality. A well-groundedness theory can provide the basic materials needed
to account for each of these five aspects of justification, both for the case
of belief and for other cases, such as that of action and desire, that will be
explored in Part II.[17]

2. DEFEASIBILITY AND PRIMA FACIE JUSTIFICATION

If we now try to characterize justification in a way that enables us to see
how one justified belief is connected with others, we encounter a problem: defeasibility. If there is any indefeasible justification, that is, justification that cannot be overridden or undermined, there is little of it. Descartes
surely believed something to the effect that one has indefeasible justification for the proposition that one exists. Simple logical truths seem to be
an even better candidate, for instance the proposition that if Jane Austen
is identical with the author of *Emma*, then the author of *Emma* is identical
with Jane Austen. But certainly the kinds of justification of greatest interest to philosophers and others who consider such matters are defeasible.
My justification for believing that the pianist wore a long dress may be
overridden by the firm contrary testimony of two others who sat closer and
who explain to me how I got a false impression.

My justification may also be undermined, as where I discover that for
some reason I have, in retrospect, mistakenly believed most of the female
soloists I have heard lately to have worn long dresses. Here the problem is
not counter-evidence that overrides my grounds (I might happen to have
good, unopposed grounds for believing this particular pianist wore a long
dress). It is evidence of my unreliability in the relevant matter: I can see
that if I was correct, it was by good fortune, not from reliable observation.
In the usual cases of overridden justification, a contrary proposition turns
out to be better justified for me. In the case of discovered unreliability,
the belief I hold simply turns out to be ill-grounded.

Even justification grounded in a standard source, then, need not be
indefeasible. It also has a second, related property: it is prima facie. The
reason is not that it is weak (though it may be), but that (at least typically)
even a basic source provides only grounds that may not, on balance, justify. Moreover, when one's grounds do justify, defeat may still occur. Even
when I am justified overall in believing that the dress was long, sufficiently
plausible conflicting testimony can override my justification. Defeasibility,
then, does not imply mere prima facie justification; defeat may befall even
justification on balance. If the belief is true, this may imply that the counter-

evidence, in turn, can in principle be defeated; but it need not in fact be defeated even if it can be. Misleading evidence need never be exposed for what it is.

The defeasibility of (prima facie) justification must not be assimilated to its eliminability. The point is not that when defeat occurs, prima facie grounds are eliminated or rendered inoperative. Just as the grounds for keeping a promise may remain even when one must break it—leaving one obligated to make an apology to the promisee—evidential grounds retain epistemic weight even when overbalanced by counter-evidence and even when undermining evidence shows that they do not carry enough weight in the circumstances to sustain (overall) justification. Compare the case of a defeated ground with one of belief arising from wishful thinking. Where I seem to remember that the pianist wore a long dress, there is some reason for thinking that she did, even if I ought to recall my frequent sartorial mistakes. There is no such reason for believing it where I have simply fabricated an attractive image and allowed myself to take it as veridical. The first case is one of epistemic mitigation, the second of epistemic irresponsibility.[18]

The defeaters just illustrated in relation to memory beliefs have a special feature. Their capacity to defeat justification grounded in memory apparently presupposes that this very faculty does produce prima facie justification. If it did not, how could testimony about the past (which epistemically depends on memory) justify disbelieving or even doubting what someone else believes? But if the defeaters we have noted depend to some degree on memory, memory is not all that they depend on. In one of the cases, a crucial factor is non-memorial justification for believing that two people credibly deny the proposition believed. In the other, two factors are crucial. The first is remembering that one has been mistaken in similar cases; the second is justification one originally had, presumably through perception or testimony, for believing that one has turned out to be mistaken.

It may happen, moreover, that the very same sense yields a defeater of a belief which it itself has produced. If an object that feels warm to one hand feels cool to the other, the justification of an initial belief that it is warm may be defeated. The balance can of course shift, as where one acquires reason to think that the second hand is hot from sunlight.

3. EPISTEMIC AUTONOMY

Far more could be said about defeasibility, and further points will emerge as we return to it in different contexts. But it raises one theoretical question that should be addressed now. Do all the defeaters of beliefs that are well-grounded in the standard sources of justification derive their defeating power from those same sources? The more general question here is whether, collectively, the standard sources are justificationally *self-sufficient*, that is, roughly speaking, self-sustaining, in providing for all the justifying grounds of belief; and justificationally self-correcting, at least in providing for all the grounds of defeat of justification. Are they, taken together, necessarily such that if a belief enjoys adequate support from at least one of them, hence is properly evidenced, and that support is not defeated by at least one other, then it is justified on balance? This self-sufficiency thesis has some plausibility, but it would take a great deal of discussion to show whether or not it holds.

We can go some distance toward appraising the self-sufficiency thesis by exploring a related question: whether the standard basic sources are *autonomous*. There are two main possibilities: first, that each source yields the justification it does independently of confirmation from any other source—call this *individual autonomy;* second, that only the entire set of basic sources meets this independence condition—call this *collective autonomy*, a freedom from the need for confirmation by any fifth source. There is also the possibility of a negative kind of individual autonomy: invulnerability to defeat by beliefs from another source, as where seeing a building yields a belief that there is a building before one and this belief is unthreatened by a memory belief that, minutes ago, a vacant lot stood in its place.

As this example indicates, invulnerability to defeat from one source may be combined with vulnerability to another. If seeing an object can yield justification that overrides that of a memory belief that the object no longer exists, justification of a visual belief may be overridden by that of a tactual one.[19] If you see a statue in the square, you probably are not justified in your memory belief that it was destroyed; yet if you feel no draperies where you think you see them, but only textured wallpaper with the right design, here touch apparently takes priority over sight.

There apparently is a measure of positive individual autonomy. Each source can by itself yield some justification. If I have a sufficiently vivid and steadfast memory impression of a vacant lot where I now see a building, I may have some small degree of justification for believing the lot was vacant (and the building has appeared quickly), even if the justification of my visual belief that there is a building before me cannot be overridden by that of the memory belief. Certainly in the normal case, justification— of some degree—from one of the four standard sources does not wait upon corroboration from other sources.

To be sure, one cannot be justified in believing that a lot was vacant unless one has the required concepts, such as that of vacancy; and it may be that one does not acquire concepts adequate to make justified belief possible until one has a complex group of interrelated concepts. This may imply that one gets no justification at all in isolation from justification for many related propositions. That possibility is, however, quite compatible with the ground of one's justification sometimes being a single experience. Epistemic autonomy is consistent with conceptual dependence. A belief might have an isolated ground without in the least being isolated in content from other beliefs.

Regarding the negative individual autonomy of a source—its providing justification that is overridable only by counter-evidence from the same source—plainly the four standard sources do not have it. To take a different example, a memorially justified belief that there was a stump in the yard can be overridden by a perception of smooth ground there. It may seem that reason—our rational capacity—is privileged as a source of justification. Strong rationalists might take it to possess negative individual autonomy. But surely some propositions, such as some in logic or mathematics, might be justifiedly believed on the basis of reflection but, in part on the basis of sufficiently plausible testimony, could cease to be justified for someone. The authority of that testimony would depend partly on perceptual and memorial factors crucial for justifiedly accepting the credibility of the attester. Thus, the overriding power of that authority does not derive from reason alone.[20]

The case for collective negative autonomy is more plausible: there is some reason to think that where a belief is justified in virtue of all four sources supporting it, its justification is defeasible only through considerations arising from at least one of those very sources. If we make the plausible but by no means self-evident assumption that defeat of justification can come only from what confers or at least admits of justification, and if we add the (controversial) assumption that all justification of belief derives wholly from the four standard sources, we may conclude that those sources are (justificationally) self-sufficient. I make neither assumption, but I would suggest that in fact these sources may be self-sufficient.[21]

There is reason to think, then, that each of the four standard sources possesses individual autonomy and, collectively, they are self-corrective and perhaps self-sufficient. Each can provide grounds that can by themselves confer justification, though it can be defeated by counter-evidence that arises from the same or a different source, and the entire set of sources may well be autonomous: self-sufficient in accounting for justification and, independently of any other sources, capable of accounting for defeaters and, in part in that way, for correction of our beliefs in the light of defeaters.

It has been plausibly argued, however, that one source, and perhaps *the* basic source, of justification is coherence among one's beliefs. Isn't my belief that the pianist wore a long dress perhaps justified by its *coherence* with the beliefs that she was formally dressed and that long dresses are traditional on such occasions? And isn't the justification of my belief that she wore a long dress later undermined mainly by its *in*coherence with the belief that people whose collective credibility exceeds my own deny that she wore one? Or at least, given that belief about others' credibility, together with other beliefs cohering with it, such as that they have no reason to lie and that one's memory is fallible, isn't the most coherent overall pattern of my beliefs one that excludes retaining the belief that the pianist wore a long dress? We must explore the role of coherence in justification.

4. COHERENCE

Unfortunately, there is no account of coherence that we may simply pre-suppose. The notion is elusive, and there are highly varying accounts.[22] But this much is clear: we cannot assess the role of coherence in justifica-tion unless we distinguish the claim that coherence is a basic source of justification from the claim that *in*coherence can defeat justification. Incoherence is not the contradictory of coherence, its mere absence. Mu-tual irrelevancy is a case of neither coherence nor incoherence. Incoher-ence has a definite negative character. The paradigm of it is blatant logi-cal inconsistency. Positive coherence is widely taken to be far more than mutual consistency, yet far less than mutual entailment.

Clearly, that incoherence can defeat justification does not imply that coherence can create it. Moreover, if it does create it, seeing this is diffi-cult because in every case where coherence is plausibly invoked as a source of justification, one or more of the four standard sources is apparently operating in a way that provides for an explanation of the justification on which *both* the coherence and the justification arise from the same elements responsible for well-groundedness. This is best seen through cases.

Consider my belief that a fan is running, grounded in hearing the usual whirring sounds. This appears to be justified by the relevant auditory im-pressions, together with background information about what the corre-sponding sounds indicate. If, however, I were to acquire a justified belief that someone is imitatively creating the whirring sounds, my justification for believing that a fan is running would be undermined by the incoher-ence in my belief system. I now find that the best explanation of my expe-rience is incompatible—hence incoherent—with my belief that a fan is running. But would I be justified in accepting that explanation apart from relying on perceptual grounds? And does the defeating power of incoherence imply that my original justification requires coherence among beliefs, including the belief that no one is imitating the sound of a fan? Does one even have that belief in such a case? It would surely not be normal to have it—as opposed to a disposition to form it—when there is no occasion to suspect such a thing.

Suppose, however, that anti-defeater beliefs (as we might call them) are required for coherence and justification. Notice how many beliefs one would need in order to achieve the relevant coherence, for example that my hearing is normal, that there is no other machine nearby that makes the same sounds—it is not quite clear how far this must go. Do we even form that many beliefs in the normal cases in which we acquire justified beliefs of the ordinary kind in question? To think so is to fall victim to a kind of intellectualism about the mind that has afflicted coherentist and opposing theories of justification alike.

Granted, if I had to *defend* my belief that a fan is running, I might have to form some of these many beliefs, and to acquire justification for them, in order to rebut various attacks on my justification. Defending oneself may require fortifications not needed in peacetime. It may be the sense that the skeptic is always lurking with objections that gives rise—chiefly among philosophers—to the view that one needs so much evidential justification in order to have any justified beliefs at all. But surely we need not take the conditions for first-order justification (roughly, justification in one's beliefs about the world) to include the capacity to perform the second-order task of showing that one has such justification (second-order because it concerns propositions not about the world but about justification of beliefs about the world). Indeed, just as one can be on solid ice without being able to show that one is, say by cutting through it to gauge its depth or by adding weight to ascertain its resistance, one can have a justified belief without being able to show that its grounding is firm.[23]

A further analogy may help. One's job may be the source of one's income, yet vulnerable to a severe depression, which would eliminate the income. It does not follow that the absence of a depression is a source of one's income. It is not. Even positive economic conditions are not a source, though one's source *depends* on them. The idea of dependence is central here. There is a negative sense in which one's job does depend on the absence of a depression. But that dependence is too negative to render the absence of depression a source (much less a ground) of income. Similarly, we might say that one's justification negatively depends on the absence of defeaters and positively depends on one's sources. But negative

25

epistemic dependence on incoherence does not imply positive epistemic dependence on anything in particular, including coherence, any more than an income's negative dependence on the absence of a depression implies any particular source of that income. The preoccupation with skepticism has tended to cause philosophers to conflate positive and negative epistemic dependence. Failure to distinguish them can provide undeserved support for epistemological coherentism.

To be sure, nothing can serve as a source of anything without the existence of indefinitely many *enabling conditions*. Some of these are conceptual. One may, for instance, be unable to believe a proposition even when evidence for it is before one; if a child has no concept of an insurance adjuster, then seeing one examine a damaged car and talk to its owner about deductibles will not function as a source of justification for the proposition that this is an insurance adjuster. Other enabling conditions are psychological, concerning our capacities or dispositions relevant to forming beliefs. If my sensory receptors are malfunctioning or if I do not respond to their deliverances by forming beliefs in the normal way, then I may fail to be justified in certain perceptual beliefs.

A source provides both a genetic explanation of where a thing comes from and, often, a contemporaneous partial explanation of why it is as it is; enabling conditions, by contrast, provide neither. Taken together, they explain its possibility, but not its genesis or its character. It is neither correct nor theoretically illuminating to construe enabling conditions as part of the source or as a ground. They are indispensable, but their role should be understood in terms of defeasibility, not in relation to sources or grounds.

The importance of incoherence as a defeater of justification, then, is not a good reason to take coherence to be a source of justification. This by no means implies that justification has no relation to coherence. Indeed, at least normally, justified beliefs cohere, in one or another intuitive sense, with other beliefs one has, typically other justified beliefs. Certainly, wherever there is justification for believing something, there is justification for believing a number of related propositions and presumably for believing a coherent set of them. A single perceptual experience—and certainly a single occasion of perception through more than one sense—provides information sufficient to justify many beliefs: that someone is playing a sonata, that there is a piano there, that there are black and white keys, and far more.

The well-groundedness conception of justification I am developing provides a way to explain why coherence apparently accompanies justified beliefs—actual and hypothetical—namely, that both are ultimately grounded in the standard sources. These sources tend to produce beliefs that are at once mutually consistent and interconnected by virtue of being explainable by their common genesis in those sources. The coherence conception of justification, however, does not well explain why the justifiedness of beliefs is apparently both dependent on the standard sources and accompanied by well-groundedness therein. Indeed, as an internal relation among beliefs, coherence may be at least as easily imagined in artificial situations where the coherence of beliefs is unconstrained by our natural tendencies. In principle, wishful thinking could yield as coherent a network of beliefs as the most studious appraisal of evidence.[24]

There is one kind of coherence that is entirely consistent with the well-groundedness conception of justification. To see this, note that one cannot believe a proposition without having all of the concepts that figure essentially in it. Whereof one cannot understand, thereof one cannot believe. Moreover, concepts come, and work, in families. This point is the core of a coherence theory of conceptual function: of the acquisition of concepts and their operation, most notably in discourse, judgment, and inference. That theory—call it *conceptual coherentism*, for short—is both plausible and readily combined with the kind of view I am developing. For instance, I am not justified in believing that there is a piano before me unless I have a concept of a piano. To have that I need many other concepts, such as that of an instrument, of a keyboard, of playing, of sound, of music—no one highly specific concept is necessary, and various alternative sets will do. In part, to have a concept of something perceptible is to be disposed (or at least to have the capacity) to form beliefs under appropriate sensory stimulations, say to believe a specimen of the thing to be present when one can see it and is asked if there is such a thing nearby. Thus, again it is to be expected that from a single perceptual experience, many connected propositions will be justified for the perceiver.

The coherence theory of conceptual function belongs more to semantics and philosophy of mind than to epistemology. But it has profound epistemological implications, and it applies similarly to the theory of practical reason, in part because belief is a central concept there, too, but also because desires and intentions are quite like beliefs in that their possession requires having a concept of their objects, in the sense of what the desires are for (or to do) and what deeds the intentions are to do. That concepts are acquired in mutual relationships may imply that justification does not arise *atomistically*, in one isolated belief (or desire or intention) at a time. This does not imply, however, that, once a person acquires the conceptual capacity needed to achieve justification, justification cannot derive at least mainly from one source at a time. The coherence theory of conceptual function is also quite consistent with the view that, far from

27

deriving from coherence, justification, by virtue of the way it is grounded in its sources, brings coherence with it. Both coherence and incoherence, then, have an important role in understanding justification. But neither need be treated as a basic source of it.[25]

5. RELATIVITY AND THE CONTEXTUAL ELEMENT IN JUSTIFICATION

If the recognition of incoherence as a defeater of justification does not imply that coherence is a basic source of justification, and if indeed coherence is not such a source, it would still be a mistake to conclude that a good theory of justification may assign only a minor role to coherence or incoherence. For one thing, at least the most common kinds of justification are defeasible, and incoherence is a prime defeater, as where one discovers that something one believes entails a contradiction and hence one ceases to be justified in holding that belief. For another, coherence can be a *mark* of justification, and important in identifying it, even if it is not a source of justification but, so to speak, a common effect of the same causes. Third, differences in the sources and defeaters of justification are essential in accounting for differences among persons in the beliefs they are justified in holding and, for a given person, in justification for different beliefs over time. I particularly want to pursue this third point.

A theory that takes even the most basic kinds of justification to be defeasible incorporates a kind of relativity that goes beyond the kind that arises from source-dependence: whether one is justified, on balance, depends on one's overall circumstances. A defeater may or may not be present; hence, the same belief can be justified in one context, say when formed as I recall what the pianist wore, and not in another context, as when I am contradicted by two credible people. There is at least this much *contextualism* in the well-groundedness view.[26]

A further reason to speak of contextualism is this. If we think not of the *property* of justification, i.e., justifiedness—which has been our main topic so far—but of the *process* of justification, of the active task of justifying a belief, by contrast with simply having a justification for it or with justifiedly holding it, then there is no doubt that in different contexts different justificatory arguments will be acceptable. In a normal sunlit room, appeals to how things look will be taken to justify color ascriptions; under colored lights in the evening, the same person might have to adduce further evidence to justify, to the same audience, the identical color ascriptions. It is not that sunlight is a missing *ground* of the justification; rather, the presence of colored light is a *defeater* of that justification. Context is not among the basic sources of the property of justification, but it is often basic to the process of justification.

6. CONTEXTUALIZED FOUNDATIONS

If the well-groundedness view is relative, contextual, and, in the way suggested, sensitive to coherence considerations, and if it takes justification to be (with at most a few exceptions) defeasible, is it nevertheless a version of foundationalism? That term has been so widely misunderstood that there is some risk in using it. On the other hand, it is established and commonly used; the kind of theory it represents is central in the thinking of most of the great philosophers; and, by virtue of both its historical and its metaphorical connections, it is usefully suggestive. Given its currency and the persisting references to it in many quarters, it seems better to clarify it than to abandon it. This is particularly so if some versions of it are unreasonably rejected because of their association with mistaken versions they do not entail. (The best-known such version is Cartesian foundationalism, which is unwarrantedly strong in ways that will be considered in Chapter 2.)[27]

Two kinds of foundationalism have been suggested so far in this chapter. Both divide a person's beliefs (with some idealization) into foundations and superstructure; both posit experiential and rational grounds as the basis of the foundational beliefs; and both countenance inference as a major building block by which the superstructure rises from the foundations. But in many other respects they differ considerably from each other. Neither corresponds to the common views influenced by Cartesian paradigms. Let me take them in turn.

The first is a psychological thesis concerning the structure of a person's belief system at a given time: it says that if we have any beliefs at all, then we have at least one which is not (inferentially) based on any further belief; and that any inferential beliefs one has are, directly or indirectly, based on some non-inferential belief one has. This thesis about cognitive structure is *psychological foundationalism.*[28] Its plausibility rests on a number of factors: that we do not have infinite sets of beliefs, at least of the kind that would make infinite inferential chains psychologically possible for us; that our beliefs do not lie in inferential circles; that in fact we do have non-inferential beliefs, beliefs based, for instance, on perceptual experience; and that generally our inferential beliefs can be traced back to non-inferential ones. Again, however, context matters greatly: particularly when queried by a skeptic, I may *form* beliefs I did not have. If I am challenged as to whether I see fabric or textured wallpaper, I may form the belief that it *seems* to me that I see fabric. Psychological foundationalism implies no absolute psychological bottom, and it recognizes fluidity between foundations and superstructure, allowing beliefs to pass from either to the other. It simply says that at any given time, the cognitive structure is foundational.

The second thesis is the more widely known stance called *epistemological foundationalism*. As applied to justification, and in a generic form, it is roughly the view that if (at a given time) one has any justified beliefs at all, then one has at least one non-inferentially justified belief; any other justified belief one has is adequately justified by, and would not be justified apart from its (positive) dependence on, at least one non-inferentially justified belief. This is a moderate foundationalism, and it is a structural thesis rather than a substantive one with commitments to any particular beliefs, or even kinds of beliefs, as appropriate foundations. Like its psychological counterpart, it posits only *movable foundations*. It allows not only the defeat of non-inferentially justified beliefs but also permits something else, such as coherence, to play a significant role in justification, so long as non-inferentially justified belief is a necessary element in it. It does not, then, imply the justificational self-sufficiency of each of the four standard sources.

So far, knowledge has been perhaps conspicuously absent from these pages. This is in part because a belief can be amply justified, and certainly rational, without even being true, much less constituting knowledge. Indeed, I think that a belief that constitutes knowledge need not be justified, rare though knowledge without justification may be.[29] The reason for this is that knowledge (apart from certain kinds of self-knowledge) is external in a way justification is not: knowledge captures some truth about something external to the believer, and it should be understood in terms of what that externality requires.

Despite these and other differences between justification and knowledge, all of the standard sources of justification I have considered, with the exception of memory, are also standard (and basic) sources of knowledge (memory is not, since what is known from memory constitutes knowledge because of grounding in some other mode[30]). Moreover, moderate foundationalism is as plausible for knowledge as for justification. What follows takes due note of the similarities as well as the differences between knowledge and justification.

If we think of theoretical reason as the domain of knowledge and justified belief, a moderate foundationalist view can provide a good account, both psychologically and epistemically, of the structure (as distinct from the substance) of theoretical reason. There is a division into foundations and superstructure; and, both causally and justificationally, experience—including reflection—grounds the foundations, which in turn ground the superstructure. Yet the ground need not be impenetrable bedrock, and the building blocks that link the foundations to the superstructure may crumble. Defeasibility cannot be eliminated. But defeat can be avoided, and there is no reason to think it is pervasive. We have seen many cases in which it does nothing to prevent experience from producing justified non-inferential beliefs. We must now consider how justification can extend from its experiential grounds into the higher reaches of cognition, and we must bring out more clearly the relation between justification and rationality.

SUPERSTRUCTURE

In the moments before the performance, I look at the full keyboard. All but its very top keys are visible to me. Noticing that the piano looks old, I recall that there still are some pianos with eighty-five keys, and I wonder whether this might be one. I then realize that I simply cannot see the top three keys, and I conclude, and in doing so come to believe, that there are the usual eighty-eight. This belief is surely justified in the circumstances; but although my perceptions help to ground it, the belief is not perceptual. It is inferential. It is based on other beliefs of mine which express reasons (or a compound reason) for it: that this is a standard American concert piano, and that such pianos have eighty-eight keys. I did not have to think of these premises before concluding that the piano has eighty-eight keys; my beliefs of them can figure as the basis of my conclusion just as surely as if I had recited them. A belief can arise from other beliefs, and thereby on the basis of premises they represent, without one's thinking of those premises; and when it is so based, then if the premises express an adequate ground for the belief, it may be justified by them. This kind of development of our belief system often takes place naturally. Our beliefs grow, and our perspective thereby widens, not only through focused reflection or laborious inference but also through our unselfconscious cognitive responses to beliefs we already hold.

1. SPONTANEOUS INFERENCE

In many cases, the spontaneity with which some beliefs arise on the basis of others parallels the direct (non-inferential) grounding characteristic of most of our perceptual beliefs. A belief can be based on a visual experience without one's having a thought of that experience. The experience, to be sure, must be in consciousness; by contrast, beliefs that express premises need only be retained in memory in order to ground a belief for which they provide evidence. This inferential grounding can occur without our formulating or even being aware of the propositions so retained, just as we can build on a foundation that remains unexposed below ground— or act on motives that do not enter consciousness at the time. Our retention of propositions in memory does, however, normally keep the grounding beliefs near to hand.

This proximity of memorially retained beliefs has at least two dimensions. First, quite without effort we can normally become aware of the propositions so believed, as where we reflect on topics that naturally bring them to mind. Second, the propositions tend to be *presuppositionally available* to us: capable—as are reasons for action—of playing a supporting role, as grounds we assume without their having to be called to mind. Given enough practice in using it, one need not formulate the Pythagorean Theorem to take it as a basis for calculating the length of a side of a right triangle. But when the need arises, as where one is asked why one believes the side of a triangle is four feet long, one can bring the theorem forward as a justification. Our experience, then, produces myriad new beliefs; many are inferential, and many, particularly perceptual beliefs, are not. I want to explore how those that are inferential might be justified by those that are not.

In a book about rationality, it should be said that in a certain way the picture of inferential belief formation just sketched is, like that of non-inferential belief formation given in Chapter 1, anti-intellectualist. I conceive rational persons not as constantly reasoning, or as always self-consciously logical, in arriving at beliefs but rather as having in some sense *internalized* rational standards which then guide them without the conscious thoughts one might cite in explicitly rationalizing their behavior. This is not to deny that rational persons must be capable of reasoning; the point is that reasoning is not the only manifestation of our rationality nor a constant element in the formation of our beliefs.

This economical conception of the human intellect is not meant to play down the subtlety of brain processes that are doubtless needed to sustain our rationality. That very subtlety may partly underlie the spontaneity and lack of self-consciousness that accompany much of our belief and action. The rapid and diverse achievements of the brain may liberate the mind to exercise reason without the labor we might otherwise have to do. Quite commonly we can recognize sarcasm in an instant, evaluate excuses as fast as we hear them, and produce good reasoning without reminding ourselves of the standards that guide it. Even apart from this, it is philosophically prudent to try to account for rationality without multiplying beliefs, inferences, or thought processes of any kind beyond necessity. This is the spirit in which I proceed.[1]

2. INFERENTIAL BELIEF

Once it is clear that a belief can be inferential by virtue of standing to one or more other beliefs in the kind of psychologically unobtrusive evidential sustenance relationship just illustrated, it also becomes apparent that a great many of our beliefs are inferential. They are based on one or more other, evidential beliefs of ours, as opposed to being non-inferentially grounded in a current experience or mental state or simply retained in memory. To be sure, a belief may only seem to be inferential. If we are asked why we believe something, reasons may occur to us that represent, not identifications of already tacit grounds on which we (inferentially) believed the proposition, but discoveries of new grounds. This is one reason for the success of Socratic teaching. It not only uncovers beliefs we already have; its questioning also leads to our discovering new evidence and new ideas.

It can be difficult to tell when we are discovering a new ground for a belief we hold and when we are articulating one that was already a tacit basis of that belief. It can be especially difficult to tell in cases where we already believe the propositions that express the new grounds. For then the question is the subtle one of whether we are just now coming to believe the original proposition *on* the basis of the new grounds as we think of them as supporting it or, without recognizing it, instead believed it on that basis before. If a pillar stands beneath a porch with its top just tangent to the bottom of the front beam, and if there is an array of other pillars jointly quite sufficient to bear the weight of the beam, it can be difficult to tell whether the first pillar actually bears weight or simply stands ready to do so—whether it is an idle, unstressed support or an unnoticeably stressed sustainer.

Even if a pillar is idle and bears no weight, it has the potential to bear it and can suddenly begin to do so because of an imperceptible downward thrust from above. A belief can be quite like an idle pillar: not merely decorative but also providing no actual support. Many of our beliefs express potential premises, and thus provide reasons for holding others. If no need for such premises arises and no association in our thinking makes a connection between them and the belief, we may never be aware of any connection or in any sense *use* those premises. It is much the same with reasons for action and the actions they support: we may have reasons for what we do that never occur to us—at least in terms of providing support for that action—and they may never figure in our motivation for anything we do.

Despite all these difficulties, we surely can sometimes determine whether a ground we consider is an actual, or only a potential, basis of a belief for which we take it to provide evidence. Even if we could not determine this, we have a great many inferential beliefs for which the question does not arise. For many of these beliefs, we have not considered our grounds for holding them, or at least we have not explicitly formed the beliefs, on the basis of a process of inferring conclusions from premises. Such beliefs might be called *structurally inferential*: they are premise-dependent as inferential beliefs typically are, yet are not inferentially grounded. Even if they have been arrived at by a process of drawing an inference, they are not at the time in question based on a process of inference.[2] When these structurally inferential beliefs are added to the more often discussed cases of *episodically inferential* beliefs—those that rest on a mental process of inference, as opposed to some brain process with no appropriately inferential manifestations in consciousness—it is easy to see that a great many of our beliefs are inferential, in the wide sense implying evidential grounding in further belief. How does that grounding yield justified belief?

Consider again my belief that the piano has eighty-eight keys, a belief held on the basis of my believing that it is a standard American grand and such instruments have that number of keys. When we hold one belief on the basis of another, so that we may be said to believe the first proposition *because* we believe the second, what relation must hold between the two beliefs in order for the first belief to be justified by the second? More broadly, given the sorts of elements described in Chapter 1 as experiential grounds for non-inferential beliefs, how are we to account for justification higher up in the cognitive structure, where our beliefs are inferential?[3] The question can be divided. One problem is what conditions must be met by a grounding belief. A second is how, when they are met, the grounded belief must be related to the former. Let us take these in turn.

3. INFERENTIAL GROUNDS

It is both natural and common to assume that unless a belief is justified, it cannot inferentially justify a second one. It is very difficult to show that this must be so. Examples suggest that it is, and we can best start there. If I do not justifiedly believe that standard American concert pianos have eighty-eight keys, my belief, as based on this premise, that this piano does so is surely not justified either. It might be thought that since a perceptual experience is not justified or unjustified and yet can justify a belief based on it, there should be no justification requirement in the inferential case either. But notice two points. First, experiences as such do not *admit* of justification, and so to require it of them would make no sense.[4] Second, we normally take as refuting a claim to be justified in believing something the point that a reason or ground the person offers as the only (or main) one is shown to be inadequate. If, on being challenged to justify my claim that a piano is American, I say that it must be, since it has eighty-five keys, and someone then credibly points out that some European pianos have eighty-five, I must either provide further evidence or give up my claim to justification.

We can better understand inferentially justified beliefs by comparing them with a major kind of directly justified belief. With perceptually justified beliefs, for instance, there is often a kind of correspondence between what we perceive and our experience of it. I am not implying that there must be interior objects, such as sense-data, with their own properties mirroring properties of what they represent. Such direct justification requires only that there be experiential properties that—in veridical perception—in some way match or reflect the objects about which their possession provides justification.[5] (Even this may hold only in elementary cases of direct justification.) The correspondence in question need not be of any highly restricted sort. I do not even claim, contrary to Locke, that colors and other secondary qualities are "in" the objects that have them. Perhaps a certain kind of functional dependence of our sensory experience on the relevant objects is enough. By contrast, the mere having of a belief on which another is based cannot in general justify the second by virtue of properties intrinsic to the former. It does not play its prima facie justificatory role in the same way. Such a premise belief may not, for instance, vary in content with variations in its grounds and, unlike an experience, can remain intrinsically unchanged while losing its evidential capacity. It can cease to be justified and thereby no longer justify a belief based on it; this is not a liability for an experience that confers justification. Its justificatory power is not derived from further grounds.

The basic contrast here can also be expressed in terms of justification and reasons. If I am not justified in a premise belief, say that standard American pianos have eighty-eight keys, then the subjective point of view constituted by my beliefs contains (at least in this premise belief) no good reason for my holding the belief based on it. I may think the belief is justified, but such thinking does not make it so, nor by itself does it give me a good reason for the further belief that is based on the first one. With a justificatory sensory experience, however, which is not the kind of thing that admits of justification, one's simply having it does the chief work of conferring justification. This is the reason that, even if the experience is hallucinatory, it may retain its justificatory power, provided it is of the right kind (chiefly in content and steadiness) to justify the belief in question.[6] A sufficiently vivid hallucination of a piano here could conceivably justify my believing that there is one before me.

Moreover, the inferential evidencing relation in question, far from necessarily exhibiting any kind of isomorphism or other direct correspondence between evidence or grounds for it and what it evidences, may be of any kind and may be highly indirect, as where it is only through a scientific theory that one can see how the premise belief expresses support for a belief it grounds. If I see a barometer dropping, I straightaway acquire a ground for believing the weather is changing; but apart from background beliefs about atmospheric pressure and the weather, this proposition would not count as evidence for me.

Roughly, the justification of a belief, and not its existence, is what matters for the justification of a belief inferentially based on it; whereas it is the existence of an experience, and not its veridicality—the closest analogue of justification for it—that matters to the justification of a belief (noninferentially) based on it. This is not to say that the "content" of an experience is irrelevant. But in order to justify a belief, an experience need not be veridical or even seem veridical to the subject (though it may fail to justify if it seems *un*veridical); whereas a belief can justify (inferentially) only if it is itself justified. One way to explain this is to describe inferential justifiers as transmitting justification and direct justifiers as conferring it.

Granted, one's knowing or justifiedly believing that an experience is not veridical may defeat any prima facie justification it provides. But that does not imply that believing the experience is veridical is a precondition of its justificatory power, nor even that justification *for* believing that the experience is veridical is a precondition. Think of children: they may be perceptually justified in some of their beliefs even before they have concepts adequate to enable them to *have* the higher-order belief that an experience of theirs is veridical. The idea of experience as true or false to "the facts" requires considerably more conceptual development than does simply achieving a measure of justification.

Suppose it is true that a belief can justify a further belief based on it *only* if the former is itself justified; under what further conditions does it justify the latter? It is clear that there should be some appropriate relation between the propositional contents of the beliefs. In what may be the simplest kind of case, if the content of the premise belief(s) deductively implies, and in that sense entails, that of the conclusion belief, then (assuming the person can understand the entailment) we should expect justification to be transmitted from the grounding belief(s) to the belief based on them.[7] In cases where the entailment is difficult to see, the better the person understands this entailment, the more justification it tends to carry from the grounding belief(s) to a belief based on them. Understanding an entailment is not a matter of going through an explicit deduction but of having the capacity to do so comprehendingly; and if I would have to labor to see the connection, then (other things equal) I do not have as good a justification as where the connection is self-evident to me.[8]

Similar principles are plausible for inductive relations between the relevant contents. This point includes any of the various kinds of inductive relation. A belief might be inferentially justified by being based on enumerative premises. One might thus be justified in a generalization about robins on the basis of observing a representative group of them. Beliefs may also be justified by inference to the best explanation. Seeing a covey of blackbirds pecking at white specks on the lawn, you might be justified in believing that they have found the bread crumbs you threw there.[9]

4. THE TRANSMISSION OF JUSTIFICATION

In the two generously diverse categories of deductive and inductive relations, a huge number of transmission principles can be formulated. We need not multiply cases. But something further must be said about one requirement suggested earlier: that for a belief to be inferentially justified, and not merely capable of being justified by the relevant premises, it must be *based on* one or more beliefs expressing those justificatory premises. Even if I have never been able to see a connection between two propositions I believe, I may still have, in my belief of the first, a good inferential ground for believing the second. The second belief is then justifi*able* by appeal to the first but not justi*fied* by it. For the second belief to be justified on the basis of the first, I must not only understand the evidential connection between their propositional objects, my premise belief must also serve as a basis of the belief it justifies. It cannot be like an idle pillar. It must actually support that belief, not merely express evidence *available* to support it.

This point can be missed if one thinks of justification as simply what is cited by an adequate answer to a certain kind of query and then supposes that a belief is justified provided the believer can cite an adequate ground for holding it. Suppose I am asked why I hold the belief in question. Especially if I feel defensive, I may cite a consideration that is not an actual ground of the belief I seek to explain or justify (I would normally seek to justify as well as explain in response to such a query). I may be merely *rationalizing,* even if I happen to believe the premises I adduce. For I may believe the proposition only on *other* grounds, whether or not I know this. Imagine a person who is asked to explain a belief that someone is untrustworthy. If it is embarrassing to cite the real reason, say the testimony of a meddling in-law, other evidences might be cited. If these evidences constitute good grounds, the proposition believed is thereby justified and the person is shown to *have* a justification for believing it. To this extent, the rationalization succeeds. But what it justifies is the proposition believed, not the believing of it. If the rationalizer's belief ascribing dishonesty is not *based* on the beliefs adduced in support of it, then it is not justified by those beliefs, any more than a porch derives its firmness from pillars that lie just below it, ready to sustain it if it falls on them but bearing none of its weight, which rests entirely on other supports. A belief is justified *by* an inferential ground only if it is based *on* that ground.[10]

This broadly causal sustenance requirement is not peculiar to inferential justification or, as we shall see in Part II, to theoretical reason. It is equally plausible to apply it to non-inferential justification, the direct kind. If my visual experience of the piano is evidence that it is longer than seven feet but (because I mistrust my visual judgment) my belief that it is longer rests entirely on testimony, then surely my belief is justified by the latter if it is justified at all. The case is an analogue of believing a proposition that constitutes a sufficient justification for a belief one holds—so that one *has* a reason to hold the second belief—but not holding the latter belief on the basis of the former one, hence not *for* the reason it expresses. In both cases, a justification that is merely possessed serves only as a rationalization for a belief: the belief is *justifiable*, but not justified, by the evidence.[11]

The illustrations of inferential relationships so far given have, for simplicity, mainly concerned single pairs of beliefs. But for many of our inferential beliefs, we have multiple premises, sometimes even many independent sets of them, quite as we can have many reasons for an action. A single premise, moreover, can justify several independent conclusions. Just as one experience can produce and justify many beliefs, a single belief can produce and justify many others. In both cases, moreover, two or more quite different experiences or beliefs can, jointly or independently, produce and justify a single belief. Sight and hearing can lead me to believe that there is a large piano before me. What I see and what I believe from memory can, jointly or independently, produce and justify my belief that the piano has both black and white keys.

Our beliefs, like our experiences, are numerous and varied; and the requirements for justified belief do not impose on our cognitive systems any single pattern or any fixed structure. The monolithic image of a pyramid, especially an inverted one axiomatically terminating in something like a Cartesian *cogito*, exaggerates the proportion of our beliefs that are inferential and wrongly suggests that foundational beliefs are like a small set of powerful axioms. This pyramidal image should be disassociated from a properly developed foundationalism. It represents bad cognitive architecture as well as poor epistemology. In shape, complexity, connectedness, content, and strength, foundations and superstructure can vary indefinitely. They vary among persons; they range over an unlimited variety of subject-matters; and, over time, they change in any of us. A better figure is that of a tree: it may develop new roots at any time and in any direction; old roots may grow or, in some cases, wither; the root system may be more than sufficient to support the rest of the tree or quite inadequate to the task; nutrients may flow upward from root to branch and foliage or downward along similar paths; and the composition of both roots and branches changes over time. The architecture of nature is a far better model of the intellect than the geometrically artificial inverted pyramid.

5. DEFEASIBILITY AND THE CARTESIAN RESPONSE TO IT

Like direct experiential justification, inferential justification is liable to both undermining and overriding. Our justification for believing that the birds are eating the bread we laid out can be undermined by our discovering that someone else also put out bread. Now their eating from that second allotment would equally well explain their congregating, and our information is no longer good reason to believe what we do. Our justification may be overridden by hearing a credible friend say that someone else replenished the supply after ours was consumed; now we have better reason to believe that the birds are not eating our bread than to believe that they are. The defeaters must, however, have, or (if they are experiential and do not admit of justification) produce, their own justification. That is the opposing force through which they work, and it, too, is apparently to be accounted for in the same framework that explains the justification they defeat. It is, for instance, because our friend's testimony justifies us in believing that our bread was consumed that we are no longer justified in our belief that the birds are eating it.

The account of direct justification outlined in Chapter 1 makes it readily intelligible that direct justification is defeasible by elements that are themselves only indirectly justified. My direct, visual justification for believing that there is a curtain before me can be defeated not only by my direct, tactual justification for believing that there is only textured wallpaper but also by credible testimony that this is what I see. To be sure, if I am not justified, perceptually, in believing something to the effect that a person is speaking to me, then there may be no defeat of my initial justification. Insofar as indirect justification depends on direct justification, the former cannot defeat the latter without ultimately deriving at least a major part of its strength from one or more directly justified beliefs. But even if, ultimately, direct justification is defeasible only through the force of other such justification, the point is that it *is* defeasible and that the immediately defeating element may be only indirectly justified. The foundations, then, may be justifiedly altered from the superstructure, even if the latter cannot float in midair and needs some grounding to gain the leverage required to alter its own foundations.

Foundations may be not only adjusted but also substantially and advantageously rebuilt from the superstructure. When we lose direct justification, we often learn something. It may be abstract, say that vision cannot always be trusted. It may also be concrete; we may acquire a tactual belief that the rough surface we are feeling is textured wallpaper. From this belief we may acquire the general belief that such paper can have the look of a fabric. Indeed, though one's justification can be defeated without one's having any inkling that this is happening, one may in other cases discover the defeat, and that discovery can lead one to reflect or to make observations. The result can be far more and even far better justification for the belief in question than one had initially. This point represents yet another underpinning of Socratic teaching. There is, however, no formula for predicting just how a given person may adjust to defeat. In principle, any discovery of the defeat of the justification of one belief could in some way affect the justification of any other belief one holds.[12]

There is, then, a strong contrast between the dynamic view developed here and Cartesian foundationalism, which has tended to dominate philosophers' conceptions of foundationalist theories (especially in philosophers whose main work is not in epistemology).[13] Cartesian foundationalism may be taken to imply (even if Descartes himself did not unequivocally assert) three major principles which, although they do not wholly define it, are central to it yet are rejected by the moderate view set forth here.

The first Cartesian principle is that only beliefs or other cognitions that, owing to, e.g., their clarity and distinctness, achieve epistemic certainty are

41

appropriate for the foundational level—call this *axiomatism about foundations*. There are other candidates for grounds of certainty, and different theorists may also differ about what sorts of beliefs are "axiomatic."[14] It would be widely agreed, however, that a belief is suitable axiomatic material *only if* it is non-inferentially justifiable. From a Cartesian perspective, this requirement would probably exclude our empirical beliefs about the external world.

The second Cartesian principle is that only deductive inferences can transmit justification, whether from foundations to superstructure or within either category. Call this *deductivism about transmission*. Deductivism is natural for anyone who takes genuine justification to require certainty (though it should not be assumed that even deductive inference must confer on one's conclusion *as much* justification as one has for one's premises). For inductive connections can reduce the degree of justification we get for a conclusion below the degree of justification we have for our premises. Suppose my degree of justification for a proposition, p, is n and that p implies q with a probability of .95. Then my justification for q, given p as my sole ground, cannot exceed ninety-five percent of n. Thus, by a chain of such inferences, in each of which I lose a corresponding degree of my original justification, I could arrive at a conclusion for which I lack any significant justification at all. This would be defeat by erosion.

If, like Descartes, we want the upper levels of our cognitive structure to be as strong as the foundations, we may take this sort of reasoning to show that owing to the diminution of justification across inductive inferences, one cannot safely build on inductive supports. Inductive pillars can never enable the superstructure to bear as much weight as the foundations themselves can sustain. Granted, the quantitative terms I have used in describing inductive reasoning represent an idealized precision about justification. But the possibility of progressive diminution holds even if we can make only rough assignments of probabilities and degrees of justification. From a Cartesian point of view, no matter how good the foundations, ultimately the upper stories could be too poorly supported to bear weight they are meant to carry.

The third Cartesian principle is that if one has appropriately strong foundations, one can or even does know that one has the relevant kind of certainty—call this *second-order foundationalism*. Such a principle is to be expected in philosophers preoccupied with skepticism; for they plainly want grounds to maintain, against skeptics, that we can know that we have certainty (or knowledge or indefeasible justification, or the like). No matter how good one's foundations are, if one does not know that they are good—and perhaps why they are—one cannot get them past a skeptical inspector. One is unlikely even to be able to defend them from skeptical attack.

None of these Cartesian principles is needed either to explain how the elements grounding foundational beliefs can confer justification on them or to account for its transmission from them to the superstructure. Certainty is not required for justification; inferential justification can surely be inductively grounded; and, as the possibility of justified belief on the part of conceptually naive children illustrates, having a justified belief does not imply the capacity for knowledge, or even justified belief, that one has it.

6. PRINCIPLES OF GENERATION, TRANSMISSION, AND DEFEASIBILITY

The principles concerning transmission of justification that I have sketched are examples of epistemic principles. The latter category also includes generation principles, those articulating conditions under which direct (non-inferential) justification arises. There is also a third kind: defeasibility principles. These lay out conditions for defeat of justification. We should briefly consider each kind (Part II will explore parallel principles in the domain of practical reason).

A quite broad generation principle suggested by some of our examples, and applicable to all the senses, is this: If a person has a clear sensory impression that x is F (or of x's being F) and on that basis believes that x is F, then this belief is prima facie justified. We might simply call this *the perceptual principle*.[15] If, for instance, I have a clear auditory impression that a bird is warbling (or simply of a bird warbling) and on that basis I believe that there is one warbling, I am (prima facie) justified in so believing. A principle similar to the perceptual one can be formulated for introspection (which yields something like impressions of its own) and for memory, which, in addition to storing and presenting images, can provide a sense of one's having learned or encountered something in the past. There are intuitive impressions as well, such as the sense of the evident truth of simple logical truths, and these impressions too can ground prima facie justification in a similar way.[16]

The status of these generation principles is a major issue. Are they, for instance, a priori or empirical, and how are we to account for their own truth or justification? All I claim here is that they are highly plausible; for it is their truth I want to presuppose, not anything specific about their status. The same holds for transmission principles. Let us consider two kinds.

One kind of representative transmission principle suggested by our discussions is this: If (a) one justifiedly believes a proposition, q, (b) q entails

p, (c) this entailment is within the scope of one's understanding, and (d) one believes p on the basis of q, then one has some degree of justification for believing p. (The entailment can be within the scope of one's understanding without one's ever considering that entailment.) A parallel principle holds for having some reason to believe p (and for rationally believing p) in place of justifiedly believing.

There is also an analogous principle for inductive transmission, where we simply substitute inductive support for entailment. But in that case an additional qualification must be made: where the initial justification is the minimal degree that can provide justification on balance, then unless the inductive support is very strong (and perhaps not even then), the belief that p will not acquire justification, or at least not enough to render the person justified, on balance, in believing p. To see why this is so, consider what justification on balance is plausibly taken to be. I shall construe it as (roughly) a degree of justification sufficient to make it epistemically reasonable for one to believe the proposition in question. This is, I think, the degree we have very commonly in mind in saying, without qualification, that someone is justified in believing something; and this, in turn, is normally such that when one justifiedly believes a true proposition to that degree (and in the absence of defeaters like those illustrated by the untoward cases showing that justified true belief is not sufficient for knowledge), one knows it. Now suppose I am at the minimal threshold of justification on balance. Then I have no justification to spare in inferential transmission if I am to acquire justification on balance for the proposition I infer; and if the inductive connection is not strong enough to preserve the full degree of justification I have for the premise, transmission of that kind of justification fails. The argument expressed earlier to help explain deductivism about transmission implies that inductive transmission *cannot* be strong enough, but I think we may leave that open. The point here is that whatever minimal justification turns out to be, if one has only this degree for one's belief that q, and if one now inductively infers p from q, then (unless one gains justification for p from some other source than q or for some other reason loses none) one loses some degree of justification in the transmission and does not acquire minimal justification for p.

The most plausible counterpart inductive principle, then, should be something like this: If (a) one justifiedly believes a proposition, q, (b) q inductively supports p, (c) this support relation is within the scope of one's understanding, and (d) one believes p on the basis of q, then one believes p with some degree of justification. Whether the belief that p is justified on balance is a matter not only, as usual, of the absence of defeaters but of whether the operative inductive relation is strong enough, relative to the strength of the initial justification, to yield an overall justified belief. The greater one's initial justification, and the greater the inductive support it gives to what one believes on the basis of it—a "quantity" that can vary independently of the initial justification—the greater one's terminal (inferential) justification.

How should defeasibility be represented in interpreting our epistemic principles? We can formulate additional principles to capture defeat wrought by undermining elements. For instance, suppose you have (undefeated) reason to believe that your ground does not, in the circumstances, support what you believe on the basis of it. Then your justification for the latter belief is undermined or at least weakened. How *much* it is weakened depends on how good your original ground is and on how great is the force of your reason for thinking the ground does not in the context support what you believe on the basis of it.

There are too many cases to consider here. It is enough that the general pattern of undermining principles is before us. Principles of overridingness are perhaps less difficult to capture in simple formulations. Here is a representative one: my justification for believing p is overridden if I have, equally accessible to me, at least as good (undefeated) justification for believing a proposition logically incompatible with p. (This holds where the incompatibility itself is readily within my understanding—otherwise I may retain some degree of justification, even if knowledge would be undermined; the further the incompatibility is from my understanding, the less it affects my justification).[17] Where the incompatibility is only probabilistic, so that it is possible, even if unlikely, that both propositions are true, the matter is more complicated. Our principle must capture the idea that the counter-evidence is good enough, relative to the probability, to outweigh the force of the original ground. If it is only as good as the original evidence, we have neutralization—a weak, merely counterbalancing overrider. If it is better, we have strong overriding, an outweighing overrider.

There is a special case that also complicates matters (and, as we shall see, has close parallels in the theory of practical reason). Suppose I have the second-order belief that my belief that p is unjustified. Does this second-order belief alone defeat my justification in believing p? Not necessarily. Ill-considered skepticism could then be the source of massive justificatory defeat. But suppose the second-order belief is *justified* (I omit the case in which it is true, for if I truly believe my belief that p is unjustified, then it *is* unjustified). This belief then expresses at least an inductive ground for thinking that either my ground provides inadequate initial support or is outweighed by one or more others. Such a second-order belief can defeat justification, but the conditions under which it does so are not easy to specify.

It seems clear that second-order beliefs of the skeptical sort we have been considering must acquire their own justification in the same ways that first-order beliefs do. The skeptic has no unique sources of justification. Moreover, the second-order status of beliefs that one lacks justification must not be taken to privilege them. A view from above ground is different from the ground-level perspective, and it may be wider. But it is not automatically better, and it may be inaccurate. Distressed that people I deeply respect deny a proposition I believe, I may go to great lengths in self-criticism and arrive at a justified belief that I lack a good justification for the proposition. But if I am quite wrong in this self-assessment, then the justification it gives me need not be sufficient to override whatever justification I originally had. A hostile wind can buffet and bend a tree without breaking a single branch.

This caution also applies to the positive second-order case: that of a justified belief that one's belief that p is justified. This belief would not automatically confer justification on the belief that p, though it may provide inductive ground to think that the belief is justified. There, maintaining the belief on that basis could imply at least some degree of justification for holding it. The theory of justification must take account of both types of second-order case in setting out the conditions for justification and its defeat. But a higher-order belief to the effect that a belief is justified need not justify it, any more than a higher-order belief that a belief is unjustified always defeats the justification of the belief it condemns.[18] The highest vantage point need not be the best. The last word is often taken to be authoritative; but it is nonetheless fallible and may be unfounded. The automatic superiority of the higher order must not be allowed to be a dogma. It is denied by a plausible foundationalism and should be rejected by philosophers in general.[19]

7. THE ROLE OF COHERENCE IN INFERENTIAL JUSTIFICATION

The epistemic principles suggested here do not mention coherence, but they do make room for it as an element in a structure of justified belief. They do not, however, demand a generation principle that gives coherence a basic role, for instance the principle that if my belief of p coheres with many other things I believe, it is thereby justified. But if coherence is understood as an internal relation among propositions (or among beliefs on the basis of relations among their propositional objects)—one that holds apart from their relations to the subject's experience—this principle is not true. One could meet this condition merely because of a subset of beliefs that arise from wishful thinking or are artificially induced. By performing rigorous deductions, moreover, a logic machine with the most fanciful axioms could create a system of mutually cohering propositions. Coherence, alone, then, is no reason to take the propositions in question to be true or to expect a belief of any of them to be justified.

It may still be true, however, that a high degree of coherence among one's beliefs is typically sufficient for the justification of at least one of the cohering beliefs. It may turn out that given how we are built, it rarely (or never) happens that a set of our beliefs exhibits such coherence unless at least some are justified. After all, if our natural beliefs arise in experience and reflection, and if these are generally good sources of justification—and if we do not introduce serious inconsistency into our belief systems by, for example, wishful thinking—then it is to be expected that many proper subsets of our beliefs are coherent (even if the entire set is not[20]). Consider the kinds of beliefs one commonly forms on entering a crowded room. These are typically governed by perception and background beliefs in a way that yields a set closely connected in content and in some way mutually supportive.

Certain kinds of coherence among beliefs may be even more than an often reliable sign of justification. Coherence may be a necessary condition for it, at least given how we are built, with our normally entrenched and often self-critical dispositions to form—and give up—beliefs on the basis of (among other things) perceptual experience and exploratory inferences. Let us make the plausible assumption—implied by conceptual coherentism—that we do not have isolated beliefs, in part because of the conceptual relations we must grasp in order to have beliefs at all. And suppose that, in part for this reason, we cannot form any justified belief without having some other beliefs with which it coheres. I cannot, for instance, justifiedly believe that there is a piano before me without having beliefs about what a piano is. Now some of these further beliefs will evidently cohere with the justified one. Hence, in any case of foundational justification, coherence can be expected as well. This is an important point; and it does much to explain the appeal of coherence as a purportedly basic element in justification.

Perhaps, then, coherence *is* in a way basic for justification, basic in the way a necessary condition must be. It is often not noticed, however, that there are at least two different kinds of necessary conditions here: *consequential* necessary conditions, those that hold because some other conditions necessary for the phenomenon in question do, and *constitutive* necessary conditions, those in virtue of which the phenomenon is what it is. Grounding in some basic source is a constitutive necessary condition for justification; coherence is apparently not. It is not by itself a basis of justification but apparently a consequence of the elements that produce justification.[21] Deduction of consequences of a justified belief, for instance, tends to transmit justification from that belief to beliefs deductively grounded on it. Nothing establishes coherence between propositions more clearly than tying them together by the sinews of deduction.

8. INTERNAL ACCESSIBILITY

The sorts of grounds and defeaters we have been considering all share an important property: they are accessible to consciousness, i.e., to reflection or introspection, taking those terms broadly. A tactual impression of wallpaper is as experiential as a visual impression of fabric; it is accessible to introspection and may indeed be by its nature an element in consciousness. A sense of the familiarity of something from the past is also accessible to introspection and perhaps necessarily an element in consciousness. A belief of a premise is also accessible to introspection; one can, with suitable efforts, become aware of the belief,[22] though a premise belief as such is not necessarily present to consciousness even when it plays a supporting role.

What is accessible to introspection or reflection need not be limited to what is concrete or mental. Relations between concepts, conceived as an essential part of the basis of a priori justification, may be taken to be accessible to reflection. Concepts and their relations are precisely the sorts of things that a certain kind of abstract reflection concerns.[23]

By contrast with internal defeaters, the mere falsity of a proposition I believe, say that there are draperies before me, does not undermine my justification—as opposed to my knowledge—in believing it. For even when we are mistaken about the facts, and our belief is thereby externally defective, we may have excellent grounds, such as clear perceptions which we have no reason to think unreliable. I am taking the grounds of justification to be, in the accessibility sense just illustrated, internal. If what defeats justification must itself have or produce justification, then it too must be internally grounded. Not every theory of justification, of course, is internalist; reliabilism, in particular, is not. In one major form it says, in outline, that justified beliefs are those produced by a belief-generating process which is reliable in the sense that it produces a high proportion of true beliefs (more than fifty percent). Reliable grounding is thus the basis of justification; and one cannot, in general, have internal access to the reliability of a belief-producing process, such as perception. This can be ascertained only inductively in relation to observations.

Much of what follows in this book is sustainable on externalist assumptions, such as those of reliabilism, but the theory of justification I present is internalist.[24] For either kind of theory, however, there is no difficulty in holding a foundationalist view or the suggested conception of defeasibility. Both one's justified beliefs and one's knowledge can divide into foundations and superstructure quite independently of whether their grounds are accessible. Indeed, it may be that for knowledge, a reliabilist, externalist, foundationalist account is best, particularly if, as some philosophers have argued, knowledge is possible without justification.[25] Justified belief, however, rather than knowledge, is apparently the closest analogue in the realm of theoretical reason to rationality as commonly understood in the realm of practical reason, and most conceptions of practical rationality are internalist. Rational conduct, for instance, is most often understood in terms of what action, from the agent's perspective, it is reasonable to expect will succeed, not in terms of what in fact does succeed, where such external success is analogous to truth in the case of belief. It is time to look more closely at the notion of rationality.

9. JUSTIFICATION, RATIONALITY, AND REASONS

Rationality, as applicable to beliefs, is closely connected with justification and can be understood along similar lines. It has important structural parallels to justification. Some of these will emerge shortly; others will be developed in Parts II and III in relation to both practical and theoretical reason. But it is important here that we take brief account of some often overlooked differences between rationality and justification. I start with skepticism as a widespread perspective that tends to cause many thinkers to miss such differences.

Skeptical influences tend to make us work with very high evidential standards. These standards, in turn, tend to lead us to assimilate rationality to justification; for we become preoccupied not only with defending ourselves against skeptical criticism, which requires establishing the rationality of the relevant beliefs (typically some kind of commonsense beliefs), but also with trying to provide grounds that would bring a neutral or even hostile party over to our side, which often requires robustly justifying these beliefs. Such grounds are often taken to imply a need to show that it is not only rational to hold such beliefs but irrational not to, which seems to imply that there is a strong justification for believing this. One could speak here of rationality as "rational requiredness." This is apparently not a sense 'rationality' normally has in non-technical contexts, and, unlike that usage, it does not apply to persons in an overall sense; but the notion is well worth keeping in mind as representing one end of a spectrum of evaluative concepts.

A different and probably less common reaction to skeptical concerns is to take a much more modest approach. Instead of trying to show the skeptic to be mistaken, one simply defends the rational permissibility of the relevant beliefs. One might thus assume that what is rational (at least in belief and action) is simply what is not irrational. We could call this the *minimal notion of rationality.* In those inclined to think of justification and rationality largely in terms of meeting skeptical challenges, this approach encourages a similarly weak conception of justification, on which it is roughly a matter of not being *un*justified in believing the proposition in question. There are, however, far-reaching differences between rationality and justification which both responses to skepticism can incline us to overlook.

To begin with, rationality is the wider notion where both apply. But there is also a global kind of rationality not closely paralleled in the domain of justification. Persons may be rational in an overall way, whereas they can be justified only with respect to something specific, such as a belief or action. We can meaningfully attribute rationality to people independently of some proposition or issue they are rational *about;* but this does not hold for justification. If I could be temporarily deprived of all beliefs, I could still be rational; but insofar as I would have justification *for* believing, it would be for specific beliefs that I might justifiedly form. Justification is in a sense *focal* rather than global. It applies to a given belief, action, policy, or other specific element that admits of direct support by reasons. Rationality may be either global or focal.

As these points suggest, global rationality is roughly a capacity concept, implying the ability to grasp certain obvious truths and to make certain kinds of warranted inferences from them, as well as the ability to reason practically (in ways explored in Part II). Justification, because of the grounding it requires, is an achievement concept. To have justified beliefs or perform justified actions, I (or my cognitive or motivational system) must have appropriately responded—often, to be sure, without consciousness of the response—to an adequate ground or adequate reason; to be rational I need only be in a position to make adequate responses.[26]

Justification seems, moreover, to be both source-specific and source-responsive in a way that at least global rationality is not. Our justified beliefs are justified by grounds provided by our sources of justification, such as visual experience provides by perception; and we must be in some way responsive to such sources if we are to have justification for beliefs. Our overall rationality does not depend in the same way on the operation of such sources. We could possess it if they yielded no grounds or, when they do, with only a lower level of responsiveness to them, as where a rational person makes pervasive mistakes. Moreover, perhaps in part because justification is source-specific in depending on a ground or a reason supplied by a source, it is also content-specific: we are justified in some particular belief, action, policy, or other element having specific content. Overall rationality does not depend in the same way on rationality concerning any particular content, if indeed it depends on that at all (a matter pursued in some detail in Chapter 8).

The differences just stressed must not be allowed to obscure connections between justification and rationality. They are especially prominent in the focal cases. A justified belief or action, for instance, is also rational, not only in the minimal sense but in the common, approbative sense that will be clarified in this chapter as well as in later ones. If we call someone's belief or action justified, we do not question whether it is rational; to say that it is not rational is to take away with one hand something given by the other.[27]

It not clear, however, that a rational action or belief need be justified. It surely need not be if certain grossly immoral actions may, as many think, be rational, even consummately clever, yet are not justified. But let us concentrate on the case of belief. Might not a belief that represents a hunch be rational even if the person has no justifying ground? Granted, there might have to be some degree of justification for such a hunch and that would derive from some kind of ground. But that possibility is perfectly consistent with the point: a slight degree of justification for a belief need not render it prima facie justified or, certainly, justified on balance. If a rational person is in any sense "entitled" to hold it, the basis for this would not be wholly this justification. To be sure, if a rational belief is not also justified, this might bear on the rationality of *acting* on it, at least where anything one thinks important is at stake. That possibility is significant in connecting justification with rationality, but it does not undermine the point that where the notions of rationality and justification both apply, possession of the former does not entail overall possession of the latter.

As these examples suggest, even in focal cases there are different standards, and presumably different associated notions, of rationality. With both beliefs and actions, 'rational' may have its minimal force, as roughly equivalent to the absence of irrationality. This notion seems operative particularly in cases where something seems odd or evidentially questionable. If there is a question of committing someone to an institution, an action may be called rational when it does not violate such basic standards as those of self-preservation, and it is thereby not irrational. If a belief seems superstitious and otherwise ill-grounded, calling it rational in defense of the person may indicate only that it is not inconsistent or "crazy," where ruling out irrationality is all that matters. More commonly, however, to call a belief (or action) rational is to imply not mere absence of irrationality but a kind of harmony with reason, understood in a way that gives the sources and transmission of justification I have described a central role. This quite common sort of rationality—the main kind that is of concern in the book—is roughly *consonance with reason*.

If the ascription of rationality in the sense that implies consonance with reason is not always laudatory, it is least minimally approbative. Particularly where it is merely approbative, justification is not implied. This is clearest for beliefs and other cognitive elements, such as judgments and expectations. Consider a juror hearing mixed evidence. We can imagine a point at which the evidence makes it rational for a juror to believe the accused is (say) innocent, but the evidence is insufficient to justify that belief. Here two jurors could reasonably disagree on the verdict. Indeed, in some such cases it might *also* be rational for the same juror to believe the accused is guilty. The same rational person might arrive at either rational belief. This does not seem so for justification. The point seems plain if we apply it to the minimal kind of rationality constituted by absence of irrationality, but it also appears to hold for some approbative ascriptions of rationality. A body of evidence can be such as to make it rational to judge a matter either way. If, however, it *justifies* one in believing p, it does not also justify one in believing not-p.

For action, by contrast, although it is true that rationality, even as consonance with reason, does not imply justification, it is *not* true that one cannot be justified in taking either of two competing courses of action. This can be explained by the point (to be developed in Part II) that whereas mutually incompatible propositions cannot both be true, mutually incompatible deeds can both be good.

The case of a trial enables us to see something more. It concerns the relation between reasons and justification. I take reasons for beliefs (and for other attitudes) to count toward their justification and, a fortiori, toward their rationality. This seems to be part of what it is to be a reason, though I do not offer it as an analysis (nor do I assume that an analysis of this central normative notion is either needed or even possible). The same holds of grounds for these elements; these may also be called reasons, but the term is less natural for non-inferential grounds, such as visual experience. What the trial example nicely brings out is that no sheer number of justificatory reasons for a belief makes it irrational not to hold it: with every such reason one acquires for believing the accused is guilty, the defense could provide a counterbalancing one supporting innocence. Even strong evidence is defeasible. Moreover, even apart from counterbalancing elements, there can be minor reasons, such as unconfident testimony on a disputed matter, which can mount up indefinitely without demanding belief. Overall justification and overall rationality are holistic notions, and the intimate relation of reasons to both must be explicated (as I seek to do in this book) by an overall theory that embodies a network of complex and often highly qualified principles.

It will help us in understanding both the relation between reasons and justification and rationality in general to consider the main kinds of reasons for believing. There are at least five major, interrelated kinds of what we might call cognitive reasons: first, normative reasons—*reasons there are* to believe something, say that there is global warming; second, person-relative normative reasons, reasons there are *for me* to believe, say for me to believe there is global warming, since I am aware of what I should (but need not) see is evidence for it; third, possessed reasons—*reasons I have*, as where I am aware of such evidence and see its purport; fourth, *reasons why* I believe something—explanatory reasons; and fifth, motivating (or actuating) reasons, *reasons for which* I believe, as where I believe there is global warming on the basis of my beliefs expressing my evidence for this. There is a great deal to be said about reasons of these sorts, and much will be said in this and later chapters. Here some preliminary points must serve.

Reasons as just described are propositions (conceived as meeting certain conditions, e.g., being true or believed by a person) and hence can all be expressed by a propositional clause, such as 'that scientific evidence indicates global warming'. But whereas a proposition, q, say, an obvious truth implying p, may be a reason there *is* to believe p, and even for *me* to believe it, whether or not anyone believes q—and thus q is in that sense an *external reason* for believing p—q must be believed by me in order to be a reason *for which* I believe p. The proposition that scientific evidence supports the hypothesis of global warming can be a reason *to* think it is occurring whether or not I believe this proposition, but it is not a reason *for* which I believe this unless I believe this on the basis of (believing) that proposition. The case of possessed reasons is more difficult: the clearest instance is believing the proposition that constitutes the reason. But suppose I have perceptual grounds, or believe propositions ("premises"), that clearly support q, which is a (normative) reason to believe p, but I do not believe q. I might still be said to *have* a reason to believe p, or at least an implicit reason. I am as it were on the verge of believing, and my evidence base entitles me to believe, a proposition that *constitutes* a reason to believe, *p*.

It is plausible to construe at least normative and explanatory reasons as true propositions, hence "facts"[28] in one sense of that term, but this does not obviously hold for reasons that are merely possessed, or for all those we cite as reasons for which we believe something (motivating reasons). If I have excellent justification for *p*, which is in turn strong evidence that there is global warming, I could properly cite *p* as my reason for believing there is, even if *p* happens to be false. My reason would not be *sound*, but it is at best unnatural to say I have no reason at all—or believe for no reason.

One could insist that I have only a "motivated" belief here and no reason for believing there is global warming. I grant that here my reason is not also a normative (external) reason, a reason *to believe* this; but I have a (to be sure defective) reason *for* believing this that is not a mere cause of my belief. My reason may even amply justify my believing there is global warming; for I have some ground, in the form of my justifying evidence, for *p*, as a basis on which *p* counts as my reason. For normative reasons, of course, there is *always* some objective ground, such as evidence for a scientific conclusion. If it is at least minimally well-grounded, this conclusion, in turn, might serve as a reason there *is* for me to believe there is global warming. Given the externality of normative reasons, the grounds for them, such as undiscovered evidence, need not be possessed by anyone, though the notion of a normative reason apparently does imply that they *could* be possessed.

There is a related notion of reasons for belief that will help in understanding all these points. Given that we do not believe *for* reasons until they enter our minds, and given that one belief of mine can be a reason *why* I hold another, we sometimes speak of certain beliefs themselves as reasons for believing. We can preserve these points, however, and achieve greater clarity, by construing reasons for believing as propositions and using 'reason state' for a belief that *expresses* such a reason, in the sense that its content constitutes the reason. Reasons proper, as abstract entities, are presumably not causes. But reason states, as concrete psychological elements, can be causal factors (of a certain kind).

Granted, a proposition can be cited as a reason why one believes *p*, and this *appears* to attribute causal power to it. But a proposition can *be* a reason why I believe *p* only if my believing it, or perhaps (where it is true) the fact it expresses, actually explains why I believe *p*: it is these elements, possibly working together, *not* the proposition itself, that play the relevant causal role. A reason why I believe *p*, such as brain manipulation that implants the belief, could, however, explain why I hold it without being a reason *for* anyone's believing this. Explaining reasons, then, though they must be "factual," need not be reason states. A false belief, to be sure, can explain why someone believes something else; but here the explanatory work is done by the fact that the person holds the belief, not by the falsehood believed.

10. RATIONALITY VIEWED AS A VIRTUE CONCEPT

There is a quite different perspective from which rationality and justification may be fruitfully viewed. Both the minimal concept and the consonance notion of rationality may well be partially derivative from the concept of a rational person, in a way the notion of a justified belief is not derivative from that of any kind of person. Very roughly, just as such virtuous deeds as labors for the poor may be conceived as beneficent because they are characteristic of a beneficent person and not because (for instance) they represent following a rule, one's rational beliefs are a kind appropriate to a rational person's holding them, whereas justified beliefs must rest on specific grounds of the kind such that, when cognitions based on those grounds are true, they tend to (or at least typically do) constitute knowledge.[29] A similar point may hold for the minimal notion of rationality. As we have seen, in some contexts, as where a belief seems strange, 'rational' may be used concessively to suggest minimal permissibility. Here again it might be held that the relevant standard is a (minimally) rational person. But even apart from the way justification is tied to grounds, it would be uncommon to speak of justification to indicate minimal permissibility, nor is it properly ascribable simply because the belief or action in question is not irrational.

Rational persons, it may be argued, constitute a standard for appraising beliefs and actions as rational or not, but it is less plausible to take them to be a standard for appraising them as justified or not. Given that rational people can sometimes have good experiential or reflective grounds for propositions that a rational person would tend to disbelieve, as where I am justifiedly convinced by a clever "proof" to take an implausible claim to be a logical truth, it would be a mistake to say that justified beliefs are equivalent to those that tend, in virtue of their content, to be appropriate to rational persons. Indeed, some justified beliefs must be arrived at by exposure to sources, including inferential ones such as proofs, that succeed only by overcoming the antecedent beliefs that are otherwise appropriate to rational persons. Paradoxes, such as Russell's famous one, illustrate this point.[30]

To some extent, however, the concept of rationality behaves more like a virtue concept than like a rule concept. Quite commonly, at least, its cognitive and behavioral instances apparently possess it more owing to their appropriateness to a rational person than on account of meeting a specific criterion for, say, rational belief or rational action.[31] This analogy should not, however, be pushed very far. For one thing, justification on the part of these elements entails their rationality. Thus, even if the main criterion of rationality is appropriateness to a rational person, that is a standard which is by no means wholly independent of the specific criteria for justification. Moreover, if I *never* achieved justification for belief, and particularly if I had sufficiently important and readily exposable unjustified beliefs—say, beliefs that direct much of my conduct and are easily seen to be ill-grounded—I could not count as a rational person in any sense rich enough for a cognition of mine to receive any presumption of rationality by virtue of being held by a rational person.

The kinds of examples just considered suggest that someone whose belief-formation processes do not accord to a significant degree with standards of justification of the kind we have been discussing here and in Chapter 1, for instance the standards governing perception, is not rational. A rational person whose senses are normal must form certain sorts of beliefs on the basis of perception and must not form certain other sorts of beliefs which are at odds with perceptual data. If, having just dropped a dog off at a kennel, I see a growling pit bull rushing toward me, I must normally form some belief or other about the dog, and I must not form the belief that I have merely fallen into a vivid dream. Moreover, even if to say that I am rational is not to attribute to me any particular rational beliefs, to ascribe justified (and hence rational) beliefs to me implies a degree of rationality: however global rationality may be, the possession of rational beliefs, and especially beliefs that are amply justified, counts toward it. Here the global is by no means independent of the focal, even if some presumption of focal rationality accrues to a belief by virtue of its being held—or at least reflectively held—by a rational person.

There is also a difference between rationality and justification in relation to both their sources and their role in discourse. In contexts where the minimal notion of rationality is in question, possessing it is a matter of minimal permissibility within the large realm that contrasts with irrationality, whereas justification is chiefly a matter of a kind of ground specifically connected with what we conceive as the standard basic sources of belief and justification: perception, introspection, memorial sense, and reflection. In many other contexts (the most common, I think), rationality is a matter of consonance with reason, which implies but goes beyond minimal permissibility but is less ground-specific. These contrasts may rest partly on the way justification of beliefs is associated with our *practices* of justification, for example of citing perceptual grounds to justify beliefs about observables, for which there is no precise analogue in the case of rationality. We do rationalize beliefs, chiefly by giving what we take to be grounds for them; but—where this terminology is not simply used as a way to describe justification of beliefs—rationalizing beliefs is quite different from justifying them, and indeed it does *not* count toward either the epistemic rationality or the justifiedness of the belief on whose behalf the rationalization is offered.[32] Rationalizing may illustrate quite well the rationality of the *person*. But that is so not because it succeeds in showing the rationality of its target: it is so because a good deal of rationality is required to produce a convincing appearance thereof.

So far, then, we have only some of the basic materials for a theory of rationality. Part III will add those needed beyond the elements that are shared between the theory of justification offered here and the theory of practical rationality developed in Part II. But these shared elements take us a long way. Like the elements central for understanding practical rationality, moreover, they are usable even in theories different from mine. In both domains, the theoretical and the practical, there are, I believe, basic sources; there is spontaneous formation of non-basic elements from foundational ones; there is transmission of justification and rationality from foundations to superstructure; there are interacting cognitions and experiences; and sometimes there is the defeat of justification, or of rationality, even at the basic level. How similar is the practical sphere, the domain of action and desire, either in the ways it embodies justification or, especially, in the ways it exhibits rationality? This is our next topic.

PART II

PRACTICAL REASON

3

ACTION, BELIEF, AND DESIRE

Belief is a response to the world we experience. Action is an attempt to make the world respond. The telephone rings early in the morning, and I believe it is my daughter. A fallen branch obstructs my path, and I move it. Both belief and action connect us with the world, and both can do so with greater or lesser success. In the light of what Part I shows about theoretical reason, we might say that successful belief rests on solid ground and reflects the world. Even beliefs about such abstract matters as logical truths may reflect the intellectual world: the world as experienced in thinking about the propositions in question, whatever their specific nature. In the domain of action, we seek more than to have a well-grounded and true picture of the world. We want to achieve our aims, and we tend to think of successful action as the kind that arises from rational aims and changes the world to match them. The world that is reflected by belief or changed by action may be external or internal. My beliefs formed at the piano recital concern not only what I see and hear but also what I feel aesthetically as the masterworks are rendered. My actions in buying tickets and traveling to the concert hall produce both external changes in conduct and internal changes in emotion and thought. Their success lies chiefly in yielding the rich musical experiences I sought.

In pursuing the musical aim that leads me to the concert hall, I am guided by what it is natural to call *instrumental beliefs:* beliefs that identify means to ends—for instance, about how to find tickets, transportation, friends who might attend. Action cannot be expected to succeed apart from guidance by beliefs. Beliefs, however, would be drastically limited apart from actions which expose us to the world that beliefs are to reflect. The

61

practical and the theoretical are intertwined and, in many ways, interdependent. But beliefs, and not actions, are true or false; actions, but not beliefs, are events; and beliefs, but not actions (apart from speech acts), have intentional objects.[1] There is analogy and disanalogy. A good theory of rationality should do justice to both. We have seen much about the structure and grounds of theoretical reason; practical reason is strikingly parallel. This chapter concerns chiefly its structure, but some of the substantive questions to be pursued in Chapters 4 through 6 begin to emerge as well.

1. A STRUCTURAL ANALOGY BETWEEN BELIEF AND ACTION

The domain of practical reason is above all that of action, and the theory of practical reason must clarify rational action, just as an account of theoretical reason must clarify rational belief and, especially, justified belief, which is closely connected with knowledge. Justified beliefs are grounded, ultimately, in experiential or intuitive elements, such as seeing or understanding, that constitute grounds for holding them and are not themselves beliefs. Rational action, too, is based at least in part on something other than itself that constitutes or expresses some ground or reason for performing it. Rational action (as I will illustrate in detail) is based on motivating elements, above all desire—in the widest sense of the term, which includes not only intention but any kind of wanting. This is the sense that 'want' bears when we ask someone who is about to plan a day, 'What do you want to do today?' An appropriate answer can cite anything you are motivated to do, including even unpleasant duties—the kind of which we might say, in another context, that we don't want to do them at all.

There is a further aspect of the groundedness analogy between action and belief. Action is based on motivation in much the *way* inferential beliefs are based on further, "premise" beliefs. This certainly applies to actions performed for a reason, which are the basic kind of intentional action. I board a plane in order to go to London; my reason for this—what I want from it—is to go to London; I believe that my boarding the plane is a means to going there; and I act, boarding the plane in that belief and on the basis of that desire.[2] My desire grounds my action much as a premise belief grounds a belief inferentially based on it; and, much as my action is connected to that desire by an instrumental belief in virtue of which the desire supports that action (since the belief indicates how the action will or may attain the desired object), an inferential belief is connected to a premise belief that grounds it by virtue of one's in some way taking the premise to support the proposition believed on that premise. The desire

62

to go to London is a motivational ground (a conative "premise") for boarding a plane, much as the belief that flying is the best way to go there is a cognitive ground (expressing a propositional premise) for buying an airline ticket.

Like actions and beliefs, desires can be rational or irrational. Take irrationality first. It is surely exhibited in some degree by a desire to do a deed, purely as a means to something else, when one should realize the action will not produce it. Given that from my general knowledge I should realize that waving an umbrella at a noisy plane will not quiet it down, my wanting to wave it, purely for that purpose as opposed to, say, expressing annoyance, would be irrational. If desires are even among the ultimate grounds of action, then practical reason differs from theoretical reason on this count: practical reason would not have, as ultimate grounds, only elements, such as sensations, that do not admit of justification or rationality.[3] Suppose, on the other hand, that basic desires—roughly desires for something for its own sake, commonly called *intrinsic desires*—themselves can have grounds (a question I take up later). Then the *ultimate* grounds of action may be like those of justified belief in also not admitting of rationality or justification.

Even apart from the extent to which intrinsic desires admit of rationality, we can understand practical reason only if we examine both motivation and action. A certain structural analogy between belief and action has already been outlined. First, actions, like beliefs, are grounded, by support relations (particularly instrumental ones), in something quite different from them that can justify them, namely desires. Second, actions are like beliefs—at least inferential beliefs—in being based on reasons. In the case of actions, these reasons are expressible by desires. There is also an internal analogy concerning the parallel between how beliefs can rest on other beliefs and how actions can rest on other actions. This internal analogy lies in the domain of the philosophy of mind, and it will pave the way for still another in that domain. We can then proceed to some analogies belonging to the normative theory of rationality.

2. COGNITIVE AND BEHAVIORAL HIERARCHIES

The simplest way to put the internal analogy may be this. Just as (normally) beliefs not themselves grounded in basic sources rest on other beliefs, so actions not performed in a kind of basic way rest on other actions.[4] There are some things we do basically; others we do *by* doing something else. Some people can wiggle their ears at will; others can do so only manually. It is through moving their hands that they move their ears, and in some sense the former action is the basis of the latter. The structure of action, then, is hierarchical: at any given time when we act, there is something we do basically, and everything we do non-basically we do by doing one or another thing basically.

The structure of belief is similar. Some things we believe are believed through, and on the basis of, one or more other things we believe. The former beliefs are inferential. But what we believe non-inferentially, through, say, perception, is not believed on the basis of a further belief. We believe it directly in response to experience, rather as we just raise a hand in greeting.[5] In the perceptual case, something outside us produces belief without our needing any prior, "premise beliefs" to ground it; in the behavioral case, something inside us produces an action without our needing to make any prior movement. In neither case is the priority temporal, though there may in fact be a temporal gap. With non-basic actions, the relation is in some way instrumental; the more basic action is a kind of means by which we perform the less basic one. With inferential beliefs, the relation is parallel; the more basic belief is the ground on which we hold the less basic one, as the basic act is the ground of the less basic one.

As we would expect from its epistemological counterpart, the hierarchical conception of action does not imply that there is any particular thing we must do or that there is any specific kind of action that must be basic for us; it simply says that if we do anything at all, then we do something basically, and whatever we do non-basically is done *by* doing something basically. The hierarchical view leaves open, then, just what *are* the basic kinds of actions for us.

Different agents have different repertoires of basic actions, as different people have different foundational beliefs. There may be some things, such as moving our bodies, that we can all do basically, much as there are some kinds of beliefs we all hold non-inferentially. But there may also be kinds of action basic for only one person. Think of virtuoso musicians and consummate acrobats. It is similar with foundational beliefs. Think of mathematicians and art critics. Some of what they believe directly others must arrive at inferentially.

It is consistent with the hierarchical view of action to regard only volition as truly basic action.[6] Imagine that I cannot (basically) raise an eyebrow, but I *try* to, say, by tensing certain muscles. In thus trying to raise an eyebrow, am I not doing something, something non-physical that we might conceive as in "the will," with the hope that by doing it I will move the eyebrow? Perhaps for every bodily action that seems basic, what is really basic is some such volitional act; we are simply not conscious of it in most cases, as opposed to those where, as in straining to move a limb that has gone to sleep, we find ourselves trying in vain. This volitional view would serve to root action internally—in the will, we may say, if we do not misconstrue this as implying a subpersonal agent.

It is illuminating to compare the theoretical case with the practical on this point. Let us take belief as the central theoretical attitude and action as the central practical element. If, in the distance, I cannot be certain the person I see is Steve and am told that I am mistaken in believing it is, I can not only intensify my gaze to improve my external information but also reflect on my own imagery and note that my impression is quite definite in some identifying features. Should we conclude that in ordinary perceptual cases, we simply do not notice that our truly foundational beliefs are not really about the perceived object but about features of our experience? I think not. The possibility of shoring up foundations from below does not imply that they are not really foundations.

The view that, in the way suggested, our truly basic beliefs have internal content would offer a kind of security. It would ground belief in the mind, as volition might ground action in the will. But basic beliefs can be well-grounded in the mind without having mental phenomena as *objects*. Images and other mental elements may both causally sustain and evidentially support such beliefs without figuring in their content. Internalism about the grounds of basic beliefs does not imply internalization of their content. And basic action can be well-grounded in the will without being volitional. It may be sustained and supported by motivation and cognition that represent the will, even if it is not itself an act of will. A deed can carry out my will without receiving a volitive push.

There is something properly called volition, as there certainly are beliefs about one's sensory states, and both can play a foundational role. It may be in part the influence of Cartesianism that sometimes makes it seem, for action as for belief, that as long as we can dig below a given level, it is not foundational. But, in the domain of action as in the realm of belief, foundations may vary in depth, and they may rest on different kinds of ground. The view that we reach them only at some ultimate bottom invites us to posit impenetrable and immovable bedrock that we do not need and may never find.

3. INFERENTIAL BELIEF AND INTENTIONAL ACTION

The second main analogy I want to explore in the theory of rationality—a further aspect of the groundedness analogy—is not between belief and action in general but between beliefs based on others that express supporting reasons for them (roughly inferential beliefs) and actions based on motivational elements that express such reasons for them (roughly intentional actions). The analogy is normatively important, but it is best appreciated if we delay normative questions and first consider the parallel between inferential belief and intentional action. In doing this, we can see how some of the conditions for rational action are similar to those that govern justified inferential belief, and in that light we can proceed to explore rational desire as an essential basis of rational action.

Motivation may be conceived in many ways. There may be no concept as representative of motivation as belief is of cognition. But wanting, in the widest sense, may be, and it is a constituent in intending, which is the other leading candidate for such a representative motivational role.[7] There are, moreover, intrinsic wants—wants for things for their own sake and not as means to something further—just as there are non-inferential beliefs. We can discover much by considering wanting as the most representative motivational element.

Just as non-inferential beliefs are not based on further beliefs whose objects are in some sense taken as grounds for them, intrinsic wants are not based on other wants to whose fulfillment their objects are taken to be in some sense a means. Suppose I ask a person to appraise an antique. This action is doubly grounded. It is not behaviorally basic, being done by, and in that sense grounded on, doing something else, such as writing a letter. Nor is it motivationally basic: it is also grounded in a reason I have for it, since I do it because I want to get an expert appraisal and believe the person can provide it. This belief links my requesting the appraisal to what I want and thereby grounds my action in my reason for it: to get an expert appraisal. Moreover, normatively this can surely be a good reason for my action (since getting an expert appraisal can be a good reason for asking one of that person). If this is so, we can see a normative parallel: the action can be based on an apparently rational desire, rather as my belief that a performance is about to begin might be based on my justified belief that the pianist has come on stage. The action can thus be rational on the basis of a good reason for which it is performed, much in the way a belief can be justified by a good premise on the basis of which it is held.

One thing that emerges here is a counterpart of psychological foundationalism in the theoretical domain. If we may assume that every intentional action is performed in order to realize some desire, then it is plausible to hold that intentional action is grounded (at least normally) in one or more intrinsic desires.[8] We might call this *the conative groundedness view* of intentional action. Like the hierarchical view of the structure of action, this view is a thesis in the philosophy of mind and is not normative. But it suggests an important normative parallel (further explored later) to the theoretical case: much as an inferential belief is not justified if it is (wholly) based on another belief that is not justified, an action is not rational if it is (wholly) grounded in a desire that fails to provide a good reason. (This is not to say the action must be *irrational*—a very strong negative description that does not follow here.)

The conative groundedness view is, however, richer than the hierarchical view of action in at least one way. In the former, beliefs play an essential role in the foundational structure, typically an instrumental role, as where one does something in the belief that it will realize (and so is a means to satisfying) a desire. I can, however, play a chord by spreading my fingers in a certain way, without having any instrumental belief about their pattern. Even to form such a belief I might have to watch myself play the chord to see how I actually spread the fingers.[9] To be sure, in the behavioral hierarchies that are central for understanding rationality, the agent is doing something *as* a means (in some sense) to the further action, and hence the agent is acting from some motive. Given the way in which motivation underlies action, it is natural to ask whether, in the light of the analogy between practical and theoretical reason, motivation may also be viewed as like belief in having a hierarchical structure.

It may be so viewed, and we thus have a third significant analogy between the theoretical and practical realms: just as I have direct beliefs as bases of other beliefs, and desires as motivational bases of action, I have intrinsic desires as bases of other desires.[10] I want my student to get a good job because I intrinsically want her to flourish; I want that for its own sake. It is not impossible to have a deeper desire, say, to fulfill my obligation as placement director. Suppose I acquire some deeper desire. This may put the first want higher up in the structure, but it need not diminish its rationality or that of an action, such as making a recommendation, meant to realize the want. It is also quite possible to have an intrinsic or other non-instrumental desire on which no other desire is based, just as one may have non-inferential perceptual beliefs on which no further beliefs are based. Even a good foundation may never be used. Some intrinsic desires, moreover, such as those that might result from jealousy or wishful thinking, may not "merit" further desires' resting on them. Still, at any given time, my action is ultimately grounded in one or more of my intrinsic desires.

To be sure, there may *be*, and I may *have*, reasons for wanting something that I in fact want intrinsically, just as there may be, and I may have, reasons for my direct belief that there is a piano before me. But just as I may have potentially foundational materials that I could, yet need not and do not, place beneath those on which I have already built, I can have potential justifiers that are not part of my actual justificatory basis of belief, and I can have potential grounds for action that never figure as a basis of anything I actually do. At any given time, however, I have some wants—say, for food and drink, conversation and reflection—that are not based, in any inferential way, on other wants.[11] Surely we have no infinite or circular chains of desires, for the same sorts of reasons that we have no such chains of inferential beliefs.[12]

If all this is so, then the psychological structure of motivation is like that of belief: if we want anything at all, we want something or other intrinsically.[13] This view is a version of *motivational foundationalism.* Aristotle implied a form of it in Book One of the *Nicomachean Ethics,*[14] and Hume affirmed a hedonistic variant in the *Enquiry Concerning the Principles of Morals.*[15] It is natural for philosophers who hold this view to adopt some normative counterpart of it, say, the view that the rationality of a superstructure desire depends on that of some intrinsic (and in that sense foundational) desire on which it is based. But that is an independent thesis. Let us begin to examine it by briefly exploring whether there can *be* any rational intrinsic desires (a question to be pursued much further in Chapters 5 and 6).

4. SOME RATIONALITY CONSTRAINTS ON DESIRES

We have seen grounds for thinking that practical reason is like theoretical reason both in having a psychologically foundational structure and in related normative respects. It does not follow from what we have seen, however, that practical reason has *normative* foundations analogous to directly justified beliefs. But many philosophers at least since Plato have taken a view that implies this. Are there intrinsic rational wants, as there apparently are directly justified beliefs?

Contrary to how it may appear, I do not mean to identify intrinsic rational wants with *intrinsically rational* ones. These would be desires that, because of properties essential to them, like their content, cannot fail to be rational. If some desires are intrinsically rational, it presumably is by virtue of their content. We need not rule out this possibility (which Aristotle seemed to think is realized by the desire for one's own happiness). But just as a noninferentially justified belief may have only prima facie justification, a rational intrinsic desire may be only prima facie (and defeasibly) rational.

Consider instrumental wants first. I begin with them rather than with intrinsic ones because in the former case the notion of rationality more clearly, or at least less controversially, applies. We can then explore rationality for intrinsic wants. In a liberal usage, a want may be said to be *instrumentally (prima facie) rational* when one believes (or at least rationally believes) that its realization will achieve something else one wants.[16] This is an instrumentalist generation principle: like the justificational generation principles cited in Chapter 1, it specifies a kind of ground of a normative status. (As one would expect from the parallel with belief, a want may be structurally as well as episodically based on another want.)

The commonest case of an instrumentally rational want is a desire for something one rationally believes will achieve something one wants for its own sake, such as conversation, rest, a good meal, or, in many cases, a fulfillment of a duty that represents a personal commitment. Relative to my wanting my student to get a job, my wanting to recommend her for it is rational. One might resist this conclusion because there are limited occasions on which it is natural to speak here of rationality as opposed to, say, naturalness. But surely someone who thinks the student utterly inappropriate for this job could say, "You want to recommend her for that! That's irrational." In this context one could go on to explain why one's desire is in fact perfectly rational.

Consider, on the other hand, occasions when one lacks an instrumentally rational want which one ought to have. Suppose that I did not want to recommend the student for a certain highly suitable job. A friend who discovered this might say that I ought to want to do it; and if I were not persuaded and I admitted that I in fact still wanted *not* to recommend her, then I could be plausibly told (apart from my citing a reason, like my believing I am the wrong person to do the recommendation) that this negative desire is not rational: it goes against my overall, grounding desire in the situation. Moreover, unlike a desire for sweets when one is trying to lose weight, it has no positive attraction to recommend it.

If the first example is one in which a want is instrumentally rational because it is for a means to satisfying an underlying desire, and if the second case is one in which an instrumentally rational want is missing, there are also cases in which an instrumental want seems to be self-defeating and on that ground to *lack* rationality. Suppose that I wanted to recommend my student to someone who is obviously the wrong person to help. If all this is very credibly pointed out to me and I believe it, yet I somehow continue to want to recommend her to that person, we would have another case of a desire that is instrumentally not rational. It is possible, but not normally rational, to want to do something (wholly) to achieve a further end when one realizes that it will tend to prevent achieving that end.

Instrumental wants are quite different from intrinsic ones. The applicability of standards of rationality to the former does not imply their applicability to the latter; and, in part owing to the influence of the Humean tradition, there has been more resistance to countenancing rationality for intrinsic desires. Can one rationally or irrationally want something for its *own* sake? Or are intrinsic desires more like brute conative givens, natural perhaps, but not properly considered rational? If they can be rational, what bearing does that have on rational action?

Again the parallel to theoretical reason is illuminating. On my view, then, a good answer to the question whether there can be rational intrinsic desires must not be framed on the model of a Cartesian epistemological foundationalism. There need be no analogue of epistemic certainty: no indefeasibly rational desires.[17] Moreover, since the foundationalism I have so far developed concerns mainly structure and not specific content, there need be no particular thing, even if there are kinds of things, which everyone wants for its own sake: a pluralism of rational ends is left quite open.[18]

The parallel between belief and desire, and, correspondingly, between inferential belief and rational action, extends to the issue of skepticism, which arises in the practical domain. Unless, in Cartesian fashion, I feel impelled to build a body of beliefs and desires to bear the added weight of skepticism about my rationality, I do not have to reinforce foundations that are already sound and thus seek intrinsically rational desires to yield indefeasible reasons for my conduct. We should not multiply foundations beyond necessity.

Indeed, supposing there are rational intrinsic desires, if they are like directly but defeasibly justified beliefs, then just as such a belief can be (normatively) defeated and thereafter irrationally held, a rational intrinsic desire can suffer defeat and then be irrationally possessed. If I come to believe, justifiedly, that a film I want (intrinsically) to see will not be in any way enjoyable, say, because I discover that it is unremittingly offensive, my continuing to want (intrinsically) to see it is not rational. I may realize that I will disappoint a friend in not going, and I may thereby have an instrumental reason to want to see it; but this is a new and extrinsic ground. Defeat of one ground may make room for another, perhaps a better one; but even foundational grounds are liable to defeat. As in the case of theoretical reason, moreover, (normative) defeat characteristically comes only from elements that have a measure of rationality themselves: from a rational belief, for instance, or, for instrumental desires, from a competing and at least equally rational desire.

There is, then, a fourth major analogy between the foundational elements of practical reason and those of theoretical reason. Just as epistemological foundationalism is committed (in this respect) only to the possibility of non-inferentially, but defeasibly, justified beliefs, its practical

70

counterpart is committed only to the possibility of non-instrumentally, yet defeasibly, rational desires. And just as one cannot in general read off the rationality of a person's belief from the content of the belief, one cannot in general read off the rationality of a person's desire from the object of that desire. One may unjustifiedly believe even a plain truth, and one may irrationally want even a plainly good thing.[19] This is not to deny that there are objects of desire, that it would be at best abnormal to want irrationally, as there are propositions, that it would be at least abnormal to believe in irrationally. But that is not because grounds do not still matter; it is because of how readily they are possessed for certain kinds of contents of desire.

Considerations of coherence, moreover, have a role in conative rationality as they do in the theoretical case. There are, again, two quite different aspects of this role. Positively, the mutual coherence of one's intrinsic desires—say, the kind of coherence based on their being jointly satisfiable and each in some way directed toward one's happiness—can count at least as a mark, as distinct from a source, of their rationality. Aristotle provides a good picture of such motivational coherence in the eudaemonism of the *Nicomachean Ethics*. Negatively, incoherence can warrant correcting basic desires, for instance where one discovers that satisfying one would thwart another. There is even a parallel to the rejection of epistemic deductivism concerning the transmission of justification: rationality may be transmitted from a foundational desire to a superstructure one even when satisfying the latter is just likely, and not certain, to satisfy the former. Thus, wanting to recommend someone can be rational even if it has only a slight chance of producing the intrinsically desired result.

5. THE POSSIBILITY OF RATIONALITY FOR INTRINSIC DESIRE

If the structural analogy between theoretical and practical reason is as far-reaching as it appears, we should also explore the analogy in relation to a fifth dimension: content. What range of intrinsic desires, considered in terms of content, might be directly rational, as opposed to being rational on the basis of, say, a practical inference? The larger question here is whether practical reason has normative as well as psychological foundations. The least controversial examples concern one's own pleasure or pain. This accounts in part for the power of egoism as the perspective from which anything whose rationality is to be shown—such as moral conduct—must be vindicated. It is both natural and prima facie rational to want to avoid the pains of being beaten and to experience the pleasures of good food.

71

Intrinsically wanting the things that constitute one's happiness is also a good candidate for a rational intrinsic desire, particularly if understood along Aristotelian lines and tied to activities whose performance can yield the distinct kind of happiness sought: the rediscovery of an old friend over a leisurely meal, a refreshing swim in buoyant sunlit waters, an effortless run through a favorite piano piece, a walk on a mountain ridge that commands a clear view of a lush green valley.

Is there any reason to deny that such desires are directly, rather than just instrumentally, rational? The view is highly consonant with what we think of as normally wanted—intrinsically—by rational persons. It is, moreover, in no way provincial or ethnocentric, either in the diversity of its proponents or in the variety of agents whose behavior confirms it. It allows for a multitude of rational ends, given the unlimited varieties of happiness. More positively, many of the desires that are directly rational on this view would gain one's approval from reflection both on their objects and on how they would fit the life plans of a wide variety of people.

A different way to see the plausibility of construing some intrinsic desires as rational is to consider how we assess the rationality of persons. Can we even conceive of rational persons who, though they have desires, have none that are plausibly conceived as directly rational, say, wanting to avoid pain and to pursue goals whose achievement is a realization of some human capacity? Can one conceive of rational persons who are, say, indifferent to their own physical freedom or to their own happiness or suffering—not in the sense that they cannot sacrifice freedom or happiness or endure suffering, for certain reasons, but in a sense that implies having no desire to achieve the former and to avoid the latter?[20]

It may be that we can be manipulated so as to have no desires whatever, at least for a time. But the question is whether one can conceive a rational person who *has* desires, but none that are both rational and intrinsic. This seems doubtful: if there must be some intrinsic desires in order for there to be any desires at all, such a person will have intrinsic desires. These might be selfish; but selfish intrinsic desires might not count against one's rationality. The question here is whether there are rational intrinsic desires, not whether there are any that are non-egoistic (a topic pursued in Chapters 4 and 6). Self-destructive (intrinsic) desires of certain kinds, however, say, wanting to burn oneself, in general would count against it.[21]

Try to imagine someone who knew, so far as one can, the pain of being burned to death but somehow intrinsically wanted such fiery self-destruction. Would the desire not be irrational? If the person has a reason, such as purgation by self-immolation, the matter is quite different; but if this reason partly grounds the desire, then the desire is not (purely) intrinsic.

To be sure, the intrinsic desire for fiery self-destruction is quite unnatural, and one might argue that this is *why* we mistakenly think it is irrational. It is indeed unnatural, and that may be the readiest term of assessment to apply. But to say on this basis that it cannot also be irrational is rather like saying that someone whose most salient problem is perversity cannot also be stupid.

One might think that there could be irrational intrinsic desires, but no rational ones (except in the minimal sense that some are not *ir*rational). Perhaps the point of view of rationality identifies, as it were, some evils, but no goods. But is nothing worth pursuing or preserving for its own sake? A minimal case, surely, is freedom from pain. Is this, however, wanted merely negatively or as an essential aspect of positive goals? It is at least not normal for anyone who rationally wants to avoid pain not to have as well a positive intrinsic desire for the peace of being without pain or at least (when suffering it) for the relief that comes with ending it. This relief, moreover, can have a positive value: it can feel good, even exhilarating, to pass from pain to normality.[22] I doubt that any plausible view explains both how it can be rational for us to want, intrinsically, to avoid pain yet not rational for us to want, intrinscially, at least the contrasting relief that follows its cessation.

More must be said on the question of rational intrinsic desire, but it is not premature to say here that there are things which it is at least prima facie rational to want intrinsically. This conclusion holds even if the only such things are avoidances of evils: the central point is that there are rational intrinsic desires; it is not about their specific content.

The same conclusion is suggested, in a less direct way, by the powerful defeating role of certain beliefs. Why is it, for instance, that it is at least prima facie irrational to want something non-instrumentally while firmly believing that it will be entirely without pleasure and wholly unsatisfying? Consider such a desire. A hungry child eating away at a box of candies might, even when stuffed and no longer enjoying the cloying mouthfuls, still have a non-instrumental desire for more. If this desire is due simply to excitement and gustatory momentum rather than anticipation of good flavor, it is not rational. It has outlived its grounds. The desire seems *irrational* if, with good reason, the child *realizes* there will be no more pleasure and no additional nourishment. We then have not only a continued desire whose grounds are perceptibly absent but persistence of a desire in the face of a realization that its object is positively unrewarding.

Still, we might ask, could such irrationality be simply instrumental? This is doubtful. It is not as if the child wanted to eat more candy as a means to pleasure and should realize—say, because it is obvious—that eating more will not be enjoyable. It may be possible to have such an instrumental want, but that is neither the case here nor the norm in pursuing things for the pleasure. The child wants more candy non-instrumentally. Perhaps the irrationality depends on the belief—or on the child's ample justification for holding the belief—that eating more would not be enjoyable. But that dependence would not show that there are no directly rational or irrational desires, only that practical rationality can depend, at least negatively, on theoretical rationality.[23] That possibility is consistent with my view of both.

Indeed, the analogy between intrinsic wants and non-inferential beliefs—particularly their similarity in being open to a kind of defeasibility by rational considerations—*supports* the view that such desires admit of rationality. Consider again the unnatural desire to burn oneself. If we should ask the person to explain it, we would respond quite differently depending on what we are told. A foolish belief that burning oneself will be simply invigorating can leave the desire merely regrettable: the person's irrationality is cognitive, and we know where to focus critical and reformative efforts. By contrast, a belief that the experience will be painful and destructive would make the desire not only prima facie inexplicable, but also prima facie irrational.

Even if we do not presuppose that pain is intrinsically bad (a question to be discussed later), irrationality seems a natural and proper notion to apply to a non-instrumental desire to burn oneself. There is a sense in which that desire does not respond as it should to reason—to a justified belief about the object of desire. This supports the assessment of the desire as irrational: it does not respond to an appropriate reason. One might say that the fact that the fire will be painful cannot be taken to be a reason to avoid (rather than want) it unless pain is intrinsically bad; but this may be too strong a claim. I find it plausible, but I want to leave open the possibility that the existence of (objective) reason to avoid the pain does not require countenancing intrinsic value.

6. DESIRES, INTENTIONS, AND VALUES

It should be easy to see at this point that the mainly structural account developed so far can be generalized. What holds for the structure of desire applies to that of all the conative attitudes, including intention, just as what holds for the structure of belief holds for all the cognitive attitudes, including knowledge. The application of these structural points is not, however, simple. Intentions may be instrumentally based on other intentions; but they need not be based on intentions as opposed to desires. I can intend to write a referee on the basis of a desire to get an assessment even when I have only a slight hope, rather than an intention, of getting it.[24] Similarly, consider judgments, understood cognitively, that is, as judgments *held* rather than as *acts* of judging. Judgments may be based on other judgments, but they need not be based precisely on other judgments, as opposed to beliefs. Grounds may be different, even in kind, from what they ground. This is also illustrated by values, in the psychological sense of *valuations*—valuings conceived as attitudes and not actions or simply evaluative beliefs. Valuations may be based on other valuations; but some valuations might be based on beliefs, or indeed on experiences, such as those one finds rewarding.

All of the propositional attitudes—of which believing, wanting, intending, and valuing are of central interest here—exhibit some kind of foundational structure. But belief and, to a lesser extent, desire have a kind of *structural autonomy:* non-foundational beliefs are always based on one or more other beliefs and may be justified by them; and typically non-foundational desires are based on foundational desires and may be justified by them, though they may also be based on and justified by beliefs, such as those to the effect that the thing wanted is good. This view of belief and its inferential role in relation to desire is controversial, since arguably one would have to *want* or at least tend to want the kind of good in question in order for the belief that something has it to justify or, especially, generate wanting that thing. I doubt this, but it is reasonable to leave the possibility open.[25]

By contrast with belief and desire, all of the other propositional attitudes seem less autonomous. They not only have either belief or desire as a component but, more important, appear to be grounded at least partly in one or more of those cognitive or conative components. For instance, for valuations, a kind of axiological foundationalism holds: if one values anything at all, there is something or other one values intrinsically (for its own sake), and in that sense non-inferentially; and any other valuations one holds are based on some intrinsic valuation. But a valuation of, say, understanding, as a ground of a valuation of consulting a colleague, succeeds as a ground in part because it embodies a desire to understand or a belief that understanding is (say) good, or both. Similar points can be made for other propositional attitudes.[26]

One further question must be answered to complete this sketch of the structure of the practical sphere. How are the superstructure elements linked to the foundational ones? If any propositional attitude stands out for a special role both in the structure and in the rationality of all the others, it is belief. Belief is the crucial connective tissue that links instrumental desires to intrinsic desires on which they are based, extrinsic valuations to intrinsic valuations on which they are grounded, and so forth. My wanting to recommend the student is based on my wanting her to flourish, not directly, but *through* my believing that my recommending her will contribute to this. My valuing exercise as a means to physical well-being is linked to my intrinsic valuing of that state *through* my belief that exercise is necessary for it.

There is less clarity about whether every belief based on another must be linked to it by a third belief. Consider my belief that the phone was answered, which is based on my further belief that the third ring was short (interrupted) and not followed by a fourth. A case can be made that there must be a connecting belief, at least if we allow that it may be *de re* (a belief *of*, rather than a belief *that*), for instance my believing, *of* an implication relation, that it holds between the proposition that the third ring was short and not followed by a fourth and the proposition that the phone was answered.[27] Whether or not this is so, there must be at least a disposition to form such a connecting belief: even if I do not believe an implication relation to hold between the two propositions in question, I am disposed to form this or some similar belief if I consider the relation between the two propositions, one of which I believe on the basis of the other. Even this is important.

Even if there sometimes is no connecting belief where one belief is (inferentially) based on a second, it would remain significant that belief plays such a connecting role in all "inferential" relations between other propositional attitudes, and that nothing else plays it in the case of inferential beliefs. Normatively, at least, and—so far as one can tell from everyday observation—causally as well, where one or more propositional attitudes justifies one or more others, belief is the main connective tissue among them.

7. FOUNDATIONALIST, COHERENTIST, AND FUNCTIONALIST CONCEPTIONS OF PRACTICAL RATIONALITY

If practical and theoretical rationality are as closely parallel as I hold, is there a practical counterpart of epistemological coherentism? There apparently is, though this possibility has not been widely explored.[28] In the practical sphere, it is instrumentalism that is the most influential view plausibly considered a kind of coherentism. For instrumentalism, although there may be things we naturally desire intrinsically, there are no rational intrinsic desires. We do, however, have rational extrinsic desires, and their rationality derives from how well their realization would, on our beliefs,[29] contribute to satisfying our intrinsic desires.

For instrumentalism, the rationality of actions is similarly subordinate to sheer intrinsic desire and may be conceived as governed only by coherence criteria. Many different criteria are possible; the leading candidate is probably a maximization standard, which (in one version) says that rational actions must contribute at least as much—in the light of the agent's beliefs—to intrinsic desire satisfaction as any (available) alternative. Above all, this standard may be taken to imply that if I do something which, on my beliefs, yields less satisfaction of my intrinsic desires[30] than something I might have done, I act irrationally, or at least I fail to act rationally. If I want a good supply of bread for the weekend, I should not take two of the loaves I like at $1.90 each when I have just seen the sale sign offering three for $5 and know that I can afford and use three. My behavior is incoherent with my desires, at least in the sense that given my beliefs and desires, I would, on even brief reflection, have preferred to do something else.

There is a deeper conception of instrumentalism. Pure instrumentalism is best viewed as a kind of *functionalism about practical rationality*. My action is rational provided that it appropriately[31] contributes to satisfying my intrinsic desires whatever they are.[32] Their intrinsic nature—especially their content—is irrelevant (apart from considerations that are not substantive, such as the logical impossibility of realizing the desire). For this reason the intrinsic nature of my actions—their act-type—is also irrelevant: no specific act-type is as such rational, since the rationality of action depends on the intrinsic desires the agent happens to have. Viewed as a functionalist position, instrumentalism can be weakened to construe rational action as needing only to provide a satisfactory, as opposed to maximal, degree of gratification of desire. This weaker position is psychologically more realistic, but does not free us of the difficulties faced by any instrumentalist conception of rationality.[33]

Instrumental desires, on this functionalist view, are to be similarly appraised. Like an action, an instrumental desire is rational only insofar as realizing it contributes to satisfying one's intrinsic desires. In the theory of practical reason, to be rational is to serve intrinsic desire. Some servants are better than others; those they serve are not good or bad, they are simply demanding brutes. If one intrinsically wants them equally much, playing the most elegant and zesty tennis game is no more worthy of desire than wallowing in a muddy ditch. A passage in *Macbeth* well expresses how indiscriminate desire can be. Testing the loyalty of his hearers as potential subjects should he become king, Malcolm says:

> ... there's no bottom, none,
> In my voluptuousness. Your wives, your daughters,
> Your matrons and your maids, could not fill up
> The cistern of my lust, and my desire
> All continent impediments would o'erbear
> That did oppose my will. Better Macbeth
> Than such a one to reign. (Act IV, sc. iii, 60–66)

By a pure instrumentalist standard, this lust is beyond reproach. Being stronger than all its conative competitors, it is the authoritative foundation of action.[34]

As a functionalist view, instrumentalism must deny not only that there are desires whose rationality is intrinsic to them but also that there are intrinsic desires rational by virtue of their non-instrumental grounding in enjoyment of the kinds of experiences they are directed toward, whether the enjoyment is active, as in singing, or passive, as in sunbathing. This functionalism can, however, treat the rationality of action as a kind of well-groundedness *relative* to the intrinsic, and hence foundational, desires one happens to have. It is thus readily conceived as a subjective foundationalism.[35]

An instrumentally rational action would, to be sure, cohere with one's overall set of relevant desires and beliefs. But that might be simply because it is grounded in this framework quite as it would be on the foundationalist view I have developed. What promotes one's system of ends coheres with it, just as a belief supported by one's foundational beliefs coheres with them. Here coherence would be at most a consequential necessary condition for rationality, perhaps an inevitable result of it and a reliable sign of it, but not a ground of it.

There is a further respect in which instrumentalism may be viewed as a foundationalist account. It gives to incoherence the same kind of defeating role that it plays in any plausible foundationalism. Just as incoherence may override a prima facie justified belief by introducing an inconsistency between it and certain foundational beliefs, defeat by an incoherence might render an action irrational relative to one's intrinsic desires when it is performed instead of an alternative that would serve them better. The same holds for an instrumental desire: one should not harbor it if realizing the desire would not (or at least, on one's evidence, one should believe that it would not) conduce to realization of any intrinsic desire, any more than one should perform an action meeting this condition. As such cases suggest, incoherence in the practical realm differs from incoherence in the theoretical domain, particularly because desires to do and not to do something, say to help a child (because the task is hard) and not help a child (because the practice is needed), are not mutually incoherent. This difference is significant and is taken into account by the theory I am constructing.

In one way, instrumentalist foundationalism contrasts with the moderate foundationalism I have developed. For instrumentalism, intrinsic desires are not subject to defeat from above or by beliefs about their objects. They can be (normatively) defeated, if at all, only by their peers, as where we can see that satisfying one intrinsic desire will frustrate another, stronger intrinsic desire. The instrumentalist's foundations, then, would be construed functionally rather than substantively; and, apart from such defects as having clearly impossible objects, they would be defeasible only by elements of the same functional kind. But they would otherwise operate much as any other foundations do, for instance in causally supporting superstructure elements and in conferring rationality on a selected class of them. At least until we have a sharper specification of what constitutes coherence, then, it seems preferable to take instrumentalism to be a subjective foundationalism rather than a kind of coherentism.

8. A PROCEDURAL INSTRUMENTALISM

Some philosophers have qualified instrumentalism by imposing procedural constraints. This yields a less subjectivist and more plausible version of the position. On one such view, my rational actions are those that appropriately contribute to the intrinsic desires I would have if, in the light of relevant facts, I reflected adequately on my intrinsic desires.[36] This rules out some possible intrinsic desires—though not necessarily the same kinds in different people—and thereby restricts the basis of rationality. There is no particular ground on which we must build or even, in any sense independent of this reflective procedure, *should* build, but we may not use materials we would ourselves reject under conditions that— procedurally as opposed to substantively—seem appropriate for making normative appraisals.

This view may be considered a procedurally constrained instrumentalism or a procedural foundationalism, depending on what we want to emphasize. It is instrumentalist in taking rational action to be action that serves desires, but it restricts the relevant (non-instrumental) desires to those that would survive certain screening procedures. It is foundationalist in taking rational action to be well-grounded, through the agent's beliefs, in appropriate foundational elements—those desires that, by virtue of capacity to survive the purgative procedure, "deserve" to be unmoved movers of conduct. But the view is not, like the theory I am developing, a substantive foundationalism, since it specifies no particular kinds of objects, not even as broad a category of objects as enjoyable experiences, as generally appropriate to rational desire. What kinds of objects these might be will be considered later, though I do not propose a closed list.

The results of applying a constrained instrumentalism to appraising human action might be quite similar to those one would get from the perspective of a substantive foundationalism. Just as we are built so that the most coherent systems of belief we can construct are apparently those that give a basic role to perception and the other standard sources, we are built so that the intrinsic desires most likely to survive the scrutiny required by constrained instrumentalism are apparently the kind that represent the common human quest to achieve enjoyment and satisfaction and to avoid pain and suffering. Even a substantive foundationalism, however, may have a high degree of neutrality regarding the objects appropriate to rational desire. It specifies only *kinds* of appropriate objects, such as those whose realization is pleasant, and so may countenance a vast range of directly rational wants. This range is at least as wide as the variety of experiences—including actions and activities—that yield pleasure.

The character of some of these kinds of objects of desire has been suggested by several of our examples. The next chapter and later ones appraise instrumentalism in detail and further explore some of the kinds of intrinsic wants that apparently are rational and the basis on which they seem to be so. But quite apart from how that inquiry turns out, the high degree of structural analogy between theoretical and practical reason should now be clear. Above all, in both the theoretical and the practical domains there are foundational and superstructure elements, inferential and causal connections between the two kinds, criteria of rationality for each kind, and a range of experiences, for instance perceptual and hedonic, that apparently provide basic grounds for the rationality of theoretical and practical elements based on them. Even apart from a more substantive parallel, this analogy provides some of the material needed for a unified theory of rationality, one that accounts for it in both the theoretical and the practical domains. Our next task is to look more closely at the sources and grounds of practical reasons.

THE SOURCES OF PRACTICAL REASONS

On a hot summer afternoon, a cool swim can be just the thing. There is no question that it would be natural to want one. There is certainly no question that it would not be irrational to want one. But suppose the rationality of an action or attitude is more than the mere absence of its irrationality. Rationality seems too positive a status to be implied by the mere absence of irrationality. If it is, one might take the position that intrinsic desires, though not irrational, are also not properly considered rational. We could consistently hold this even if we maintained that intrinsic desires can, as ultimate motivational premises or unmoved movers, *confer* rationality on actions performed to satisfy them. This thesis is indeed the heart of instrumentalism, which is held not only by Humeans but by a number of philosophers who simply do not believe that there is anything intrinsically good.[1]

The proper appraisal of instrumentalism has many dimensions. In the end, however, it must be assessed in comparison with well-developed alternatives. The leading positive view that provides a good contrast is the position that there are substantive criteria for the rationality of intrinsic desires. I want to develop a theory of the nature and grounds of such desires. This requires exploring the character, sources, objects, and satisfaction of intrinsic desires.

1. THE PHENOMENOLOGY OF INTRINSIC DESIRE

To assess the case for the rationality of certain intrinsic desires, we must first consider precisely what intrinsic desires are. They are not easily understood, and some natural misconceptions about them allow their assimilation to instrumental desires or to merely non-instrumental desires, like a desire to get one's pliers, retained after one distractedly forgets what they were needed for. A desire that is merely non-instrumental is not thereby intrinsic; and an intrinsic desire is not a special kind of instrumental one.

Intrinsic desires are not equivalent to mere non-instrumental desires because unlike the latter, intrinsic desires must be understood positively in terms of what their object is wanted *for*. Wanting something for its own sake entails not only having a conception of the thing wanted—a requirement for any want—but also having a sense of some apparently intrinsic characteristic of the activity or state of affairs in question. Moreover, we do not want a thing for its own sake unless there is some such characteristic for which—roughly, on account of which—we want it. When I want to have a cool swim for its own sake, what appeals to me about it is the anticipated enveloping feel of the surrounding water, the sense of movement within it, the ambient sustenance of it. And when I experience these things, it is on their account that I tend to want to continue swimming.

The point is not that what I want is these qualities of swimming in themselves: that they are the object of my desire to swim. Once more, there is a significant parallel with theoretical reason. Wanting something *for* certain (intrinsic) qualities of it is like believing something on the basis of experiential evidences of it: I believe that the phone rang on the basis of auditory sensations; it does not even make sense to say I believe those sensations. I can believe I am *having* them, just as I can want to *experience* the natatory qualities for which I want to swim. But I need not have such self-referential beliefs in order to believe, on the auditory basis of hearing a phone ring, that it rang, and I need not want specifically to experience the natatory qualities I anticipate in a swim in order to want to swim on account of those anticipated qualities.

To suppose that wanting a thing, or to experience something, for certain of its qualities does entail wanting those qualities themselves is to invite a regress. If wanting to swim for its own sake entails wanting qualities thereof, then we must suppose that these can be wanted for their own sake if we are to avoid a regress whose next element is wanting those qualities for a further reason, such as the experience of instantiating them, which would entail wanting *its* qualities, and so forth. We must surely grant that at some point something can be wanted, other than on the basis of a further want. But if we deny that every such object of desire is wanted brutely, for no reason, we return to the natural picture I am sketching, in which what is wanted for its own sake is wanted for some quality taken to be intrinsic to it.

82

To say, however, that intrinsic and instrumental desires are irreducibly different is not to say that the two cannot coexist toward the same object. In a normal case of swimming for its own sake, I may or may not regard the swimming as instrumental to something else I want. Moreover, others who want to swim for its own sake may or may not be attracted to it for the same qualities that attract me. All of us, however, seem to be drawn to activities we take to be in some way pleasurable, and one powerful tradition, that of hedonism, maintains that it is only for pleasure (or for the sake of some other hedonic element such as pain reduction) that we want anything intrinsically. In the language I have used to characterize theoretical reason, all practical generation principles posit pleasure or some other hedonic element as grounds of reasons for action. Even apart from whether such hedonism is sustainable, the role of pleasure as providing reasons for action is important. Without understanding this we cannot adequately understand practical reason.

When I intrinsically want to swim, I usually want it *for* the expected pleasure. But when I do want it for pleasure, I do not thereby want it as a *means* to pleasure; nor does the specific concept of pleasure, as opposed, say, to that of a nice swim, have to enter into my conception of what I want. The wanted pleasure is *in* the swimming as I envisage that activity. The pleasure for which I want to swim is not some further end. There need be no question of anything further—say, of exercise or of any additional end not intrinsically tied to swimming and achievable by doing something other than swimming. If, however, the pleasure is in the swimming, what more can be said of such pleasure?

2. PLEASURE AS AN OBJECT OF INTRINSIC DESIRE

To reflect the sense in which the pleasure of an activity is properly seen as in the activity itself, we could call what is wanted for pleasure a *constitutive means* to it. The same point, however, will hold. A constitutive means to the pleasure of swimming is something which, pleasurably done or pleasurably experienced in the envisaged way, will *be* the wanted natatory pleasure. By contrast, a means to something, in the usual, instrumental sense of 'means', is not constitutive of it and can in principle be replaced by a different means to it. This is why instrumental value is taken to be derivative and relational rather than intrinsic. It is not intrinsic to a thing that it produce or tend to produce something further; and it is not intrinsic to a thing that it be produced by a given, distinct thing. Thus, if we consider a constitutive means to be instrumental at all, we must keep in mind how different it is from the standard instrumental means. Both notions, however, are essential for understanding rationality.

We can now see more clearly why it is that what we intrinsically want *for* pleasure is not properly said to be wanted as a means to pleasure. Wanting something for pleasure is wanting it for (presumed) intrinsic qualities of it that make it attractive to one *as* pleasurable; it is not wanting it as a causal or other contingent producer of pleasure. To want something for pleasure is to want it in the anticipation of pleasure *in* realizing it. One anticipates engaging in the enjoyable activity, having the attractive experience, possessing the cherished object. To take pleasure in something is, in turn, roughly equivalent to enjoying it; and there are as many kinds of enjoyment as there are enjoyable activities and experiences. In this sense pleasure is experiential: we cannot enjoy things unless we do or experience them.[2]

What is it to enjoy an experience? Part of the answer is surely that an experience—including an activity—that we enjoy *engages* us. We are not left cold by it; we spontaneously attend to it; we tend to smile about it, or from it, and often to voice our pleasure in it. There is laughter at good jokes, smiling at receiving happy news from friends, and the spontaneous 'mm' when the soup is just right. Much that we enjoy doing we also do with a certain zest. We go forward with a kind of momentum and often with a pronounced rhythm. We flourish in the performance. Intense pleasures are often characterized by a positively visceral engagement. The devotee of the opera is moved to shivers by a great aria, the swimmer invigorated by easy movements through perfect water, the racquet enthusiast delighted by success in a fast, artful rally, the lover, in passionate moments, suffused with sensations. The visceral elements of some pleasures can also be subtle, and can easily combine with aesthetic appreciation. Think of being moved by a great dramatic rendition of Prospero's farewell to his art in *The Tempest.*

Most pleasures, however, do not have visceral elements. If pleasure is an experiential engagement with its object, it need not be visceral. Think of viewing a painting one simply likes, as opposed to being stirred by a moving passage in a sonata. Or take what may be an intermediate case: one can be pleased, piqued, and stimulated by a good cognac, without being zesty in the ingestion of it. Like good background music in a restaurant, the cognac can be an enjoyable part of the ambience rather than a main focus of attention.

Even in pleasures with strongly felt visceral manifestations, the elements one feels are not the whole of the pleasure. Nor is pleasure itself a kind of sensation, something one simply has. Sensations may be assessed as pleasant or not; it is doubtful that any kind of sensation is, simply as sensation, intrinsically pleasurable. Even a favorite food can utterly fail to please. It might perhaps be otherwise with pain. But if there is any kind of sensation that is intrinsically painful, it still need not be identical with the pain; it might be a necessary feature of experiencing it. Pleasure is experiential not because it is an autonomous object of experience but because it takes its character from the *way* in which one experiences the thing that one enjoyably does or undergoes.[3] We are all familiar with the difference between disappointment in eating a favorite dish and enjoying it. We can want to do or have a thing for just the kind of quality experienced in the one case and not the other.

It is, to be sure, possible to want something as a means to pleasure. I might think that if I don't have some fun I will go crazy. I might then want to do something, like visit an amusement park, because doing that is fun and visiting the park will therefore cause me to enjoy myself and thus help me retain my sanity. But this is not wanting to visit the park *for* pleasure. It is only wanting to visit in order to *cause* pleasure in myself, hence as a means to pleasure I need. The distinctive pleasures of visiting an amusement park are beside the point and may even be largely unknown to me.

There are analogous cases in the domain of theoretical reason. Just as one can do something to cause a desire for pleasure, one can do something to cause a belief with a certain content, say, that an injury will quickly heal. There is a related normative analogy. Just as I can have a *reason* to cause myself to want to have pleasure, and hence can have a reason for instrumentally wanting something on account of the pleasure it will produce, I can have a reason, and thereby a ground for instrumentally wanting, to cause myself to believe life will be good (which I want to believe so that I can face the future). A practical reason to cause oneself to believe something contrasts with having a reason *for believing* this; and just as it provides no normative reason to believe the proposition, my reason to cause a desire for pleasure in doing something does not justify (or make rational) an intrinsic desire to do it that I may induce in myself. Reasons *to* cause are not reasons *for.* I can have such a desire without any of the characteristic anticipation: I may not be looking forward to visiting the park at all. Doing it is more like taking a pill that will cause pleasure in something else. Doing something to *cause* pleasure in oneself is not doing it *for* pleasure, and it is compatible with having no inkling of what kind of pleasure it will produce. One might think that even if we can do things as means to pleasure rather than—as befits an "intrinsic end"—for pleasure, the character of such an end prevents our wanting it as a means. But even pleasure can be wanted as a means. I could want to have pleasure for what it will produce, as where, though I dislike a certain playwright, I want to take plea-

sure in his or her play so that my companions will be pleased by my refor-
mation and enjoy the performance.[4]

For desires in general, intrinsic as well as instrumental, we can have not
only more than one reason but more than one *kind* of reason. When I want
to do something, such as visit a park, as a means to pleasure, I may also, as
I think about what the visit would be like, come to want to visit the place
for pleasure. It is certainly possible to want something both intrinsically and
instrumentally. There can be dual instrumental and intrinsic reasons for
wanting something, just as there can be both perceptual and testimonial
grounds for believing something, say, that a storm is approaching.

What we might call a *purely* intrinsic want, however, is based only on
intrinsic grounds. Similarly, a purely instrumental want is based only on
instrumental grounds. Nonetheless, intrinsic wanting need not be considered a distinct kind of wanting; rather, it is wanting on a distinct kind of
ground. This yields a simpler theory than one that multiplies kinds of wanting. The difference is, to be sure, reflected in how one wants—intrinsically
as opposed to instrumentally, with all that this implies—but apart from this
and the associated differences in kinds of reasons, we need not posit different kinds of motivational states.

3. ELEMENTAL DESIRES

It may be that our psychologically most elemental intrinsic desires concern
pleasure or pain that we are directly experiencing. Any normal child knows
the pleasures of being cuddled and suckled, of bathing and eating, of
motion and quiescence—and the pains of indigestion. These experiences
are the birthplace of both desire and aversion. If I had never experienced
a cool swim on a hot day, or something I take to be like it, I would not
intrinsically want one now. And if I am (intrinsically) averse to backaches,
it is probably because I have had one and, on account of its excruciating
qualities, intrinsically wanted it to stop. Let us look more closely at a case
of something wanted on account of how it is directly experienced.

Particularly when it is intense, pleasure is an experiential engagement
with its object. One might think that what underlies it is gratification of
intrinsic desire: we are engaged in the pleasurable experience because we
want it for its own sake. But must this be true of me every time I am enjoying a swim? That may seem so because I must in some sense *like* what I am
doing, and then I am at least disposed to want to do or continue it. But
liking—which is at least a close cousin of enjoyment—is often the origin
of desire and, at least initially, does not entail its presence as a precondi-

tion. Sometimes we do not want an enjoyable thing at all until we have actually found ourselves enjoying it. Suppose, however, that I do want to continue swimming for its own sake. What is it that I like about it, in virtue of which I intrinsically want to go on doing it? For me, it is the enveloping feel of the surrounding water, the sense of movement within it, and the ambient sustenance of it. These are qualities of my experience.

The qualities of my swimming in virtue of which I want to do it can (as noted earlier) themselves be objects of desire, in the special sense that one might want to instantiate precisely those qualities, for instance to experience the cooling quality of the water. But wanting to swim *for* those qualities does not require a further want *of* them, a want specifically to have or realize them. To say that it does is to invite assimilation of an intrinsic desire for something on account of its qualities to an instrumental desire for it as a means to realizing those qualities. That assimilation is tempting in just the way it is tempting to say that to believe that there is a piano before me on the basis of my visual impression of one is to believe it on the basis of a more specific (perhaps implicit) belief to the effect that I have that impression. This view assimilates beliefs based *on* experience to beliefs based on premises *about* experience. I normally do not conceptualize or form beliefs about the shape and colors of the instrument, even though the perception of those shapes grounds my belief that there is a piano there; and when I believe there is a piano before me, it is normally not on the basis of beliefs about my experience.

The same sort of point holds for the case of pain. Consider a backache. When we want relief from a backache, what are the object and basis of our wants? I want the pain to stop—its cessation is the object of my want; and I want this because I am averse to the unpleasant qualities of my immediate, painful experience. Once again, the cessation of the pain is not wanted as a *means* to elimination of the unpleasant qualities. It is wanted for that prospect, at least if their elimination is constitutive of the desired relief from the pain, as the presence of the pleasant experiential qualities for which the swim is wanted is (at least partly) constitutive of enjoying it when the swim is wanted for pleasure.[5]

In a great many cases of intrinsic desire, the qualities for which the object is wanted really are intrinsic to it. The enveloping presence of water, for instance, is essential to swimming. But suppose I want to swim for a sense of liberation from the ground, yet I then do not get that sense. This is like swimming for pleasure and not enjoying the swim. One can want an experience (or other thing) for a quality it does not have, and this holds for qualities one takes to be intrinsic to it as well as for others. There is a difference, then, between the way the qualities for which something is wanted figure in the wanting of it and how they figure in the experience that satisfies the want. In the content of a prospective want, say, to experience something, the qualities in the abstract are those for which the object is wanted; when the wanted experience occurs, if it has those qualities, then one can be aware of concrete instances of them (tokens of them in one terminology). In this case, one's wanting to continue the experience can be based on a consciousness of concrete qualitative elements of it. If one finds the experience lacking in those qualities, one tends to be disappointed: the qualities for which one wanted it are not *encountered* in the would-be gratifying experience.

If we think of intrinsic wanting as wanting based on a certain kind of ground, as where one wants to see a sculpture for the pleasure of viewing it as opposed to determining its value, and if, as is plausible in general, we allow one's having a ground to play a supporting (and even prima facie justifying) role even when one's having it implies a false presupposition or a mistaken belief about the object of desire, then mistakes of the kind in question—and accompanying disappointments—should not be surprising. They may occur even where we are acting rationally. We are often justified but mistaken in beliefs about what an experience will be like, and in many such cases would not have wanted the experience had we known what it would really be like apart from the mistake.[6] We may find the sculpture clumsy and shapeless or find a much anticipated meal dominated by a spice we dislike. The qualities for which—perhaps quite reasonably—we wanted the aesthetic or gustatory experience are not instantiated therein.

The possibility of such errors is important. Our problem is largely whether an intrinsic desire can be rational; and if it can be in some sense mistaken—or at any rate embody mistakes—in resting on false beliefs or mistaken presuppositions about the intrinsic qualities of the object, then it can certainly be ill-grounded. If it can be ill-grounded, one would expect that it can be well-grounded when it is free of the relevant vitiating basis, and that well-groundedness would take it at least close to one kind of rationality. To see whether this is so, we should further explore ill-grounded intrinsic desires.

It can be foolish to think that certain things are enjoyable. Unjustified beliefs or presuppositions are among the major factors that render intrinsic desires ill-grounded. When we discover such a mistake, as where we try to do a stunt that looks like fun but is clearly beyond our training, we sometimes chide ourselves for having had a foolish desire. But we also make mistakes even when we are justified, nor need all errors about prospective experience concern their hedonic aspects. We may be mistaken in believing an activity to have an invigorating quality, but *justifiedly* wrong because we had good grounds for thinking that it would have that quality. Here the (objectively) ill-grounded intrinsic desire is an analogue of justified but false (hence objectively ill-grounded) belief. We would not be thought foolish in wanting the experience, as we would be if our error in expectation were the result of our ignoring ample evidence and credible good advice.

It is also significant for understanding rational desire that we are surprised at what some people do want (intrinsically) and what others do not want, and that if we care about someone, especially a child, we often give reasons—practical reasons—for or against wanting various things. This practice is especially appropriate where action to get them is or may be in the offing. Still, even if one believes (for instance) that a child will not take hard drugs, one may offer reasons for thinking that the experiences they produce are not desirable and should not be wanted. Wanting something that is undesirable is a bad thing not just because it may lead to action to realize something undesirable but because it may preoccupy a person, if only in fantasies about the desired thing; it may suppress action for preferable competing ends; and it may preserve in the storehouse of memory a goal that would not be harbored in a sufficiently informed and generally rational person.

I have suggested that if intrinsic wants are liable to the kinds of negative appraisals I have cited, one would expect them to be subject to counterpart positive appraisals and so to be capable of being well-grounded when those appraisals apply to them. Perhaps such desires can even be in a sense sound, or can embody soundness, including justified as opposed to accidental soundness, as where one is both justified and correct in believing that a swim will yield a pleasing sense of ambient sustenance. The possibility of well-grounded intrinsic desires may not by itself decisively establish that an intrinsic desire can be rational, as opposed to having only some other positive normative status; but it does take us at least partway toward that conclusion. At this point, I am going to regard the conclusion as plausible and set out a conception of rational desire that will provide further support for it as part of an overall theory of practical reason.

4. AGENT-CENTERED ASPECTS OF DESIRE

In order to find the most salient examples of the grounds of desires that are both intrinsic and apparently rational, I have concentrated on cases with a limited range of objects, such as my desire for a cool swim or for cessation of a sharp pain. It is time to begin exploring the breadth of the range of objects of rational desires.

In one way, this range might seem quite narrow. There is a sense in which the apparently rational desires so far examined are self-interested. This is not to say that they are selfish. That would be a matter of how they are related—and how I as their possessor am related—to other people. But they are intuitively of the kind which it is in one's own interest to satisfy. Suppose they are self-interested. It still does not follow that they are *egoistic*. We can view intrinsic desires as self-interested without conceiving them as truly egoistic. A missionary's most cherished and quite selfless project may be to help starving children, which is activity the missionary engages in for their sake. But imagine that church funds are short. Then the missionary's arguing for their use mainly in that cause might still be said by proponents of other projects to be self-interested. It is an irony of usage that when helping others is one's dearest project, the notion of self-interest can be stretched to apply to altruistic behavior.

To see the difference between the merely self-interested and the egoistic, take a self-interested desire that is more likely to seem egoistic, in the sense of being directed toward one's *own* well-being, not just toward something one *cares* about. Think of the desire for relief from a backache. I want the pain to stop. Does this require that I want specifically that *I*, or *my back*, be free of it? Surely not, though this could be how I would express my desire to a concerned person who asked if there was anything I wanted.

None of this is meant to deny that I might have a self-centered desire like this. The point is that it is not the primitive case, the most elemental and most basic case, of a desire to be rid of a backache: neither conceptually nor psychologically. The primitive case is a kind of occurrently experiential desire: a desire, regarding something that is being directly experienced, for it or for its absence. My simplest desire here would be just that *it* stop. Feeling pain is also apparently prior, in human development, to having a concept of it. Something akin to *disliking* it may also be prior to intrinsically wanting it to stop, just as (in a certain range of cases) liking something or a similar positive experience may be prior to intrinsically wanting something to occur. Disliking is akin to pain, and especially to *being pained by*, but is not equivalent to the latter; liking is akin but not precisely equivalent to enjoying.

Granted, the realization of my want that the backache stop, or of my desire to swim, is an experience *of mine*. I am its referential anchor; others can want to have the same kind of swim, but there is no way to specify what swim I realize other than by reference to me as the swimmer. Similarly, although the qualities for which I intrinsically want something can be the basis of a similar desire for it on the part of others, my desire for it can be rational on account of those qualities only if they are (or have been) in some way encountered in my experience, if only (with sufficient vividness) in my imagination. But neither of these points about the epistemic and genetic aspects of my wants entails that I myself must enter into the content of those wants.

To be sure, if what I want is quite specifically that *I* swim, then in *some* way I do figure in the content of my desire.[7] But this is not the primitive case even of action-desire, desire to do something. Doing is rather like having: just as, in the simplest cases, when we want to have something, our focus is on *it*, and the object of the want is something like the thing's being present (or wherever we are or want it to be), so when we want to do something, our agency is as it were presupposed and the object of desire is the doing. This is particularly so when we want to do whatever it is purely for its own sake, so that we need not think about doing it in a way that brings about a desired result. In wanting to swim for qualities intrinsic to it, for instance, I am focused on the whole experience of the swim with the anticipated qualities; I do not need to conceptualize my action as mine or to attribute the qualities to it conceived as mine. Granted, if there is some question of someone else's swimming instead and I am not content to be supplanted, I will want specifically that *I* do it. But where there is no such question and no other ground for my contrasting myself with anyone else, my goal is simply *to do* the thing. In this way, my wanting to do something is conceptually prior to my wanting that *I* do it.[8]

5. THREE KINDS OF DESIRE

These examples illustrate three kinds of desire that should be distinguished in the theory of practical reason ('want' is an often preferable term, though slightly wider in some uses). There is objectual wanting, which is directed to a thing, including an action or experience or property, that one is aware of, as where one wants the pain to stop. There is behavioral wanting, which is directed to one's own action, as in the case of wanting to swim. And there is propositional wanting, which is directed to a state of affairs expressed subjunctively, as where one wants that there be no more war or has a desire that all children be adequately fed.[9]

With wanting as with believing, these different cases need not coincide even when they concern the same object. Just as, even if I am the man I see in the mirror, I can believe the man in the mirror to have a stain on his coat, without conceiving him as me (or as anyone in particular), I can want the backache to stop without conceiving it as mine (or as belonging to anyone in particular, though I am *disposed* to conceive it as mine if ques-

tions about it arise for me, thereby forcing me to conceptualize it in relation to myself).

It is, of course, generally easier to identify oneself as the subject of one's
experiences than to identity external things as objects of one's experiences,
but that point does not imply that either having those experiences—or
having beliefs or desires concerning them—must wait upon or even embody such identification. It may even be that having beliefs and desires
concerning our experiences or their objects is a precondition for arriving
at a clear conception of ourselves. In the natural genetic order of conceptualization, the external may have a certain priority over the internal.
We do not build the world from within; we build within from the world.

There is an economy as well as a naturalness in this view of the most
primitive cases of intrinsic desire. Nature seems to incline us to form no
more complex attitudes than the situation requires, and to build the more
complex from the less so. Like believing, wanting is in a sense under-
determined by experience. When I see a tree-lined field before me as I
step out on a friend's deck, I do not normally form all the beliefs I could—
about the height of the trees, for instance, or their distance from me. When
I simply feel like swimming, I naturally focus first on the attractive activity
I want to engage in: the cool swim. I need not conceive it as mine. If my
initial focus is instead on the complex prospect of swimming in a certain
kind of lake with certain kinds of companionship, then it is likely that what
I want is in fact that larger experience. Particularly after enjoying a complex activity as such, one can come to form, directly and without contemplation, intrinsic wants for similar complex activities. But in the natural
order of human development, complexity of content apparently arises from
integration of simpler elements.

Quite apart from how desires arise, we must resist the temptation to
multiply or expand them simply because of what their satisfaction can be
anticipated to imply. Specifically, wanting something, whether its object is
an experience or anything else, while knowing that it *has* certain properties, such as belonging to a particular person, no more entails wanting the
entire complex—the object *as having* those properties—than believing a
proposition, while knowing that it has certain implications, entails believing the proposition conjoined with all of those others (one could fail to
believe the others at all). In order to want to experience something, one
need not even be thinking of the experience as having all the properties
one knows to belong to it, just as one can believe (and come to believe) a
proposition without thinking of implications one knows it to have. I can
simply want to swim without imagining the stimulating waviness of the
lake—or the vegetation that I know will cling to my limbs.

To be sure, if I do think of something I want and it now occurs to me that it has a certain property, then if I find that property attractive, I tend to *come* to want the object as having that property, say, the swim as having a relaxing rhythmic waviness. But not all properties of experiences I want, including properties essential to my having those experiences—such as their being mine—have any bearing on what makes them attractive to me, just as not all the grounds in my ken that support a proposition I believe need have any bearing on why I believe it.[10] The grounds of a desire do not enter into its content and need not enter into the content of any other, such as a desire for a further end, just as the basis of a belief does not enter into its content and need not enter into that of any other belief, such as one expressing a premise for the first.

One might think that since (for instance) my wanting a backache to stop *is* just my wanting the cessation of what I conceive indexically as *this* pain, I do enter into the content of this want for cessation of the pain. For here the indexical, 'this', may seem to mean 'the ache *I* now have'. It surely does not mean this, though some such phrase would be natural in identifying the *referent* of 'this'. Nor must I conceive the pain under such an indexical notion—though if I am asked to identify it, I may be disposed to conceive it in that way. It is not clear that simply wanting the pain to stop because of its felt unpleasantness requires conceptualizing it at all, as opposed to responding to its qualities, or perhaps conceptualizing *them*.

The point that a self-concept need not enter into desire regarding oneself can be easily missed because it is natural to represent and analyze such self-referential desires through locutions one uses to ascribe them to oneself. It *is* true that *self-ascription* of my desire that the pain stop may require an indexical; my simply having the desire does not. To self-ascribe it—indeed, even to articulate it as a premise in practical reasoning—I must say something like, 'I want this (or my) awful pain to stop'; but I can have such a desire even before I have a self-concept. If some indexical notion is part of the content of my want, we should construe that content referentially, not conceptually: the relevant indexical terms are not abbreviatory, but demonstrative. They serve to identify the desired object, not to build an individuating concept of it by projecting it into a special relation to oneself, as if to assign it coordinates on an egocentric grid of consciousness.

In the primitive cases, then, what we intrinsically want, whether it concerns something experienced here and now, such as pain, or something quite distant, like visiting Finland next summer, need not be wanted egoistically.[11] We need not want such things *as our* experiences, even if we see ourselves as their subject. I may want that I visit Finland, but the visit's being mine is not what makes it desirable to me. I want it for the company of friends, the beauty of the landscape, the pleasures of discovery. We *locate* desired experiences in relation to ourselves; we must do so in order to bring them about. I cannot visit Finland if I have no conception of a path from me to it. But this referential line extending from my present consciousness of what I want to the object of my desire does not make the content of that desire egoistic.

6. PLEASURE, PAIN, AND THE GOOD

Pleasure and pain are universally appreciated as natural objects of desire and aversion. They have also been frequently taken to be the only things having intrinsic value or disvalue. Indeed, for the common conception of (positive) intrinsic value as roughly what is worthy of intrinsic desire, i.e., intrinsically desirable, it seems fair to say that if any theory of value has approached dominance in the history of philosophy, it is probably hedonism. In value theory we may take this to be the view that pleasure and freedom from pain, or at least relief from pain, are the only intrinsic goods.[12] It is edifying to explore the relation between hedonism and rational desire.

To say that something is pleasurable (or, for that matter, intrinsically good) is not equivalent to saying that it is always rational, on balance, to want it for its own sake. For one thing, I could presumably believe, mistakenly but justifiedly, that something is intrinsically bad, when it is in fact intrinsically good; it might then be rational not to want it. But intrinsic goodness does seem to meet two conditions: first, something's having it provides, or at least entails that there is, a prima facie reason to want it intrinsically for some intrinsic quality of it; second, wanting something for its intrinsic goodness, or—more basically—for a quality in virtue of which it is intrinsically good, is prima facie rational. (I say, "more basically" because intrinsic goodness is possessed in virtue of one or more other properties—"natural properties," in a sense that is difficult to elucidate—and wanting something for those properties is in a certain way prior to wanting it for its intrinsic goodness, at least in the sense that we cannot adequately understand the intrinsic goodness of any given thing that has it except in terms of such underlying properties.) Pleasure, conceived as enjoyment of some experience, seems clearly to meet these conditions. (I leave open that there may be further conditions for intrinsic value—a full analysis is not needed here.) If, when Marie is asked by a skeptical friend why she wants to hear a youth symphony, she says that the players are very proficient and hearing them will be enjoyable, no one would normally doubt that she had given a good ground for wanting to hear them or that wanting to do so is prima facie rational. Imagine someone's saying 'So what?' Would we know what to make of this?

Saying 'So what?' to a person's adducing enjoyment as a ground for wanting something could perhaps be a misleading way to suggest that there are far *more* enjoyable things to do with one's time; but that would only confirm that the prospect of enjoyment is a ground for desire. It would be both normal and rational to want to hear the concert just for the musical pleasures anticipated. One could also argue that there are better kinds of things to pursue. But this is quite consistent with pleasure's being intrinsically valuable. If, as many philosophers have thought, there is a plurality of intrinsically valuable things, some may be better than others, and the former may thus provide better reasons for desire and action than the latter. To be sure, these and other points I have made do not constitute a proof that pleasure is intrinsically good. But they are well explained on that premise and are independently plausible.

The notion of intrinsic goodness is highly practical. If, for instance, pleasure is intrinsically good, then there is reason to want it intrinsically—though on my view that reason is itself grounded in the hedonic experiential qualities of the object in question, such as the enjoyable melodies and rhythms of a sonata. On the plausible assumption that what there is reason to want intrinsically there is (prima facie) reason to seek, there is reason to seek pleasure. This implies that there is reason for certain kinds of actions: reason to do enjoyable things. I am inclined to agree with hedonists that pleasure is intrinsically good and pain intrinsically bad; but I do not hold that these are the only intrinsic values. I want to develop a theory of value, and of reasons for action, that is more pluralistic.

We can seek a theory of value more pluralistic than hedonism without denying that hedonism at its best is by no means monistic. On any adequate understanding of pleasure and the absence (or reduction) of pain, they are different values. Indeed, the reduction, or at least perceptible diminution, of pain is surely a good that is not necessarily a case of either pleasure or pain. Similarly, in many cases, the perceptible sense of improvement in the quality of something we are doing, particularly when it is a task that engages us, seems to be an intrinsic good distinct from pleasure, from the fulfillment of the desire to complete the task, and from the actual accomplishment of that task. Moreover, if pleasure is understood in a broadly Aristotelian fashion, as an activity concept, then it alone is as diverse as the multifarious activities that yield it. It is even more diverse construed more broadly as also arising in experiences in which one is not agent but patient. The pleasures of reading differ from those of viewing paintings. These in turn differ from the pleasures of swimming, which are quite different from the relatively passive pleasures of a backrub, wherein the subject is not acting but only having an experience. (Mill's examples of pleasures exhibit this kind of diversity; but although his hedonism is really pluralistic in content, he sometimes represents it as monistic, or at least dualistic, having the two basic elements of pleasure and pain.)

Is it not possible, however, to experience, say, a conversation as intrinsically rewarding without taking pleasure in it? Some conversations are engaging and interesting, but they are too laborious or too fraught with tensions to be enjoyable. A hedonist might say that if they are intrinsically rewarding but are not found enjoyable, this is because the pleasure they give is mixed with discomfort and obscured by the labor of comprehension. Or, it might be claimed that the rewarding quality is really instrumental: one learned something. Certainly these points sometimes apply to a rewarding conversation; but I cannot see that intrinsic rewardingness *must* be reduced to some kind of pleasure. Indeed, one can clearheadedly want to do something for its intrinsic interest or intrinsic intellectual challenge, even when one thinks it will not be enjoyable and may at times be somewhat unpleasant. (This is how some people view certain lectures or visits to some museums.) Moreover, if there is, as there seems to be, intrinsic moral value, for instance in disciplining avarice and in making a just distribution where one could take more for oneself, there is yet another reason to consider hedonism too narrow.

It must be granted that rewarding experiences, even when they are not pleasurable, share with pleasurable ones the tendency to *engage* us, for example to keep us interested. This engaging quality is surely one kind of reward. It may well be that a sense of satisfaction, even when not pleasurable, as opposed to pleasing in some way, is another. Moreover, the most characteristically rewarding experiences that are not pleasurable have a further property: they employ some of our more complex faculties in an engaging way. The scholar comprehendingly reads a difficult but interesting passage; the athlete plays a losing game of tennis with an elegance of style and a closeness to success that minimize disappointment; the musician muddles through some difficult sightreading that is too laborious to be enjoyable, yet too good not to look back on with an intrinsic desire to try again.

There is, however, a difference between the way a pleasurable experience produces spontaneous attention and the way certain other kinds of experiences do. Pleasure tends to be more exclusive: to reduce consciousness of things other than the object of enjoyment, more than experiences that are rewarding without being pleasurable. Compare enjoying a play with simply finding it dramatically worthwhile: valuing the performance for its own sake but without the positive sense that goes with pleasure. Such a rewarding experience will not have the same tendency to make one smile, and certainly may lack any visceral manifestations of the engagement with its object. Nonetheless, wanting such an experience, which may take the form of a desire to do an arduous and complex task, may surely be rational. And can wanting this not be a desire to perform the task on account of its yielding a non-hedonic good, say, some kind of intellectual good? This seems possible; and if it is, then hedonism is too narrow as an account of the grounds of rational desire.

Perhaps it is largely because pleasure and pain seem capable, and perhaps uniquely capable, of motivating people prior to any education that hedonism, at least in its psychological form, is as plausible as it is. It could be that if we were not built so that, especially in our early years, we enjoy some things and are pained by others, then we would not or could not learn to want other things for their own sake. But it is essential to distinguish here between genetic primacy and motivational or valuational hegemony. The former does not entail the latter. It may be that we would not learn to value non-hedonic goods intrinsically if we were not first motivated by hedonic ones. But non-hedonic desires that we come to have only as civilized people need not be subordinate to hedonic desires, and they can be stronger. Our early years under the tutelage of pleasure and pain need not prevent our developing autonomous desires. I reject, then, the two-dimensional model of motivation so natural for hedonism: the idea that all motivation resides either directly in hedonic desire or in desire instrumentally based on it.

To be sure, once we *regard* something as good in itself, we tend to take pleasure not only in realizing it but also in the thought of doing so. Sometimes it is as if the childhood teacher returned to encourage the adult accomplishment. Pleasure is perhaps the most primitive and enduring kind of reward in human life, and it is important in learning to value other goods. But this does not entail that we seek all other goods for the pleasure of their realization, nor does pleasure in contemplating the realization of a good entail that one seeks it *for* pleasure. We can take pleasure in the thought that we will resist temptation, even though we know that doing so will be unpleasant and that we will be doing it not for pleasure but to keep our word.

The idea that we can intrinsically want things only for pleasure, or to avoid pain, is too narrow. But in one respect, namely its emphasis on experience as the locus of value, hedonism seems correct. Even where something is wanted for qualities other than those conducing to pleasure, it may be wanted for qualities one experiences. We can go well beyond hedonism in broadening the objects of intrinsic value and still hold what might be called *axiological experientialism*, the view that only experiences have intrinsic value.[13] This allows that one can rationally want something for someone else's sake, even if it will not bring anyone pleasure or reduce anyone's pain. It is not just one's own experiences that are the bearers of intrinsic goodness, and pleasure need not be the only intrinsic good.

7. EXPERIENCE AS A LOCUS OF VALUE

It may be, however, that even axiological experientialism provides too narrow a conception of intrinsic value. Might it make sense to want intrinsically that the world continue to contain beautiful landscapes, even if one believed no one would experience them? And could this want not be rational and indeed directed toward something of intrinsic value, namely the existence of beauty? A natural reply here is that anyone who reflectively believes this is thinking of the beauty as valuable because experiencing it *would* be valuable. One might call such things *contemplatively valuable* to suggest that the intrinsic value they point to is really in the rewarding contemplation of them and not in their mere existence.

To this move in defense of experientialism, one might rejoin that although people's rewarding experiences of something may be our way of *knowing* that something has intrinsic value, such value can nevertheless exist unexperienced. Our knowledge that there are physical objects comes through experience; it does not follow that they would not exist apart from it. Here an experientialist might grant that the mind-dependence of intrinsic value does not follow from any of the points made in support of it, but stress a disanalogy with the physical realm. Whereas physical objects and their properties can explain our experiences, intrinsic value, conceived as mind-independent, as instantiated by objective beauty, for example, cannot. Suppose for the sake of argument that this is so. It is far from self-evident that we should accept the underlying *explanationist realism*—the view that only what has explanatory power, or this kind of explanatory power, exists.[14]

A simpler objection to experientialism arises from reflection on the content of both desires for what is intrinsically good and second-order desires to have them. If anything is of intrinsic value, it would seem that wanting it for its own sake is intrinsically good. Surely it does not seem that wanting this is merely instrumentally good. For the content of the want is apparently the good in question, and this is intrinsic to that want; satisfy-

98

ing the want need have no instrumental value.[15] Its satisfaction is, however, a realization of intrinsic goodness. Similarly, it would appear more than instrumentally good to have a second-order desire that one want (for its own sake) what is intrinsically good. Desires, however, are not experiences (though there are experiences *of* them); there would thus be non-experiential intrinsic goods, namely first- and higher-order wants whose content is appropriately related to what is, experientially, intrinsically good.

There is plausibility in this objection, but what is sound in it can be accommodated by experientialism. First, a thing need not be intrinsically good overall just because it has one intrinsic property, such as a certain content, that counts non-instrumentally toward its goodness. Intrinsic goodness might be a more organic property than that implies.[16] Perhaps, moreover, what makes the content of a want, for instance a friend's happiness, seem good in itself is that the *realization* of this want in experience would be intrinsically good. The content of the want is more like a representation of the desired good than an instance of it. The good is constituted by the experiences that *are* the happiness. It still may be true that wanting something which is intrinsically good, and wanting to have such wants, are themselves intrinsically good. But I cannot see that this must be so, or that the argument just given is plausible independently of what makes the general idea for non-experiential value plausible: the argument that some things simply deserve approval or promotion on the basis of what they are, whether or not they are experienced. Wanting something intrinsically good (for the features in virtue of which it is intrinsically good) seems to be a case in point; but I do not see a decisive argument for this.[17] Whether it is such a case can be better appreciated in the light of further reflection on what sorts of things might be intrinsically valuable.

8. INTRINSIC VALUE AND INHERENT VALUE

It can help in thinking about intrinsic value to imagine that a Cartesian demon—or a technology of the future—causes us to have experiences intrinsically just like those we find enjoyable (or otherwise intrinsically valuable). If only experiences have intrinsic value, then it would seem that playing Beethoven's *Appassionata* with great pleasure is no better, intrinsically, than a perfect hallucination of doing so. From the inside, the experiences are indistinguishable. If one thinks that the veridical experience is, in itself, better, the best explanation is that one ascribes some intrinsic value to a non-experiential element such as truth—or at least ascribes some negative value to falsity (one would believe, or at least be disposed to

99

believe, falsely, that one is playing the sonata). If one thinks that the veridical experience is not better, then one should be ready either to maintain that the best ideal for human life might be to create such a technology and find a safe way to produce the best experiences in us that it possibly can, or to explain why not. I do not believe it is obvious that this kind of example refutes experientialism; but it surely puts an additional burden of proof upon it. The prospect of even the finest kinds of hallucinatory pleasures does not seem to exhaust intrinsic goodness.[18]

For my purposes here, there is no need to presuppose experientialism. My theory of rationality allows, but does not require, that there be things of intrinsic value other than experiences (construed in a purely psychological sense not entailing the existence of mind-independent objects) and their qualities. If there are, however, surely the awareness of their value is acquired at least in part *through* experience. Consider a moving poem. What is good about it is appreciated in the reading of it; in itself it does not enter our lives and, if utterly unnoticed, seems to have its value, as it were, unfulfilled. In part for this reason, non-experiential good things may be said to have *inherent value*, as distinct from both intrinsic and instrumental value: roughly, they are such that properly contemplating them, or in some other appropriate way, experiencing them for their own sake (say, a poem for its striking metaphor) is intrinsically valuable. Thus, they are not valuable independently of their relation to contemplation (or experience), hence not intrinsically so, yet they are not means (in any ordinary sense) to the value of experiencing them, since they are partly constitutive of that experience.[19]

Moreover, things that have intrinsic value are by their nature *necessarily* capable of being a component in intrinsic value, since they would be essential to any experience that is *of them*.[20] Hence, unlike things of instrumental value, by their very nature they necessarily provide occasions for the realization of intrinsic value. If experientialism is combined with a theory of inherent value, then, it can have the same substantive axiological implications as a view that allows an indefinite variety of objects to be bearers of intrinsic value. It will imply, for instance, that we have non-instrumental reasons to preserve what is, like a beautiful forest, an inherent good.

Even aside from the point that countenancing inherent value makes experientialism more plausible, it is the experientially grounded rationality of intrinsic desire that chiefly concerns me in accounting for the foundations of practical reason. Consider again the basis of rational intrinsic desire. It is in our experience; it is above all those experiential qualities intrinsic to pleasure and pain and to the happy exercise of our capacities, including conscious states of rewarding contemplation, whether aesthetic,

100

intellectual, religious, or of any other kind.[21] If there are non-experiential intrinsic goods, they provide us with non-instrumental reasons for action. But we still need experience of them or something relevantly similar if they are to provide us with basic reasons for action, reasons not dependent for their normative force on any further reasons.

There is no limit to the range of experiences appropriate to ground rational intrinsic desire; they may be active or passive, physical or mental, mundane or otherworldly. I want to swim for the ambient sustenance of the experience; I want to converse for the rewards of exchanging ideas; I want to play a sonata for the auditory and performative experience. Indefinitely many kinds of things may be rewarding. I offer no analysis of rewardingness in the sense in which it seems equivalent to intrinsic goodness, nor of its opposite as equivalent to intrinsic badness. But each notion is anchored and unified by the open-ended range of examples I have given.

The rationality of our rational intrinsic desires is grounded in the kinds of experiential qualities we have been considering: the ambient sustenance of the water, the insight that comes with good dialogue, the melodic resonances of Beethoven.[22] I encounter these qualities in my own experience, but the rationality of wanting things *for* those qualities is grounded in the qualities themselves, not on these qualities *conceived* as experienced by *me*.[23] Even when the object of a want is realizable only *in me*, I need not want it *for me*. Our experience is our route to discovering the qualities that ground rational desires, and those desires are realized in it. But the basis of their rationality is not egoistic and may be the same in kind for us all.[24]

Once the distinctive qualitative character, and in a sense the impersonality, of the grounds of rational desire is fully grasped, the grip of egoism on our conception of practical reason can be broken. There is no good reason to think that the only way to show a desire or action to be rational on the part of a particular person requires showing that it will produce pleasure or some other intrinsic good *for* that person, in the sense of an experience of, or something of personal benefit to, the agent. It is true that the experiential grounds of practical rationality are internal; but they are not egocentric. They are communicable to others and repeatable in their experience.[25]

9. A COGNITIVE ANALOGUE OF BASIC RATIONAL DESIRES

We have seen an epistemological analogy to rational intrinsic desire. It will help in understanding practical rationality to explore it further. Think of perception, and take seeing as one paradigm. Our visual experience is the ground of our justified visual beliefs. My experience contains (phenomenally) the colors and shapes of furniture and books, and I thus believe that these things are here. It is true that I see the colors by virtue of *my* visual impressions; but this does not require me to experience *myself as* experiencing the colors and shapes, nor do these impressions enter into the content of those beliefs. Doubtless, if asked why I believe these colors and shapes are here, I will say that I see them. But I answer from a second-order perspective. I cite the basis of my belief, and my *citing* it requires self-ascription of the belief which is explained or justified by my citing that basis of it. Our original question concerns what, prior to my citing that basis, justifies my belief. The question is not—though it is often taken to be—a request to defend the belief, and the self-reference necessary for citing the basis of this belief must not be imported into the content of that basis.

Many philosophers have conflated the question of what justifies a belief with the problem of how it can be defended. That is understandable: both issues preoccupy us in trying to show, in the face of the pervasive skeptical challenges, that we have justified beliefs; and in this context self-ascription of visual experience is easily taken to express a premise for the belief grounded in that experience. But we must not let a preoccupation with skepticism make us assimilate consciousness of objects to self-consciousness regarding the experiences through which we know them. The basis of my justification for believing that there is a tree before me is a particular visual experience I have, not my visual experience specifically marked *as* mine. I am not part of the object of the experience that justifies my belief. The presence of a tree in my visual field justifies me in believing there is one before me; I need not imagine, or even believe, myself to be seeing a tree in order to have that justified belief. That the visual experience *is* mine must be noted to establish the second-order claim challenged by skepticism: that *I* justifiably believe there are colors here. But what justifies the first-order perceptual belief is my experience of those colors, not an experience of myself as seeing them, or a set of my beliefs about arboreal appearances in my visual field.

It may be thought that our primary perceptual beliefs are that *we* see, hear, feel, taste, or smell the things about which experience gives us justified belief, and that therefore we ourselves must enter into the content of the grounding experience. This inference is invalid: my visual experience of a tree may justify beliefs *about* me—say, that *I* see a tree—without being an experience *of* me, or of anything *in* me, such as sense-data. My role as subject of the experience does not imply that I am part of its object. And this experience can justify my belief that I see a tree without being an experience of my seeing it.

There is a more subtle mistake underlying the argument from self-referential belief as the basic perceptual kind to the conclusion that we ourselves enter into the experiences grounding perception. This mistake lies in the intellectualistic reasoning that typically leads to accepting the premise about perception. Let us grant that if, because I see a piano, I believe there is one here, I am *disposed* to believe that *I* see it. Still, I need not actually believe this, as I would if there were some question whether, for instance, I see it or see only a picture of it; and once we carry through the distinction between dispositional beliefs and mere dispositions to believe,[26] it should begin to become clear that self-referential beliefs need not be taken as primary in perception. Indeed, a belief that I see a piano is far more complex than a belief that there is one out there: having the former belief requires having the concept of seeing, and that concept, in turn, has at least a causal and experiential component.[27]

The epistemological analogy I have been developing leads us to reject, as central for theoretical reason, a stance parallel to egoism in the theory of practical reason: call it *epistemic egocentrism.* The analogy has a related dimension supporting the view that the most elementary grounds of rationality are qualitative and, in an important sense, impersonal rather than egocentric. Just as, when we see a house only partially, or merely glimpse it in passing, we can believe it to be green without conceiving it *as* a house or indeed forming *any* specific conception of what it is, we can have a desire regarding an experience without conceiving it as any specific kind of experience.[28] We can want a stabbing pain to cease even if we do not conceive it *as* a stabbing pain, or even as ours.

This point is perfectly consistent with a contrasting one that might seem to lead in a different direction. To have a desire regarding an experience, such as a pain one wants to be rid of, requires that it discriminatively affect one. This implies one's having a capacity to identify discerned features of the experience in a certain way, just as believing a house to be green implies that it discriminatively affects one through some (normally identifiable) connection between oneself and its properties. It also implies a responsiveness to changes in the experiences, as where our desires alter as the experience ceases to be painful. But our discriminative capacity to identify qualities of what we want apparently underlies our associated powers of both indexical reference and accurate conceptualization; it is not a product of prior, self-referential thought.[29]

In order to want something, then, we do not have to conceptualize it as bearing some relation to ourselves. In some cases it is only when we need to explain why we want it, or at least to *say* that we want it or think of ourselves *as* wanting it, that we form a concept of how it is related to us. Wanting, like believing, can connect us with its object without our having to conceive ourselves as part of the object. Indeed, the primitive conative and cognitive connections I am describing may be a precondition for arriving at an adequate self-concept in the first place.

The analogy between the foundational aspects of the theoretical and practical sides of rationality is profoundly important. If I have been correct so far, a further question arises. Is the practical analogous to the theoretical in respect of the autonomy of theoretical sources? Above all, can practical grounds of rational desire and rational action provide reasons for action without positive dependence on some kind of theoretical endorsement of their normative power? The question is best answered by first considering skepticism about practical reason, but fully answering it will require at least the work of the next chapter as well.

10. PRACTICAL SKEPTICISM AND THE EGOCENTRIC POINT OF VIEW

Rather as skepticism about theoretical reason has shaped concepts of rational belief, encouraging a certain egocentrism, skepticism about practical reason, in particular the skeptical view that because practical reason is wholly instrumental, there are no rational intrinsic desires, has influenced conceptions of rational desire. The theoretical skeptic may allow that deductive inference can justify beliefs once we have at least one justified premise belief to start with but tends to deny that we have much in the way of justified belief to start with. The practical skeptic allows that given intrinsic desires as inputs, practical inference may yield instrumentally rational actions and rational instrumental desires but denies that we have rational intrinsic desires as motivational premises based on autonomous grounds of reasons for action. The main difference is that the practical skeptic (as conceived here), being a functionalist about practical reason, sees no need for rational motivational premises: intrinsic desires as such are unmoved movers, capable of conferring a kind of rationality though they have none.

This practical skepticism runs deeper than it may appear, however: the rationality conferred is subjective and entirely relative. Nothing is beyond intrinsic desire if one is attracted to it; and what is rational for one of us, say, avoiding an icy crash through a thinly frozen lake, may be irrational for another, who, owing to some anomaly, intrinsically wants to be chilled to the bone despite its producing cries of agony.[30] A standard of rationality that is this permissive is not one that sets a high normative ideal.

With either kind of skepticism as a dominant concern, the effort to vindicate reason in the skeptical tribunal promotes the tendency to posit the self in the content of the experiences that ground rationality. It is almost as if one wanted to find an observer who can give firsthand evidence of the presence of the experiential qualities that one takes to ground the justification or rationality. This *projectionism,* which is characteristic of both egocentrism in epistemology and egoism in the theory of practical reason, is a mistake, and it gives undeserved plausibility to egoistic conceptions of rationality. If the evidences the observer cites are sufficient, they can perfectly well do their work without anyone's viewing the process.

The projectionist mistake is abetted because, as we learn to distinguish appearance from reality, it is often natural to form beliefs about our experience *as* ours, such as the cautious belief that it seems to me that it is Steve in the distance. Similarly, in contrasting my experience with another's, I may conceptualize it as pleasant for *me.* But these are not the primitive cases. They are our first position in retreat; they are not our normal front-line stance.

Even if projectionism were true and the primitive cases of belief and desire were self-referential, this would not help to explain the justification of any direct beliefs or the rationality of any intrinsic desires. If my visual experience itself could not justify, my sense of *my* having it could not either. If it could not be rational to want to hear music for the qualities intrinsic to hearing it, it could not be rational to want, for those qualities, that *I* hear it. As a belief is justified by sensory experience, a desire may be rational on the basis of rewarding experience. The belief that we have such experiences is normally necessary for giving our justification for a belief or citing the grounds of an intrinsic desire. But if what we offer in giving a justification or citing grounds does not do the job of grounding what we defend by appeal to it, our simply believing that we have the experience in question will not make it succeed.

If we choose to be thoroughgoing realists, we might say that—in some way—sensory experience points toward truth, rewarding experience toward goodness. But the analogy I have been drawing between theoretical and practical reason does not strictly require a realist interpretation. It is enough if there are experiential grounds of rationality in each case: for belief and other theoretical attitudes and for action, desire, and other practical attitudes. The experiential status and internal accessibility of these grounds should not be taken to imply either that there are no objective standards of rationality or that the only intrinsic goods are experiences or their properties. An objective standard can be applied from the inside, or even *on* the inside; and even if everything intrinsically good can be an object of experience, it does not follow that it is simply an element *in* experience or a property thereof. Assuming it is such an element, however, there can be kinds of experiences, such as those that are enjoyable, which are good from an impersonal point of view. Their realization will depend on the subjects who have them; but their status as intrinsically good, and as providing impersonal grounds for rational intrinsic desires, is not subjective. It is intersubjectively ascertainable, apparently universal, and objective.

11. DESIRE AND VALUATION

What holds for rational desire is generally also true of other motivational elements. The one that is specially important here is rational valuation. If it is rational to *value* what it is rational to want intrinsically, then my conclusion about rational desire implies that the rationality of values—of valuations of things—is also grounded, in the primitive cases, on qualities of experience, and that altruistic values can be perfectly rational. Valuing, as a practical normative attitude, is quite analogous to desire in its structure and grounds. (There is a use of 'valuing' in which it designates evaluative belief; but this propositional use is not the central one nor of direct concern here.) We value some things intrinsically if we value any at all, and it is rational to value things intrinsically for the same sorts of qualities that make them objects of rational intrinsic desire. There is, however, at least one major difference. Unlike mere intrinsic desires, intrinsic valuations imply a positive attitude toward the object. One is at least disposed to believe that it is in some way good in itself.

Intentions, like valuations, can be rational or irrational, and their assessment as such can be guided by the criteria for rational belief and rational desire. They will be considered later in relation to rational action, but this much can be said here. If it is rational to want—on balance—to do something, then it is prima facie rational to intend to do it. There are, however, other factors, such as whether it is rational to believe that one can do it. Furthermore, not everything it is rational to want intrinsically can be rationally wanted *on balance*. My cool swim might preclude my fulfilling an obligation that I properly see as much more important to me. Hopes and other attitudes can be appraised in respect of rationality in similar ways. If, moreover, believing and wanting are the fundamental cognitive and conative attitudes, at least from the point of view of rationality, then we now have some of the materials for assessment of all the other propositional attitudes.

The rejection of egocentrism in epistemology and of egoism in the theory of rationality does not underestimate the role of the internal, and particularly of experience, in rationality. Rationality may be rooted internally, in qualities of experience to which we have access by introspection or reflection; but this does not make it subjective, either in the sense that whatever I believe is rational for me is so, or, more plausibly, in the sense that there are no general standards of rationality applicable to persons as such, and that the only intelligible standards apply, like the instrumentalist one, merely to individuals depending on what they happen to desire. There are general standards of rationality, including the widely held standard of pleasure and pain as generating good prima facie reasons both for action and for desire.

I have not tried to account for the epistemic status of the thesis that there are experiential standards of rational intrinsic desire, or even for the status of the view that there are rational intrinsic wants. For all I have shown so far, one could give an empiricist or a rationalist or indeed a noncognitivist account of the rationality of intrinsic desire. At least much of what has been said can be accounted for from any of these perspectives. This is a topic to which I shall return when more of the theory of rationality is laid out. But I would emphasize again that I seek to exhibit structural features and basic elements of theoretical and practical rationality in a way that is useful from a number of theoretical perspectives, including some quite different from my own. Our next task is to build a more detailed account of practical reasons and to explore analogues of epistemic transmission principles: how practical rationality is extended from foundational elements that have it to concrete actions based upon them.

DESIRES, INTENTIONS, AND REASONS FOR ACTION

Rationally wanting to hear a concert gives me a reason to buy a ticket; rationally wanting to swim gives me a reason to go to the beach. These are not points about mere desire. In isolation from my experiences and beliefs, or under conditions that render these desires irrational, they would not give me reasons of the kind in question—practical reasons. They would also fail to do so if, for instance, I had no beliefs, or at least a basis for beliefs, about how to satisfy them. A desire for something that one has no idea how to get, even when it is insistent, does not point in any particular direction. If, agitated by such a desire, I think about my plight, I may form a further desire: to do something about my discomfort. That desire may be guided by beliefs about how to discover the needed means. But even if an utterly unguided desire can give rise to a further desire, it is not a spur to directed action. Desire without belief has no direction. If desire can express well-grounded reasons for action, it does not play its motivationally basic role entirely alone. Beliefs are also essential in this role. Without them, even if there could be rational desires as foundations for practical reason, there would be no adequate means of building a superstructure.

1. DESIRE AND INTENTION

The behavioral directionlessness of much desire is one reason we might hesitate to consider desire to be the fundamental practical attitude, that is, as basic in expressing practical reasons. A desire need not even be to *do* something. We want to know as well as to do, to be a certain kind of person as well as to do certain kinds of deeds, to experience some things passively, as well as to do some actively. Furthermore, much of what we want is outweighed by something else we want, and in many such cases no question of actually realizing the counterbalanced desire ever arises. We cannot read everything we want to read, travel everywhere we want to go, or please everyone we want to please.

What we intend, by contrast, has normally won out in any such competition there may have been among desires that pull us in different directions.[1] There is a kind of *motivational commitment* to what we intend, parallel to the kind of cognitive commitment one has to a proposition in virtue of believing it. Neither commitment is the kind that must be *made*. These commitments are attitudinal and not behavioral. Intending, then, differs from mere wanting both in necessarily having a behavioral—hence practical—content and in having a certain executive character: a tendency to act which will normally be realized if the agent has the ability and the opportunity to do the intended deed and does not change in motivation or belief.[2]

It is in part because intention has this executive character that it is not rational to have intentions that one should see cannot be jointly satisfied, or even two that one has ample justification to *believe* cannot be. Here intention contrasts with desire. For desires, including clearly rational ones, plainly incompatible objects are commonplace, say, to visit Italy on a spring holiday and to visit California during that same respite. To understand practical reason fully, we must consider not only further aspects of desire but also intention and some of the conditions for its rationality.

The kind of action tendency just described does not, of course, come with conditional intentions: roughly, intentions to do something *if* a particular condition obtains. Until an appropriate cue occurs, conditional intentions do not produce a tendency to do the intended deed. The cue might be seeing the fulfillment of the condition: if I intend to give Rosetta a book if she asks for it, then when she does ask I may immediately reach for it. We need not settle the question whether I must form a further belief, say, an appropriate instrumental belief, or whether I can, if I know exactly where the book is, act "automatically." We may also leave open whether I must form the *un*conditional intention to give her the book, as opposed to simply acting on the conditional intention given the cue. My point here is simply that conditional intentions do not produce the intended action (or even unconditional tendencies to perform it) without some kind of *instrumental mediation*, whereas unconditional intentions are practical attitudes in a stronger sense: to produce the intended action or a tendency to perform it, they require at most some trigger, such as a thought that now is the time to get out of bed.[3]

Conceiving intending rather than wanting as the fundamental practical attitude can lead to certain mistakes. One is to overextend the parallel between intention and belief, even to the point of taking intending—despite its not admitting of truth or falsity—to *be* a kind of belief.[4] Another is to think that since intending is the *fundamental* practical attitude, it must be unanalyzable. But a fundamental *practical* attitude need not be, in the order of analysis, a fundamental attitude, and there is some reason to believe that intending is a complex of cognitive and motivational attitudes.[5] A third mistake is to think that if intending is the (psychologically) fundamental practical attitude, it is the motivational attitude basic in the order of practical reasons. It is this error that I particularly want to avoid. Most of what I have to say in this chapter is compatible with the other two positions.

The simplest point here is that a want can provide a reason to act without one's intending to realize its object.[6] Wanting to read a certain long book can be like this. There is a related normative point. I may have good reason, and rationally want, to read the book, but better reason to read two others instead. Here I do not have good reason—or at least not adequate reason in the context—to decide or even to intend to read the long book. By and large, if I do not have good reason to do something, I do not have good reason to intend it either.[7] But by virtue of my ground for (rationally) wanting to read the book, that desire provides a practical reason to do so, and it may significantly affect my planning even if it does not warrant my forming a corresponding intention.

A related aspect of the contrast between wanting and intending bears more directly on their roles among the practical attitudes. Whereas wants can provide reasons to do something without our intending to do it, every intention is either based on some want as supplying a reason for intending the action, or at least has a desire component whose status is crucial for the reason-giving power of the intention. My reason for intending to read the two books is to keep up with the topic. This is *my* reason in virtue of my wanting to keep up with the topic. This desire plays both an explanatory role and, if it is adequately rational, a justificatory role toward the intention. When, however, I intend to take a cool swim and I swim for its own sake, there need not be any further want expressing a reason for intending this. Still, a major aspect of my intending is my wanting to swim; and if my wanting to do this is not rational (say, because I believe I will not enjoy the swim), neither is my fully corresponding intention, i.e., the intrinsically motivated intention with the same object: to swim (for its own sake).[8] I may, to be sure, rationally intend to swim for an instrumental reason, say, to mitigate the effects of my mosquito bites. We can want, intend, or do a single thing not only for many different reasons but also for different kinds of reason. But the rationality of intending to A presupposes, and so cannot explain, that of wanting to A.

There is another respect in which wanting seems, as a practical attitude, prior to intending. It may be quite rational to intend to take the swim because it is rational to want to do so; but it would be a mistake to say that wanting this is rational because intending it is. We do allow intentions to explain why we *have* desires, as where I explain why I want an extra loaf of bread by saying I intend to freeze one of the two. But here it is implied that the intention itself is based on a want, say, to store bread. Where intending explains wanting, in the reason-providing way just illustrated, it is by virtue of some want embodied in the intention or appealed to in the context. This is why, in the broad sense of 'want' relevant here, 'Why do you want to A?' can be used to query the grounds of any intention to A.

Nothing I have said in comparing intending with wanting rules out the possibility that in some respects intending *is* the more fundamental of the two. In at least one respect it is. Again the analogy with belief is instructive. In a very wide sense, our beliefs indicate the content of our intellects: our map of the world—at least of our world. In a similar way, our intentions indicate the content of our wills: our overall plans to change the world. Kant saw this and accordingly took the goodness of one's will to be determined by what one wills, which he apparently conceived as a matter of intention.[9]

Similarly, for a person to be good from a cognitive point of view is largely to have the right sorts of beliefs. It is not entirely this. For reasons to be brought out in Chapter 8, poor reasoners are cognitively defective no matter how good the content of their belief systems. Nor is truth the only relevant standard here. Appropriate justification is crucial for having the right kinds of beliefs from the point of view of rationality, as appropriate grounding is essential for the kinds of good intentions that count toward good will. Neither true beliefs that are unjustified, and thus held on inadequate grounds, nor good intentions whose good content is based on reprehensible motivation—and so are also ill-grounded—are significant here. Intending, then, is central for appraising the will, believing for appraising the intellect. This parallel between intending and believing indicates that intention is the most fundamental practical *commitment*, as belief is the most fundamental theoretical commitment. But fundamentality in the order of commitments does not imply fundamentality in the order of attitudes. Once this is seen, we can do justice both to the parallel between intention and belief and to the place of wanting as the basic attitude that enables intention to play the pivotal role it does in defining our practical commitments.

111

2. RATIONAL DESIRE AND REASONS FOR ACTION

If, as I believe, we may treat wanting as the fundamental motivational element, particularly in constituting our basic rational conative attitudes, then practical reason must be understood partly in terms of an account of rational desire. That there are experiential sources of rational intrinsic desire was argued in Chapter 4. To maintain the parallel with theoretical reason, I call what these sources uniquely provide, such as enjoyable aspects of experience, *grounds*, and I refer to the wants rational on the basis of them as foundational wants. We can also call those wants basic, and in some contexts this is appropriate. But that term suggests that a specific content is crucial, as where desires for shelter are called basic because of their presumed centrality in human life. A desire basic in that way could, however, be instrumental, being based on desires to avoid pain and enjoy comforts. Thus, as contrasted with 'foundational', 'basic' does not always capture the functional role of foundational desires: being grounded in experience on one side, and, typically, sustaining instrumental wants on the other.

If there are rational intrinsic desires, there are reasons for action—at least if there are suitably related beliefs, or at any rate capacities to form them. This second qualification is crucial, at least for understanding *having* a reason: if I could not even form a belief to the effect that doing something would achieve the object in question (say, comfort), then having that desire would not give me reason to act. By contrast, the possibility of having reasons for belief may not similarly depend on desires. Indeed, perhaps there could be, and perhaps persons could have, reasons to believe certain propositions even if there were no desires or even tendencies to form desires and, therefore, no actions (or in any case no intentional actions).[10] This is perhaps one reason why the concept of a pure intellect is a more nearly self-sufficient ideal than the concept of a pure will.

Some philosophers would argue that the existence of certain kinds of desires is necessary, as well as sufficient, for the existence of reasons to act: that if there were neither desires nor tendencies to form them, there would not be, from any source, reasons to act—or at least we would have no such reasons. This claim is plausible because—in a useful metaphor—whereas belief succeeds when it appropriately reflects the world, regardless of whether we do anything, action is plausibly thought to succeed only if it changes the world in the desired direction. Without desire, it may seem, there is no possible success, and without possible success there is no reason to act.

There is, however, the possibility that reflection, and in that sense "reason," might show the desirability of a state of affairs, say, self-sacrificial altruism, even if there is no actual tendency to want to achieve it. If reflection can do this, then the most one might say is that one must be *capable* of wanting something in order to have reason to bring it about. There is no need to foreclose the possibility of such cognitively grounded reasons for action, and I will return to the possible basis of these reasons shortly.

It appears, then, that the possibility of one's forming a belief about how to realize a desire is a condition for that desire's providing one with a reason for action, that is, providing what we might call a *normative direction* for desire, roughly a direction in which it ought to take one. The reason why belief itself is not required for such normative direction is that one can have a reason to act even where one only has some (accessible) evidential ground for an appropriate instrumental belief, and thereby at most a disposition to form such a belief. One need not actually have the belief. Given my wanting to understand a certain problem, I can have reason to read a certain book even if I have no beliefs about that book but, if I were to begin reading my journals, *would* form the justified belief that I should read it.

There are various ways of having grounds for believing something, for instance justifiedly accepting a proposition that can be seen to imply the one in question, or holding a theory that obviously implies it though one has simply never drawn the inference.[11] Some ways of having grounds for a proposition take one closer to believing it than others. Other things equal, the easier it is for us (normal persons) to see that the grounds imply it, the closer they take us to believing it. Moreover, the closer they take us to belief, the better our reason for an action supported by the belief, other things equal. There is no need to describe these cognitive tendencies that fall short of belief. We can work quite adequately here with the notion of belief. What is less controversial is that belief, or something similarly informational, is needed to provide *behavioral direction* for desires. Typically, unless I have an actual belief regarding how to realize a desire, it does not move me to action. Until I believe, for instance, that a given book will provide the facts I want, the desire for those facts does not move me toward the book. It is true that even an inkling that the book provides the facts could produce some disposition to act. But I can have normative reason to read the book without even an inkling that it contains the desired facts.

I emphasize the contrast between reasons for action and reasons for belief because action and belief are the primary representatives of the practical and theoretical domains (at least if knowledge, which is essential in understanding theoretical reason, is constituted by belief of a certain kind). But if action is the chief practical element in our lives, in the sense that it is central in our practices and is the primary fulfillment of our purposes, desire is apparently the chief practical attitude; and there the contrast with belief is less extensive. It is less extensive, at any rate, if, just as there could be reasons for one to believe even if one had no desires, there could be reasons for one to desire even if one had no beliefs, or at least none indicating anything positive, instrumentally or intrinsically, about the object of desire. There surely can be reasons for desire that do not *positively* depend on one's (actual) beliefs, though there is a dependence on potential for belief formation. Consider a case in which in enjoying something, such as a refreshing drink, I acquire a reason for (intrinsically) wanting it, or to want it in the future. This requires *concepts*, but perhaps not actual beliefs about the drink and certainly not beliefs about what I have reason to want or to do. By virtue of having the relevant concepts and experiences, however, I would be *disposed* to form beliefs in the situation. Here we have a disanalogy between desire and belief, since a being with beliefs and reasons for *them* might *not* have to have a counterpart tendency to form desires. There remains, then, a significant difference between desires and beliefs in the extent to which each depends on the other for its rationality. Here the conative depends on the cognitive more than the cognitive depends on the conative, if indeed there is any such dependence.

3. THE AUTHORITY OF THE THEORETICAL OVER THE PRACTICAL

There is a related contrast we should recall. Whereas the rationality of intrinsic desire is defeasible by beliefs, that of beliefs is not defeasible by desires. If I believe, or at least if I rationally believe, that a swim will not be in any way enjoyable or rewarding, this defeats the rationality of intrinsically wanting one. If, by contrast, I have even a rational desire concerning the content of a rational belief of mine, say that it not be true, this does not defeat the rationality of that belief.

To be sure, in the special case in which my belief is about a desire, say, that I do not have it, the desire might play a defeating role. Suppose I falsely believe, of a desire I consider shameful, that I do not have it. It might be pathetically clear to everyone else that I do. Here, however, the desire defeats the would-be justification of my belief not because of anything about it *as* a desire but because it is an object whose existence so plainly counts against the truth of the belief. Another special case occurs where the existence of a desire is evidentially relevant to a belief, as when my wanting, upon noticing gross insensitivity, to escape someone's company is evidence against the belief that the person is a potentially good friend. Cases of these sorts do not undermine the basic contrast between the normative dependence of desires on beliefs and the relative independence of beliefs from desires.

114

It is also true that whereas desires cannot render beliefs rational (apart from such special cases as just noted), beliefs *can* render (intrinsic) desires rational. For instance (as I have already suggested), a belief that something will be enjoyable may render it rational to want it intrinsically. Beliefs of this kind represent an exercise of theoretical reason that yields practical content, and, when justified, such beliefs also have normative authority. Even an appropriate readiness to form a belief can have normative power. It can supply the directional element needed for a want to provide reason to act—a practical reason. Recall the book I have reason to read. Until I form the belief that it is important for my work, I have no desire to read it. But if I am now reading a journal and am about to discover the importance of the book, or should discover it if I am conscientious, may I not have a reason to go to the library, even before I come to want this book? I am, after all, about to come to want it, and in a reasonable way. Call this conative disposition (which itself rests on a cognitive one) an *implicit reason*, since it is in a way inoperative until the want is formed. Even apart from being manifested in actual desire, it has some normative significance. If I am interrupted and never get the book, I fail to do something I had reason to do.

Implicit reasons of this sort might be called *psychologically unrealized reasons*, since they are not represented in any propositional attitude and—in that sense—not realized (though they are in a way present) in the agent's psychology. They are analogous to the kind of justification for a belief one has in virtue of an experience that can yield, but has not produced, a belief of a justifying premise, as where one sees the shape of a traffic sign in passing, but one forms no belief about it.

If we countenance reasons that are not expressed by any propositional attitude, we must bear in mind that unlike the usual reasons for action, which are expressed by desires and related beliefs, they do not have the same explanatory or predictive power. To see this consider two contrasting cases. In the first, I want a ticket and believe I must write a check to get one. My reason—to get a ticket—is *realized*, at least in being represented, in my desire and my instrumental belief. If the reason is not outweighed by counter-reasons, it warrants some degree of expectation that I will write the check, and it can explain my doing that. The second case is the one just described, in which I am about to conclude that the library contains literature bearing on my work. Suppose I am interrupted and do not draw this conclusion. If I nonetheless do not forget what I have read that supports it, I now have an implicit reason to go to the library which has neither of the properties mentioned: it does not provide a basis for expecting the action it supports, and it is not the kind of psychological element that adequately explains such an action. The implicit reason must first yield desire, which, in turn, will be behaviorally directed only given an appropriate belief. The implicit reason is thus at least one step further from action than the desire it may engender. Such implicit reasons must be taken into account by the theory of practical reason, but they are not central cases. I turn to those now.

4. INSTRUMENTALLY RATIONAL ACTION

On the assumption that rational intrinsic desires can express adequate reasons for action, under what conditions is an action rational in the light of such desires? Belief plays a crucial role wherever the pattern is instrumental: so long as what I want is something other than to perform a basic action, there is no action that, in the light of that want, is rational for me apart from what I believe (or have appropriate warrant for believing), since I must find a means to satisfying this want. If, however, all I want to do is walk, just for the sake of walking, which I like doing, then, since walking is a basic action for me, perhaps I need not believe any instrumental proposition, even the trivial one that all I have to do to walk is simply walk. Here the path from desire to action is perhaps not mediated by belief. In this case, at least, perhaps knowing *how* does not require knowing *that*.

This line of thought is plausible; but if it shows that belief is not essential in all intentional action, the exception is a special case with limited significance. It would show that belief is not essential to *directing* action, not that belief, or at least justification for holding it, is inessential to the rationality of action. After all, if the desire to walk is intrinsic, I want to walk for certain qualities of walking, such as the sense of free movement. This point has two significant implications. First, I presumably do believe that walking in the relevant case will have such properties, or at least I am disposed to believe it. Second, if I do not at least have some justification for believing this (whether I do believe it or not), then, just on the basis of my desire, it is not rational, though it may be natural, to walk. If, in the special case of intrinsically motivated basic action, belief itself is not necessary for the rationality of the action, some degree of justification for belief is essential. This is another illustration of the authority of theoretical over practical reason.

In standard cases of instrumental action, there is much less reason to consider belief dispensable. If I write a check in order to get a ticket, I surely believe that (say) writing the check will suffice for getting the ticket.[12] But even here, it is one thing to say that belief is required for a want to provide

116

a reason and another to say that rational belief is required. My having the belief connecting my writing a check with my getting the desired ticket can be essential to my desire's providing a reason to write the check without the *rationality* of the belief's being essential to that. Indeed, the classical decision-theoretic view of rational action does not require the rationality of such beliefs as a necessary condition for that of the action they guide.[13]

Is the latitudinarianism of classical decision theory a mistake? Suppose my belief that writing the check will suffice is patently irrational, because, say, from reading a prominent warning that cash is required, I should know that the check will not be accepted. Is it still reasonable for me to write one? If I did so and it was rejected, would I not think I had made a mistake and even acted stupidly? One might say the mistake was simply in not getting the concert ticket. But my self-criticism is not like that of someone who tries hard (and reasonably) to fix a leaky hose with heavy tape and, when it fails, mutters, 'I might have known better'. In the check-writing case I have not done anything like the best I can. I lacked even a reasonable hope. I had, unfortunately, a motivating reason, but lacked a normative one—or certainly one sufficiently powerful to render an action based on it rational. An action is not well-grounded merely by stemming from a good ground. The stem must be strong enough to bear the weight it is to carry.

5. BELIEFS AS UNDERLYING ELEMENTS IN RATIONAL ACTIONS

The question explicitly pursued in the past few paragraphs is whether, if an action is rational for an agent in the light of a reason for it, then the agent has some rational *connecting belief:* some rational belief that exhibits the action as appropriately contributing to satisfying the desire. Apart from the case of basic action, the answer surely is positive, and it commonly holds for actions that one is considering as well as for those actually performed. An important further question (already touched on) concerns the way in which a reason we have for an action bears on the rationality of the action in the case in which we actually perform it. Specifically, let us ask whether a deed actually performed is made rational by a reason one has for it only if one performs it on the *basis* of that reason. I want to begin with cases in which a good reason we have for doing something is not in fact the reason for which we actually do it.

Again, the analogy with belief is clarifying. Just as one can have a reason for believing something yet actually believe it for a different reason, one can have a reason for doing something yet actually do it for some other reason. And, I think, just as a belief is rational in the light of a reason for holding it only if held on the basis of that reason, an action is rational in the light of a reason for performing it, only if performed on the basis of that reason. Wanting to bring toys in from a heavy rain may make it rational for a child to go out and get them. Yet the child may happen to do so only for another, bad reason: to annoy its mother by getting wet, where this is a bad reason both because (we may assume) the desire to annoy her is irrational *and* because it is foolish to think that getting wet on such a responsible mission will annoy her. The good reason is available to rationalize the action but does no work in grounding it. The grounding reason, on the other hand, on which the child acts, is not good. In Kant's terminology, the child is acting in conformity with reason, but not from it; and the deed does not count toward the child's rationality, in the way performing a rational action should. It counts quite the other way. Too many such acts and we have not just irrational action but an irrational child on our hands.[14]

If beliefs are the main connective tissue in rational action, can they also yield foundations of it, in the sense that they can be a basis for rational intrinsic desire? That they can defeat the rationality of intrinsic desire, for instance where one realizes that one will not enjoy something one wants, we have already seen. They can also eliminate some intrinsic desires, and they commonly do so when one learns disappointing facts about something one wants. But neither of these points implies the positive role in question. I have already indicated, however, a reason for an affirmative answer, partly based on what might be called cases of expected reward. If I believe that playing a piece would be enjoyable, this can surely provide a reason to play it: that I would enjoy playing it.

It might be replied that cognitively anticipated pleasure in an action can render it rational only given a *prior* want for pleasure. But surely the experience of the kind of pleasure in question is enough. I might need to be *justified* in believing that I *would* enjoy playing the piece; I need not already want some enjoyment of the relevant kind. Indeed, contrary to what is sometimes called a Humean view of motivation, there is also no cogent reason to deny that such a belief can, independently of the causal power of other desires, produce a desire to act accordingly. Still, my belief will not be rational apart from my having had certain experiences of a kind that enable me to appreciate, prospectively, playing the new piece. If (as suggested in Chapter 4), those experiences could not have qualities in virtue of which wanting them, or wanting to experience something essentially involving them, is rational, it is difficult to see how believing an experience to have these qualities would be capable of justifying an intrinsic desire for it. Beliefs can render intrinsic wants rational, either by making it rational to form and harbor such a want or by rendering rational an intrinsic want one already has; but they cannot, I think, do so independent of experiences which, more directly, render at least some intrinsic wants rational. Beliefs can supply reasons with this normative power only if they themselves are well grounded, and the needed grounds will be experiential.

6. SOME MAJOR KINDS OF REASONS FOR ACTION

More than one kind of practical reason has figured in our discussions so far, and it will help us to have a more explicit sketch of those kinds and some other sorts of reason that must be kept distinct. There are at least five main kinds of reason for (or directed toward) action (each with belief parallels, as described in Chapter 2). First, there are *normative reasons:* reasons (in the sense of objective grounds) there *are* to do something, say, to take a cool swim on a blistering day or to comfort a dying friend or to keep one's promises. Second, there are, derivative from the first kind, *person-relative normative reasons:* reasons for (say) *me* to take a cool swim (e.g., that it will keep a lonely friend company). Third, we should recognize *possessed reasons* (which are in that sense subjective): reasons I *have* to take a cool swim, for instance my wanting the relaxation it would provide. Fourth, there are *explanatory reasons:* reasons *why* I take a cool swim. These are typically also reasons I have. But we should allow that something else, such as post-hypnotic suggestion, might explain why someone does (or believes) something, without providing either a normative reason or a reason that the person has, and hence without being in any of the respects important for the theory of practical rationality, a practical reason. Finally, the richest kind of reasons in the practical domain are *motivating reasons:* reasons *for which* I take a cool swim.[15]

The first two kinds of reasons are abstract elements—propositions, in the case of contents of beliefs and other cognitive attitudes, and states of affairs in the case of the contents of desires and of other conative attitudes—and thus not likely candidates to be causal factors. Normative reasons are objective: when a normative reason is propositional, it is true; when it is not propositional, it in some way corresponds to a truth. For instance, suppose there is an objective reason for me to relieve a friend's suffering and that it is expressed, as it might be, infinitivally: to fulfill my promise. This reason corresponds to the truth that it is a promissory duty to relieve this suffering. (If doing this is not a duty for me and is in no other way good, then there only appears to be an external, normative reason to do it.)

In the third case, that of reasons one has, it is the psychological states, such as desire and hope, that express these reasons. The psychological states may or may not exercise causal power. As in the case of beliefs, we may speak of *reason states* in reference to desires that express the sorts of abstract elements which constitute normative reasons of the first two kinds. Some such states may be ineffectual: we are not actually moved by every reason we have, whether it is a reason for acting or believing. But possessed reasons for action are internal to one's motivational system in a way that makes their producing action tendencies expectable. They apparently always produce them if—as where a possessed reason is also a reason for which we act—we have a belief that indicates an action we take to be a means to realizing a desire that provides the reason. There may, however, be little or no action tendency if the reason is possessed in a merely implicit way, for instance when one has only a disposition to form the desire in question (say, to consult a physician) or an appropriate instrumental belief regarding its object.[16] We should also acknowledge a use of 'have a reason' in which the reason may not seem even implicitly possessed. I might ask, of a new administrator, "Do I have any reason to worry about him?" where I have no suspicion or fear. In my view, either '*Is* there a reason?' or '*Should* I have any reason?' is, depending on the context, preferable (and in any event one could possess a reason, as I use this phrase, without realizing it). But even if a non-possessional use is adopted, no substantive point I make is affected. We might still consider the use "internal" by virtue of its apparent connection with the interests of the agent together with related propositions the agent could discern.

By contrast, reasons *why* (the fourth variety) are always (sustaining) explainers, and for them the parallel to belief is very close. On the plausible assumption that true propositions are equivalent to facts, we can also take reasons *why* to be facts: explaining ones. Such reasons need not, however, be even prima facie justifiers, since an action can be produced or causally sustained by factors that have no justificatory value; these factors might be manipulations of the brain and not mental elements at all, even if, in order to produce genuine action rather than mere behavior, they might have to work by inducing the presence of certain mental elements. Motivating reasons—the fifth kind—are explanatory, possessed, and, even when they do not coincide with external reasons (as they commonly do), have whatever minimal prima facie justificatory power (if any) a reason must have to be a basis of *action*.

Wants can provide all five kinds of reason; but not every want does so and those that do must operate in different ways, above all by *expressing* normative reasons and *constituting* causal explanatory ones. A rational desire, say, to listen to a beautiful aria, can express a normative reason to act, as well as a possessed—and in that sense subjective—reason to act, and it can constitute an explanatory reason for acting. An irrational desire, however, does not provide the agent with any kind of normative reason, though it can explain an action. Beliefs, like desires, can also provide all five kinds of reason for action, though—in contrast to their autonomous role in giving us reasons to believe—they provide normative reasons for action only *because* of what one should want, where the 'should' is that of rationality. Still, since wants themselves provide reasons for action only in combination with beliefs or dispositions to believe (or at least reasons to believe that can so dispose one), a reason for action can always be expressed by an appropriate ascription of a belief to the agent. Paradigms are instrumental beliefs to the effect that the action is a means to the object of the want or beliefs indicating something desirable about it. Whether we *cite* a belief or a desire or both or neither in explaining or justifying an action is largely a matter of what can be presupposed in the context. Asked why I put ice in my stew, I might say I was in a hurry; encountering a puzzled look from someone who cannot see the rising steam, I could adduce a belief I had presupposed and say that I think this will quickly cool it without thinning it.

To be sure, beliefs, by contrast with wants, are not quite as usefully described as reasons for action, or even as *providing* such reasons (the more accurate terminology where the reason in question is normative, e.g., a proposition linking an action to producing pleasure or avoiding pain).This is because, apart from what one should, in some objective sense, want—which is very often something someone does want—there cannot be normative reasons for one's action. There would be nothing desirable for one.[17] Even if, for example, a belief that listening to an aria will be enjoyable provides, by itself, a reason to listen to it, it also provides a reason to want to listen to it, and it could not yield the former reason apart from providing the latter. By contrast, a belief can express a reason for a further belief quite apart from what one wants, or from any non-cognitive attitudes.

It might seem that, in addition, if one *intrinsically* wants something, then there is reason to act in quest of the desired object regardless of what one believes or should believe. This very important idea is by no means clearly true: if a desire (even an instrumental one) provides a reason to act, there is surely some positive characteristic of its object that one should believe the object to have. The theoretical 'should' here is the counterpart of the objective sense of the practical 'should' that goes with the notion of desirability: there is a kind of believability, or belief-worthiness, that is like desirability, or desire-worthiness, in implying a normative reason. Suppose there is (normative) reason for me to do something I want to do, since I will much enjoy it, but, given what I justifiably believe, I am unable to see that I will and hence am puzzled that I want it. Prior to having certain musical experiences, I might even have good reason to think, regarding a beautiful aria I can listen to, that it will be terrible. Still, if I will enjoy it and I can realize this, then in some partly objective sense I should come to believe this upon adequately considering the matter. As the example perhaps suggests, it could turn out that wherever an intrinsic desire provides a reason to act, it is because of something that the agent does or should believe about its object, where this implies at least an appropriate disposition to form the belief. Hence, that reason can be in some way registered in the agent's cognitive system.

7. THE NORMATIVE POWER OF DESIRE

In speaking of intrinsic desires as expressing reasons, I have so far left open an important matter that bears directly on the status of instrumentalism. In my main examples of such desires, they have valuable objects, and I have argued that at least these intrinsic desires can be rational. But so far I have not directly pursued the question whether intrinsic desire *by itself* can ground rational action, at least where the person does not have certain defeating beliefs. Does just any intrinsic want provide a (normative) reason for action, that is, a consideration that counts to some degree toward the rationality of an action based upon it? I have not ruled this out, but I suspect that such a desire can provide a reason, as opposed to a motive, only where there are already equally good reasons for and against an action and it tips the balance one way or the other.

On this issue, instrumentalism gains unwarranted plausibility from our natural constitution. We just do not tend to want things, intrinsically, unless we either take them to have certain attractive qualities or at least are drawn to them *for* certain qualities, and in either case these qualities tend to be very much the sorts in virtue of which it is rational to some degree to want the things in question. So far as pleasure and the avoidance of pain account for our basic motivation, this is obvious. Moreover, since our intrinsic wants tend to be in some ordinary sense rational, it seems correspondingly plausible to say, of virtually any of the representative ones, that they provide at least some reason to act.

There may be a still deeper explanation of the plausibility of instrumentalism, one that has not to my knowledge been noted. Intrinsic desire seems to have a non-contingent (and probably a priori) connection with certain feelings. For instance, if we come to believe that we will not get something we intrinsically want, we tend to feel disappointment.[18] If I intrinsically want to attend an opera, I tend to feel disappointment on hearing that the tickets are all taken. Now even if disappointment is not *necessarily* unpleasant, it is clear—and it is arguably a conceptual truth—that there is prima facie reason to avoid disappointment. On the plausible assumption that rational agents in general believe (or are rationally disposed to believe) that if they do not get something they intrinsically want—at least something they want on balance—they will be disappointed, they thereby have reason to act to get it. But here the *ground* of their reason is not the desire but the hedonic or other valuational consideration generated by the prospect of disappointment. If instrumentalism gains plausibility from this point, it is trading in part on the merits of an incompatible theory.

It will help us to compare the case of belief. Our non-inferential beliefs are typically based on grounds which, unlike wishful thinking, confer some degree of justification. But a belief's merely being non-inferential surely does not confer any degree of justification (or rationality) on it. Granted, a merely non-inferential belief is analogous to a merely non-instrumental desire, not to an intrinsic one. The real analogue of an intrinsic desire is a belief of a proposition *for* its experiential or intuitive attractiveness, as exhibited in, for instance, a supporting sensory experience. I believe there is a paneled wall before me not merely non-inferentially but because my visual field contains a series of knotty, long-grained woody strips. Yet even here, I could believe something on the basis of experiential qualities that do not lend it support, as I could want something on the basis of qualities that I should not, by my best lights, find attractive. There may seem to be no harm in taking any intrinsic desire that is not objectionable on broadly logical grounds (say, by being for a clearly impossible state of affairs) to provide some minimal reason to act in order to satisfy it. But, as will be apparent shortly, we are not bound to do so, either by the analogy between practical and theoretical reason or on any other count.

8. DIFFICULTIES FOR INSTRUMENTALISM

The theory of reasons I am developing is best understood by contrast with instrumentalism, and I want to pursue the contrast in a direction that seems largely unexplored. For instrumentalism, since the role of reason is to serve desire, reasons for action are grounded in and *only* in desire. The reason for this is not that the satisfaction of intrinsic desire is considered intrinsically *good*. Far from it; anyone who countenances intrinsic goodness is at best unlikely to be an instrumentalist, since intrinsic goodness would apparently provide reasons for action—such as pursuit of things that have it—even apart from any actual desires. It is, for example, scarcely coherent to say such things as that enjoyment of a symphony is intrinsically good but there is no reason to pursue it. There might be "internal" criteria that a normative objectivist sympathetic with instrumentalism would impose in devising a hybrid version; for instance, the agent might have to be *capable* of believing that the wanted object has certain desirable qualities, or at least be capable of wanting it on their account. But this constraint, like many others plausible from an objectivist point of view, is not substantive and would leave the hybrid position quite far from instrumentalism.[19]

Instrumentalism in its pure form, then, is at once very permissive about what sorts of objects intrinsic desires may have and very restrictive in its grounding of reasons for action exclusively in actual desires. On the second count in particular, it is more odd than is usually realized. It implies that if, for even a moment, one were bereft of desires, one would have no reasons for action. I would not even have a reason to step out of the way of an advancing brush fire, though I might know that I *would* want to avoid the burns once they began to hurt.

It is common for instrumentalists to deal with such difficulties by ascribing reason-giving power to *hypothetical* desires, such as those one would have upon suitable reflection.[20] That those desires may have it is perhaps a plausible claim; but according it to them is a major departure from the aseptic functionalism of the pure theory. For pure instrumentalism (as we have seen), the function of reason is to serve desire, not hypothetical desires, or even the durable actual ones that would be retained on reflection.

To see a rationale for this functionalist notion central for the pure theory, one might think of instrumentalism as based on the conception of foundational desire as something like an agitation that naturally tends toward quiescence. The means it calls for, which we naturally and—perhaps on that account—rationally seek, may be of any kind. This will depend on the kind of agitation we experience and on what, in the situation of action, attracts our attention in the right way. An appropriate action may cool what is burning, moisten what is dry, contain what is exploding. We swim to cool the body, drink to wet the parched tongue, throw up our arms to relieve the pressure of anger. If the function of reason is not to serve the desires we actually have, and in the end is construed hypothetically, so that some desires are suitable foundations of rational action and others are not, then we are owed an account of the added conditions. It must not presuppose an independent standard of practical reason.[21] What might it be?

One good explanation of why hypothetical desires should have the normative power to confer rationality on action or would-be action is that their objects are intrinsically valuable. Since instrumentalists do not appeal to the notion of intrinsic value, they might reply that a better explanation is that we naturally *tend* to want the things in question, for instance to avoid burns, and would tend to want them even if there should come a time when we in fact have no desires. Suppose there is such a tendency. Imagine that at present I do want, quite strongly, to be burned, though I would want even more not to be burned, once the flames reached me. It still seems that I have at least better reason to avoid the flames than to wait for them. But, for instrumentalism, why should a mere tendency to want have any force in comparison with an actual want, even if the potential (non-existent) want is stronger?[22] If the instrumentalist grants that it should, one might surely suspect that a tacit attribution of value or disvalue, or of some other desire-independent ground for action, is subliminally at work. Being burned, after all, is virtually universally taken to be a bad thing and, even more basically, to have qualities that ground a rational desire to avoid it. Even apart from this, it is commonly taken to be a bad thing—and a paradigm of imprudence—to do or permit something now, because of my present desires, that will frustrate my later desires that are vastly stronger and, at least in that way, more important to me.[23] Neither notion of badness is derivable from pure instrumentalism.

Once the points so far made in this section are taken seriously, another important aspect of instrumentalism should become clear. At least for pure instrumentalism it makes no difference whether a desire is intrinsic or merely *non-instrumental*, as where one forgets why one wanted something, such as to go into the study, but still does this. The action is a response to the desire and may occur even when one has forgotten, but does not realize one has forgotten, why one is going there. *That* one wants something other than as a means is all that matters. This point is entirely consistent with the related psychological point that believing we do not know why we want something can eliminate our wanting it, especially if we believe we originally wanted it as a means. The normative point here is that for instrumentalism the desire is not only not irrational but can provide a reason for action, say, to open the study door. A merely non-instrumental desire can be as insistent as an intrinsic desire, crying out for satisfaction; it combines with instrumental belief in the normal way to produce action; it can explain action performed in order to satisfy it; and its object can be, in one's view, as natural as any other object of one's desires.

Wanting something purely as a means, then, can (on instrumentalist grounds) provide a reason for action *derivatively* from a non-instrumental desire to which the instrumental want is subordinate, even if this desire is not intrinsic and would be easily given up. The reason is, however, *entirely* derivative—otherwise, even where one wants A purely as a means to B, one could be credited with two reasons to A—that one wants to A and that one wants to B—which, together, could outweigh an intrinsic desire to C stronger than the desire to A. At that rate I could, on the one hand, prefer swimming to boating but, on the other hand, since the strength of my desire for the latter, together with the strength of my desire to rent a boat, as a means to it, could be greater than the strength of my desire to swim, I could have better reason to go boating. And this could be so even if I have forgotten why I wanted to go boating (say, to meet a friend across the lake) and would hardly know what to do with the boat having rented it. Here conative agitation unsettles me after all, even though I do not know its cause or how to achieve quiescence.

It might be pointed out that a merely non-instrumental desire is "alien," in the sense that one does not identify with it or has a second-order desire—or disposition to form a second-order desire—not to have it. But not all merely non-instrumental desires are like this. It feels natural to want to enter my study, even when I cannot remember my reason. A deeper point is this: a pure instrumentalist is apparently unable to account for *why* a desire's feeling alien should matter in itself or why the potential of a desire to be wanted by the agent should bear on its capacity to ground rational action. The higher-order strategy also invites a vicious regress, since the second-order desire could be similarly in need of grounding. But the main point is that merely non-instrumental desires can guide action and can cry out for satisfaction no less urgently than intrinsic ones.

The implied parity between intrinsic and merely non-instrumental desires leads to a further oddity of instrumentalism. I can have reason to enter the study, since I want to, but be utterly unable to say on what account I want to. I may be able to explain the genesis of the want as undoubtedly due to, say, finding myself without something or other I needed; but at present the desire itself is utterly ungrounded. Surely the rational thing is to regard it, not as a reason for the desired action, but at best as a reason—or as giving me a reason—to find the reason I *had* for that action.

Consider the belief analogue. I forget my premises for a thesis that, without them, does not seem plausible to me. I am puzzled by my own belief of it. I may have faith that there *is* a justification for the belief; but it is surely not justified now.[24] It would seem, indeed, that one's having no idea why one believes something or what one wants something *for* is in general a defeater of the rationality of holding the belief or pursuing the action. Even an intrinsic-desire-satisfaction theory of reasons for action has trouble

126

enough here. But if instrumentalism cannot solve the parity problem (as I shall call it), if it cannot properly motivate distinguishing mere non-instrumental desires from intrinsic ones, it becomes still less plausible.

9. HEDONIC VALUE, DESIRE, AND REASONS FOR ACTION

It may be thought that the experientialist view of rational intrinsic desire, at least so far as it depends on hedonic grounds for action, is in the end tarred with the same brush. For it might seem that there is nothing distinctive about pleasure or pain, over and above the qualities of the experiences that yield them. To enjoy a swim, it may be held, is simply to want to continue it for its own sake; hence, to take enjoyment as a source of the rationality of an intrinsic desire is in effect to grant reason-giving power to the having, or anyway, the satisfying, of intrinsic desire.[25] But is this so? Does the difference between enjoying a swim and simply having it consist just in what one wants regarding it? Surely I can enjoy it without wanting to go on doing it for its own sake when I am *disposed* to want that. And at the *last* moment I enjoy it, need I even be disposed to continue to want it? I think not.

More positively, is there not a certain zesty feeling that partly constitutes this kind of enjoyment, or at least the pervasive sense of absorption noted in the discussion of rational desire in Chapter 4? Is it not because of this and similar feelings that one *does* want to continue? And when one is disappointed by a swim one does not enjoy, is the problem just that one found one did not want to continue it for its own sake? Is there not a sense of disappointment? Admittedly, the zesty feeling may be grounded in elements of the experience which can be non-hedonically characterized. My enjoyment derives from the feel of the water, the sense of free movement, the tingling of cool currents. But these surely are phenomenally distinct pleasurable elements, and they need not depend on what one wants at the time. It may be that the tendency to want to continue enjoyable activities for their own sake is the only—or at any rate the most prominent—thing they have in common. But this is explainable in terms of its being produced by pleasurable qualities. It does not imply that any such desire is constitutive of pleasure.

We should also look at the intrinsic desire theory of pleasure—call it *the conative theory of pleasure*—from the other direction: can one not want to continue something for its own sake without enjoying it? Consider a stimulating and valuable, but also difficult and tense, conversation with a senior colleague. Granting that one might not be able to want to continue it for its own sake if one were utterly suffering throughout, it still appears that pleasure (or pain avoidance) is not the only case in which one has such an intrinsic want to continue something one is not at the time enjoying. Pleasure is not the only thing intrinsically wanted; and even if it were, it can be qualitative in a way the conative theory of pleasure does not allow.

Once again it is illuminating to compare desire with belief. As we have seen, the analogue of intrinsic desire is not mere non-inferential belief but the normal kind of non-inferential belief, the kind grounded in experience. Recall my belief that there is a paneled wall before me. This belief is grounded in my visual experience and is a natural response to it as I seek a typical example of an experiential belief. On the same perceptual basis, I could have formed a belief that there is a wall which is more than three-fourths of an inch away; but although I had a disposition to form this belief on considering the distance, I did not: belief formation is (normally) a discriminative response to experience (as indicated earlier).[26] Our cognitive system is selective in what it inclines us to attend to, and we form beliefs mainly on matters relevant to what we are doing or are inclined to do. Apparently, for both evolutionary and pragmatic reasons, we form far fewer than the huge number of beliefs that, given our experiences, we could, psychologically and justifiedly, form. I suggest that intrinsic desire is similar to experiential belief on this count. What we want for its own sake we want for certain of its qualities. We do not just want it on no account at all, as we do the object of a merely non-instrumental desire.

A merely non-inferential belief will be neither justified nor capable of conferring justification on any belief grounded in it; for similar reasons I suggest that a merely non-instrumental desire will tend to be neither rational (though it need not be irrational) nor capable of conferring rationality on any desire or action grounded on it. If such a desire is a response to experience at all, it is not discriminative. It is not based on anticipation of pleasure, aversion to pain, engagement in conversation, aesthetic contemplation, or any other aspect of experience for which one might want the object in question.

Pure instrumentalism, then, cannot solve the parity problem. It has no adequate way to explain why a merely non-instrumental desire should not play the same role in conferring rationality as our intrinsic desires, which (normally) represent discriminative responses to experience. Modified instrumentalist theories can deal with the problem by one or another qualification, but they still owe us an account of how, apart from assumptions that undermine instrumentalism entirely, one can deny this parity between intrinsic desires and merely non-instrumental ones.[27]

128

10. THE INTERNAL GROUNDS OF RATIONAL ACTION

In the light of the many points that have emerged, I believe that we have intrinsic wants as a foundation of our motivational structure and that, contrary to instrumentalism, if we have any rational desire, it is in virtue of our having one or more rational intrinsic desires. It also appears that our instrumental desires often have a quite integrated grounding, since so many of them are built upon important intrinsic desires, such as wanting to care for one's children. Suppose further that our rational actions are those that are well-grounded in these basic elements, as where an action is rational because we rationally believe it will avoid pain (where the rationality in question is roughly consonance with reason and not merely the absence of irrationality). What sorts of transmission relations and principles explain how a rational intrinsic desire can confer rationality on an action performed to satisfy it?

The crucial element that links the rationality of action to that of a desire it subserves is the connecting belief, the belief to the effect that doing the deed will contribute to realizing that desire. There are various sorts of connecting beliefs, each corresponding to a different kind of practical argument that the agent might, but need not, go through in preparing for action to realize the desire in question. When an action is based on actual practical reasoning, such an argument is *realized* in consciousness. Where the action is performed for a reason but not, in that way, *reasoned,* the connecting belief still plays an essential role. A connecting belief may express necessity, sufficiency, adequacy, optimality, or mere probability. One may, for example, believe, of a recommendation, that it is necessary to help the candidate, that it is sufficient, that it is adequate, that it is optimal, or that it has some probability of helping. And there are many other possibilities: as least as many as there are presumptive means to one's end. Well-groundedness of the action requires that at least one crucial connecting belief be rational.

Here, as with inferential belief, defeasibility is possible. There is defeat of the rationality of the foundational element, as where the rationality of the intrinsic want is undermined or overridden. There is also defeat of the rationality of the connecting belief, as where one discovers that one was foolish to think an action would be sufficient for one's end. Defeat of the foundational desire can come from beliefs, say, a belief that satisfying the want will not be worthwhile, or from beliefs together with wants, as where I discover (hence come to believe) that realizing the want will prevent satisfying one that is more important to me. (The required kind of importance is itself a topic for exploration.)

If one has a reason that is undefeated, then if it has sufficient strength relative to what it is a reason for, it makes it rational to do something one justifiedly believes will fill the bill: to get the vegetables one needs, to take a certain route to one's destination, to satisfy one's editor—the reason needs greater strength depending on the importance of the item in question. This transmission principle captures part of the important idea that an action supported by a sufficient reason is rational.

This principle does not imply that an action supported by a sufficient reason must be what one has *best* reason to do. For one thing, we often have equally good reasons for different options, any of which it is quite reasonable to take. The problem of determining what one has best reason to do is difficult and goes well beyond determining when a reason is undefeated and sufficient. I have argued that mere intrinsic desire does not tell the whole story, but I would grant that when one is choosing between two actions concerning which other things are equal on some clearly rational basis, one might then reasonably prefer one of them if, in addition, it satisfies a mere intrinsic desire.

This apparent reason-giving capacity of mere intrinsic desire may suggest that such desires can serve as a *conditionally basic* source of reasons, rather as coherence among beliefs may be argued to be a conditionally basic source of justification. The idea is this: *given* that there is already reason to A, one's intrinsically wanting to do so can by itself make it more rational to A than to B, where apart from this desire B would be just as good an option. Even this weak thesis, however, is doubtful: it may be that the reason-giving weight we find in such cases is due wholly or mainly to the presumption that one would not intrinsically want something (or non-inferentially believe something) for which there is no prima facie reason on the basis of the normal experiential grounds, or perhaps to the presumption that an unsatisfied want can cause frustration and thereby provides an instrumental reason to satisfy it. In either case, mere intrinsic wanting would not by itself confer a reason. It would do so because of its connection with what is independently valuable or otherwise capable of conferring reasons.[28]

As I conceive rational action, then—in the sense in which rationality implies consonance with reason—it is action that is at least minimally well-grounded: it must be based on some rational ground by some rational cognitive connection.[29] It is, as this suggests, normally intentional, but something done knowingly yet not intentionally can still be rational. For instance, offending x as a foreseen but not desired consequence of nominating y may be rational though it is only consented to and performed non-intentionally. Still, whenever any non-intentional action is rational, it is apparently by virtue of some intentional action that is. We might call such non-intentional rational actions *indirectly well-grounded:* being wanted neither as ends (intrinsically) nor as means (instrumentally), they are not motivationally grounded directly in any desire; and being rational on neither of those counts, their rationality is also indirect.

The possibility of rational action that owes its rationality to indirect grounding shows that rationality is like justification in being transmissible to items other than its primary bearers. Consider perceptual evidence. It can justify for us a proposition we are only disposed to believe, as where our view of the people in a normal dining room justifies the proposition, which we neither believe nor disbelieve, that there is no one in the room over 9.89 feet tall. Moreover, sympathetically entertaining a proposition that is justified for me, without believing it, is somewhat like non-intentionally doing something that is rational for me: in both cases we have something that is rationally appropriate in the light of, but is not a full-blooded response to, the relevant ground. The will does not embrace, but only permits, the action; the intellect does not adopt, but only sympathetically considers, the proposition. To be sure, non-intentional action is still action, whereas entertaining a proposition is not believing it. But the two cases are alike in this: neither is well-grounded by virtue of the kind of connection, characteristic of both rational action and rational belief, that links them to the ground on the basis of which, by a chain of instrumental beliefs or evidential support relations, they are rational.

The notion of rational action has a further characteristic worth noting and also belonging to the conception of justified belief developed in Part I. The notion of rational action is apparently *internal,* in the sense that it requires that the agent can, by reflecting with sufficient care, arrive at the relevant ground and a connection between it and the action it supports, even if not under descriptions of these abstract kinds. There can be external (normative) reasons to act, as where there is a good case for treating people with respect. But unless I have appropriate access to these reasons, they are not reasons *for me,* nor can they render an action I perform rational unless they become so. Perhaps there can be no normative reason, for action or belief, to which *no one* has access. It would be like a ground that nothing could rest on. But there can be impersonal reasons for types of acts so long as someone has access to them and can act on the basis of them.[30]

11. THE MUTUAL IRREDUCIBILITY OF PRACTICAL AND THEORETICAL REASON

Given the parallels between rational belief and rational desire, and given the pervasiveness of the concept of belief in any plausible account of practical rationality, one might wonder whether practical rationality is somehow reducible to theoretical rationality. We have seen by implication that neither is reducible to the other. Beliefs and actions are, for all their parallels, irreducibly different; and the rationality of each is at most in part a question of the rationality of the other.

Few have even suggested that rational belief reduces to belief based on rational action, such as surveying evidence and granting assent. In any case, once it is seen that it can be rational to cause oneself to believe something which it is not rational *to believe*, this strategy will not even appear to be promising (as will be argued further in Chapter 8). Believing is simply not an action; and if it can ever be produced by assent, the act of assent is still not a belief.[31] Even beyond this, assenting can itself be rational or not, and it is difficult to see how to avoid taking its rationality to depend on that of some connecting belief which links the evidence to the proposition in question, say, a belief to the effect that the evidence supports that proposition.

Still, one might say, isn't the goal of belief to get us around in the world, and so should not belief be judged by how well it fulfills its goal?[32] There are at least two difficulties here. First, belief does not literally have a goal. Neither belief in general nor individual beliefs are (directly) voluntary, or, in part for that reason, aimed at anything. *We* have goals in criticizing beliefs; but although this makes it natural to think that beliefs have related goals, such as getting us around in the world, those ends should not be ascribed to beliefs themselves and are best understood as goals we should bring to bear on influencing our beliefs. Second, do we not need to judge the success of our overall system of beliefs—by relying on our beliefs? And do we not need to presuppose the rationality of some of them in deciding what else it is rational to believe? What good is a judge who is not rational? Perhaps a kind of coherentism may seem to suffice here, but I doubt it can, for the sorts of reasons offered in Chapters 1 and 2. A coherentist element is accommodated by my framework, but a pure coherentism gives experience too small a role in providing basic reasons for belief.[33]

There is perhaps more reason to take practical rationality to reduce to theoretical rationality than to expect the converse reduction. If we suppose that some beliefs have motivating power, then even if we grant that actions are very different from beliefs, we can say that actions are well-grounded when they are motivated by rational desires and justified by the relevant rational beliefs.[34] But it is far from clear that beliefs in themselves do have motivating power—though they may be expected to be accompanied by motivation *in rational persons*, and plainly they can cause desires, especially but not only in rational persons. If they do have that motivating power, and if they can justify enough of our basic motivation to ground all our rational action, I think it is surely because what makes these beliefs rational *also* makes certain intrinsic wants rational. If that is so, there is little theoretical gain in trying to reduce practical to theoretical rationality.

What makes reduction of the practical to the theoretical attractive is the idea that beliefs, which on this approach emerge as the basis of practical reason, can reflect *truth*, which is an accomplishment that seems a fitting ground of rationality. But even if, as strong motivational internalism may imply, there should be truths whose *adequate* grasp makes a person practically rational, I cannot see that explicating them—and the relevant notion of an adequate grasp of them—would be any easier than explicating how the appropriate awareness of certain qualities of experience makes it rational to want experiences of that kind.[35] A practical belief, say, that cool swims on hot days are (intrinsically) good, can be well-grounded, and can be most plausibly considered motivating, only if it is experientially grounded in much the same way as rational desires for that kind of experience.

Even on the assumption that some beliefs about what sorts of things are good, say, the general belief that enjoyable experiences are good, are a priori, surely these beliefs can be justifiably held only if one has some minimal knowledge of the nature of such objects of experience. It is highly doubtful that one could adequately know what they are like without relevant experiences.[36] And those experiences presumably are just the kind that make it rational to want the things believed to be good. To stay with the case of pleasure, the experiences would be the kind we have in enjoying a cool swim, a beautiful aria, or a zesty conversation.

On balance, then, I conclude that some of our intrinsic desires are rational because they are experientially well-grounded and not because of— though of course not regardless of—what we independently believe about their objects. Practical reason depends on theoretical reason at crucial places, but it has a significant measure of autonomy. Theoretical reason takes us, often by way of instrumental beliefs, from rational grounds for action to the rationality of actions supported by those grounds. Such actions constitute a practical analogue of rational inferential belief, and (as we have seen) there are also analogous transmission principles linking the rationality in intrinsic desires to that of desires or actions based on them. But theoretical reason does not by itself supply all of the basic grounds of action. The beliefs about action that provide reasons for it can do so only if they are themselves well-grounded; and the kinds of grounds they require for this task include experiences that are themselves more basic sources of practical reasons than beliefs themselves.

The autonomy of practical reason can be seen in the context of profound parallels between theoretical and practical reason. In the fundamental cases, the formation of intrinsic desires, like the formation of non-inferential beliefs, is a discriminative response to experience, whether sensory or introspective or reflective or of some other kind. There are features of experience that apparently play basic normative roles in both the practical and theoretical spheres. Action is a discriminative response to desires and beliefs that arise in our experience—and is thereby also a response to reasons for it. These conative and cognitive elements are rational when they are well-grounded.

Well-groundedness is experiential for intrinsic desire, as it is for our normal non-inferential beliefs; it is inferential in the case of instrumental desires and inferential beliefs; and it is also inferential—in the practical sense—in the case of actions. This does not imply the inferentialist view that every rational action arises from an actual piece of practical reasoning. But rational action is grounded in reasons that provide the materials for a supporting practical argument should one be needed for explanation or justification of the conduct in question. This is a compressed summary of a complex theory of theoretical and practical rationality. Some, but by no means all, of the essential details have been presented above. More are needed. Toward that end, the next chapter explores how far the theory can take us toward providing a foundation for ethics.

OTHERS AS ENDS

Sense experience justifies a multitude of beliefs about the world; reward-ing experience, whether sensory or not, warrants a multitude of desires. My visual experience of the colors and shapes of a piano before me justi-fies me in believing that there is one there; my enjoyable experience of the melody and harmony of the sonata I hear makes it rational for me to want to listen to the performance. Sense experiences vouch for the truth of the propositions they tend to cause us to believe, and thereby ground the justification of our believing them; rewarding experiences vouch for the value of what they tend to make us want, and thereby ground the ra-tionality of our wanting it.

Both theoretical and practical reason have experiential sources, and both belief and desire are rational chiefly on the basis of their relation to those sources. The fundamental relations, both psychological and norma-tive, are direct. Perceptual and other direct beliefs rest on experience with-out the mediation of other psychological elements: direct beliefs are not inferentially based on other beliefs. Similarly, intrinsic desires are not based, via instrumental beliefs, on deeper desires to which they are instrumen-tally subordinate. This is psychological directness. When these direct be-liefs and intrinsic desires are rational, their rationality normally derives from their grounding in experience. This is normative directness. The direct-ness of the relation of these grounding cognitive and conative elements to experience is not, however, brute. Although these beliefs and desires are not inferentially mediated by other beliefs or desires, direct beliefs and intrinsic desires are discriminatively responsive to their experiential grounds, and they can be supported (or defeated) by other grounds, directly or inferentially. My belief that a violin is being played across the street is a direct response to, and rational on the basis of, what I hear, but it could be supported by testimony. My desire to hear more is a response to, and rational on the basis of, the beauty of the qualities I discern, but it could also be supported by a belief that I would enjoy hearing more.

Many beliefs, however, are inferentially justified, as many desires are instrumentally rational. A multitude of beliefs are justified on the basis of other beliefs; a multitude of desires are rational on the basis of other desires. Inferential extension has no fixed limits, if it has any at all. Rational superstructure elements are well-grounded through beliefs that connect them with foundational beliefs or desires, and those, in turn, are experientially grounded. But over time, both the foundations and the superstructure can change. Restructuring can occur through elimination, addition, discovery of deeper foundations, and in other ways.

1. RATIONALITY FROM THE INSIDE OUT

Although the learning that children must undergo in order to achieve rationality proceeds from the outside in, it is perhaps easiest to understand both theoretical and practical reason from the inside out, beginning with one's own case. Moreover, if we are to understand how reason supports morality, one thing we must find is a path that takes us from the inside— from our own experience—to the external world. Rational desire, in particular, is most clearly exemplified by desires for one's own pleasure or for relief from one's own pain. This is in part why egoism, in the theory of value as well as in psychology, is so appealing.[1] The central question that its persisting appeal raises here is whether rationality is grounded in the way egoism claims.

Recall the desire for a cool swim, and consider again how its rationality is grounded. Suppose it is a hot summer afternoon. As I think of the enveloping wetness of the cool water, the sense of free movement within it, and its ambient sustenance, it is easy for me to see my desire as rational. When I vividly think of these qualities of the experience, it seems to me that I would be crazy not to want it. I need not, however, clearly envisage these natatory qualities, or even envisage them at all, in order simply to have a desire for a cool swim. If I do not clearly envisage them, or if I become absorbed in something else before they can come home to me, then I may have either no desire to swim or one that is gratuitous in a way that prevents it from being rational. I might also have duties that give me an overriding desire to do something else, and this desire might prevent my clearly envisaging the swimming. But none of these points shows that it is not full-bloodedly rational to want to swim when I am clearly envisaging the swim as having the properties that make it attractive to me. The comparison with belief yields a similar conclusion: I need not believe there is a piano before me if, though it is indeed there, I have no clear impression of one in my visual field; and even when I have that impression, the (prima facie) rationality of my belief that there is a piano before me can be overridden by other, contrary beliefs of mine. Normally, of course, it is not.

If others are fundamentally like us (and I assume we have good reason to think this), we might expect that their experiences can be enjoyable—or painful—in much the way ours are and can provide grounds of practical reasons for them. For many of us this sense of the similar humanity of others makes it natural to want them to have enjoyable experiences. It is obvious, to be sure, that other people can be means to one's own ends. Egoists about human psychology think that this is all they are to us. An egoist can certainly allow that I want something for someone else and thus can account for *beneficent* conduct; but beneficence need not be altruistic. If egoism is true, I cannot *intrinsically* want something for another, since then the other person would in some sense be an end for me. The psychological egoist denies that this ever happens; the valuational egoist would condemn it if it did. But if it is really for the qualities of an experience that I want it, it should be possible, with those qualities in mind, to want someone else to enjoy the same kind of experience for those same qualities. And it should be possible to want this intrinsically: not for my sake but, for instance, for the sake of my daughter.

Granted, one may have to care about others in order to have such a want. Indeed, to care about others *is*, in good part, to want, intrinsically, things that one takes to benefit them. Such desires may in fact be prior, conceptually as well as genetically, to the attitude of caring, rather than conversely. Granted, too, that caring about others may have to start inside. If I never experience pleasure or pain in a way that leads me to have the normal intrinsic desires regarding them in my own experience, there is no reason to expect me to develop the counterpart intrinsic desires for the realization of pleasure and the avoidance of pain in the experience of others. But if my experience is normal, I may develop a measure of something of great importance in moral life: empathy.

Empathy radiates beyond us, even if its origin is in us. The necessity of starting inside (if this is necessary) does not confine us there. Perhaps nothing guarantees that I will intrinsically want my daughter to have a swim; but, as I think of her experience of the cool wetness and free movement, I can be aware of how good it would be for her to experience them, much

137

as I can feel its desirability in my own case.[2] Imagining her experience of them may be much like imagining my own: in neither case do I actually experience them; in both I project outward from my memories of swimming to a new instance of it.

Suppose, however, that there is only one swimming ticket, and I am nearly prostrate from the heat, while my daughter is not uncomfortable. Is it still rational to want intrinsically that she have the swim? It surely is. Must it be otherwise if we substitute a friend or even someone I do not know? I think not. Nothing stops me from imagining the same refreshing qualities in their experience that make swimming attractive to me. This is especially so if I can remember my own swimming, on similar occasions in the past, as having those qualities. For even though the experience I remember was mine, it is not now occurring; and the distance between my present and past experiences is, if not similar to, then at least a model for understanding, the distance between my experience and theirs. Memory can at least overcome the tyranny of the present self-conscious moment in our conception of rationality and goodness. That can be a first step toward overcoming an egocentric view of their grounds.

It can be my imagining the qualities of a friend's experience, rather than, say, a sense of duty, that leads me to hesitate to use my swimming ticket myself. Empathy can motivate, with or without the help of duty, and sometimes better. I take it to be feeling *with*, not just feeling *for*, someone else, as sympathy may be; and feeling, especially feeling of this empathic kind, can motivate. To be sure, in the end it may not be rational to act on my desire that my friend have a swim, as opposed to the self-directed one: my own desire to swim. This could be because the latter desire is better grounded; it could also be because it is just equally well-grounded but stronger. Given equal quality, a difference in quantity prevails. One possible explanation of this apparent fact is that disappointment, which there is reason to avoid, tends to be greater in proportion to the strength of the unsatisfied desire.[3]

There are many occasions where self-directed rational desires provide better reasons for action than competing altruistic ones. Egoism can gain undeserved plausibility from that fact. For it may appear that when it would not be rational for me to *act* on a want that is thus normatively outweighed, say, the desire that my friend have the swim, it is not rational for me to *have* the desire. This is not so; the desire is entirely natural, nor does it crowd my mind. Indeed, if I did not have it, I would not be so ready to give my friend the ticket if I am suddenly called away. Furthermore, overall weight of reasons is an organic matter like overall goodness. Imagine that despite the extent to which a little girl would enjoy a swim, she is being punished for a mean trick and the temporary deprivation is deserved. Then the overall good of the child requires our denying the swim despite its intrinsically good aspects. It would be a good she ought not now to have: it would be good *for* her in one sense of 'for', but not good *that* she have it.[4]

Suppose, then, that altruistic wants—intrinsic wants for something on account of its benefiting another (or being taken to do so)—are rational, in a sense implying that they are fully consonant with reason. This point is entirely compatible with their sometimes being overridden as prima facie rational grounds for action. A prima facie rational element whose rationality is overridden need not cease to be rational to the original degree. Defeasibility does not imply eliminability; defeat is not annihilation.[5]

2. ALTRUISM AS A RATIONAL DISPOSITION

If altruistic wants can be rational for the reasons I have emphasized, there is some reason to think that altruism as a trait of character can be, rationally speaking, a virtue. More specifically, it can be fully consonant with reason to want the good of another purely for that person's sake; and a long-standing, stable pattern of such desires as a feature of one's character may surely count as a virtue. It does not follow that a rational person who thinks of specific things about others, such as their enjoying food and good health, that it seems rational to want, *must* want these things for others. Circumstances matter greatly; starvation, fear, and depression may profoundly affect a rational person's altruistic inclinations.

To be sure, there is no need to suppose that altruistic desire, even in people of altruistic character, must be *pure:* one could want the good of another both for its own sake and as part of one's effort to maintain a flourishing relationship with the other person. Nor need the altruistic desires in question have great strength. As long as the altruistic component in the desire is strong enough to sustain an appropriate kind of other-regarding conduct—and could exist without support from instrumental desires for the same thing—we can take it to be the sort of desire that goes with the virtue of altruism as a feature of character. Even given this moderate conception of what is needed to achieve altruistic desire, however, we cannot take it to be a strict requirement of rationality: it would not be irrational to lack an altruistic desire in such a case.

To see what a weaker rational requirement of altruism there may be, it should again help to bring to bear the comparison between practical and theoretical reason. The common tendency to understand rationality in general primarily in terms of one's view of theoretical reason may unduly encourage a negative answer to the question whether altruistic desires are rational from the point of view of practical reason. There are certain elementary facts, say, about gravity, and many self-evident logical truths, which can be plausibly thought to be such that every rational person on earth must believe them, or at least be suitably disposed to believe them immediately on considering them, as where one considers an obvious logical truth that has never come remotely to one's attention. No comparable tendency to have altruistic desires seems to exist in rational persons. Even in those cognitive cases, however, we are assuming a certain range of experience. We shall soon see that when the rationality of altruism is considered in relation to a certain range of interpersonal experience, the contrast between the theoretical and practical cases diminishes.

To begin with, this range of examples from the theoretical realm is the wrong basis of comparison with the practical sphere. The relevant theoretical case is that of experientially grounded belief of empirical propositions. Thus, we would not expect rational persons to believe (perceptually) that there is a piano before them if they could not see or otherwise perceive it, nor to have visually grounded beliefs if they were congenitally blind. Similarly, if they have reason to think they are being visually tricked, we would again not expect them to believe there is a piano before them. Rational beliefs arise on the basis of one's experience only if it has qualitative content appropriate to ground those beliefs. Why should it be otherwise with rational intrinsic desires? If, as I have argued, their formation in us is a discriminative response to experience, we might expect that they are rational only when their objects are wanted for properties of them that the person is experiencing, has experienced, or has reason to expect to experience.

The question to ask, then, is whether, relative to a certain range of beliefs and experiences, a rational person must have some altruistic desires, where 'must' expresses not the strict requirement whose violation entails irrationality but the moderate requirement whose violation entails some deficiency in rationality. It matters greatly what capacities one has and what kind of life one has led. Some of us have thought more than others about what it is like to be someone else. Some have reflected more than others about what it is like for one person to express love to others.[6] Some of us are simply more easily influenced by the perception of pleasure we evoke, or of suffering we relieve, in our fellows. Similar points hold for belief. If one does not look at paintings in a certain way, one cannot be expected to see the subtler patterns they contain, much less be able to form aesthetically based beliefs that do justice to those patterns. Aesthetic cases are illuminating in relation to desire as well. If I do not view paintings, I do not experience their colors and shapes, contrasts and balances, shades and textures, in the rewarding way that evokes a desire to view paintings for their own sake. But if I do contemplate them in ways that are rewarding, it is rational for me to want such contemplation.

We may perhaps go further. Surely my aesthetic rewards might be such that I would exhibit some deficiency in rationality if, under conditions that bring the rewarding contemplation vividly to mind, I did not tend to want such experience for the color and shape and texture I take it to realize for me. The vivid thought of an experience of a kind I have found rewarding should, when there is no reason to be negative about it, produce some degree of desire for something similar. To be sure, it is different if I have come to believe that I would no longer enjoy the experience, or that it would later cause pain to me or someone else. Here, as so often, we find defeasibility. But normally the vivid thought of contemplating a beautiful painting is itself pleasant. Such anticipatory pleasantness often indicates value in the anticipated experience and is in any case a prima facie reason for wanting to have a similar experience.

How far might we extend these points? If I have experienced the rewards of a cool swim on a hot afternoon, and I bring to mind what it would be like for my daughter or my friend to experience them, would it be entirely rational, at that moment, to lack any degree of intrinsic desire for them to experience those rewards? Some support for a negative answer is indicated by the following kinds of considerations. In my own case, I want it for its qualities; and in the basic case, I do not want it for *my* experience of those qualities, even though the experience I envisage is in fact mine. It is the qualities themselves that make the experience attractive to me; they are not attractive to me as features of *my* experience. Why, then, should not those same qualities, envisaged in their experience, or indeed the experience of anyone toward whom I have no negative feelings, make their having that experience attractive to me in a sense implying that it seems desirable to me? It is quite similar with pain, and the point may be more evident in that typically simpler, often more vivid case. The vivid contemplation of their pain should tend to arouse in me, as a rational person who is averse to my own pains on the basis of the same kinds of qualities I take them to feel, some degree of desire that they be rid of the pain. This is quite consistent with my wanting *more* that they endure it; all I suggest here is a tendency to have some degree of altruistic desire. We cannot go so far as to say—in this kind of case—that to lack it is to show a deficiency in rationality. It would certainly not be irrational. But the tendency is both natural and consonant with reason. What we may perhaps conclude at this point is that a pervasive *pattern* of such failures bespeaks some deficiency in rationality. That would be significant.

One may think that my example trades on the normal closeness we feel to our children and friends. This closeness certainly bears on the degree of desire that is likely and on the readiness with which such desires are formed. But the tendency to form desires of the kind in question is not limited to close relationships: it is characteristic of those who want the good of others for its own sake. It is also in part constitutive of empathy, as a common underpinning of altruism—and doubtless sometimes an essential precondition for it—that one tend to form desires of the kind in question. It may be that what is so hauntingly disturbing in Meursault, the principal character of Albert Camus's *The Stranger,* is that he seems bereft of empathy, certainly without any trace of developed altruism, and lacking in the desires one might expect—including desires to avoid harming others. His virtually motiveless killing is possible because he is an easy victim of hostile impulses or even of the sheer pressures of circumstance. His killing is gratuitous. If it is not irrational, it is as least not rational. It is not consonant with reason. If he has even a motivational reason for it, it is not a good reason, nor is the deed either reasonable or even expectable on the basis of his self-interest or his beliefs and desires in general.

There are, to be sure, at least two complementary ways in which an experience can be attractive to me: cognitively and conatively. I have so far concentrated on the latter, arguing that the kinds of grounds that render self-directed desires rational can also render altruistic desires rational. It must be admitted that the altruistic considerations in question count more obviously toward justifying positive cognitive evaluation than toward justifying a desire for what one takes to be good experience on the part of others. It is, for instance, clearer that in the kind of case imagined one should believe the other's enjoyable experience to be good than that one should tend to want it to occur. If, as I hold, the primitive cases of rational desire are not egoistic, then in the situations I have described there is as much reason to believe others' experience to be good as to believe mine to be good; and the same holds for their experience's being valuable, rewarding, worthwhile, or the like.

This point would hold, though less obviously so, even if the primitive cases were in a certain way egoistic, provided that what *makes* something egoistically wanted is not tied to oneself, but impersonal. Our examples argue that this point in fact holds. Even if I learn the value of swimming in my own case and want that *I* swim, my wanting to swim for its own sake is still a case of wanting to swim not for *my* sake, but for *its* sake—for certain qualities I anticipate in the swimming. The more empathic I am, the more I tend to feel attracted—conatively perhaps even more than cognitively—to a similar experience for someone else.

We should not simply assume, however, that rationality strictly *requires* empathy here. Although it is both natural and rational in such cases, not to feel it is not a case of irrationality, nor would irrationality follow from lacking a related altruistic desire, say, to give a delicious morsel to someone else. Suppose my friend's rewarding experience of swimming seems as good to me as mine—as it surely should insofar as I am rational and adequately informed. We cannot say that it follows that if it is rational for me to want to have such an experience myself, then it is not rational for me to fail to want my friend to have it. That may, however, still be true. Seeing why it may be is in part a matter of being able to see more vividly how swimming is alike in one's own case and someone else's. This is a capacity important for empathy, though it does not entail feeling it.

A parallel case in the theoretical realm is instructive. Compare having one's own evidence with believing that someone equally competent has exactly similar evidence: my visual impressions of a forest fire on a distant hilltop are no better reason to believe there is one than my companion's visual impressions of it from a point right next to me, and it is natural for me to believe there is one if, though I cannot see the hilltop myself, I realize that my companion has those impressions. I am, however, more likely to believe it, or at least to believe it strongly, on the basis of my own visual experience than I would be to believe it on the testimony of my companion, if my line of sight were obscured. This can hold even if my confidence in the reliability of the testimony is as great as my confidence in my own visual acuity. But the greater psychological power that our own grounds have over us does not imply their normative superiority to those of others. Just as I should believe the proposition that there is a fire on the basis of the adequate grounds for it that I am aware of, whether or not they occur in my experience, I should have a desire for someone else to swim on the basis of the adequate grounds for its desirability that I am aware of, whether they are in my experience or not. In each case, the grounds are of the same kind regardless of whose they are; and much as our beliefs should be guided by evidence of truth, our desires should respond to grounds for desirability.

The theoretical analogy can be seen in another way. Consider skepticism about the external world. There is surely nothing inconsistent about believing one has experiences of color and shape that could be caused by external objects, yet refusing to believe that there are such objects, and I want to grant for the sake of argument that reason may not absolutely force that conclusion on skeptics who accept empirical propositions only about their own experience. Refusal to accept it does not entail irrationality. Must we say, then, that this skeptical restriction of empirical belief to the internal world is rational? I very much doubt it.[7]

143

This is not to imply that experience provides entailing grounds for propositions about the external world, but I do believe those propositions are adequately supported (though not entailed) by the kinds of experiences we apparently all have. If we need not consider failure to form external world beliefs rational, why may we not refuse to apply that term to the counterpart failure on the part of people with the normal kinds of experiences of the impersonal grounds of desirability who fail to form altruistic desires for the things that, on those grounds, are clearly desirable? In each case, we have people who have strong normative grounds of certain externally focused beliefs and desires, but fail to form them. Even if we grant a difference of degree of departure from rationality in the two cases, they are profoundly similar. To be sure, warrant to withhold an ascription of rationality is not necessarily warrant to attribute a deficiency in it. But there is some reason to consider that attribution plausible.

These points about the similarity of theoretical and practical cases have implications that go beyond the analogy between beliefs about the external world and desires regarding external experience. They lead us to recognize truths about others that have additional normative authority. Let us again consider the status of *beliefs* about the value of others' experience. If, as I have argued, I have the same kind of (equally good) adequate reason for believing my daughter's and my friend's (qualitatively comparable) experience to be good as I have for believing mine to be good, then, assuming its essential similarity in the relevant qualities, I am also justified in believing theirs to be as good as mine. If I am justified in holding this belief, I would be rational in intrinsically wanting theirs to occur, as I may rationally and intrinsically want my own to occur. Now suppose I do justifiedly hold the belief. If, when I vividly contemplate their qualitatively comparable experience, I do not have *some* degree of intrinsic desire that they have it, I would be in some way criticizable from the point of view of rationality. My lacking any such desire, though it does not entail irrationality—a very strong notion—is nonetheless not consonant with reason. Such a desire is, then, a requirement of reason in a moderate sense of 'requirement'. Call it a *demand* of reason. It is demanded in part because, in fully rational persons, there must be an integration between cognition and motivation. If I believe their experience as good as mine and am fully aware of the qualities underlying the goodness of this kind of experience, then if I have no intrinsic desire for their realizing that good, my desires are not adequately *integrated* with my beliefs.[8] The appropriate degree of desire is left open by this line. The point (in part) is that our desires should respond, in some way, to our evaluative beliefs. This pattern (to be explicated later is an aspect of the integration essential in rational persons. This integration between belief and desire is part of what it is for rationality to be not merely the absence of irrationality but consonance with reason.

3. THE LIMITED PRIORITY OF THE NEAR AT HAND

There is often a great distance from desire to action. Weak desires, moreover, have little tendency to produce it. We must, then, consider the degree of altruistic desire appropriate to rational agents if we are to assess how the approach to practical rationality I am developing bears on conduct. Recall my altruistic desires toward my daughter. Even if I must have some degree of intrinsic desire that she have good experiences, it must be granted that I need not, simply as a rational person, want her good as *much* as I do mine. In explaining how this point is consistent with what I have maintained, we can see the basis of some of the resistance to the view that a measure of altruistic desire is, under some conditions, required of rational persons, in the moderate sense in which failure to meet the required standard implies criticizability from the point of view of rationality.[9]

To begin with, it cannot be denied that, both cognitively and motivationally, we are closer to our own desires than to those of others. I can more clearly envisage the qualities of my own swim; and my doing so motivates me more readily than my thinking of the qualities of anyone else's swim. We are most easily motivated from the inside. As I have stressed, other things equal, the stronger of two competing desires provides a stronger reason for action, though the reason need not be overriding. I could have better reason to give the ticket to my friend even if I want more to use it for myself. This point is similar to one noticed by Hume: the greater motivating power of nearer objects of desire as compared with more distant ones.[10] It does not, follow, however, that a gain to be realized now is a better reason to act than a competing, greater gain that is (certain) to be realized tomorrow. Nonetheless, there is a certain naturalness in giving some priority to the present and to the nearby, if only because in practice it may never be certain, and usually seems uncertain, that a distant good is as likely to be realizable as one we have at hand. The theory of practical reason allows for that priority, to this extent: other things being equal, we may rationally prefer a nearer good to a more distant one.

This limited priority of nearer goods is a rational permission; it is not a rational requirement. If other things are not equal but, for instance, the attraction of the present temptation is very strong in contrast with the less vivid future greater good, we do not have that permission. We may still have

145

an excuse for pursuing it, despite a measure of imprudence in doing so; but this does not make pursuing it rational. Moreover, the more nearly we approach inability to resist, the better our excuse tends to be; and where resisting is itself costly, as where excessive self-sacrifice by a parent will have bad effects before the future good is realized for the child, the balance may shift.

The limited priority of the near at hand applies to interpersonal cases as well. When it comes to attending to the good of others, we often consider them rather abstractly, and we commonly do not think vividly of their wants and needs. Their good is often not just further from vivid consciousness than our own, but not near at all. Practical reason does not have precise standards governing just how often we should vividly and concretely call the good of others to mind, nor is there any uncontroversial way to establish a precise standard.[11] That is one reason why plausible ethical theories differ as much as they do regarding the extent of our obligations of beneficence. But this does not undermine my main point: when we do vividly and concretely call the well-being of others to mind, then for those of us with a sufficiently clear grasp of how others can experience the qualities in virtue of which our own intrinsic desires are rational, and particularly for those of us with a measure of empathy, rationality demands some degree of altruistic desire.

A related point holds for the cognitive side of altruism. We are not justified in believing our own rewarding experiences to be better than the same sort of things in others; but we may often be justified in believing more *strongly* that such experiences are, in the relevant ways, good. We are closer, experientially, to the qualities in virtue of which our experiences are rewarding and satisfying our desires is rational. Similarly, standards of rationality allow, for the same sorts of reasons concerning the closeness of the qualities that make the objects of desire seem rewarding, that we have stronger desires in our own case.

These two points, in turn, imply that it may be rational to act on a self-directed desire rather than an altruistic one, even when the two sorts of experiences are qualitatively comparable. For at least when an intrinsic desire is rational, its strength enhances its power as a reason for action; and when other things are equal, the stronger one's belief that an action will achieve an end, the stronger one's reason for taking that action.[12] It is easy to see, then, how altruistic desires can be commonly outweighed by rational self-interested ones. Nonetheless, an altruistic desire, even when thus outweighed, can be not only consonant with reason but a demand of reason. Wanting something can be, in this way, required by rationality even where overall rationality licenses a stronger desire for some competing end.

146

This is parallel to the point that an intrinsic good, such as ecstatic pleasure, remains good even when the overall state of affairs in which it occurs—
such as constant enjoyment of life on the part of a person supposed to be
rigorously doing penance—is intrinsically bad.

None of this implies a precise standard regarding just how much rational persons ought to *do* for others whose needs they clearly perceive.
For some people in some circumstances a great deal of other-regarding
conduct is rationally appropriate or may be demanded. But, in addition
to the factors already cited as allowing a measure of self-preference, the
same sense of value that leads us to regard rewarding experiences as good
makes us dislike being used merely as a means to the ends of others and
resent the pains it tends to bring. This is how a rational person is likely
to feel at the prospect of an overriding obligation to maximize happiness
in general, as one must apparently do on a classical utilitarian theory.
For given the sorry state of the world, this would in most cases require
great self-sacrifice. If, however, one finds happiness in extreme self-
sacrifice, the prospect is quite different, and making that sacrifice may
be rational.[13]

An important qualification here is that one can exhibit some degree of
deficiency in rationality not just by what one does or does not want but in
the *strength* of one's desire. One can, for instance, want something too
much. The point is obvious for instrumental desires: it would not be rational to want something purely instrumentally, say, to exercise daily, more than
one wants what one takes it as instrumental *to*, say, good muscle tone. Even
a pure instrumentalist can grant this. It is a case in which the superstructure would be invited to bear more weight than its foundations will support. A pure instrumentalist cannot grant, however, something that is surely
both true and important: that an *intrinsic* want can be stronger than is
consonant with rationality (even apart from conflicts with other such desires). If I believe that my friend needs a swim as much as I and would
equally enjoy it, then if I am fully rational and conditions are normal (for
instance, I am not burning with fever), I will not want vastly more that I
take it. That would be unconsonant with my beliefs as well as dispropor-
tionate to my sense of what is good in each envisaged experience. I may
want somewhat more that I take the swim, in part because the prospect of
my realizing its qualities is clearer. But if there is a huge difference between
the two desire strengths, for instance so much disparity between my desire to take the swim and my desire for my friend to take it that I cannot
feel any tension between the two, my desires are neither well integrated
with my beliefs nor appropriately responsive to reason. I could perhaps
explain, but could not justify, this disparity.

147

4. TOWARD A REASONABLE ALTRUISM

So far I have developed two lines of argument for the rationality of altruistic desires. I began with a case for the naturalness and rationality of altruistic desire in the light of how rational desires are grounded. I went on to make a case that, in addition, assumed certain rational normative beliefs and concluded that rational desires are in a moderate sense required by reason. Let me recapitulate.

The first line of argument proceeds from the qualitative basis of rational desire to the conclusion that, given an awareness of relevant aspects of this grounding and given certain eminently rational beliefs about others, it is both natural and rational to have some degree of altruistic desire. The idea is roughly that in a rational person, some degree of altruistic desire should arise from the vivid contemplation of the qualities in others' experience that constitute one's own basis for the counterpart desires in oneself, just as the vivid contemplation of my companion's visual impression of a forest fire I cannot see should tend to evoke in me a belief that there is one. If my sense of your having the evidential visual experience provides me with a reason to hold the indicated belief, why should my vivid sense of your experience of desirable qualities of a swim not provide me with reason to have the indicated desire, i.e., to want, to some degree, that you have it or continue it? If I should respond to the vivid sense of your ample grounds for belief by believing the proposition they indicate, why should I not respond to the vivid sense of your ample grounds for desire by sharing your desire? Granted, the belief is shareable in a way the experience is not. But the *kind* of experience is shareable: my naturally and rationally wanting a swim myself in no way prevents my wanting one for you; and it is a contingent matter whether we can in fact both have one, as it is also contingent whether we can in fact believe the same proposition.

The second line is an argument from integration. Here the point is that we ought to have beliefs that capture the similarity of others to us in respect of what makes their lives desirable, and, given the requirement of integration between evaluative belief and desire, we should have altruistic desires appropriate to those beliefs. Both arguments bring out ways in which rational persons must be responsive to reasons—in the wide sense that includes grounds—but whereas the first appeals not to any normative belief but to the way in which desires should respond to a vivid *awareness of normative grounds*, which are not necessarily conceived as such, the second appeals to *normative beliefs concerning grounds*. The first, we might say, is an argument within the domain of practical reason; the second is an argument that links it with theoretical reason: it proceeds from the rational

demand for integration between evaluative belief and desire to the conclusion that, given certain other-regarding beliefs, a rational person tends
to have some degree of altruistic desire.

I now want to pursue a third line of argument, this time focusing on a
concept allied to rationality. I refer to reasonableness, which a number of
philosophers have contrasted with rationality.[14] It is clear that nothing
reasonable fails to be rational; but a rational person, or stance, can surely
fail to be reasonable. What is reasonable is not only minimally consonant
with reason, say, by conforming to logical and sound epistemic standards,
but also the sort of thing one would expect of a rational person who is at
least moderately thoughtful and balanced. In this light, it makes perfect
sense to say that some skeptical positions are (at least minimally) rational,
but not reasonable. Moreover, one can have minimally rational beliefs and
minimally rational desires that, quite apart from skepticism, it is not reasonable to have. It can be perfectly rational, but overoptimistic and not
reasonable, to believe one will finish an essay by tomorrow, and it can be
altogether rational, but not reasonable, to want a friend to change long-
standing travel plans to help one with a project.

There are, then, two kinds of things to be considered if we are to understand the reasonable as compared with the rational: persons and, on the
other hand, their attitudes, particularly beliefs, desires, and intentions, and
their actions. From what has just been said in this section, as well as from
points made earlier, several things should be clear. Let us first consider
persons and then proceed to attitudes and actions.

First, as applied to persons, rationality is more nearly a capacity concept,
entailing less about actual conduct than does reasonableness (in some uses
the former is doubtless a capacity concept). This is not to deny that either
can be possessed over time without being manifested in conduct; but
whereas a rational person, even one more than minimally rational, could
for a long time act in unreasonable ways, this does not hold for a reasonable person. If, for months on end, I acted unreasonably—or if I had an
accident that made such action inevitable for me pending treatment—I
would have ceased to be a reasonable person.

A second and related point is that reasonableness requires a greater
responsiveness to reasons than mere rationality. Indeed, if we speak of
merely rational *beings* rather than of rational persons in the full-blooded
sense of 'rational', a capacity to respond to reasons is all that is required,
as with very young children. But, apart from special lapses as may be caused
by, say, abnormal fatigue, a reasonable person must actually respond to
reasons when they are offered or otherwise encountered. Responding to
reasons does not entail acting on them, but it does require at least an ap-

propriate kind of consideration of them and sometimes a change in belief, desire, or some other attitude.

Part of what this implies is brought out by a third important point: being a reasonable person requires a measure of good judgment and is incompatible with pervasively bad judgment (everyone is, to be sure, entitled to bad judgment in certain special cases, particularly if it does not lead to significant bad decisions). An aspect of the required level of good judgment is—in rough terms—a tendency to treat like cases alike and to be prepared to give a reason for doing otherwise. This holds both in the theoretical realm, for instance in scientific matters, and in the practical domain, say, in prudent classification of risks and benefits and in the treatment of people.

If reasonable people must, within limits, have good judgment, must they also unfailingly act on it? This would preclude some major kinds of weak-willed conduct; and although such action may be prima facie irrational and, if frequent in people's behavior, counts against their reasonableness, there is room for some such action even in the lives of reasonable persons—and more room in the lives of merely rational people who are not reasonable.[15] There is no good way to quantify this fourth point; but a related, fifth point helps to clarify it: there are limits to how much a reasonable person may be governed by mere whim, in the sense (roughly) of desire not grounded in one's long-term projects and arising from sudden attractions, and these limits are lower for merely rational persons, i.e., persons who are rational but not reasonable. One kind of defect is so many whims that even if they are resisted, there is interference with normal conduct; another kind is certain sorts of unresisted whims, say, to dangle by one's toes.

A sixth point supports both the fourth and fifth: reasonable people are to some degree self-critical, at least in the sense of being disposed to think about and correct tendencies that have gotten them into trouble. They are normally also self-critical in a more positive way. They are disposed to review and to try to alter their own desires, including whims, or even passions, whose presence or satisfaction they regard as interfering with their main goals in life.

None of this is to take the notion of reasonableness to be intrinsically moral. Indeed, in part because I want to argue that considerations of reasonableness support adherence to certain ethical standards, I do not presuppose that moral commitments are intrinsic to it. But it is plausibly taken to embody some substantive standards, including those we have seen to be central for theoretical and practical reason. If people could even survive without generally forming beliefs on the basis of their sensory experience and desires on the basis of their experiences of pleasure and pain, they would certainly not be reasonable. Again, however, the threshold is lower for rationality (even as implying consonance with reason) than for reasonableness.

There is a related contrast between rationality and reasonableness—my eighth point—concerning conduct that is foolish or even morally wrong. Irrationality, when extreme, is excusatory and, even when moderate, mitigatory; unreasonableness is neither. Some children and many of the mentally deficient illustrate the former point; much of the human error we see in everyday life illustrates the latter.[16]

Nothing said so far entails that a reasonable person must be a social being. The last person in a dying world would not necessarily cease to be reasonable. If, however, we think of a social being simply as one *capable* of social interaction, our conclusion may be different. The concept of a reasonable person does seem to be social in this capacity sense. But we may say more. A reasonable person cannot be unwilling even to consider cooperative relations with other people; and when reasonable people live in human societies of the kind that concern us, they actually maintain such relations.

A stronger point is warranted here, however (my ninth): reasonable people must, in a suitable proportion of their relations with others, be willing to give reasons to them and to consider reasons given by them. Someone who "won't listen at all" is not reasonable. By and large, neither is someone who, even to intimates, will not give any reasons for significant kinds of conduct. None of this entails highly specific standards of conduct. But if we can presuppose rationality and the kinds of beliefs and desires I have argued are expectable in rational persons given a normal kind of human experience, then we can see how the interpersonal aspects of reasonableness can be expected to lead to a willingness to negotiate and even—in ways to be indicated shortly—to moral agreements. Far more could be said here, and there are also complicated constraints on the ways in which reasonable people must respond to reasons. Some are implicit in what has been said in this book so far; others will emerge later in this chapter and in Part III.

There is no way to summarize in a phrase the points that have so far emerged about reasonableness for persons, but in rough terms we might say a reasonable person is (minimally) *governed by reason*, whereas a merely rational person (one who is rational but not reasonable) is only capable of such governance and too often fails to achieve it. With this in mind, we are ready to pass from the notion of reasonableness for persons—global reasonableness, which is a kind of *developed* rationality—to that of reasonableness for attitudes and actions—focal reasonableness.

In contrasting rationality with justification earlier, I maintained that the former is more nearly a virtue concept. A similar point holds for reasonableness. It is not equivalent to a virtue—except in the sense of a *strength* of character, indeed one crucial for realization of the usual virtues—but it has much in common with virtues. We might even call it a second-order virtue, given how strongly it bears on what patterns of feeling, thought, and action one nurtures or maintains in oneself. However this classificatory question is settled, reasonableness in persons is to reasonableness in attitudes and conduct much as virtues such as justice and veracity are to the attitudes and actions that bear those names. This is not to say whether the trait concept or the attitudinal or behavioral ones are more basic; in either case, we can understand the latter in good part on the basis of understanding the former, and conversely.

My suggestion, then, is twofold: it is fruitful to think of reasonable attitudes, such as beliefs and desires, as the kind that are appropriate to a reasonable person, and similarly for reasonable actions; and it is also fruitful to think of them as the kind that constitute appropriate responses to reasons for them. Often, these conceptions require relativization to circumstances or to those together with individual elements. It is unqualifiedly reasonable to believe certain a priori propositions; it is reasonable in the light of certain data to believe that there is some global warming; and it is reasonable for me alone to believe that a certain student can finish a Ph.D. thesis by next spring. Similarly, given data we all have that provide reasons for a view about a certain military dictator, a negative attitude toward him may be reasonable; but in the light of my reasons, but no one else's, it may be reasonable to believe the student will finish the work next spring. Moreover, although wanting to finish a thesis soon is generally quite reasonable for a student doing one, I might have grounds on which I reasonably want my student not to finish it so fast. All these examples confirm that the reasonable is also rational; but many of our examples show that what is rational need not be reasonable. I might be unreasonably rigorous with a student and so unreasonably want a delay. This desire and the associated attitudes may still be at least minimally rational.

If we now consider whether it is reasonable to have altruistic desires (and not reasonable to lack them entirely), we can surely take the kinds of considerations I have been stressing to support this conclusion for at least normal persons with a good sense of the respects in which we are in general alike. Granted, one might suffer excusable ignorance or have excusable false beliefs about others' experience or indeed about one's own. But there is much that is uncontroversial about pleasure, pain, and other good and bad things in human life; and in the light of an appreciation of such everyday facts, a rational person who lacks a good measure of altruistic desire is not reasonable.

It should be plain that I am not taking the reasonable, in desire or in conduct, to be always strictly required by reason. The conclusion that, for normal people with a certain typical range of experience, altruistic desires are reasonable is thus weaker than the view (which I think may also be true) that they are, up to a point, strictly rationally required. This conclusion is perhaps more easily seen if we assume—what is surely plausible—that such people are already rational. It may be useful to think of reasonableness here as a *demand* of reason, even if not a strict requirement. Surely there is a normative domain that lies between mere permissibility and strict requirement and in which deficiency counts significantly against one in respect of reason. This is the domain of rational demands. I have argued that under certain conditions a measure of altruism is a demand of reason, and indeed a requirement of global reasonableness, though much of what I want to show may require only that altruism is rational in the sense of consonance with reason. What the reasonableness of a measure of altruism implies for interpersonal conduct in particular and for ethics in general is less clear and remains to be considered.

5. OBSTACLES TO RECOGNIZING THE RATIONALITY OF ALTRUISTIC DESIRES

The case for the rationality of altruistic desires needs more than the positive considerations so far set forth. To overcome the egoistic conception of rationality, we must at least appreciate some further reasons why altruistic desires seem to many philosophers to be at most rationally permissible rather than, at least in certain cases where one vividly imagines the experience of others, consonant with reason or even demanded in reasonable persons. There are at least five points here.

First, when we must justify or explain our actions at the deepest motivational level, we often say that we did the thing in question because we wanted something, where the want is often self-directed and, precisely because we are ascribing such a want or some other motive to ourselves, is in any case presented and conceived as ours and not impersonally expressed in terms of the qualities for which we want the object. Even if, for example, I do a good deed from beneficence, it will be because *I* wanted to help someone. In short, much self-explanatory discourse is prima facie egoistic; and it can nearly always be made to seem so by emphasis on the agent's *own* stake in the action. Even when I explain an action of mine as taken for an altruistic reason, I represent it as *my* reason. But, in giving perceptual justification for an observation statement, I indicate what *I* see; and just as what justifies my perceptual belief is the experience and not the second-order belief that *I* have it, what grounds my altruistic action is not my wanting to satisfy *my* altruistic desire but my wanting some good for the person I am trying to help.

Second, the conditions under which altruistic desires arise are highly variable compared with those that produce self-directed desire. We all suffer pains and, if only in elemental cases, virtually everyone experiences pleasures. But many people have not had much occasion to acquire a vivid awareness of others' experience and a sense of its likeness to theirs. This may be in part because it is quite possible to go through life with little vivid consciousness of the ways in which, despite our many differences, we are alike. Indeed, this is an age in which our differences are commonly stressed and often resolutely preserved. Still, the need to tolerate, and indeed celebrate, our differences must not be allowed to obscure how much we have in common and how many grounds there are for at least some degree of altruism.

Third, when altruistic desires do arise, they are often overridden by stronger, self-directed rational desires. What is overshadowed is easily lost from view, even if it ought not to have been overshadowed and exerts its own pressure for recognition. The good of others is often not concretely felt, and can be obscured from view, or distorted in prospect, by ignorance, prejudice, or sheer self-absorption. One can get on in the world without much in the way of altruistic desire. Prudence makes this especially easy. Prudence can skillfully mimic altruism. It ably sees the desires and needs of others, but often produces no inclination to feel them.

Moreover—and this is the fourth point—since prudence is a paradigm of a trait endorsed by practical reason, its worldly success can easily obscure the softer voice of altruism. If practical reason is conceived only as the faculty that enables one to get on in the world—an outlook encouraged by some evolutionary ethical perspectives—it is natural to think that it does not extend to taking others as ends. But one can also get on in the world without many beliefs which one would, with appropriate experience, justifiedly hold. In both the cognitive and the motivational domains, what rationality requires is relative to the range and depth of one's experience. In neither case should we construe rationality so minimally that demands for self-preservation are taken to exhaust its basic standards.

The fifth point is easily seen in the light of the third and fourth: much of rationality is instrumental; and many of our failures to achieve rationality are deficiencies in adapting means to ends. Much of our conduct can be seen as rational simply in the light of its suitability for some appropriate intrinsic end of ours, without the character of that end, much less its being egoistic or altruistic, coming into question. This gives instrumentalism an advantage: if our natural, often self-regarding, intrinsic desires are presupposed as major elements in judging our rationality, a person whose actions are instrumentally rational relative to these desires will tend to seem quite rational overall. Even if we think of overall rationality as normally including some altruistic desires, we often find that in efficiently pursuing their own interests, people accord prudent, and sometimes affectionate, consideration to others. Moreover, given how much of rationality has to be, as it were, devoted to survival, it is natural to take its basis to be largely or wholly its instrumental contribution to that end. But even if this contribution is part of its basis, and even granting that rationality at least normally requires some self-interested intrinsic desires, a prominent necessary condition must not be inflated into an account of the whole.[17]

6. ALTRUISM AS A BASIS FOR MORAL DISPOSITIONS

If altruistic desire is rational for the reasons explored here, then a case can be made that a suitably informed, rational person would adhere to certain moral standards. What I have in mind draws on both the argument from the qualitative basis of rational desire and the argument from integration. It might be called the argument from the interpersonal character of reason (we may also speak of the impersonal character of reason, but that may unwarrantedly suggest that persons as such do not matter from the point of view of reason). Some of the main points have already been made in setting out both the argument from the qualitative basis of rational desire and the argument from integration, but they warrant brief review. We have seen that rational persons have at least some rational intrinsic desires among the motivational foundations of their conduct. What they want regarding the things in question is not, in the primitive case, that *they* have them, but the things themselves. When I have pain, I want *it* to stop. That it is mine need not enter my mind, and I need not conceptualize it as mine in order to have a rational desire to be rid of it. As tiny children, we are acquainted with pain and pleasure; and, in virtue of their phenomenal qualities, we rationally want elimination of the former and realization of the latter. These hedonic desires arise even before we have a self-concept. At least these grounds of rational desire, and thereby some of the basic normative reasons for action, are impersonal.

The interpersonal character (and, in a sense, impersonality) of the grounds of rational desire is clearest when the desire is experiential: a desire concerning something actually being experienced, as with wanting that the backrub one is enjoying continue. When what is wanted is in prospect, particularly where the object of a desire is to *do* something, the non-egoistic character of its grounds is more difficult to see, but it is no less important. Consider an aesthetic case. Even when I develop a self-concept, my viewing as mine the literary pleasures that I seek when I want to read Shakespeare for pleasure does not make them seem any better. I want to read Shakespeare for its aesthetic rewards; I want it for its sake, not mine. This point is pivotal; for if it is sound then even if, in content, the basic reasons for action are in some way egoistic, their normative force does not depend on this. Even if, in order to want to read Shakespeare for its aesthetic rewards I must see them as mine, I would be unjustified in believing that what is good about those rewards, or what makes it rational to want them, is their being mine.

I doubt, however, that, even for actions in prospect, our reasons must be egoistic. What I want is *to* read Shakespeare: to do a reading of him. I can see that it will be mine, but I need not want it in terms of a self-concept that determines the exact object of my desire. I need not specifically want that *I* read him. I can want that—for instance where just one of us is going to read a sonnet aloud and I want my interpretation heard. But I may not be in a comparative situation in which I see what I want as possibly going to someone else. I then tend not to conceptualize what I want in a self-referential, ostensibly egoistic way.

These points are quite consistent with the point that my wanting to do something requires an indexical sense of what it is. Without that sense, I would not be in a position to find a means to it—to get from "here" to "there," say, from the sofa to the book on the shelf. But my wanting to do something does not entail wanting *that I* do it, where some self-concept enters the content of the desire. Wanting, and learning, to do things precedes the development of a self-concept. I can want to read a sonnet, and can have a sense of a path from me to it, without wanting specifically that *I* read it, just as I can aim at and hit my target without thinking of it as mine. What I cannot do is *say* that I want to read it without specifying myself in the attribution, any more than I can say that I am aiming at my target without specifying myself. This is one among other cases in which the language in which we describe our cases may be richer than the phenomenological data and misleading as to the character of our experience.[18]

The interpersonal character of reason has far-reaching implications. In a world like this, rational, generally informed persons have justified beliefs to the effect that other people are much like them in rationality, motivation, and sentience. Others can reason and discern facts; they want food, shelter, and company; and they can enjoy conversation and suffer from the cold. It is thus reasonable for rational persons to believe that others' experiences are, in familiar situations, qualitatively similar to those that they themselves would have in these situations. This point, in turn, makes it reasonable to believe that what I have found painful or pleasurable, you, in similar circumstances, will find so (or, more cautiously, any person like me will find so). It is a short step, though admittedly not a step that formal logic, as opposed to substantive reason, requires us to make, from here to the view—which is independently plausible—that certain kinds of things, for instance aesthetic and social enjoyments, and physical and mental suffering, are human goods and evils. And if there are goods and evils realizable in the experience of anyone, then there are reasons for acting in certain ways toward anyone at all. Given how many other people there are and how many competing rational concerns I may have, the good of any single one may ground at most a weak and plainly overridden reason for my action; but a reason that is overridden is not thereby eliminated.

The points in this section take us some distance toward establishing that it is rational, in a full-blooded sense that implies a significant degree of justification, to hold certain moral principles and, given the normal altruistic desires reason demands we have, to act accordingly. Let us explore how great this distance is.

7. ALTRUISM AS A PATHWAY TO MORAL PRINCIPLES

The kinds of basic moral principles I want to consider are pervasive and generally familiar. Three of the fundamental and most pervasive are, in rough formulations, these. First, we are to abstain from killing or causing pain: beating, burning, cheating, taunting, and all too many other familiar offenses. Second, we are to treat people equally in distribution and retribution: rewarding people equally for equal services, burdening them equally in compulsory contributions to community life, punishing equally for the same crimes. Third, we are, sometimes, to contribute to the pleasure or at least the well-being of others, for instance, to provide food or shelter, to liberate from bondage, to instruct in the ways of self-development, to nurture and love. I know what I want in regard to most such elemental matters; I may believe you want similar things. To be sure, my obligations under these principles are not absolute but prima facie, and there are difficulties about how to deal with conflicts between (or among) the obligations. But those difficulties arise for any plausible moral position and can be laid aside here.[19]

157

How are these principles supported by the account of rationality developed in this book? What is good in what I want is impersonally good; it is thus normally quite reasonable to take this kind of object of desire to be as good for you as for me. Selfishness may oppose my acting accordingly. The point is that it is still reasonable to act so. I need not favor others over myself; but I have no rational ground to favor myself, as such, over others. Where a self-interested want is stronger than a conflicting altruistic one, I may sometimes rationally satisfy the former; but not just any disparity in such desire strengths is rational. The qualitative, interpersonal character of the foundations of practical reason, when guided by the sorts of justified beliefs about others we have noted, requires that we view the basic worth of others as on par with our own and allows only limited differences in the strengths of our self-interested wants in comparison with our altruistic ones. The intrinsic desirability of our pleasures, like the rationality of our wanting them, is grounded in *what* they are, not in *whose* they are. Nothing becomes intrinsically better just because it is mine. No deed is rational simply because I do it. Similar points hold for non-hedonic grounds of rational desire and for desirability characteristics in general. If this is so, and if, as seems clear, there is no other basis for thinking that there is overall reason to promote or respect one person's good more than another's, then we are surely justified in viewing one another as prima facie equal in at least one major kind of basic worth: our experiences can have the kinds of qualities that ground basic reasons for action. Given this belief, only moral principles that embody a prima facie requirement of equal treatment of persons will be justified for us. (One reason the requirement must be prima facie is that people differ in relevant ways, most notably in doing things that warrant censure or punishment rather than the usual kind of altruistic treatment that has been my concern.)

If we proceed along these lines from the foundations of practical reason and from justified beliefs that they warrant, two further points seem warranted. First, we find some of the basic ingredients of a good argument for a version of the intrinsic end formulation of Kant's categorical imperative, which says roughly that we must treat persons as ends in themselves and never merely as means.[20] Second, we find a plausible basis for treating human happiness and relief from human suffering as intrinsic goods that ought, prima facie, to be promoted. The Kantian principle reflects the intrinsic valuation of persons implicit in regarding the coercion of persons as prima facie wrong and in taking them to have desires whose satisfaction is a good thing or can at least be rationally considered to be good; and (especially in its universality formulation, which may be argued to be implicit in the intrinsic end version) the principle accords with, even if it does not quite capture, the reasonableness of treating persons equally which is implicit in the qualitative, interpersonal character of rationality. Perhaps the principle does capture this if we take it to imply that we are to try *equally* hard in each case to treat people as ends and to avoid treating them as mere means. A prima facie obligation to promote happiness and to reduce suffering is similarly consonant with that valuation of persons (I have in mind mainly human happiness, but the position I have developed provides reasons to take account of animals—and other kinds of sentient beings that might exist—as well).

If something close to these principles can be shown to be the basic moral principles or even among the basic moral principles, we would have much of the materials needed for a systematic rational account of the grounds of moral principles.[21] I do not claim to have established these principles. It is enough to show how the theory of practical reason makes it highly plausible to affirm them or closely similar principles that figure in many plausible ethical theories.

In interpreting the arguments of this section, we must again distinguish the cognitive from the motivational rationality in question: the theoretical rationality of holding such principles and the rationality of the desires needed to motivate conduct that accords with the principles. That a suitably informed rational person with sufficiently wide human experience should believe them is one thing; that such persons should have the relevant desires is another; and that those wants should, sometimes or always, override competing ones is still another. The task of assessment here is very difficult. We should first consider just what beliefs and desires are in question.

Although I have given examples of specific rational desires and of rationally defensible moral principles, I have not implied that every rational person must have precisely those desires or believe precisely those principles. Given how different each person's experience is, and given how finely desires and beliefs must, as intentional attitudes, be individuated, it is quite sufficient for our purposes if there is a suitable range of altruistic desires and moral principles that, in the context of adequately reflective human experience, are demanded by rationality.[22]

Moreover, acting morally, as I understand it for purposes of assessing its rationality, does not entail acting partly on a belief of a moral principle. It is enough if one acts on grounds that adequately reflect a moral commitment. Perhaps keeping a promise out of a sense of obligation can be prior to believing a principle to the effect that one must keep one's promises. Such a sense is not equivalent to wanting to do the deed in question—and probably does not entail such a desire. It is more a matter of an attraction to doing it on the basis of taking it to have certain features, such as being promised, being required by justice, or being the only decent thing to do, and it is partly constituted by a disposition to form certain beliefs and draw certain inferences. Certainly, acting from a sense of obligation, together with a related disposition to believe some such principle, is sufficient for acting morally. Even a broadly Kantian ethics may not be committed to the view that acting morally must be motivated by belief of a specific moral principle, particularly if it is accompanied by a disposition to form such a belief on proper reflection. But certainly not every ethical position is committed to this view, particularly those in the virtue tradition. I stress this point because the stronger the requirements for acting morally, the more it will take to show that such action is rational.[23]

Once the matter is seen in this way, our first question is whether a suitably informed, appropriately experienced person must have beliefs, or at least dispositions to form beliefs, of something like the Kantian and (weak) utilitarian principles sketched, at least upon reflecting on them extensively in the light of the relevant experiences, say, of pleasure and pain, and of reasonable beliefs about the nature of human beings. If my case for the rationality of altruistic desire is sound, there is good reason to think so, particularly if we focus on people who are not merely rational but also reasonable. The case for rationality of altruistic desires and beliefs (e.g., beliefs to the effect that the good of others is as valuable as one's own) can justify moral principles because those principles express plausible necessary conditions for realizing the good of others. This point may help to explain the rationality of such specific desires as an intrinsic want to treat one's children equally. But that desire can be rational even apart from a commitment to moral principles.

It may turn out, then, to be less difficult to show that moral principles are rationally defensible than to show that acting morally, in the narrow sense, is so—where so acting is not merely doing the morally required thing, but doing it for some distinctly moral reason. Acting altruistically, say, from friendship or love, is not acting morally in this narrow sense. Friendship and love may supply good reasons—and I think they do—but these reasons are not distinctively moral. They are, however, at least next door to the moral. Consider having two children and imagine giving one an obviously much better bicycle than the other. The thought of their reactions, especially that of the one with the lesser bicycle, can certainly make the prospect both generally unappealing and morally repugnant. Is it the sense of a child's unhappiness, which is not moral but affectional or hedonic, or the sense of inequality, which is moral rather than affectional or hedonic, that colors this prospect? Perhaps at the level of felt discomfort it is the unhappiness. If this should be all there is to ground the aversion to the unequal treatment, we can see some support for the utilitarian view that moral values, though instrumental in contributing to non-moral goodness, are not intrinsic values.

There is a danger of going too fast here. Even if one does not find an inequality in itself aversive, one can, in the course of contemplating it, form the belief that it is an injustice. And if this belief is warranted, then (as the argument from integration indicates) it may itself be a ground of the rationality of wanting, *on account of* its injustice, to avoid the inequality. Suppose there is a sense, then, in which the most basic source of the rationality of wanting to avoid a certain kind of inequality is non-moral, contemplative experience. This point is compatible with the same experience yielding cognitive justification that, in turn, warrants a specifically moral intrinsic desire.

Given some elementary facts of human psychology, the point is perhaps even expectable on the assumption that moral properties are grounded in non-moral ones that are (by and large) more easily known; for we should then expect that the experience of the latter properties is our normal basis for attributing the former. It might be true that, as Mill apparently thought, one develops a sense of injustice partly through experience of, and sensitivity to, human happiness and suffering. But it does not follow either that the concept of justice is definable in terms of happiness and suffering or that well-grounded beliefs about injustice cannot by themselves warrant rational intrinsic desires.

Even if all we can expect to show is that it is rational—consonant with reason—for a normal person with normal self-concerns to have intrinsic moral desires, and not that such desires are rationally demanded in suitably informed, appropriately experienced persons, this would be significant. For one thing, if we can assume, as I do here, that certain moral principles are justifiable, even if it should be (as I believe it need not be) derivatively from non-moral grounds, then we can justify creating incentives for the development of moral desires as intrinsic motives in human conduct.

This last point presupposes that justifiedly holding moral beliefs can, in people with a normal range of interpersonal experience, ground rational intrinsic desires, for instance, that justifiedly believing that causing pain is wrong can ground a rational intrinsic aversion to it. But that presupposition seems reasonable. It is particularly so if the moral beliefs themselves are grounded in experiences that justify regarding others as relevantly like ourselves in their capacities for the kinds of experiences that it is rational to want for their own sake. If intrinsic desires grounded in (for instance) desires to avoid causing pain are rational, and if having them conduces to morally acceptable conduct, there can be good reason to cultivate and nurture them. If some of those intrinsic desires are also specifically moral, as are desires to avoid injustice, to treat people fairly, and to lead a moral life, there is no less reason to think that they too can be rational.

8. THE STATUS OF MORAL REASONS

Among the remaining questions about grounds for being moral, one in particular should be addressed in some detail. This is the question whether, when a specifically moral intrinsic desire is rational, it always (normatively) overrides competing non-moral wants. Some philosophers, particularly a number of Kantians, have believed that moral reasons are invariably over-riding. Discussions of this issue have not always distinguished between two possibilities we have seen to be distinct. One is that there is always better overall reason to do what morality requires than to do anything incompatible with that. Call this *the thesis of moral supremacy;* it says that moral requirements are supreme; they have normative precedence over all others, collectively or individually. The second view is that a specifically moral requirement always provides a better reason for action than any particular competing non-moral reason. Call this *the moral priority thesis;* it says in effect that a morally overriding reason is superior to any such competing non-moral one.

The priority thesis can hold even if the supremacy thesis does not. A moral reason might prevail over any other kind of reason taken by itself, but might be overridden by a coalition of non-moral reasons of different kinds. The supremacy thesis may, however, seem to entail the priority thesis, but under special conditions supremacy would not imply priority. Suppose non-moral reasons, for instance prudential ones, were necessarily *aligned* with moral requirements in such a way as to support morally required conduct over competing options. Then, although the moral requirements themselves need not provide reasons that prevail over any other kind, they would never occur without allies sufficient to warrant their prevalence. We could mark this case by speaking instead of moral *dominance* and reserve 'supremacy' for the case in which moral reasons *alone* are dominant, and in general I will follow this practice and understand the supremacy thesis accordingly.

Nothing in my account of rationality implies either the supremacy, dominance, or priority thesis. Nor does it imply a related view that can be invoked to support at least the priority thesis: the view that moral reasons are *paramount*, in the sense that they are the best kind of reason to act on when the same action is indicated by a moral reason and one or more other kinds of reason. If this paramountcy view is true, then even if moral reasons can be overridden, still, so far as we can affect how much we are motivated by moral and other reasons for the same acts, as where duty and love cooperate, we should cultivate the moral motive over others. Someone who thinks moral virtues are the highest might hold this thesis; proponents of certain theological views, or of an ethics of love, would reject it—possibly in favor of their own paramountcy thesis. Neither the paramountcy of moral reasons nor any other strict hierarchy of kinds of reasons is implied by the theory of rationality developed here. On my view, each kind of moral reason for action must be judged on its merits. The supremacy view might seem to follow from the point that the "function" of morality is to regulate our conduct against any conflicting inclinations. But even if this thesis is true, the supremacy view does not follow except on the assumption that this function is supreme in the order of reasons. That is far from self-evident, though it may seem self-evident to those who are committed to the moral life as their fundamental goal.[24]

On the side of the moral priority view, there is one argument in particular that, related to my conception of reasons for action, is quite forceful. Since, in the imagined kind of case of conflicting reasons, a rational person in the disadvantaged position would want the moral thing to be done, not doing it represents a preference for oneself over others that cannot be justified on the basis of the qualitative grounds of practical reason. If I would (rationally) want you not to break a certain kind of promise to me on the kinds of grounds I now have for breaking such a promise at your expense, then my wanting to break it, even if rational, should almost certainly not override my obligation to keep it. Indeed, I very likely have better impersonal (hence interpersonal) grounds for keeping it.

This argument has much plausibility, but it is far from clearly sound. Here are two difficulties. Suppose I believe, on plausible grounds, that moral reasons are not supreme and that self-interested ones are. Second, imagine that I have a rational desire to do something that I simply cannot do if I keep my promise, and that this desire is much stronger than my moral and altruistic ones concerning the promise. These difficulties deserve separate treatment.

Regarding the first difficulty, beliefs about the status of a reason one has do not affect it in any simple way: they may defeat it or strengthen it, but they may not affect it significantly at all. A student emerging from a lecture with a hastily reasoned belief that skepticism is true and that there is thus no justification for believing in external objects is—I think—scarcely less justified than before in believing that there was an instructor making the case. The issue is in part how well-grounded the second-order belief is relative to how well-grounded the moral reason is and in part how the second-order belief applies to this particular case. Not every second-order doubt about the status of moral reasons in comparison with others need affect the moral reason one now has. As to which do and which do not, although some generalizations are possible, there is no substitute for wisdom in deciding such matters.

Concerning the second point, morality allows rational persons a certain latitude: if my life would be significantly altered by keeping the promise and you would be only inconvenienced by my breaking it, then my breaking it, while prima facie wrong, may be excusable. Here, of course, a rational person would perhaps not want it kept—or at least would not unselfishly want that. It is as if morality were designed to protect itself against being rationally overridden and so excuses truly rational lapses from its standard directives. This would be expected, of course, if the standards of morality are grounded in those of rationality in the first place.

It seems to me not clear whether in the end we must say that moral reasons always have priority over any other kind of practical reason. I cannot see that a good theory of rationality or of morality must imply this priority thesis, though I find it plausible. In any case, I suspect that even if moral reasons have priority over any other kind taken by itself, moral reasons are not always supreme and that the moral supremacy thesis is thus mistaken.[25] A good theory of rationality must, however, make it plausible to believe, even if it need not enable us to prove, that there are good reasons to hold moral principles and to act in accord with them.

A good moral theory should go at least this much further. It should explain how it can be rational to have specifically moral intrinsic desires: how they can be rational, as opposed to rationally *cultivated* as a means to producing non-moral results, such as enhanced human happiness. But it need not yield a general result, applicable to every case, concerning the status of moral reasons versus non-moral ones. What we may tentatively conclude about rational conduct in relation to moral conduct is that a rational person, when suitably informed and adequately experienced, will *tend* to act morally. But it does not follow (and is not true) that such a person always actually does the morally required thing. The least controversial reason is that there are errors of memory and of calculation that, while they yield moral violations, need not bespeak irrationality. One might argue that a *fully* rational person will always act morally. But even leaving aside the question of just what constitutes full rationality, this is at least not obvious. It may be true that it is never irrational to act morally, but that is a different and weaker point.[26]

9. PRACTICAL REASON AND THE EPISTEMIC AUTONOMY OF ETHICS

We have traced a reasonable route from the qualitative interpersonal character of the foundations of practical reason to experiential grounds for altruistic desire. Some of these same grounds provide significant support for both beliefs of moral principles and the kinds of desires that enable us to adhere to those principles. But there are two important possibilities which this approach to justification leaves open, one in moral epistemology and the other in the ontology of ethics.

Many philosophers have held that certain moral principles are self-evident, at least in the sense that understanding them—even if it requires reflection—is sufficient to justify believing them.[27] W. D. Ross and other intuitionists are representative proponents of this view.[28] Nothing I have said is incompatible with this thesis or with the weaker view that some moral knowledge is a priori.[29] Once it is seen that many beliefs capable of direct justification can also admit of inferential justification—that many foundations can be buttressed by deeper or wider foundations—this should not be puzzling. More generally, one can derive both the justification of moral principles and the rationality of moral desires from a theory of practical reason without denying that ethics has a kind of *epistemic autonomy:* that moral principles can, in their own terms, be seen to be true on the basis of adequate reflection on the concepts that figure in them—concepts such as that of a person, a promise, a duty of fidelity—and on the kinds of human situations to which the principles apply.[30]

It is, however, a further step, though a very natural one, to the conclusion that moral reasons for action, such as the consideration that an action is required by justice, are, on their own account rather than instrumentally, good reasons for action. To derive this conclusion one needs a theory of the grounds of rational action, and that, in turn, requires at least a partial account of rational desire. It may be true that a person who believes a moral principle *can* be motivated to act accordingly. But even if it were impossible to believe such a principle and fail to be so motivated, it would not self-evidently follow that an intrinsic desire to act accordingly is rational; this would depend on the overall conditions for the rationality of desire. The argument from integration is intended to show that in normal persons those conditions can be satisfied by justified non-instrumental beliefs about the experience and worth of others.

Much of our critical discourse about both moral principles and human conduct suggests that we do tend to view ethics consistently with the picture of it I am presenting. We offer moral reasons, such as that one must keep a promise, as if they were both basic and compelling; and we talk as if certain moral principles are common knowledge: children are often said to have known that lying is wrong and to have had no excuse for it. That morality can derive support from elsewhere does not imply that it lacks credibility of its own. On the other hand, if the support from elsewhere is sufficiently far-reaching, we may be in a position to unify moral principles in a way intuitionists have thought we cannot. Perhaps we may (as suggested in this chapter) exhibit moral principles as justifiable (given certain other plausible points) on the basis of the impersonal grounds of practical reason and thereby of rational desire, and as largely functioning to preserve, without preference for any single dimension of human life, the many kinds of things that are appropriate objects of rational desires.

10. COGNITIVISM AND OBJECTIVITY

I have been assuming a cognitivist view on which moral principles and judgments, even if they have an essential expressive function, are true or false. This is one reason why I have not endorsed motivational internalism, according to which, in a generic form, it is intrinsic to holding (or in some way endorsing) a moral judgment that one have some degree of motivation to act accordingly. This view is far less plausible on cognitivist assumptions, since it would appear quite possible to grasp the truth of any particular proposition without thereby having to have any specific desires (or other motivation). We may, however, leave this open.

Cognitivism certainly allows one to leave open, as I do, the possibility that in a *rational* (or highly rational) person moral judgments are to some degree motivating. Much of what I have said can also be adapted to non-cognitivism. For instance, much of it does not imply that there are mind-independent, objective moral facts. Nor does it imply moral realism, in the sense of a commitment to the existence of moral properties, though some such view is the most natural ontology for a cognitivist position and certainly for my position.

If the account of rationality developed here is taken realistically, it has more explanatory power. If, for instance, there really are properties like the hedonic or aesthetic value of an experience or the injustice of an action, then desires and aversions can be seen to be rational—and "correct"— as a reflection of normative reality rather as many beliefs can be seen to be true and justified as a reflection of observable reality. A piano, through its perceptible colors and shapes, is causally responsible for, and its presence implies the truth of, my belief, based on my sense experience, that there is a piano there; and that causal grounding of the belief in perception contains as a part of it the sensory basis of the justification of the be-lief. The melodic and harmonic qualities of my musical experience are causally responsible for, and their presence implies, the "correctness" of my wanting it for the sake of those qualities; and that causal grounding contains the experiential basis of the rationality of my wanting to hear the music for those qualities.[31] Justified experiential belief is discriminatively grounded in evidential features of experience, those that count toward the truth of the belief they evidence; rational intrinsic desire is discriminatively grounded in rewarding features of experience, those that count toward the goodness of the experience.

It is important to realize that the objectivism of the account of practical reason could be retained without its realism. Just as our experience can contain sensory qualities in virtue of which, even if we are systematically hallucinating, it is rational to believe there are objects outside us, an expe-rience can contain aesthetic or moral qualities in virtue of which, even if there are no properties of, say, musical value or justice, it is rational to want experiences like it. But I see no good reason to give up realism in the second instance if it should be maintained in the first—which is not to say that there are no reasons to give it up in the first. Indeed, a case can be made that moral properties play a role in explanations of concrete phenomena. This causalist realism has much to recommend it, but it is not the only kind of realism.[32]

My conclusion in this chapter is that, in various ways, others can and should be among our ends, and indeed among our reasonable ends. This parlance is of course metaphorical. Ends can be *realized;* substances, prop-erly speaking, cannot be. Our desires can be realized; *we* are already real. Our self-realization is largely a matter of the satisfaction of certain of our rational desires, which in turn is largely a matter of what we experience. But the experiences, states, and activities of others can be our ends, just as our own can be. If others are as much like me as it seems reasonable to believe they are, then I can easily take them as ends. I can intrinsically want them to have experiences they will find rewarding. I assume that they will find such experiences rewarding in much the way I do. When our lives are structured by normal human relations, particularly those characterized by cooperation, friendship, and love, it is natural to make such assumptions, to feel a good measure of empathy, and to have a significant degree of altruistic desire. It is clear that such desire is consonant with reason. I have argued that, in lives that are normal in civilized societies, it is also de-manded, even if not strictly required, by reason.

The things I want for others may or may not be highly similar to those I want for myself. I must start with an understanding of my own experience if I am to understand others. But the paths that originate in what I am acquainted with in my own case can range, by analogy and imaginative extension, far from me. Empathy and perceived likeness may ease the way toward altruism, but when they do, it is because I transcend my absorption with myself. The most general grounds of altruism lie in some apparently universal characteristics of persons. It is to rewarding features of our experience that rational desires are a natural and discriminative response, as rational experiential beliefs are natural and discriminative responses to the sensory array that pervades our lives. When action is suitably grounded, through rational belief, in rational desires, it is rational. When it is both rational and, in a certain way, other-regarding, it is moral. Morality at its best carries a commitment to impartially caring about others in the way we naturally care about ourselves.

PART III

RATIONALITY AND RELATIVITY

7

RELATIVITY, PLURALITY, AND CULTURE

Rational beliefs are well-grounded in the features of experience that are conducive to their justification; rational desires are well-grounded in the features of experience that render them consonant with reason; and rational actions are characteristically well-grounded, through rational beliefs, in rational desires. Justifiedness in beliefs and rationality in desires are themselves indications of something further. The features of experience that are conducive to justified beliefs count toward the truth of their content, and the features of experience that render desires rational count toward the goodness of their objects. But people differ greatly in the range of their experiences, and over time the experiences of any one person may change dramatically. What it is rational for me to believe, then, may not be rational for another; and a desire rational for me now may not be rational for me later. Reasonableness is similarly variable.[1]

If there are kinds of experience that we all have, there are also experiences each of us has that no one else does. Nearly all of us, however, share a culture with those whose lives overlap ours. A culture is usually a pervasive element in the lives of those who belong to it. This applies to something as large as "Western Culture," as well as to social frameworks as narrow as, say, the culture of the Parisian Left Bank in the 1920s. Do cultures also supply their own standards of rationality to those who belong to them? And is the apparent universality of certain standards of reason and morality mainly the result of the contingent fact that those who discuss such questions share deep cultural presuppositions? It is certainly appropriate to wonder how the theory of rationality developed here can be squared with differences between individuals and cultures. Can there be universal, objective standards of rationality and morality that apply to people despite their individual and cultural differences, or are standards of rationality, in some deep-going way, relative to persons, places, and times?

1. RATIONALITY AND THE SPACE OF RELATIVITY

The first point to consider is that the conception of rationality I have set out is, in some ways, quite permissive. None of the proposed standards implies, by itself, that there are certain propositions that all rational persons must believe, or even certain specific ends they must pursue.[2] In this sense, rationality is largely a structural and relational notion. Its experiential grounds profoundly affect its substance but place only limited constraints on its content. It may be a requirement of rationality that a rational person who comprehendingly *considers* a luminously self-evident truth would believe it and that a rational person who suffers excruciating pain would want it to stop. But it is perhaps not necessary that a person ever consider such propositions, and it is not strictly necessary that one suffer pain, even if a life without it would be artificial.

There are, to be sure, generic substantive requirements for rationality. There do seem to be *kinds* of beliefs and desires rational (human) persons must normally have *if* they have any at all. There are also kinds of beliefs and desires that a rational person must *not* have. But a rational body of beliefs or desires—or of propositional attitudes of any kind—must above all exhibit a certain structure. It must have experiential foundations and a superstructure that rests on them by virtue of beliefs that connect the two. Rational beliefs and desires must, then, be appropriately related to experience—well-grounded in it, if I have been right. But just what elements belong in such structures depends on the experiences of the person in question, and human experience is highly varied.

The partly structural character of rationality and the plurality of substantive standards for it are tempered by the universality of certain basic sources of it in human cognition. There are at least four: sensory experience, introspection, memory, and reflection. There are also universally basic sources of rational desire. Pleasure and pain are the most widely recognized. The inescapable promptings and vulnerabilities of the body, together with pleasure as a characteristic accompaniment of rewarding experiences and pain as a characteristic accompaniment of "punishing" experiences, help to make pleasure and pain seem the only basic grounds of practical reasons. Indeed, pleasure is itself one kind of reward, variable in nature and—as Mill argued, in value—depending on the experience that yields it. The same holds for pain; and achieving relief from pain can be a closely related but distinct kind of good experience. But the rich and varied responses of the emotions, the engagements of the aesthetic sensibilities, and the life of the intellect all seem to yield rewards, and rational desires in response to them. Not everyone has all the normal sense modalities, however, and some might have other, quite different sources of cognition or desire, whether sensory or of some other kind.[3] Rationality does not require that one have beliefs or desires from sources of all the common kinds, and it does not close the list of sources.

New sources of rationality must, to be sure, earn their credentials through appropriate connections with standards we already have. This is most obvious for beliefs: a sense of impending dampness can become a source of non-inferential justification for believing that it will rain, only if its deliverances are first correlated with rainfall as ordinarily perceived; a felt attraction toward sky-diving can make it rational to want intrinsically to do it, only if there is some reason for those who feel the attraction to take sky-diving to be in some way rewarding.[4] The reason may be cognitive; one may have a justified belief to this effect. It may also be experiential; one may have been through something similar, such as high-diving into water, and liked it. But the mere impulse to pursue something does not make wanting it for its own sake rational.

There are, however, no a priori restrictions on what new sources of non-inferential belief or of intrinsic desire might turn out to ground rationality. If new sources should arise and should come to play a sufficiently large role in our determinations of rationality, our conception of rationality might change considerably. There may be no reason to expect major changes of this kind, but some gradual evolution seems likely, particularly in the wake of major biological or cultural upheavals. Nonetheless, it is probably more the differences that already exist among people, rather than the changes we could undergo in our standards of rationality, that pose a challenge to an objectivist account of rationality.

If we do differ greatly in the range of our experiences and if, owing to our personal and cultural characteristics, we may also differ extensively in the content of our rational beliefs and desires, one should expect that in certain ways rationality is relative. But there are many kinds of relativity, and the term is often used ambiguously. Several kinds must be explored.

2. RELATIVITY TO GROUNDS

An internalist view of rationality by its very nature embodies a kind of relativity that goes a good distance toward accounting for individual differences without implying that there is no universally applicable notion of rationality, or that we differ from one another in ways that make us ultimately unintelligible to each other. I refer to relativity to grounds: the dependence of the rationality of one's beliefs, actions, or desires (or other propositional attitudes) on one's grounds for them. There are two main cases of such relativity. The rationality of these elements may depend, positively, on one's grounds *for them;* it may also depend, negatively, on one's total grounds relevant *to them.* Much the same holds for justification and for reasonableness.[5]

Consider the positive dependence on grounds first. Our (propositional) attitudes and actions are rational, not absolutely but only in relation to our grounds, which are highly variable. My beliefs, for instance, are rational when well-grounded in *my* experience or reflection. They may thus be very different from your rational beliefs, depending on how different your experience is. Still, we are sufficiently similar to make it likely that in the same environment we will share many beliefs, and form a number of similar desires and aversions. Walking out together into an unexpected snowstorm, we will each believe it is snowing; and if the wind is bitterly cold, we will each have some kind of self-protective desire. The degree of cognitive and conative overlap among persons is a contingent matter, but if we communicate as well as we seem to (however imperfectly) there is substantial overlap.

If we distinguish beliefs from dispositions to believe, we can see why it may not be absolutely necessary that there is any particular proposition that all rational persons must believe. From the same kinds of raw materials, vastly different structures can be built, and no two need be exactly alike. On the basis of common human experience, we may all be disposed to believe, for instance, that we cannot jump to the moon by earnestly wishing to; but a rational person need not actually have that belief. Must it be different with propositions that are more familiar or more useful? It is simple logical truths that are most likely to seem to falsify the suggestion that rational persons need not believe any particular proposition, since we seem to reason in accordance with such logical truths so often, whereas the proposition just formulated plays no role in the normal person's thought or action. The capacities entailed by rationality certainly do imply that there are many logical truths which rational persons are at least disposed to believe. Take the proposition that if it is either snowing or sizzling outside, and it is not snowing, then it is sizzling. If one considers this under normal conditions, one believes it. But perhaps a rational person could go through an entire life without considering this or any other logical truth; and even apart from that, although *dis*belief of certain simple logical truths may be ruled out by rationality, there may not be any *particular* logical truth which every rational person must believe, either constantly or at any given time.[6]

For empirical beliefs, and for specific desires, similar points hold. Might there, however, have to be some logical truth or other that one believes at any given time when one counts as rational? If, as seems possible in the limiting case, the cognitive system could be emptied of beliefs without destroying the capacities essential for rationality, the answer would be no. One need not have in one's experience any grounds to which one is not rationally responding, and one would be (globally) rational by virtue of one's readiness to respond to grounds. Rationality can be a capacity to respond to grounds even if one has, under special conditions, no grounds to respond to.

The second kind of relativity to grounds is negative and is based on a notion that I have throughout taken to be central in understanding normative notions: defeasibility. We sometimes have grounds that would justify a belief we hold or render a desire of ours rational if it were not for our having other grounds that defeat our would-be justification or rationality. There are times when I would be justified in my belief that a student will meet a deadline, if I did not also believe, or have good reason to believe, that on most such occasions the student has requested extensions. Something similar occurs with desire. My intrinsic desire for a certain mountain hike would be rational if I could not easily remember how arduous that route is and that the view is now obscured by overgrown trees. In the first case, we have defeat by a justified attitude (or by justification for forming an attitude) of the same kind, a cognition. In the second, we have defeat by a different kind of attitude: the rationality of a desire is defeated by beliefs that bear on what it would be like to satisfy it.

The case of defeasibility indicates a third kind of relativity to grounds, derivative from the first two: *temporal relativity*. Since one's grounds for an attitude may change, holding it can be rational at one time but not at another, when its rationality is defeated. There are at least four cases here, each most easily illustrated with beliefs. First, I may gain grounds where I had none. Second, I may simply forget the grounds I have, as where I can no longer remember the rationale for a strange view I once could justify and am now somewhat embarrassed at rediscovering in conversation with a colleague.[7] Third, I may acquire defeating grounds that outweigh the grounds I had before. And, in the fourth case, I may acquire undermining grounds: roughly, reasons in virtue of which I cannot take my positive grounds to justify me, as where I acquire excellent evidence to think that someone on whose testimony I relied was lying. The rationality of a particular attitude, then, is not in general fixed by its content, any more than that of an action is generally fixed by its abstract type. In each case, the actual sustaining grounds are crucial, and these can change with time. Here its rationality is not intrinsic, but relative to its grounds.

175

Relativity to grounds encompasses yet another kind of relativity, some-times predicated of reasons: *agent relativity*. What are called agent-relative reasons are sometimes cited as constraints on conduct that would maxi-mize intrinsic value yet be wrong because it uses someone merely as a means. Suppose I could save one hundred innocent people from a death by biological contamination if I executed one innocent person. May I not decline on the agent-relative ground that *my* deepest standards forbid so using a person as a means, even if I believe my doing so would do more to enhance intrinsic value, impersonally and non-relatively conceived, say, in terms of the total happiness of all who are affected? Suppose I may. Is there any obstacle that prevents my theory from accounting for the rationality of this choice? I think not.

Granting that what I may do is relative to my particular grounds, does not the force of my agent-relative reasons ultimately depend on my over-all reason for action, where that reason is understood organically, in rela-tion to my moral standards as well as to my contribution to enhancing in-trinsic value impersonally conceived? We must not be misled by the term 'agent-relative': the agent and the specific situation of action are crucial, but only in a way that has identical normative significance for any exactly similar agent in exactly similar circumstances. It is certainly not obvious that the force of one's agent-relative reasons is not derivative from one's contribution to intrinsic value, organically conceived, together with deontic considerations that are also organically conceived. There is, then, no good reason to expect a disparity between a sound moral judgment made on the basis of agent-relative reasons and a judgment properly made in the light of the same factual information on the basis of the highly pluralistic theory I am defending. In both cases, the relativity is to grounds, which is what we should expect on a well-groundedness account of reasons and rationality.[8]

3. GENETIC RELATIVITY

Relativity to grounds is not equivalent to something easily confused with it: genetic relativity, a kind of causal relativity. The confusion is abetted by the partly causal character of the grounding of the rationality of beliefs and other attitudes, but here the point is that a causal relation is not just necessary for genetic relativity but also sufficient. To illustrate, the genetic version of relativism in question says, in part (and this is often said), that what we believe is relative to our culture and upbringing, in the sense that it depends on that and, in the case of many of our beliefs, is (in a causal sense) determined by it. In the light of this view—which we might call *causal genetic relativism*—beliefs, desires, and other propositional attitudes are thought to be relative to what produces or sustains them in the sense that they are determined by it and they vary with changes in the relevant causal factors. But this thesis about causal determination is not a philosophical view, and it is consistent with various anti-relativist normative views. It is a relativism concerning what beliefs and other attitudes we *have*, not about conditions for their rationality.

There is, however, a related genetic view that is philosophical: the thesis that the rationality of our beliefs and other propositional attitudes is relative to their genesis, in the sense that it automatically varies with their causal basis. Call this *normative genetic relativism*. Rationality might be thought to be relative in this way because the ascription of genetic relativity to beliefs and other attitudes is easily confused with the view that their rationality is relative to grounds. For (in my view) grounds, when they justify attitudes or actions, *do* causally produce or sustain what they justify, and that work is genetic.

Even on the view that justifying grounds produce or sustain an attitude they justify, normative genetic relativism is too strong. Causal work is not the *only* kind done by justificatory grounds; nor is their doing such work sufficient by itself for justification. For one thing, the brain could be manipulated in such a way that one's believing a good premise for something (say, a theorem of arithmetic) could cause one to believe the latter though one cannot see the relevance of the former to the latter. One would then "have" a justification one cannot see to be even a support. Moreover, not just any change in what sustains a belief affects its justification. My belief that a loved one is dying of cancer can darken my outlook in such a way that it causally reinforces my evidentially justified belief, of a seriocomic play I attend, that it is depressing, yet the first belief expresses no evidence for the second belief and need not affect its justification. I need not lose this justification even if my depressing belief cooperates in sustaining my interpretive one; and I certainly lose none if that evidentially irrelevant causal factor is eliminated.

To say, then, that beliefs and other attitudes are relative to—determined by–their causal basis is not equivalent to saying that *rationality* is genetically relative in this sense. Causal genetic relativism does not imply normative genetic relativism. Rationality *is* relative to grounds, which in turn are causal factors; but it is not produced or affected by just *any* causal grounds, and the sense in which it is relative to its causal bases is captured by the notion of relativity to grounds.

If the thesis of normative genetic relativism were weakened to say that the rationality (and justification) of beliefs and other attitudes *may* vary with changes in what sustains them, it would be true (it need not vary because, e.g., one sustaining normative ground can immediately be replaced by an equally good one). But it would hold in virtue of the factors that warrant affirming relativity to grounds, and to say that rationality is genetically relative in this way would add nothing of interest to that thesis. Genetic relativity must not be taken by itself to imply anything about what it is rational for a person to believe or want, or about the basis on which beliefs or wants are rational. *What* we believe and want may be genetically determined by, and in that sense relative to, causal factors, without the *rationality* of what we believe or want being determined by those factors. Normative grounds encompass causal ones, but are not exhausted by them.

4. RELATIVITY OF RATIONAL CONTENT

Once the relativity of rationality to grounds, as an aspect of actual attitudes and actions, is understood, it is a short step to a related kind: relativity of rational content. This concerns mainly *prospective* attitudes or actions, as opposed to those one actually holds.[9] It may also concern abstract elements, for instance propositions or types of acts: a proposition or course of action is rational for me relative to my grounds for it. This kind of variability might even be called *prospective relativity* to emphasize that it applies mainly to would-be elements rather than to attitudes or actions one has or performs at the time.

To say that rationality is relative in this hypothetical sense is to take the view that what one (rationally) *should* (or may) believe, or want, or do, is relative to one's pertinent grounds. Here the focus of relativity is on a prospective rather than an existing attitude or action: on what content is rational *for* us, not rational *in* us. The question may concern the future, but we may also ask what it is rational for us to want now as an alternative to what we do want. But the basis of the relativity is the same as in the case of relativity to grounds: it is the grounds one actually has relative to the attitude or action in question.

The difference between relativity to grounds and relativity of content is that whereas to understand the former concept we keep fixed a given belief or attitude a person holds and consider possible variations in its rationality as the grounds for it change, to understand the notion of relativity of rational content we keep fixed a person's grounds (such as one's evidence base for beliefs) and consider the various contents toward which, on those grounds, the person may hold a rational attitude, such as belief or desire. If (quite unbeknownst to me) I am observing a piece of paper in yellow light, my visual grounds make it rational for me to form the belief that it is yellow; if you view it in sunlight, your grounds make it rational for you to form the belief that it is white; and if a shade is opened and I realize that I am only now seeing the paper in normal light, I too may become justified in believing the paper to be white. If Pauline enjoys rigorous hikes and Paul does not, then it is likely to be rational for her, but not for him, to want to take one. And what I should want to do in response to a request to give a paper is relative to (among other things) what I have to say on the topic and how much time I would have to write it. Differences in grounds warrant differences in content.

There is, however, a constancy that underlies relativity of rational content. We are alike in having visual grounds and in the (prima facie) rationality of our visual beliefs which derive from them; and we all find some experiences rewarding and others not. There is much overlap in what visual grounds we will acquire if we make normal observations in the same physical circumstances; and there is considerable overlap, if less, in the motivational grounds we will acquire if we undergo similar experiences in similar psychological circumstances. In both cases, the more elemental the circumstances, the more alike we tend to be. We react similarly to extremes of hot and cold, light and dark, starvation and nourishment, drubbing and massage. These common human experiences provide some of our basic grounds for belief, desire, and action.

Something similar holds in moral cases. People with little children normally have grounds of obligation to nurture them. But our experiences, capacities—and children—differ. The content of my obligation may thus be quite different from the content of yours; I may have to provide for voice lessons where you must provide for piano lessons, and there may be instruction in sports, second languages, and so forth. In this sense, moral obligation is relative. But its relativity of content does not imply that its existence is relative: for instance that, under certain conditions, one might have *no* moral obligations to one's children.

5. CONCEPTUAL RELATIVITY

So far, we have been exploring how rationality might be relative on the assumption that there is a univocal concept of it, so that in speaking of rationality, in different contexts, we are speaking of the same thing. This may be challenged, as it has been for moral notions such as rightness.[10] One might hold that just as there is no rightness simpliciter, but only rightness in a system, such as that of a given society, there is no rationality simpliciter, but only, say, Western rationality or scientific rationality or Australian aboriginal rationality.

The thesis in question is *conceptual relativism:* the view that there is no absolute concept of rationality, but only a range of related concepts each anchored in a cultural and linguistic context that determines what properties are crucial, what inferences are permissible, and so forth. We could also call this relativity a kind of *multivocality,* since the claim is that there are different meanings of 'rational' and related terms depending on the context governing their use.[11]

Conceptual relativism is difficult to assess. For one thing, there is no sharp distinction between using a term in two senses and using it in accord with different theoretical commitments about what it designates. For another, what looks like multivocality may be the change in dominant criteria of application that occurs from one context to another, for instance from the context of science to that of art, and from that of belief to that of desire. Perhaps my theory of rationality can largely account for the diversity here through two points. First, the notion of well-groundedness is wide enough to apply very differently in different domains, such as those of belief and desire. Second, there are of course different *conceptions* of rationality, in a psychological sense of 'conception' akin to that of 'theory'. These conceptions are, however, apparently connected by virtue of each being a conception of a way the relevant element can be grounded: for instance, in experience, in coherence, or in social practices.

Quite apart from these considerations favoring a multiple-conception view of rationality over conceptual relativism about it, I prefer not to multiply concepts, or senses of terms, beyond necessity. I will take it that there is a (common) concept of rationality to be clarified by philosophical theory (a claim supported later in connection with the practice conception of rationality). If, however, this univocity view is mistaken, there is still a task for a philosophical theory of rationality: accounting for why the different concepts of rationality are all concepts *of it,* and explaining the apparent overlap among them. The theory of rationality I propose can do much to complete this task even if in the end the wisest course is to countenance different concepts of rationality rather than, as I prefer, different conceptions of something appropriately viewed under a single concept.[12]

6. DOXASTIC RELATIVITY

Neither relativity of grounds nor relativity of content nor even conceptual relativity implies a further kind: doxastic relativity. To say that rationality is relative in this sense is to claim that it is relative to what one believes is rational. The most common expression of the view employs that elusive little word 'for'. "What is right for one person may not be right for another," people often say. Those who sincerely speak so would certainly tend to say the same sort of thing using 'rational'. These locutions are ambiguous between 'What one person *believes* to be rational may not be believed to be rational by another'—which is simply a point about what people believe—and a genuine relativism: the view that beliefs about what is rational for one make it so.

There is also a perspectival use of 'for' on which 'right for me' can mean roughly 'right relative to my commitments'. Given sufficient self-understanding and inferential power (enough to see what one is implicitly committed to by, above all, the relevant beliefs and desires), what I believe is right for me will be what is perspectivally right for me. But we can be wrong about what *is* perspectivally right for us. In any event, despite appearances such *perspectival relativity* is not doxastic, but a special case of relativity to grounds. Our perspective in the relevant sense is largely a matter of the grounds we stand on. Our vision of these may be obscured, and we may misappraise them.

Our grounds may also be inadequate to justify an action or attitude based on them. What is grounded in our perspective, and in that sense "right for us," is rational only if it is *well*-grounded. Perspectival relativity is important in understanding the notion of being true to oneself. Failure to be true to oneself may be criticizable in various ways and may manifest a deficiency in rationality—depending largely on the soundness of one's constitution—but being true to oneself is no guarantee of rationality.

Doxastic relativism is a counterpart of the position that our actual obligation is to do what we believe is our obligation. In its most plausible form, the position requires that this pivotal normative belief must be rational. Such a view is probably less plausible for rationality than for moral obligation. To start with the negative case, we have seen that although a rational belief that another belief or a desire is irrational *can* undermine its rationality, it does not always do this. Certainly a mere belief to this effect need not. As to the positive case, a rational belief that another belief or a desire is rational does not make it so. One can even quite justifiedly believe one is obligated to do something without being so obligated, though in some such cases there is a sense in which one ought to act on the belief. From general knowledge, I might be amply justified in believing that my letter of nomination must contain reasons in support of the candidate. Given that justified belief, as a rational person I ought to give reasons. But I might still be incorrect in this belief (since I am assimilating a nomination to a

181

recommendation) and I might not have an obligation to include reasons. In that sense, then, it is not true that I ought to do so.

Doxastic relativity represents a kind of subjectivity. If rationality were doxastically relative, then in a sense it would be a matter of opinion whether a belief or desire is rational. But rationality does not wait upon opinion. Our beliefs and desires can be rational without our believing that they are and irrational when we believe they are not.

One might think that an internalist view of rationality must ultimately be subjectivist. But despite its far-reaching relativity to grounds, my view does not imply either doxastic relativity or any radical subjectivity. What it is rational for me to believe depends on my experience; but *that* it is rational to believe what I do *given* a normal response to my experiences does not depend on those experiences. Nor is it up to us just what our basic sources of belief or desire are. The standards of rationality, though internal, are in this twofold sense objective. Being internal, experiential, relational, and, to a high degree, content-neutral, the standards are multiply applicable. They allow for the rationality of beliefs and desires very different in their contents, whether in a given person over time or in different people. Being universally applicable, the standards are not doxastically relative.[13]

7. RELATIVITY OF NORMATIVE STATUS

If, for the kinds of reasons I have suggested, doxastic relativism is mistaken, we can see that content relativity does not imply a further kind: relativity of status. To affirm this kind of relativity is to take the view—commonly expressed among lay people and presupposed by many social scientists— that the applicability, and hence the normative authority, of the basic rational standards is not universal across persons, but depends on certain variable factors, such as beliefs, circumstances, and culture. This kind of relativism about normative standards—*status relativism*—might also be called relativism about normativity. It may seem to be implied by conceptual relativism about rationality, but it is not. The latter allows the former, but is compatible with the existence of universal standards of rationality common to *each* of the various concepts of rationality. Thus, once we specify a concept of rationality, say, "the" Anglo-American one, the standards are determined. They need not eliminate all indeterminacy, as where a certain question, say, about whether lower animals have rights, may simply have no answer. But *that* the indeterminacy exists will itself be a matter concerning the application of the standards.

Status relativism is widely held for judgments of morality as well as for judgments of rationality. It derives some plausibility from the persistence of disagreements between apparently rational persons, but I believe that it is mistaken. Certainly persistence of disagreement is at least often explainable without assuming status relativism, as many would grant is the case with typical scientific disagreements. On my view, the basic standards of rationality take account of our differences and even of striking disagreements. But once these differences are taken into account, the way is open to seeing that the standards are universally valid. Wanting to view the paintings of Picasso is not rational for everyone, and one might think that this kind of difference implies relativity of normative status. But such differences do nothing to undermine the plausible view that it is—universally—rational to want to view them *given* that one enjoys it.

There is an important source of support for status relativism that must not be misunderstood: the existence of valuational ties. Two of us may have equally good cases for opposing policies; two or more competing activities may seem to a single person equally good. This may appear to imply that there is no universally valid standard for making the evaluation in question. It does not; a universally valid standard may support the conclusion that two or more options are equally good and that therefore choice of any of them is rationally permissible—or may be reasonably made on grounds of individual preference. If we want to stress how important a role personal preference can play when there are two or more options—including propositions vying for acceptance as well as competing courses of action awaiting decision—we could speak of *preferential relativity*. But this kind of relativity is entirely consistent with the existence of objective standards by which the two or more options in question present us with such matters of preference.

Indeed, given the organicity of overall intrinsic value, we should perhaps expect to encounter wide differences in rational judgments regarding how the elements yielding such value are interconnected and how much they contribute to the overall value of the thing in question. This may or may not yield disagreement in normative judgment; where it does, it does not follow either that there is no correct judgment or that every incorrect judgment is not rational. Where it does not, as when two buyers for a museum regard two paintings as equally good, there may remain a rational (though not a rationally required) difference in their preferences for one or the other of the equally good options. There may be a *compositional relativity* in many complex cases: a plurality of ways in which, with equal warrant, sensitive rational persons may judge the whole on the basis of its parts or aspects.

The idea that where such valuational differences occur, either only one view is sound or the standards in question are merely relative is a mistake natural for those who want to be right or have a naive conception of evaluative standards. There is no support for status relativism here, but only for preferential relativity. The preferential relativism in question may also figure in some cases of agent-relativity: where there is a valuational tie, two different agents could, in the light of their individual preferences, choose different options with equal justification.

There is another source of felt support for status relativism which we should examine. It is *instrumentalist relativism:* the view (explored in Chapter 5) that actions which are rational for us are those that, on our beliefs, appropriately contribute to our desire satisfaction. What is rational for me, then, is relative to my beliefs and desires, and it may be diametrically opposed to what is rational for someone with different desires. This point, however, shows that instrumentalism is committed to relativity to grounds, not to status relativism. The same point could be made about our respective *beliefs*, given different experiences as grounds for them—and this could hold on a universalist, objectivist view of theoretical reason.

To be sure, instrumentalism is subjectivist: what is rational for me is not only relative to my grounds; my conative grounds, at least, are not constrained by any substantive universal standards, hedonic, moral, or even prudential.[14] But the question whether an action is rational for a person does *not* have a different answer in different cultures. It is indeed answerable by an objective method for determining what a person's desires and beliefs are—at least if the instrumentalist does not place implausible constraints on the crucial instrumental beliefs. If, for instance, one required that our beliefs about desire satisfaction be rational *and* one disallowed objective criteria for rational belief, then objective psychological inquiry could not determine what actions are rational for us. This, however, is not how instrumentalists have generally proceeded. They have tended to use common-sense, objective standards for instrumental beliefs. This is illustrated by the many political philosophers who, at least since Hobbes, have argued from the assumption of shared basic desires (such as a desire to live in society as opposed to a state of nature), together with factual beliefs about their satisfaction, to the rationality of certain social actions.

Our experiences and capacities vary; on that ground, then, such universal standards as the principle that enjoying something makes it rational to want it should be expected to warrant different desires in different people. Much the same holds for scientific theorizing: proper applications of scientific method should be expected to lead to different beliefs in people with different experiences and capacities. This is indeed what we find, and there is no need to posit status relativism here either. In both cases, once the relevant capacities and confirmatory experiences are held constant, what it is rational to want or to believe does not vary beyond certain limits. For beliefs, desires, and actions, at least, rationality is well-groundedness, however different the grounds we stand on.

8. THE PERMISSIVENESS OF RATIONALITY

This objectivist conception of rationality may sound very strong, and in a way it is. There are, however, several points about the account of rationality that help to place its strength in perspective. They concern both the degree of the rationality in question and the latitude the account allows for rational disagreement.

First, we are talking about what is prima facie rational. Normal adults have a multitude of beliefs and desires, including some that yield self-critical dispositions. We know that appearance does not always correspond to reality, that pursuing desires for what looks appealing may disappoint us, and that beliefs are sometimes influenced by wishful thinking. Our prima facie rationality in our ordinary visual beliefs or normal affectional desires, then, like our justification for them, may not be sufficient to yield overall rationality (or justification), and even when it does, that rationality may later be defeated. Granted, then, that it is of the first importance that there are universal sources of prima facie justification and universal standards that demand respect for those sources, even a universally acceptable coin may be of too little value for the needed purchase.

My second point here is implicit in what has just been said. If the pervasiveness of defeasibility indicates a major element in rationality as I have portrayed it, the nature of the relevant defeaters does nothing to support status relativism. The standard sources of normative grounds are crucial in grounding defeaters of justification and rationality. Defeaters very often gain their subversive authority from the same sources they impugn.[15] The proper weighting of conflicting sources of rationality cannot always be formulated in precise principles. But even the rough-and-ready generalizations, such as those that, in simple observational matters, tend to weight the evidence of the senses over that of memory and that of objective measurement over that of visual appearances, seem universally applicable. A visual impression of the height of a building normally outweighs a memory impression that it was taller; a measurement of two walls that finds them equally long outweighs a visual appearance of differing length (though its doing so presupposes warrant for confidence in one's memory of, among other things, the visual impression that the measurement contradicts).

The third point to keep in mind here is that a rational belief or desire, in the common sense that is of most concern in this book, is one that a person may, consonantly with the appropriate standards, have; it is not to be conceived as one that it is irrational not to have. Hence, the universality of the standards does not imply that the rational beliefs and rational desires of rational persons are beliefs and desires they *must* have. Indeed, the notion of rationality seems to admit degrees in a sense that allows for the possibility that one may rationally hold a belief, or rationally perform an action, even if it would not be reasonable to hold it and would be better, and *more* rational, to hold a different one or do a different thing. There is a tendency to deny this latitudinarian character of rationality because one imagines comparing the relevant propositions or actions with a view to deciding on one, and given an informed comparison for this purpose, it *would* tend to be irrational not to believe the best grounded proposition or perform the best justified option, provided one realizes that there is a fully justified winner and not a tie. But *consideration* of options is a further experience and can enhance both the number of one's grounds and the strength of some of them. With different grounds, what is rational for us may change; that is the basic truth underlying both relativity to grounds and relativity of content.

A fourth, related point is that we must not in general judge, on the basis of a hypothetical comparison *we* make, the rationality of a belief formed without the *believer's* making a comparison of the various relevant potential grounds for it or for alternatives to it. If reason always demanded such a comparison, things might be different. But to think that it does is to succumb to a kind of intellectualism that invites us to adopt an infinitely regressive notion of rationality. For if a belief or action could never be rational unless we considered alternatives to it or at least appraised the proposition or action in question, we would finish scrutinizing one belief or action only to be confronted with an obligation to repeat the procedure. It is not only not rationally required of us, but is in general positively unreasonable, to compare our alternative routes to getting across the yard to pull some weeds.

A fifth qualification is needed to clarify what the objective conception of rationality implies concerning differences between persons regarding the same propositions or options. Given the relativity to grounds, I may be not only rational, but justified on balance, in believing one thing where another person may be justified on balance in believing its negation. Our different lives yield different evidences. If I *learn* that someone else is so

justified, I should in many cases reconsider my own view. I should, moreover, try to learn, in certain important matters, whether anyone else *is* so
justified.[16] But even when I find that someone is fully justified in an incompatible belief, I may still retain my own overall justification, at least if
I can explain how the other person can be justified to the degree in question and still be mistaken. Such explanations can neutralize a defeater. It
is not as though one could have a genuine justificatory ground only if
anyone else considering that ground would have to be convinced of the
proposition in question. Skeptics have often so conceived justification, but
there is no good reason to take its grounds to be always psychologically
compelling in this way.

Knowledge is different from justification in this interpersonal aspect.
Knowledge is of truths, and incompatible propositions cannot both be true.
But it is quite possible to be justified in believing a proposition without
knowing its truth. It can also be rational to *claim* to be justified in cases in
which it would not be rational to claim to know the proposition in question (as where one has made a very careful but inconclusive check of a
mathematical result). The point is not that one should generally expect
to be justified and correct without expecting to know; it is that the kinds
of grounds required to warrant the higher-order claim to know are different from those required to warrant the higher-order claim to be justified.
Moreover, often two or more people can each be warranted, respectively,
in conflicting higher-order views concerning the normative status of a given
belief, desire, or action.

Practical reason is analogous to theoretical reason here: I can be rational or even justified in performing a kind of action that is not rational for
you, and we can each justifiedly view our conduct as rational. But suppose
we are looking ahead to the *same* options, as in discussing a policy issue we
must resolve by joint action. Then, even if there is a valuational tie, we
cannot both be successful in selecting contrary options, and we should
devise a fair procedure for aligning our final preferences. Any of us, moreover, can be rational in performing an action that does not *maximize* whatever interests we are serving by it. To be sure, as I have suggested, in general one may not rationally do something that one (rationally) believes or
should believe is *less* good, overall, than an available alternative action, and
one may not rationally believe something one (rationally) thinks or should
think is less well-grounded than an alternative or competing proposition.
But it does not follow that we must always make comparisons, or always try
to maximize, either in deciding what to do or in forming beliefs, if only
because the calculation costs may be too great. There is, however, also a
disanalogy between the theoretical and practical cases: whereas one or

more of us can believe incompatible propositions, we cannot jointly perform contrary actions, say, enact an overall tax reduction and an overall tax increase.[17]

Where we do disagree in major matters, it is important to reconsider them and, often, to form second-order beliefs about the quality of our evidence or about the rationality of our relevant desires. It could turn out that one of us, while continuing to think that our preferred option is rational, will decide that it is more rational, or at any rate better on balance, to choose the option favored by the other. Such a decision is facilitated by the internality of the notion of rationality: we can regard others who disagree as rational in the light of their experience, even though when we hold mutually incompatible views, we cannot each know we are right.

What emerges, then, is a pluralistic theory of rationality. Rationality is grounded in a variety of sources; and although the objectivity of the standards associated with these sources allows a great variety of rational beliefs, desires, and actions, those standards are universally valid.[18] If there is a plurality of sources, however, then diversity of rational attitudes from one person to another is to be expected. On the other hand, because rationality requires well-groundedness and there are universal experiential and rational ("intuitive") sources of belief and desire, we can readily achieve communication, arrive at substantially overlapping cognition and motivation, and reach compromise in resolving disagreements. As differing individuals, we derive happiness, develop intrinsic desires, and form beliefs, from experiences with quite different things. But we are enough alike to be capable of understanding the grounding of most beliefs and desires of most other people, and the objective standards of rationality accommodate wide differences among people without impugning their rationality.

9. THE PRACTICE CONCEPTION OF RATIONALITY

Reason, both theoretical and practical, crosses cultures. Both kinds of rationality are essential *in* a culture but are not mere products of it. Yet reason (in various ways I have illustrated) leaves the specific content of rational belief and desire largely open. Elementary perceptual experiences and biological needs normally yield some of that content; but much of the most important content, and the content in which people differ most, is supplied by one or another aspect of culture. Reason would have us value, and intrinsically want to pursue, what we find rewarding, most obviously the activities we enjoy. Many of these engage our complex faculties, but doing so is not part of what it *is* for an activity to be enjoyable or even rewarding.

It is arguable that other things being equal, if two activities are equally enjoyable and one engages more complex faculties than the other, then that activity is intrinsically preferable. This is often so, but I cannot see that it is necessary.[19]

It is culture that supplies many of the activities that, in their different ways, people enjoy, especially those that are social, aesthetic, intellectual, and religious; and the resources of a culture, such as its institutions, provide most of the social and educational conditions for achieving rationality, especially in complex matters. Reason can embrace indefinitely many cultures. It constrains how they contribute to rationality, but not, beyond broad limits, *what* they contribute to it. There are no a priori limits to the variety of rewards experience can provide. Reason would have us pursue activities we find rewarding; but it provides no precise list of these, nor does it endorse as final the cherished list of any one culture.

One way to think of how culture bears on rationality is to view culture as partly constituted by practices, especially those that are intellectual, moral, political, religious, aesthetic, and recreational. A practice will embody its own standards of reasoning and conduct. And when one is engaging in a practice, there is a sense in which the rationality of one's conduct and belief is relative to that practice. A rational judgment in art criticism, for instance, will depend on a kind of trained perception, not merely on ordinary sensitivity to color, shape, and texture.

This kind of embeddedness of judgments in practices might incline some who are impressed with the pervasiveness of practices in our lives to construe rationality as *practice-relative*, in the sense that what is rational is always dependent on the standards intrinsic to a social practice and, to that extent, dependent on the culture that contains the practice.[20] But consider the art critic again. Surely the rationality of aesthetic judgment is, in substantial part, based on prior perceptual and rational capacities. If I cannot discern one color from another, I cannot even respond to aesthetic training of my visual perceptions. Relativity to practices may come in at higher levels, but at the most elemental levels there is far less reason to posit it.

To be sure, if we take the notion of a practice broadly enough and speak, for instance, of our perceptual practice to refer to our pattern of dependence on sense perception in forming non-inferential beliefs, then rationality is relative to practices in the same way it is relative to grounds. But this dependence on sense perception is not only universal, but largely involuntary. If we use the term 'practice', as is standard, only for patterns of behavior that are voluntary and variable from one culture to another, then it is no longer as plausible to call rationality practice-relative.[21]

If rationality is not in general practice-relative, however, the rationality of certain specific beliefs and behaviors is. This latter point goes a long way toward explaining what makes the practice conception plausible. For much of what we believe is associated with a structured domain, such as a branch of science or a practical art; and the same sort of thing holds for much of what we do. These domains often have rules that form a presupposed background of rationality for the beliefs or behavior they govern. Even here, however, the basic sources of justification must operate as usual. One cannot do science or write poetry or play chess without perception and memory. Far from the normative authority of the basic sources being derived from these practices, it essential for that of the more specific standards constitutive of those practices.

Practical rationality is like theoretical rationality here. It is not exhausted by the special standards of rationality characteristic of practices. Quite the contrary: the practices that account for many human differences tend to presuppose the general standards of practical rationality explored in Part II. Just as we cannot learn rules without perception, we cannot acquire or conform to social customs without acting for reasons. Both the acquisition of social practices and the criticism of those who deviate from them presuppose standards of both practical and theoretical reason that seem constant from one practice to another.

We have been exploring rationality *in* a practice. There are also questions about the rationality *of* practices. Even a practice with positive features relative to which certain conduct is, in a practice-relative sense, rational may not itself be rational in the unqualified sense that concerns us. Brutality can be rational as part of certain terrorist practices, and terrorists can be criticized as stupid for letting their natural kindness prevent it. But those practices may themselves not be rational, either instrumentally or intrinsically.

Must we, then, posit a higher practice, a metapractice, to define a perspective from which first-order practices can be appraised? We could speak of almost any unified pattern of responses and discourse as a practice, say, of our perceptual practice and our deductive logical practice. In this wide sense, certain practices *are* required by standards of rationality. But I would stress again that it is not clear that these practices are even voluntary, in the sense that we can control not just how we engage in them but whether we do so. They are also distinct from practices in the familiar sense in being basic to the latter. The distinction is important in part because both the voluntariness of practices in the usual sense and the relativity of their standards of rationality may be wrongly applied to beliefs and desires grounded in more fundamental ways in the experiences and activities—such as introspection and reflection—that ground justified beliefs and rational desires. These patterns are not on a par with practices in the cultural sense. In that standard, cultural sense of 'practice', practices differ from one culture to another in a way the justificatory functions of the basic experiential and rational sources apparently do not.

The objections I have raised against practice relativism must be balanced by at least two points. First, social practices are certainly a source of concepts, beliefs, and modes of thought that profoundly affect what justified beliefs and rational desires we form even directly from the basic sources. As compared with the novice, the art critic may, upon simply seeing a painting, have different visual impressions of it, and certainly different noninferential beliefs about it. Concepts provide a framework within which both percepts and thoughts do their genetic work. The richer the relevant conceptual scheme of the perceiver and thinker, the richer and more interconnected the beliefs and desires that tend to arise from experience of the world or from performance of rewarding activities. Second, social practices are a source of defeaters of justification and rationality. Scientific practices, for instance, yield beliefs or techniques that can override even quite steadfast sensory results.

Both points illustrate a sense in which rationality, justification, and indeed reasonableness as well, are *contextual*. Different contexts may contain different experiences, different conceptual schemes brought to those contexts, different potential defeaters, and indeed different standards for achieving justification or rationality in the light of these special features of the situation. If contextualism about rationality is the view that rationality is, in this way, contextual, it is an affirmation of relativity to grounds and relativity of rational content, and it is perfectly compatible with the theory of rationality developed in this book.[22]

10. OBJECTIVITY AND REALISM IN THE THEORY OF RATIONALITY

Objectivism tends to be closely associated, epistemologically, with the antiskeptical view that there is knowledge and, ontologically, with realism in the sense in which it is taken to require a commitment to "correspondence truth." Objectivism is often contrasted with relativism. The internalist objectivism defended here can (as indicated earlier) be squared with a realist ontology about normative properties and with an accompanying cognitivist, objectivist moral epistemology. I now want to defend further its consistency with the kinds of relativity affirmed in this chapter as characterizing rationality. Even if rational desire, for instance, is grounded in certain characteristics of the experience of its object and is in that (limited) way subjective, it may be that there really are desirable features of experience: that, say, pleasure really is an intrinsic good in virtue of which an enjoyable experience can have objective value. I would reiterate that the epistemic objectivity of judgments of rationality does not entail a realist ontology that posits normative properties as its grounds. It does, however, go well with such an ontology, and I have left the question of realism open.[23]

Despite the popular association of noncognitivism with mere emotivism, the former need not be relativistic in any deep-going way. Suppose noncognitivism is true. Suppose that in saying, for instance, that a desire is rational I simply express *my* positive attitude towards it. There may be, and I may have, good grounds for such attitudes. From a judgment of rationality being an expression of the speaker's attitude rather than an assertion of a proposition, it does not even follow that these grounds are substantially different from the considerations that, on the theory I have proposed, count toward rational desire. When I sincerely assert a proposition, even a simple one about what I see, I also express my belief; this says nothing about its basis or the standards on which it should be judged. And the sorts of considerations that can make it plausible to believe that intrinsically wanting something, say, to listen to Bach, is rational are very much the kinds of things that can ground the rationality of a positive attitude toward this desire.

Although I want to make room for noncognitivism as a position from which at least much of my theory of rationality can be employed, a cognitivist non-skeptical epistemology is more consonant with my view and seems on balance more plausible.[24] Surely we may justifiably believe, and may even know, principles corresponding to the objective standards I have stressed. It is eminently reasonable to maintain—and quite consistent with accepting relativity to grounds—that a belief based on sense experience is justified by that grounding. When a belief that there is a piano before me is based on a vivid and steadfast impression of those distinctive pianistic colors and shapes, surely it is justified. It also seems to me that my justification in holding such an epistemic principle is a priori; but my overall account of rationality does not depend on that position.[25] Even if the justification of epistemic principles is ultimately empirical, it can have the kind of objectivity appropriate for construing rationality as, in turn, objective in the qualified sense I have sketched.

The case of perception may be thought to be too favorable to my account to serve as a good example. Perceptual justification may seem unrepresentatively straightforward and solid. But we have seen that it is not so straightforward, and the literature of skepticism will convince anyone who needs persuasion that, compared with the a priori justification possible for simple logical truths, it is not so clearly solid. It may still be held that practical rationality, compared with even perceptual justification, is fragile and too highly variable to be universal. I have tried to show that although rationality is relative in important respects, this claim is mistaken.

Human experiences may be more nearly alike in the respects relevant to perceptual beliefs, and, thereby, to our beliefs about the world, than in the respects relevant to intrinsic desires. But this difference should not be exaggerated. Is it any less common to dislike being burned when one grasps the handle of a smoking-hot skillet than to believe that there are trees before one when one looks at them in conditions which make an arboreal visual impression as likely as burning makes a painful experience? And is the aversion to being burned any less rational in the former case than the belief that there is a tree before one in the latter case? In many instances, desirability, in the sense implying that it is rational to want to have or to avoid the thing for its own sake, is as clearly indicated by a rewarding or punishing experience as believability, in the sense that implies the rationality of non-inferential belief, is indicated by sensory experience.

Admittedly, there may be masochists who would insist that they like being pained, but there may also be people who refuse to accept the testimony of their senses. Indeed, even masochists have reason, in the painful qualities of the experience, to be averse to being burned; but they might also have reason, in virtue of other qualities of it, to want it. If this conflicting-reasons picture is appropriate, then the role of painful qualities of experience in yielding a ground of rational desire is not disconfirmed by masochism. We can understand it in part on the basis of relativity to grounds and the defeasibility of the reasons they provide.

There are some differences between theoretical and practical reason that I have not indicated, but I believe that none of them undermines the main analogies that I have drawn. Structurally, theoretical and practical reason are strongly parallel. Experiential grounding of rational elements is common to both and explains the relativity of each to the grounds of those elements. This grounding accounts for two quite different and even ostensibly conflicting sides of rationality: its internalism and its objectivity. Its objectivity enables us to formulate some universally applicable standards. Its internalism enables us to account for the possibility of widely differing rational beliefs and desires.

Pluralism appears in both the practical and the theoretical domains, but not in a way that implies normative relativism. We differ in the range and content of our experiences but not, I believe, in the ways in which our experience justifies our beliefs, desires, and, thereby, actions. Rational disagreement is possible and indeed expectable. But this does not imply any relativity of a kind that undermines the possibility of universal objective standards for appraising persons from the point of view of rationality. Relativity to grounds and relativity of content can be accommodated by the well-groundedness account of rationality; genetic relativism, in the causal sense, is no threat to the account and, taken in the normative sense, is mistaken; conceptual relativity poses a challenge to the account, but seems, on analysis, to constitute no insurmountable obstacle; doxastic and status relativisms are mistaken; and perspectival relativity, preferential relativity, practice relativity, and contextual relativity, on their plausible interpretations, may be understood as either species or consequences of one of the sound forms of relativity.

The same sources that make it rational for different people to hold conflicting beliefs and to have disparate desires can make it possible for them to resolve disagreements in rational ways. In sharing the kinds of experiences that, in others, ground beliefs and desires different from our own, we can sometimes come to believe or want the same things they do. Even where consensus is not possible, its unobtainability does not imply normative relativism, nor does it preclude good communication. Often, we can also come to appreciate how and why others might rationally differ from us. The objectivity of the standards of rationality makes this appreciation possible; the internality of its grounds makes the plurality we can thus appreciate natural.

8

GLOBAL RATIONALITY

Beliefs are the basic elements of theoretical rationality. Our beliefs determine our map of the world. Desires are the basic elements of practical
rationality. Our desires determine our itinerary, our destinations in the
world as we see it. These two sides of rationality, the cognitive and the
conative, are structurally parallel. Experience contains the underlying
ground on both sides; belief is their main connective tissue; inferential
relations anchor their higher elements in their grounds. Normatively, the
rationality of beliefs and desires depends on the multifarious experiences
that anchor it. Causally, rational beliefs and desires are also grounded in
those experiences.

Our rational beliefs and rational desires are major elements in our psychology. But we ourselves, as persons, may also be rational or irrational.
How is the global rationality of persons related to the rationality of these
elements?[1] This overall rationality of persons is important in describing
us, in understanding human behavior, and in articulating normative ideals for human life as a whole. Most people want to be rational; perhaps
even more want to avoid being irrational; and for many of us the notion of
a rational person is a guiding ideal.

The notion of a rational person is also essential for understanding many
other notions. Some are even more global, such as the concept of a rational society, others far less so, for instance the concept of a rational strategy.
The notion of a rational person is not, however, basic. Persons are rational in virtue of the rationality of certain of their properties, above all their
psychological properties and their actions. First, I want to present a conception of the rationality of persons that gives due weight to both their

propositional attitudes and their actions. Second, I want to show how the conception can lead to an account of their overall rationality.

1. THE RANGE OF CRITERIA FOR GLOBAL RATIONALITY

Whatever else is important to the rationality of persons, beliefs are. I could not be rational without having some rational beliefs, indeed, some that suitably influence my behavior.[2] If one has enough rational beliefs covering sufficiently pervasive subjects, this counts significantly toward one's rationality; and, of course, having certain kinds of irrational beliefs counts heavily against it. I begin by connecting rationality with justification and reviewing some of the main criteria for justified belief systems.

Justified beliefs are rational; and rational beliefs tend to be justified. But, as we have seen, rationality is both a more permissive and a more global notion than justification. Let me recall four central points. First, an unjustified belief need not be irrational; it may stem from a quite understandable mistake in reasoning. Second, a rational belief need not be justified, even if the person must have *some* degree of justification for it. There are, third, rational beliefs that arise from an exercise of sensibility, as in judging novels; and in some such cases justification is absent and may come, if at all, only later when one gains evidence. Finally, as aesthetic matters often illustrate, whereas one can have divided evidence—with some evidence supporting one proposition and some supporting a second that is obviously incompatible with it—and rationally believe either, this does not hold for justification. If I have good enough ground to be justified in believing a proposition, this precludes my being justified in believing an obvious contrary.[3] Despite all these points, the similarities between justification and rationality are more prominent than their differences, and I shall often consider rational belief on analogy with justified belief.

The diversity of everyday judgments of people's rationality suggests that there are many kinds of criteria for rational belief systems. To begin with, the criteria may be behavioral: certain kinds of actions, such as self-preservational ones, are evidence of cognitive rationality. But we also use non-behavioral criteria, for instance psychological ones such as a belief's accord with sensory experience. Our criteria for rational belief may be internal or external, depending on whether they construe the rationality of beliefs, as determined by factors to which one has access by reflection or introspection.[4] The analogy to justified belief also extends to structural properties: our criteria for a rational belief system may, for instance, be foundationalist or coherentist.

196

Most of the criteria mentioned so far have a common feature. They are *manifestational*, in that they exhibit cognitive rationality as determinable by its manifestations: above all in behavior, in inference, and in the formation of further beliefs. This requirement will seem natural if one takes global rationality to depend on what manifests it, say, actions. It also reflects an important point I have illustrated in many places already: that rationality is very much a kind of responsiveness to reasons and grounds. One might, however, stress *trait-based* criteria instead. The rationality of a belief system is then a matter of cognitive traits, such as good habits of observation and inference and a tendency to get one's beliefs into reflective equilibrium. One might then claim that the rationality of manifestations of these traits, far from being the ground of the rationality of the system, is itself based on these manifestations' reflecting the appropriate traits. This view is an analogue of virtue theory in ethics.[5]

From the perspective of trait-based criteria of rationality, certain behavior and certain individual beliefs count toward a person's rationality, but not *constitutively:* they count indirectly, insofar as they reflect the appropriate traits. The causal language is no accident. The trait-based view takes the actions or states of a person to count toward the overall rationality of the person's belief system only if they are appropriately caused or sustained by that system.[6] But non-causal criteria are sometimes used. A belief system might be considered rational provided that for a suitable proportion of its elements, there *is* an appropriate experiential foundation, whether or not it plays a causal sustaining role. Most of the leading conceptions are causal; but a strong internalist account may be non-causal, at least if accompanied by the view that causal relations are not introspectively accessible.[7]

There is a further division, within both causal and non-causal views. It turns on different judgments concerning, on the one hand, the importance of the route one takes in forming an attitude and, on the other hand, the importance of the basis one has for it, regardless of the route to its formation. The central distinction here is between *process criteria*, which require that rational beliefs be produced, sustained, or in some way backed up by an appropriate process, and *capacity criteria*, which require only that such beliefs be produced, sustained, or backed up by an appropriate capacity, such as a potential to defend them. A process theory sees rationality as a sort of precipitate of an appropriately constrained process; a capacity theory sees it as supportable by appropriate grounds, whether or not they involve an evidential or confirmatory process.

The leading process views impose inferentialist criteria, which demand actual (even if subliminal) inferences to underlie the rationality of rational beliefs (unless these beliefs are foundational).[8] The paradigm of a rational belief would be one formed by obviously valid inference from propositions one rationally believes. The plausibility of this view derives partly from the obvious fact that inference is a case of reasoning, which is in turn associated with rationality and sometimes taken to be the mark of truly rational beings.

Non-inferentialist criteria require some other, usually less elaborate, underlying state, even if they allow that one *can* in principle construct a supporting inference. These, then, are most commonly capacity criteria, though a non-inferentialist could require justificatory processes (such as episodes of awareness) other than inferences. A paradigm of a rational belief of the sort backed by a justificatory capacity is one that is sustained by perception or intuition and could be defended by appeal to its grounds. Asked why I believe David is in the audience, I might say that I can see him—he is simply too bundled up for most others to recognize. Here I appeal to perceptual recognition as a ground.

The causal view of global rationality may or may not impose process criteria. A causal sustaining relation can hold between one belief and a second based on it without the mediation of any process, such as inference. If I know Liz is late, then when the phone rings, I may immediately believe that Liz is calling. If there *is* an unselfconscious inference, the causal view will still take the structural grounding relation between the inferential belief and the underlying premise belief(s) to be causal. This structural inferential grounding relation between beliefs is commonly instantiated by one belief's being based on other beliefs where all of them are dispositionally held and stored in memory; but a causal view in its inferentialist form also takes the relevant inferential connections to be causal.

The non-causal view, which also may or may not impose process criteria, either takes inference to be non-causal or, more plausibly, simply makes the *availability* of inference crucial as backing for rational beliefs. It allows either that they not arise from inference or, where they do, that the inferential process be only their rational ground as opposed to their causal basis. Consider a non-causal, inferentialist, coherentist capacity theory. It could allow that one have a non-inferential rational belief; but, as a capacity view, it would require that one be *able* to infer its propositional object from some suitable set of premises one believes.

The most plausible criteria for a rational belief system will not be merely causal or wholly "descriptive" but also normative. Even if the property of having a rational system of beliefs is grounded in one's natural properties, it is itself a positive normative property, in a sense implying at least that having the property is intrinsically good or is a state that one ought to be in. It might be argued that the rationality of a belief system is just a matter of fact of the kind ascertainable by purely scientific procedures.[9] Consider reliabilism about justification: a rational belief system would be roughly one produced or sustained by belief-producing processes such that a large proportion of the beliefs they produce are true. Whether such a "descriptivist" account of rationality can succeed seems doubtful but may be left open from the point of view of the main position of this book.

As all this suggests, criteria of rationality may also be relativistic, in any of the senses described in Chapter 7, or non-relativistic. The main kinds of relativism about rationality pertinent here are conceptual relativism, which denies that there is a univocal concept of rationality, and status relativism, which denies the objectivity of the notion of a rational belief system. The reasons for taking the rationality of persons to be relative to prevailing cognitive practices are perhaps better than those for taking the rationality of individual beliefs to be so. Above all, a rational person might be supposed to follow such practices. There is some truth in this idea; but what was said about relativity in Chapter 7, including the endorsement of relativity to grounds, should accommodate that truth. I see no need to take the concept of a rational belief system, or indeed of a rational person, to be relative to prevailing cognitive practices in any *further* respect.

There are many other kinds of criteria for a rational belief system, but those cited give us much to work with. Moreover, the criteria can apparently be applied to all the other propositional attitudes. Let me illustrate this with respect to desires, which, like beliefs, are fundamental in understanding global rationality.[10]

2. DESIRE, BELIEF, AND WILL

We have seen that desires are not only capable of rationality and irrationality but can also stand to other desires in a close counterpart of inferential relations. Wanting one thing for the sake of another is much like believing one thing on the basis of another. If I want to read a novel for diversion, my wanting this effect is a basis of my desire to read it and is analogous to a belief of a premise, where this belief grounds my believing a conclusion I infer from that premise; and just as I in some way take a premise to support a proposition I infer from it, I take the diversion the novel affords as a reason (thus as support) for my reading it.

On the basis of this parallel between wanting and believing, we can imagine both internalist and externalist criteria for the rationality of wants. Internalists may argue that wants are rational by virtue of such internal criteria as the person's justifiably believing their realization to be pleasurable; externalists might argue that wants are rational by virtue of their satisfaction's *actually* contributing to some appropriate end. If foundationalist and coherentist criteria, as well as internalist and externalist criteria, apply to wants, surely the other criteria I have sketched, for instance process and capacity criteria, may also be applied to them.

It is widely thought that the rationality of actions derives from that of the beliefs and wants that explain actions, or at least that the rationality of action is a matter of facts about the agent's beliefs and wants: the former as sources of subjective probability, the latter as sources of subjective values. For instance, on a plausible interpretation of the maximization of expected utility view, the subjective utility of my reading the novel is determined by how much I want the consequences I take it to have; the subjective probabilities of such outcomes are determined by my beliefs, for instance in terms of probabilities I would assign to the outcomes; and the overall subjective utility of the action is determined by adding the products obtained by multiplying each of these values by its subjective probability.

Like most views of rationality, the maximization of expected utility view of rationality is usually combined with a conception of belief that takes it to arise non-voluntarily. But it may also be developed in the context of an opposing conception of belief associated both with Descartes in particular and with some philosophers who stress radical freedom as central for rational persons. I refer to doxastic voluntarism, roughly the view that in at least a significant range of cases, belief formation can be accomplished at will. In some versions (including perhaps Descartes's) the paradigm of a justified belief is one formed by appropriately choosing to believe.[11] On this view, although beliefs themselves need not be taken to be actions, accepting propositions commonly is action, and rational beliefs are either those chosen in the light of suitable grounds—call these beliefs rational in the primary sense—or such that one would so choose them if one were able to contemplate the grounds one actually has for them in a situation in which one could freely choose whether or not to believe the relevant proposition. It would take a great deal of space to assess doxastic voluntarism in detail. All I can do here is briefly amplify some points made in Chapter 5.[12]

Unless it is restricted to a small range of beliefs, doxastic voluntarism misconceives belief formation. Do we ever choose *to believe*, as opposed, say, to choosing to bring it about *that* we believe? People do say such things as 'You choose not to believe his claim; I choose to believe it', or 'You accept it, and I do not'. But in most such cases the choice is directed to *conduct:* you will, for instance, proceed as if he were innocent; I will not. There are also cases in which one is not sure whether a proposition is true and can choose to resist it—say, to go on wondering—or to stop questioning and to proceed as if it is in fact true. Here, too, what one actually chooses is not *to believe* but to do something that typically inhibits, supports, or produces belief formation.[13]

Suppose one can choose, directly, to believe propositions, and thereby come to believe them, as we can choose to raise our hands. Surely we must then (as Descartes probably saw) distinguish rational and irrational, justified and unjustified, choices. And it seems plain that the only basis of assessment here is the same kind as for other actions: our beliefs and wants. One may object that when, for instance, I am vividly aware of what looks like paper, I may transcend the influence of my antecedent wants and beliefs and rationally choose to believe there is paper before me. But if I am really rational and free in choosing, do I not need to *note* (or, say, realize) that I am aware of such a thing, and take account of this in choosing? If, however, I have no *want* (or reason to want) to take account of my experience in choosing beliefs, why should I choose to believe there is paper before me? On the other hand, if I do want this, why is that want a guide to rational belief formation? Is it brute, or is it justified by my *belief* that experience is my best guide? But how would that belief be justified?

The problem, then, is (partly) this: a choice (or an acceptance) is a good basis of rational belief only if it is itself rational or meets an appropriate normative standard; but every appropriate standard seems to presuppose some independent criterion of rational belief. If we lacked such a criterion and had to presuppose that a rational belief is one rationally chosen, then in order to choose a belief rationally, we would have had to choose a belief to guide the choice; and that belief would have to be rational, and hence rationally chosen, in order to play its proper guiding role. The result is a vicious regress: to choose a belief rationally we must already have a rational belief, which in turn must have been rationally chosen.

It appears that the only promising criteria for rationally choosing (directly) to believe, where this is understood as implying that the belief so chosen is thereby rational, depend on the standard experiential criteria for a belief's being rationally held. Thus, even if there should be such a thing as choosing to believe—as opposed to causing oneself, by some indirect means, to form a belief—determining criteria for rationality in such choices presupposes, and cannot replace, criteria for appraising the rationality of beliefs considered as (roughly speaking) dispositional properties of persons. Those criteria, I have argued, are the kind that go with good cognitive grounding, which, in turn, requires that sensory experience play a major role.

Apart from a radically subjectivist notion of reality, this is how we should want things. If our beliefs are to provide our map of reality, they should discriminatively respond to the reality they are to reveal. Without a good map, we cannot expect to reach our destinations; and to draw a good map, we do not choose beliefs for the purpose of writing in the routings. Instead, we survey the territory to be charted and record the information that perception reveals. If our desires determined the map without our relying on that information, they would undermine their own satisfaction. It is hard enough to get what we want with a realistic map; we would at best find it even more difficult if our only routes were determined in the subjectivistic way to which a thorough-going voluntarism seems committed.

3. THE RATIONALITY OF ATTITUDES AND EMOTIONS

What we have seen in this chapter, and indeed in this book as a whole, is that propositional attitudes are the basic elements that underlie rational actions and that both rational propositional attitudes and rational actions are central in the rationality of persons. I have not so far directly discussed either emotions or attitudes other than belief and desire. All of these must be accommodated in any comprehensive account of the rationality of persons.

A case can be made that the basic constituents of our attitudes are beliefs and desires. For instance, attitudes of approval and disapproval toward other people seem to be complexes of one's evaluative beliefs regarding them and desires appropriately connected with those beliefs.[14] If attitudes are so constituted, it should be clear that their rationality is determined by that of their constituent beliefs and desires. My approving of an appointment, for instance, is rational provided that both my belief that the candidate was (say) best for the job and my desires connected with this belief are rational. No doubt the belief is the more important element for appraising the rationality of the approving attitude, and it largely determines both what the associated desires are and whether they are rational. But there could be a disparity between belief and desire: I might, even with the belief that the candidate is best, unreasonably want to delay the appointment, and this desire could adversely affect the rationality of my overall attitude.

The emotions, however, are apparently not constituted by beliefs and desires, in part because in some cases emotions have phenomenal aspects not implied by beliefs or desires. One cannot be terrified or embarrassed or indignant without feeling something or other, even if one can perhaps be proud of someone without the feelings that sometimes go with pride. Fortunately, we do not need a detailed conception of the emotions here.[15] It is widely agreed that they have cognitive elements and that these are crucial for their rationality. Their conative elements also play a part in their rationality. Their affective elements, moreover, such as the feelings of trepidation that go with some fears, may, on the basis of the person's beliefs and desires—and indeed mainly on the basis of their rationality—count for or against the rationality of both the emotion they are part of and the person who experiences them. Trepidation is not voluntary action and is neither rational nor irrational; but it is to some degree voluntarily suppressible, and my trepidation can thus count against my rationality if I am quite irrational in thinking the object I fear is dangerous or if the degree of my trepidation is very high relative to my assessment of minimal danger.

Emotions are especially prone to irrationality—or at least to deficiency in rationality—when they are grounded in irrational beliefs, as indignation might be grounded in an irrational belief that a friend has wronged one. Moreover, like attitudes, they are capable of being irrational when a constituent desire is inappropriate to them in either content or strength. Indignation could lead one to want to shoot a person who, having delayed one's viewing of a film, plainly deserves at most a chiding. This is a desire inappropriate to what one's beliefs are—or should be. Indignation could also, and more likely, lead one to want so passionately to chide that for a time one cannot think of much else. This would be an unduly strong desire. Such a desire might cause one to do the chiding at a highly inappropriate time. That would be an irrational action.

If emotion is to be fully understood, it must be distinguished from feeling, even the kind characteristic of it. For instance, a feeling not unlike that of anger commonly goes with resentment, though it is not equivalent to (occurrent) anger. This feeling is not constituted by cognitive and motivational elements, but can cause their formation. One might feel disturbed by an action and in part for that reason become resentful about it; or a feeling of sadness on hearing a musical passage can make one sad. Both feelings may play an evidential role: the former can be a sensitive response indicating that one has been wronged; the latter can warrant a view about the musical passage. The perceptions that in principle could more directly evoke or justify beliefs may first arouse an affective response. People differ in how they respond to similar evidences of phenomena to which emotions such as anger or jealousy or indignation are appropriate. In some, feeling is often first, and in some it may be first on one occasion, second on another, and absent altogether on a third.

Feelings can be responses to experience in something like the elemental way intrinsic desires commonly are. Feelings of the kind in question— feelings *of* as opposed to propositional feelings, feelings *that*—though not constituted of desires or beliefs, may produce and even ground them; and emotional feelings, the kind characteristic of an emotion (and there apparently are such feelings for at least most emotions), can produce the emotion in question, just as they can be produced by beliefs or desires. A feeling of anger can produce the full-blooded phenomenon and may contribute to (even if it does not suffice for) its justification. A belief that one person has cheated another can both produce and justify anger or angry feelings. But just as the experiences grounding a rational intrinsic desire are not rational or irrational, the kinds of non-propositional, occurrent feelings that play a similar experiential role are not. A tendency to have them at inappropriate times may bear on rationality, though if they do not tend to produce the corresponding emotions it may bear more on psychological well-being. But that is a different matter.[16]

Far more could be said about attitudes, emotions, and feelings, but enough has been said to suggest how both the rationality of attitudes and emotions and also their bearing on the rationality of persons can be accounted for by a theory in which the rationality of propositional attitudes, conceived in the experientialist way described in this book, is the basic ground of the rationality of persons. The central question is how the constituent beliefs and desires, and the affective elements, belonging to attitudes are to be appraised and how our attitudes and emotions weigh in an overall account of our rationality. There is no formula for determining this, but enough has been said to indicate how it can be determined on the kind of well-groundedness, reasons-responsiveness theory of rationality I have developed. This is not to imply that a rational person must, at all times, *have* attitudes or emotions. Life would be impoverished without them. But emotional and attitudinal poverty—in the absence of experiences that in some sense require them—is not necessarily a deficiency in rationality, even if it bespeaks truncated humanity and indicates limitations in the quality of rational life. Given that we have emotions and affective attitudes, however, they cannot be ignored in appraising our rationality.[17] A beautiful garden need not have every kind of flower, and it can be lovely with a small selection. But those it does have must in themselves possess certain fine qualities, and these must be related to the other flowers in a way that sustains the beauty of the whole. It is similar with global rationality.

4. STRUCTURAL FEATURES OF GLOBAL RATIONALITY

If actions and propositional attitudes are as important as I think they are in understanding the rationality of persons, we should be able to describe, in psychological and epistemic terms, some structural features of a rational person. I begin with belief, and I assume a moderately foundationalist (capacity) view of rational belief, the kind of view outlined in Part I. Four ideas are central in a plausible structural view of rational belief. If one has any rational beliefs, then first, the structure of one's body of rational beliefs is foundational; second, the rationality of the foundational beliefs is, at least typically, defeasible; third, the inferential transmission of rationality, whether from foundations to superstructure or within the superstructure, may or may not be deductive; and fourth, non-foundationally rational beliefs need not derive all of their rationality from the foundational ones, but only enough so that they would remain rational if (other things being equal) any other sources of their rationality that may exist (such as coherence) were eliminated.

As we have seen, in a typical case, a person will have a foundation of non-inferential beliefs rational on the basis of experience or reason and a vast superstructure of beliefs based on them, directly or indirectly: directly if they are based just on foundationally rational beliefs, indirectly if their connection to foundational ones is by an inferential chain with an intermediate conclusion. In either case, on the most plausible foundational theories, there is a causal grounding relation such that foundational beliefs play at least a partial sustaining role with respect to superstructure beliefs.

Many rational beliefs are, to be sure, directly rational by virtue of grounding in memory. Moreover, there need not be inferential processes to mediate between foundations and superstructure even where rationality is transmitted by a psychologically realized inferential relation. On the structural, anti-intellectualist view in question, foundational grounding is possible without cluttering consciousness with inferential, observational, or even recollective processes. A rational belief, on the proposed view, is one that is well-grounded; and since normal rational persons have some rational beliefs, they have some rational foundational beliefs.[18]

The same kind of structural thesis applies to desires and values, and there is reason to think that a foundationalist view can also account for the rationality of the other propositional attitudes. Indeed, even actions can be so conceived: on the reasonable assumption that every intentional action is grounded in some desire, all intentional actions can be traced to some intrinsic desire. This is what in Chapter 3 is called the behavioral groundedness view, a view about our psychological structure apparently held by Aristotle and by philosophers as different as Hume and Kant.[19] One would have not only a psychological but a *normative* behavioral groundedness view if one added that (apart from overdetermination, at least) the rationality of actions depends on that of their foundational want(s). This view is confirmed by many examples and arguments given in earlier chapters.

If the normative behavioral groundedness view is correct, the implications for the notion of a rational person are profound. For actions are the only elements other than propositional attitudes and emotions that are clearly crucial in judging a person's rationality. If the rationality of actions is, like that of emotions, derivative from that of propositional attitudes, then the latter are the primary criteria for global rationality. It is not enough, however, that a reasonable proportion of the beliefs and desires one has be rational. One might *also* need some particular kinds, depending on one's experience and capacities, perhaps including some *framework beliefs*, such as beliefs of some simple logical and empirical truths and procedural beliefs to the effect that one should not judge a population by members of it that do not constitute a fair sample.[20] This kind of belief guides much of our intellectual life.

At least as important as framework beliefs are *response tendencies*, both theoretical and practical. If I have perceptual experiences to which I do not appropriately respond, for instance in failing to believe that people are speaking to me when this is utterly plain and I have no sensory deficiency or good reason to doubt it, this is a defect in rationality. If I am pained and form no desire to be free of the pain, again something is amiss, this time with my practical rationality.[21] The rationality of persons is determined not only by that of their propositional attitudes but also by their having an appropriate set of such attitudes (and perhaps emotions as well) relative to their experience and capacities. Rational persons must respond to their experience by acquiring certain attitudes, and certain dispositions to form them, appropriately grounded in it.

The relations among propositional attitudes are important because it might be possible for someone whose beliefs and desires are all rational to lack tendencies to draw on them in the appropriate ways, for instance tendencies to combine believed propositions into a rational outlook, to bring instrumental beliefs to bear in satisfying desires, and to try to harmonize the strengths of one's desires with one's beliefs about the probabilities of their joint satisfaction. If all propositional attitudes are combinations of beliefs and wants, further simplification would be possible. Such an analysis—or at least one adequate to capture the aspects of the attitudes relevant to their rationality—seems to be far from obviously impossible, but I do not assume it and will consider other attitudes besides believing and wanting.

There is a difficulty for the account of rationality just sketched. We have already noted that rationality can be defeated by dependence on unwarranted inference. Suppose that one makes many such inferences, yet lacks a *belief* that they are warranted. It might appear that the account must (implausibly) take this lack of self-critical cognition to be excusatory, since there is no unjustified or even false belief on which to pin the prima facie irrationality. Should we say, then, that one must at least implicitly believe the principles of inferences one uses? I think not. This intellectualist position seems even less plausible if we distinguish between dispositional beliefs and dispositions to believe. It is then reasonable to argue that one need only be disposed to believe the principles instantiated by one's typical inferences.[22] The solution to the problem, then, must lie elsewhere.

My suggestion is this. Surely the rationality of my belief of some proposition can be defeated by my simply *having* justification for an incompatible proposition. I need not actually believe that proposition, hence need not have such justification through a belief. For one thing, given an experience, say, of a cool breeze, I might have justification for believing that there is a cool breeze. This is another reason that we cannot take global rationality to be based wholly on *actual* propositional attitudes. Indeed, that conclusion is to be expected in the light of the importance of response tendencies for rationality. As illustrated earlier, there are times when *lacking* a belief or desire indicates a deficiency in rationality.

The significance of the point that global rationality is not based wholly on actual propositional attitudes should not be exaggerated. In both cases of irrationality not due to actual beliefs, there is a propositional attitude which the person *would* be rational (or not rational) in holding: given what I know and am justified in believing, I (rationally) ought not to believe the relevant inference principle, and ought to believe the incompatible proposition (or at least that it is probably true). Perhaps, then, we may still say that global rationality is grounded at least *indirectly* in a combination of those (properly interrelated) propositional attitudes one holds *and* one's dispositions to hold such attitudes in the suggested rational ways.

5. INTEGRATION AND COHERENCE

Even if this revised combination-of-sources thesis is true, it leaves us a long way from an account of the structure of rationality in persons. It is not as though one could be rational only if *all* one's propositional attitudes are rational. A few that are irrational may pose no threat to one's overall rationality, particularly if their influence on one is minor. This latter point is crucial: some beliefs, wants, and other attitudes are far more important than others for global rationality. A weak, readily eliminated irrational belief that one can win a tennis game counts little against one's rationality compared with a strong, entrenched belief based on the gambler's fallacy, for instance that a double six is almost certain on the next toss.

The difficulty here is better understood in the light of the question whether there are *composition principles* that enable us to determine the rationality of a person given the rationality of the person's propositional attitudes. There seem to be at least no simple ones; and even determining focal rationality is often very difficult. Both points indicate why it is at best misleading to say that rationality is *rule-governed*. There are rules of inference, theoretical and practical, whose blatant violation counts against rationality; but often it is only after we discern how a belief, desire, or action is rational in the light of its grounds that we can frame any generalization plausibly considered a rule.[23] Still, there are some very general principles we should note. The basic idea can be seen from a sketch of some that apply to belief.

Both the *strength* and the *entrenchment* of a belief are relevant to its contribution to global rationality. Strength is roughly degree of conviction; entrenchment is roughly degree of resistance to elimination. Other things equal, the stronger or more entrenched a belief (or other propositional attitude) is, the greater its significance for one's overall rationality. If it is rational, then its strength counts more in a positive way; if irrational, that counts more in a negative way. This is in part because we are more likely to act on, or to have other propositional attitudes stem from, a stronger belief; and if the belief is entrenched, these things are more likely to occur. The stronger an entrenched desire to avoid crossing shadows, the more it tends to count against the rationality of its possessor. Moreover, the strength and entrenchment of such elements, say, desires regarding the welfare of others and beliefs about their rights, to some degree determine how much they are a part of one's *nature*. Insofar as rationality is like a virtue concept, we might expect that just as the more a virtue of character is part of our nature, the more it counts toward our excellence, the more an element that contributes to global rationality is part of our nature, the more it adds to our rationality. It is similar for elements that detract from global rationality.

Strength and entrenchment connect with a third variable: *scope*, roughly the variety of significantly different topics on which the belief bears. The rationality of a belief about persons in general is, other things equal, more important for one's rationality than that of a belief about one particular person. Still another variable is psychological *connectedness*, roughly the number of other propositional attitudes and potential behaviors likely to be affected by the belief, for instance eliminated if it is lost. Other things equal, the greater the scope or psychological connectedness of a belief, the greater its importance for global rationality. This principle suggests one of the ways in which the notion of global rationality is organic. It is more a matter of relationships than of a totality of atomistic quantities.

Two further kinds of variables are suggested by the well-groundedness, reasons-responsiveness conception of global rationality. They are easiest to see for the case of belief, though there are analogues for the other propositional attitudes. First (as suggested at several earlier points), in a rational person there is a certain *fit* between experience and belief and between reflection and belief. If I am looking in the direction of unobscured white paper in normal light, I should experience white and either believe there is white paper before me or at least be disposed to believe it. This example suggests a criterion of *experiential harmony*, calling for a proper relation between beliefs and experiences relevant to them. Similarly, if I am considering an obviously valid syllogism, I should either believe or be disposed to believe that its conclusion follows from its premises. Here we see a criterion of *intellective harmony*, calling for a proper relation between the content of the intellectual field and beliefs appropriate to that content.

A rational person, then, responds to both the sensory and the intellectual contents of experience. No simple set of principles captures these response tendencies. A single sensory experience warrants many beliefs; and from any given proposition many others can be easily seen to follow. But for a huge range of cases we are far from ignorant in deciding what kinds of beliefs are appropriate to rational persons in response to experience and thought.[24]

There is a range of principles here, but the most general one is that overall rationality demands an appropriate fit between experience and beliefs (or dispositions to believe) and that, other things equal, an improper fit counts significantly against the person's rationality. The idea can be seen through a simple example. There are sound epistemic principles saying such things as that (assuming a grasp of the relevant concepts) if one has a clear impression of green grass, one is (prima facie) justified in believing that there is something green before one. The belief system of a rational person must be in certain ways harmonious with principles like this. A person who has the relevant impression and is not even disposed to believe the justified proposition is not properly responding to perceptual grounds. This kind of disharmony between such sound epistemic principles and cognition is one sign of deficiency in rationality.

Another important variable that should be taken into account is *integration:* a kind of unity in the entire system of propositional attitudes. Other things equal, the greater the unity, the more rational the person. Consider beliefs first. The simplest kind of unity in the belief system—and perhaps the philosopher's favorite—is axiomatic. As we are actually structured, however, there is most likely to be a framework of beliefs, some general and some singular, which divide into foundations and superstructure in such a way that at least many of those with the greatest unifying and explanatory power are, unlike axioms, *not* foundational. Some of the unifying beliefs are, for instance, scientific. Others concern the nature of persons. Still others concern ourselves: our past, our plans, or our values.

Integration is a kind of coherence, and here coherence does far more normative work than in the contexts where it is commonly appealed to, such as the justification of belief. Integration is a paradigm of coherence both among propositional attitudes and among them and experiences; it illustrates unifying threads of both causal and intellectual kinds. The status of coherence as a criterion of rationality does not, however, depend on epistemological coherentism. It is indeed partly understood in terms of the idea that beliefs non-inferentially supported by a common experience tend to receive a measure of integration from that shared basis. The integration is often explanatory as well as evidential: the same experience or belief can both explain why one holds a set of beliefs and justify them.

Now consider other propositional attitudes. Certain kinds of wants can help to unify the motivational system. Consider wanting to realize one's human capacities. Given various beliefs about how one can do so, this want will produce many desires that are more specific. Like beliefs, wants generate more of their kind given certain behavioral connecting beliefs—beliefs to the effect that by doing a certain thing one will (or may) achieve the desired object. If I want certain information, believing it is in the library tends to make me want to go there. Rational persons who want the end also tend to want the (believed) means.

Moreover, beliefs and wants may be mutually integrated, as where one both intrinsically wants to realize one's human capacities and believes that this is intrinsically good. Some philosophers (perhaps Aquinas) have held that one wants things only under the aspect of the good; other philosophers have held that if one believes that something one can achieve is intrinsically good, one must want it. I have not endorsed either view, but I suggest that part of what makes both plausible is that intrinsically wanting something and believing it intrinsically good *are* normally a well-integrated pair and, in rational persons, tend to occur together. In addition, desires quite diverse in content can be unified by beliefs to the effect that a single action will satisfy them all. Integration, then, is possible both within any system of propositional attitudes and among the systems. Each kind of integration counts toward global rationality; and without some degree of integration, it is doubtful whether a person could be rational.

6. VOLUNTARINESS AND AUTONOMY

Some criteria for global rationality are in a sense *functional*, bearing on how the mind works rather than on its compositional properties. I have already stressed reasoning capacities. A quite different aspect of our functioning that may be considered essential for rationality, at least in conduct, is free- dom. But suppose I am manipulated in such a way that I neither act freely nor even have, through my thoughts, the normal influence on what I want and value. I can behave rationally in certain ways, being perhaps very adept at achieving my (imposed) ends. Can I, however, be a rational person? Much depends on how the case is specified. As a prisoner subjected to torture and brainwashing, I might still remain rational. For example, I might rationally want to avoid pain, and rationally believe that writing a propaganda speech will achieve this. My writing it, though compelled, may still be rational; and even if it is compelled, I may control *how* I do it and may, to indicate my anger, fuse participles and split infinitives in alternate paragraphs. Freedom, then, is not necessary for the rationality of an ac- tion. This point does not preclude that some degree of it may be in some way necessary for at least the highest degree of global rationality.

There is, moreover, a sense in which one can do voluntarily what one is compelled to do, and this may indicate a kind of voluntariness that is more plausibly taken to express a functional constraint on rationality, at least for action. Even when I am acting under compulsion in such a way that, in the ordinary sense, I cannot do otherwise, I may be acting rationally in fulfilling my aim, say, to make my life as good as I can. I might be a little like the child in Dylan Thomas's "Fern Hill": "Time held me green and dying, though I sang in my chains like the sea."

Suppose, however, that demonic neurosurgeons so manipulate my brain that no matter what my natural desires are, and no matter what beliefs I have to the effect that I should not do a certain thing, I do it, and do it *because* of the wants and beliefs they have induced, such as wanting to pro- pagandize for their cause. In effect, they step up the motivational power and the influence of the induced want and belief so much that these bring about the action, in what *looks* like the normal motivated way, no matter what else I want and, let us assume, with a degree of motivation unaffected in strength by any counter-wants I may have. Here, although my conduct is determined by reasons I have for it, they are not integrated into my motivational system: they are immune to the counter-influence of my other wants and beliefs, which cannot overturn or, as I am describing the case, even weaken, their tendency to cause my action. Here I am reduced to a spectator of my own behavior. I have lost not only my freedom but my *autonomy*,[25] roughly, my self-governing power to bring reasons to bear in directing my conduct and influencing my propositional attitudes. I do not act rationally, for my action is not even minimally under the control of my system of reasons. It is not voluntary even in the way my writing a propaganda speech to avoid torture can be. I do not act *for* the reasons I have; they do not function as grounds but are instead means by which I am forced to do what I do.

To be sure, I might still have second-order desires not to have my (first-order) desires manipulated, or (especially if I have no inkling that I am being manipulated) second-order desires to be rid of my propagandistic desires. But second-order desires too can be manipulated, and a clever enough manipulator would exploit this vulnerability. The point, however, is not that my second-order beliefs and wants are or might be manipulated. Second-order beliefs are a significant variable, but their manipulation is not decisive in undermining my autonomy,[26] nor does my case require their manipulation. What seems crucial is that my thoughts and wants relevant to my own compelled actions are deprived of significant influence on what I do. I am more an instrument of my manipulators than an agent.

Similar points hold for beliefs and other propositional attitudes. If I am right about the relevant cases of maximal compulsion, then a measure of autonomy may be necessary, not only for the rationality of actions and propositional attitudes but for global rationality: rational persons must apparently be able at least to influence, even if not to overturn, their own tendencies to act, believe, and desire. This can hold even when they are not free. Freedom requires the possibility of *alternative action;* autonomy requires, above all, the possible influence of *alternative reasons* and can survive even when freedom is undermined.[27]

Intuitively, a being in whom reason lacks this minimal control—which is a matter of one's reasons' having an adequate influence on one's behavior—is not rational, even if we need not ascribe irrationality (I am as usual taking rationality to be consonance with reason rather than merely the absence of irrationality). Without some degree of autonomy, a creature may have *intelligence* and may act *efficiently;* but it cannot be rational or act rationally. It can plot, but not deliberate; it can monitor and adjust its aim, but not its motives. Some degree of autonomy, then, behavioral, cognitive, and motivational, is required for global rationality, and, other things equal, the more autonomous a person, the more rational.

By implication, these points about autonomy, together with much of what is said earlier in the chapter, reveal something very broad: the importance of a capacity to do and appropriately respond to theoretical and practical reasoning. It is not that a rational person as such must engage in these, though it is unimaginable that a rational person going through life as we know it would not do so quite often. The point is that to be unable to engage in and respond to them is to be unable to realize, in a process of reasoning, the connections between grounds and what they imply; these connections are crucial for the transmission of rationality from foundations to superstructure. The connections can be and sometimes are achieved "automatically," without reasoning; but to be unable to do such reasoning is to lack an important element in rationality. It would be as if I could read music and sing it in key, but could not hear it, even in my mind's ear. A momentary existence might afford a rational person no occasion for reasoning; a normal existence requires it regularly. A capacity to do and respond to it is essential for global rationality. How well one exercises this capacity is an important element in determining how rational one is.

7. SUBSTANTIVE ELEMENTS IN RATIONALITY

So far in this chapter, little has been said about what, if anything, a rational person must believe, want, or do, apart from what is implicit in believing principles of logic. A structural account of rationality does not require any specific beliefs, actions, or desires, and I have so far left largely open what sorts of beliefs and actions might be expected in a rational person with a normal range of experiences. What is the range of non-formal, substantive constraints on rationality?

We have seen some (non-formal) inductive constraints. Even Hume said that "none but a fool or a madman will ever pretend to dispute the authority of experience," though he also treated induction as if it were mere inference that did not represent patterns deserving to be considered reasoning.[28] Whatever his commitment to skepticism, his working notion of rationality (whether or not he would use that term for the positive status he was describing) implies an epistemically authoritative role for experience. But suppose we go beyond this general authority and beyond logic broadly conceived. Must a rational person believe or presuppose non-logical principles, or have any definite aims? And are there any external, say, social, criteria? Let us start with the last case.

One might think there are social constraints on rationality. Is not someone who is completely out of touch with what everyone else believes irrational? This does not hold of necessity. Experience might justify different beliefs: I could be the sole victim of demonic manipulation that makes my behavior eminently rational given my vivid hallucinations. Granted, certain kinds of deviance provide good reason to consider a person irration-

213

al. But deviance in action or in (empirical) belief alone does not entail irrationality and is only a derivative criterion for judging rationality. Apart from knowing why someone is deviant, we may not be able to tell the difference between madness and genius.

Similar points hold for factual constraints on rationality, at least regarding propositions about the external world. No matter how strange my beliefs about the world, they may, relative to my experience, still be eminently rational. If one's beliefs do not accord with one's *own* experience and reflection, this counts against one's rationality; but the relevant standard here, experiential harmony, is neither factual in an ordinary sense, nor external, nor behavioral.

Quite as justified belief need not be knowledge, rational action need not be *successful;* and for realists about value and desirability, rational valuations and rational wants need not be "correct," and similarly for the other propositional attitudes. Just as one can rationally believe a falsehood or rationally seek a goal by insufficient means, one can rationally value or have rational desire for something, such as a drug-induced experience, that turns out to be worthless. External normative criteria *do* apply to the elements that admit of rationality; the point is that such elements can be rational without satisfying those external criteria.

Normative elements can even be analogous to justified true belief that is not knowledge. Suppose I am given a hallucinogen but luckily hallucinate a fine sonata I have never heard. Suppose further that the technician in charge uses a random procedure to determine whether I "hear" a good performance rather than a bad one. I may now value something—hearing this fine sonata—that *is* valuable and indeed value it *for* the desirability characteristics it has that make it valuable, yet because I have only hallucinated those characteristics and am only defectively acquainted with them so far as this sonata is concerned, I am lucky to have a correct valuation, in the way one is lucky to have a true belief when, at ten after ten, one looks at one's normally accurate clock to determine the time and, unaware that it stopped at that time twelve hours ago, forms a true belief that it is ten after ten. Here one has justified true belief but not knowledge. We might say that the analogous rational but only fortuitously correct valuation is not *sound.*

Perhaps the best way to approach the question whether there are (nonlogical) substantive criteria of rationality is to recall the controversy over the status of practical reason. Consider the view that it is purely instrumental. It implies that practically rational persons are simply those who, relative to their beliefs, efficiently seek realization of their desires. Practical reason, then, is not as such subject to substantive constraints. This view was

214

examined and rejected in Chapter 5. The opposing, objectivist view, which credits reason with yielding substantive goals, is found in Aristotle and (at least in some passages) in Kant. For objectivists, there are goals that rational persons ought to pursue. Thus, non-instrumental motives can be rational when they are directed toward those goals. There is more to motivate us, and to provide a standard of rational conduct, than what we actually desire; there is something for which instrumentalism apparently leaves no place: what is (intrinsically) *desirable.* Let us explore this objectivist position further by first considering Aristotle's view.

8. THE SUBSTANTIVE LATITUDE OF THE CONCEPT OF HAPPINESS

I believe that Aristotle was mainly right in treating happiness as intrinsically good and central in the life of rational agents. He sometimes speaks, however, as if contemplation were the only genuine happiness, and I cannot accept his view so interpreted.[29] But I share his conception of happiness as, at least for paradigm cases, an activity concept: happiness occurs, above all, in virtue of one's doing something in a certain way, with something like enjoyment or in a way that is rewarding. Passive experience can also provide a measure of happiness. But it is not clear that a happy *life* could center only on such passive pleasures.

There is (as Chapter 4 stressed) a kind of zest that tends to mark doing something with pleasure, and by implication to characterize some kinds of happiness in doing something; but it falls short of being a defining property of either pleasure or happiness. This zest is difficult to characterize phenomenologically, but reflection on, say, the pleasures of a cool swim or of a lively conversation, indicates the sort of thing it is. Happiness in doing something, and certainly pleasure in doing it so far as this is different, do not reduce to doing it in a way that counts as fulfilling an intrinsic desire to do it. That is compatible with doing a thing quite without enjoyment. If everything one does yields a sense of fulfilling such desires, perhaps one could be happy *with* one's life. But this approbative, attitudinal sense of 'happiness' suggests mere satisfaction more than the kind of hedonically positive, and often zesty, response that largely makes happiness a basic human end. One could, through certain kinds of errors and imbalances in one's appraisal, be happy with one's life without being happy *in* it.

In any case, it is plausible to take, as one substantive principle of rationality, the idea that rational persons (with some degree of experience of happiness) want their own happiness, under some appropriate description and for its own sake. Call this the *eudaemonistic principle.* It reflects much of what is plausible in the view that it is rational to seek one's self-interest, but is free of the egoistic tenor of that view. One may seek one's happiness in that of others (as I believe Aristotle's eudaemonism allows up to a point). Even here, one need not want or seek one's happiness under that altruistic description. The principle is schematic and requires only that one want things *for* qualities in virtue of which one sees their attainment (under some description) as yielding happiness. The specific goal varies with the person and the kind of thing so wanted.

It is not easy to argue for this principle. There are at least two cases to be considered: that of present happiness—roughly, enjoyment—and that of prospective happiness—roughly, the kind anticipated from something one looks forward to. First, imagine someone's enjoying something, yet denying intrinsically wanting to do it, or claiming to want to do it *only* as a means. These claims seem intelligible,[30] but are prima facie far from being rational. It is surely not rational to fail to want intrinsically (to some degree) to do what one is enjoying doing (even if one quite rationally *also* wants to stop, say, because the behavior is sadistic).[31] Indeed—and here we come to prospective happiness—if one is asked why one (intrinsically) wants to do something, say, to do dangerous mountain climbing, a good answer, and one which is never irrelevant, is that one enjoys it.[32]

To reiterate a central analogy between theoretical and practical reason, it looks as if, rather as the justification of my belief that there is paper before me is grounded in my visual experience of paper, the rationality of my intrinsically wanting to listen to Beethoven's *Appassionata* is grounded (at least partly) in my enjoying my doing so. But the point that enjoyment is a ground for wanting does not by itself entail that rational persons must want their own happiness. Still, on the assumption that their desires correspond to what there is reason to desire and that their lives contain some enjoyable experiences, that general desire is to be expected.

Indeed, it may be that such responsiveness to reasons (in the widest sense, in which reasons encompass grounds) is the most fundamental global property of rational persons. In broad terms, the theory of global rationality I am developing may be seen as a responsiveness view, much as my theory of focal rationality is a well-groundedness view. The two are complementary: the crucial responsiveness to reasons is to those that are well-grounded. By itself, however, it is not substantive. In both theoretical and practical cases, moreover, memory may preserve the normative status of our propositional attitudes and hence keep our rationality intact. This is important: if only conscious states could justify those attitudes or render them rational, then either precious few of the attitudes would be rational or our consciousness would be filled with experiences, in a way it surely is not. The grounds of justification and rationality preserved in memory may have to be in some sense accessible to consciousness; but they need not reside there. Too much memory loss, however, and a person cannot be rational even at a time, much less over time. Imagine forgetting elementary facts about the world and the basic skills of self-preservation and communication.[33]

In part because the reasons to which our practical attitudes should respond are variable in strength as well as content, there may be no minimum level of strength or pervasiveness of rational intrinsic wants; and in some people such a want may be, from the point of view of rationality, too weak or perhaps too strong relative to other important wants they have. One can want even a good thing too much, just as one can lack motivation where one should be keen. But if we can conceive someone who, from the point of view of rationality, excessively desires some enjoyable activity, or even happiness itself, we probably cannot conceive of a rational person who does not to any degree want to be happy, under *some* relevant description (or is not disposed to want to be—an exception important at least for rational depressed people, whose desires can be inhibited). One can expect happiness in the strangest activities; but apparently one cannot be rational and lack even a disposition to care about one's happiness. This would be worse than imprudence; it would undermine the very basis of prudence.

If the eudaemonistic principle is correct, it would seem that some kind of similar *hedonic principle* is also true: given the common kinds of pleasant and painful experiences, rational persons tend to have intrinsic desires to have the former and avoid the latter. But pleasure is a narrower notion than happiness, and perhaps the kinds of life experiences necessary for the development of global rationality need not include it or even nurture a conception of it. If one has suffered but has never enjoyed anything, one might rationally want relief from pain, but wanting pleasure is a further matter. Granted, if one's experience did not give one any sense of pleasure as a reason for action, and one had no desire for it, one's rationality would be in a way *narrow;* but one could still be rational to a significant degree. For people at all typical of humanity, however, the hedonic principle holds.

Perhaps one could rationally fail to want the relevant things under *descriptions* that are at least approximately equivalent to 'pleasurable' and 'pain-avoiding'. But it is doubtful that a rational person who has experienced pleasure and pain of a remotely normal range can fail to want some things *for* the pleasure they yield or the pain they avoid. The pleasure may be lofty, and the pain avoided may be spiritual or mental; but some pleasures and pain avoidance must be wanted by a rational person with the appropriate experiences of them. A rational person may, for a purpose, strongly want to suffer pain, and perhaps even intrinsically want certain pains—if with ambivalence. But, at least if we consider people who have had the kinds of pleasures and pains that go with remotely normal child-rearing, it would count to some degree against rationality to have *no* intrinsic desire to avoid any kind of pain or to have any kind of pleasure. In either case, one would fail to be pursuing one's interest in the sense in which doing so is a condition for rationality.

9. THE PLACE OF OTHER-REGARDING DESIRE IN GLOBAL RATIONALITY

The principles so far suggested are self-regarding and do not take us beyond the notion that rational desire is rooted in the rationality of self-interest, broadly conceived. But for reasons that emerged in Part II, we can see that not all principles governing rational desire are self-regarding. If it is, as it seems, rational for normal, minimally educated adults to regard others as relevantly like themselves in being rational, sentient, and similarly constituted in other major ways, such as motivation—thus similar in the things apparently crucial for basic worth—it would seem to be rational to have intrinsic wants for others' happiness and for their enjoying themselves and avoiding pain.

It is a further question whether, other things equal, lacking such desires, at least when others to whom one stands in friendly relations are prominently present, counts to some degree against one's rationality. Recall that one wants the relevant experiences not in the abstract, but *for* certain desirability characteristics. Let us now reintroduce a dimension of the integration argument (given in Chapter 6) for the rationality of altruistic desires. If, as a person with rational beliefs and the kinds of rational desires just described, one regards others as capable of similar good experience of these characteristics, then a kind of consistency—or at least a need to avoid a kind of incoherence—would seem to demand that one intrinsically want (to some degree) that they too have the relevant experiences.

This is not to say that altruistic desire is entailed by rationality simpliciter; it is rather demanded of rational persons, and clearly of reasonable persons, *given* certain desires and beliefs (of a kind they normally, or at least commonly, have).[34] The closer other people are to us, and the more vividly we see their needs and capacities, the stronger the demand. Second, even if one does not actually believe the experiences in question, such as enjoyment of food, to be good, it is arguable that as a rational person one must be *disposed* so to regard them, and thus, again in order to preserve a kind of consistency (or at least avoid a kind of incoherence), one should be disposed to consider them good for others. A *rational* person so disposed, I believe, will thereby also be disposed to want intrinsically that others have the experiences. For rational persons—and certainly those who are also reasonable—tend to want intrinsically for themselves what they take to be intrinsically good; and again a kind of consistency (or avoidance of incoherence) apparently demands a similar attitude toward others. These considerations do not yield a conclusive argument for my view, but they help to make it plausible.

These reflections suggest an *altruistic principle:* rational persons—provided they believe something to the effect that others' experiences are qualitatively as good as their own, and given that their experience includes other people in friendly relations—tend to have some intrinsic wants for others' happiness when others are vividly present to their awareness. The tendency is stronger in a reasonable person than in one who is merely rational. The closer others are to one, the greater the presumption that one should have some such desires. Let me now suggest some qualifications which may help to support the principle.

First, unlike a capacity to respond to experience and to reason, the principle expresses a conditional demand of rationality: one that comes into play only given certain beliefs about, and experience of, others. Second (as explained in Chapter 6), rationality does not in general demand wanting others' happiness and freedom from pain as *much* as one's own, though there may be limits to the extent of self-preference consonant with rationality. Third, the deficiency indicated by failure to have any altruistic (intrinsic) wants is not sufficient for *ir*rationality. It is also true that a preferable critical term for such people is 'self-centered', though we sometimes also call them unreasonable. Still, even if the altruistic principle derives from the eudaemonistic and the hedonic principles, together with some commonsense beliefs about others and some related principle of consistency (or at least avoidance of incoherence), it is a substantive principle of rationality.

It is even more difficult to secure agreement on principles less closely associated with one's own happiness, pleasure, or pain. Consider things widely taken to have intrinsic value, such as the growth of knowledge, the creation of art, and the flourishing of love. Could a rational person understand what they are and have some rewarding experience of them, yet have no tendency to value them intrinsically? I doubt that this would be consonant with reason, even if it is consistent with minimal rationality. It would clearly not be reasonable. To be sure, how *much* deficiency in rationality the lack of such a tendency indicates would depend on the range and qualities of the person's experience.

A modest principle suggested here is that an appropriately experienced rational person must be *disposed* to have positive intrinsic desires regarding such things as knowledge, art, and love. I find this idea plausible, particularly given that the disposition need be manifested in actual valuations only when the person has had adequate experience to reveal what these things are like. Intuitively, wanting, for their own sake, the growth of knowledge, the creation of art, and the flourishing of love needs neither explanation nor, more important, justification. Surely a rational person, given suitable information and adequate experience, tends to want, and to value, for their own sake, things the person is justified in taking to be intrinsically good. Call this the *valuational principle*. Depending on what has intrinsic value, there may be many specific valuational principles.[35]

There is no way to prove any of these substantive principles, not even the eudaemonistic and the hedonic ones, which are fundamental if any are. But at least these two seem to be both presupposed in our discourse about rational persons and intuitive in themselves.[36] Perhaps people who ultimately care only about their own pleasures need not be irrational.[37] But if, in people who have the general knowledge that goes with, say, completing a decent secondary education, and who also have wide experience of the world, one probes why they do not care about others, one is likely to find hatred or prejudice or even imbalance. These may tend to count to some degree against their rationality, as where a prejudice is a tissue of irrational beliefs or where hatred of a few people influential in one's life leads one to treat people in general as mere means to one's own ends.

It may be objected that the unmitigatedly self-centered are often rational enough to succeed in life and to conduct themselves quite shrewdly. Perhaps some such people are rational. The absolute concept of a rational person, however, is vague, and there is simply no uncontroversial baseline. This is why I stress how the various criteria count for or against rationality (though I have not taken time to develop subprinciples, such as that, other things equal, it is rational to have stronger intrinsic wants for activities in proportion to the extent to which they engage one's rational and sentient capacities). We could take as our basic notion *being more rational than*, where degree of rational integration, as well as appropriate proportionalities of the sort just cited, is a major element in the relevant degree. We could then adjust our baseline in different cases. Perhaps it can be agreed that the self-centered agents I have described are *less* rational than they would be if they had certain altruistic desires. In any event, even if we cannot agree on conditions under which a person is rational overall, if we know what sorts of things conduce to rationality we should criticize indifference to them and encourage their development.

10. REASON AND MORALITY

The status of other-regarding motivation returns us to the classical question of the relation between reason and morality. Must a globally rational person be moral? I have not implied that. Suppose, however, that there are readily knowable moral principles. A relevantly informed person with a rational belief system might then have to believe them. Still, it would not follow that a rational person, even if aware of such moral truths, must be moral overall, since any moral motives such a person must have as a result of knowing moral truths might be outweighed by self-regarding ones.[38]

Perhaps a *fully* rational person, relevantly informed, must be moral. Might a kind of consistency (or avoidance of incoherence), together with a principle to the effect that, even if it is sometimes rational to act immorally, it is not rational to do so pervasively, imply that such a person cannot fail to be generally moral? I do not know that even this can be shown. If what I have said so far is sound, however, then a rational person who knows the basic moral truths would at least have some reason to want to be moral and so, under normal conditions, would to some degree actually want to be moral, even if only out of limited altruism. Again, a person who failed to meet this standard need not be irrational, but, other things equal, would be *less* rational than one who did.

It may seem that we can go further. The *point* of the institution of morality might be said to be to provide reasons that override non-moral reasons when there is a conflict. Thus, moral reasons arguably *are* overriding, and a thus informed rational person must act accordingly. In the light of earlier chapters, this argument can be seen to be invalid. Granting that our commitment to the institution of morality is in part grounded in a presupposition that we *need* rules that override self-interest, it does not follow that the relevantly informed, rational person will always act morally. This conclusion is a motivational counterpart of the thesis of the supremacy of moral reasons. The conclusion may seem to follow from various truths about the institution of morality because of the overriding *function* we tend to attribute to moral rules. But the thesis does not follow. Moral rules can have the function of overriding other sources of reasons, and indeed it can be rational to support the institution of morality as having such a function, even if, given the character of some rational persons, in some cases moral rules would not always fulfill that function.

It remains true, however, that an overridden moral rule is not nullified or inapplicable; there is simply an opposing reason of greater weight from the point of view of rationality. Thus, indifference to the moral reason would not be rational, even if acting contrary to it might be. If moral rea-

221

sons need not always rationally override, they do always rationally count. This *principle of the ineradicability of moral reasons,* as we might call it, does partial justice to the close connection between reason and morality without forcing us to assume that morality can derive from reason only if its rules are always motivationally or at least rationally overriding.

11. RATIONALITY, REASONABLENESS, AND IRRATIONALITY

Both the structural and the substantive criteria of rationality I have suggested are in a sense permissive. They are readily satisfied, to some degree, by normal adults. This is appropriate, for in some ways the notion of rationality, understood as consonance with reason, represents a quite moderate standard. There are ideal cases of rationality that no one achieves, but in most contexts we assume that people are rational unless we have good reason to think otherwise. A rational person, however, need not be reasonable. One can be rational, yet excessive in pursuing pleasure. Not only can we say to rational people that we wish they would be reasonable; we even presuppose their rationality in so exhorting them.

The suggested criteria of rationality are also quite pluralistic. The reason for this is largely that although experiential grounding of beliefs and desires is a unifying element in the explication of rationality, the criteria allow that rational persons have widely differing experiences. Our perceived environments may differ drastically—something of fundamental importance for theoretical rationality. Our happiness can come in as diverse forms as the activities whose performance yields it—something of fundamental importance for practical rationality. Assuming that any other substantive criteria of rationality there may be are no stronger than those suggested, have I made it too easy to qualify as rational? And how is irrationality possible?

Consider belief and action. There is no doubt that irrationality in both is possible.[39] We may overlook or foolishly misappraise evidence. We may make culpably unwarranted inferences. We may act, or believe, from blind prejudice. We may do foolish things because we have a disproportionately strong desire, as where wanting something now leads us to forgo something that we want, or would on brief reflection want, far more. We may act against our better judgment, and thereby irrationally, or we may irrationally avow, through self-deception, propositions against which we have what we should see is preponderant evidence. This is not to say that *every* case that meets these descriptions is an instance of irrationality. Rationality and irrationality are to be conceived holistically, and there are exceptions, as can be seen in relation to self-deception and weakness of will.[40]

The kinds of failings in rationality just described must be kept in perspective. We cannot even attribute such failings to people without making some minimal assumptions about their rationality. For instance, we can justifiably hold that people acted against their better judgment only if their behavior is intelligible enough to warrant our attributing to them both the judgment in question and the intentional action against it.[41] Still, nothing I have said precludes the possibility of justifiably judging that a person is irrational. For one thing, even a highly irrational person can be frequently intelligible, in speech and other behavior. With instrumental irrationality, in fact, it is essential to see the action as aimed at satisfying some desire; otherwise we could not consider the deed instrumentally irrational in virtue of how badly it is aimed.

My account, then, is neither unrealistically demanding nor excessively latitudinarian. Depending on one's specific standards, one can fill it out so as to arrive at a stronger or weaker notion of a rational person and indeed of a reasonable one. My emphasis has been on the criteria, on what counts for or against rationality, not on a minimal notion for use as a standard. Let the standard vary from case to case; my chief concern is the kinds of materials that go into its construction.

There may, indeed, be other sorts of raw materials of rationality besides those I have identified. I claim only to have set out what seem the major kinds of basic criteria. There are other, derivative criteria, and there may be some basic criteria not covered here. But whatever the criteria, they should not assimilate rationality to reasonableness. The latter requires a good measure of success on the part of the elements of the former. We cannot be reasonable without being rational, but reasonableness is a kind of achievement; rationality is a kind of gift.

12. THE INTERNAL CONSTITUTION OF RATIONALITY

I have stressed the analogy between rationality and justification. Given the association between justification and knowledge, one might wonder why I have not said more about the analogue of knowledge in the theory of rationality. The main reason is the internalism of my account. Rational beliefs as such need not be true, except in certain a priori matters and perhaps sometimes in relation to one's own consciousness, and in these cases the relevant grounds of belief seem internal in being accessible to reflection: introspective in the case of empirical elements, conceptual in the a priori case.

Rational persons must, however, by their very nature tend to seek truth, in at least some cases and under some description; and there is an analogue of truth for the conative attitudes, roughly (intrinsic) desirability. When an intrinsic desire for something that is desirable is suitably grounded, it is sound; and its status can be explained along internalist or externalist lines analogous to accounts of knowledge. For instance, if I intrinsically value hearing a sonata for the intrinsic properties of the experience in virtue of which that experience *is* intrinsically desirable, and no defeating factors are present (such as good reasons to believe it lacks those properties), my desire is sound. But soundness is not the crucial focus for discussions of rationality, any more than knowledge is crucial for discussions of justification. Rationality in some way counts toward soundness, as justification of belief in some way counts toward knowledge. But such objective success is not entailed in either case. As a justified belief may be false, a rational valuation may be unsound.[42]

It would be a mistake, however (for reasons given in Chapter 7), to take my account to be subjectivist because it is internalist. The standards of rationality, though internal, are intersubjective and cross-culturally valid. This applies to the cognitive criteria of strength, entrenchment, scope, connectedness, harmony with experience and reflection, and integration; and the same holds for the application of these criteria to other propositional attitudes. The crucial standards are, then, epistemically objective. Moreover, belief is fundamental in the account, and it is plausible to suppose that our rational empirical beliefs, especially perceptual ones, are by and large produced by the realities they represent.[43] Hence, it is plausible to suppose that truth suffuses the cognitive foundations of the system of propositional attitudes fundamental to the rationality of a rational person. It would be a mistake to say that all the other rational propositional attitudes derive their rationality from that of beliefs. But rational persons can at least bring their beliefs to bear in assessing the rationality or appropriateness of any of their other propositional attitudes, and this gives reason and experience a special place in self-criticism and self-direction.

There may be a far-reaching theoretical explanation of why global rationality is not grounded in belief alone. Recall the parallel between rationality and justification. Our justified beliefs about the world are grounded in experience. Without experience, particularly the sensory kind that occurs in perception, we could at best have *beliefs about perceptibles*, say, beliefs to the effect that there are trees around us. We could not have *perceptual beliefs*, or even beliefs grounded in the kind of experience, say, visual sensation, crucial in perception. Similarly, if we simply had beliefs about the values of things, and never had *experience* of something valuable, we could have only *beliefs about value*, that is, about what sort of thing is valuable, and not *valuational beliefs*, that is, beliefs grounded in valuing a thing for intrinsic properties in virtue

224

of which it is valuable. I doubt that beliefs merely about what is valuable can render a valuation rational. As in the counterpart case of wanting, one can rationally value something on the basis of believing it to have certain desirability characteristics, only in the light of rewarding experiences of it, or of adequately similar things, as having those (or similar) qualities.

Thus, if there is any sense in which beliefs could be the ultimate grounds for global rationality, then—contrary to at least one version of Platonism—some of the crucial ones would at least not be wholly cognitive: not simply attitudes toward propositions. If beliefs are to render rational our intrinsically wanting the kind of thing they represent as valuable, they have to be grounded in experience sufficient to show us concretely what that kind of thing *is*. Just as, without experiencing green, I do not know what the green of a tree is no matter how extensive my abstract knowledge of color, so if I never experience something like the beauty of a sonata, I cannot have a rational intrinsic want to experience it *for* its beauty. I can believe that this sort of experience is good, and can want to bring it about on that (abstract) ground. But I cannot want it for its own sake until I have an experiential acquaintance with certain of its properties or adequately similar ones. This is another domain in which intellectualism must be resisted. If there is some way in which global rationality could rest entirely on our beliefs, they must at least have a suitable experiential basis.

If there are substantive principles of rationality, such as the eudaemonistic, hedonic, altruistic, valuational, and moral ones I have proposed, they can be discovered by rational persons and brought to bear in guiding and developing desires. Moreover, surely rational persons are so constructed that their beliefs about what is intrinsically good, such as promoting activities that yield happiness, will have some tendency to elicit motivation to act accordingly. Bringing such beliefs to bear in our conduct, whether internal or external, is part of the exercise of autonomy.

There is a plurality of intrinsic goods and evils; and rational persons, depending on their conception of their happiness, seek some good things for their own sake and will have a commitment to realizing them that is a foundational element in their motivational system. Rational persons need not be good, but they cannot be wholly indifferent to everything that is good, even if in the main they seek it selfishly or are preoccupied with avoiding such evils as pain rather than with realizing anything positively desirable. Such rational goals as happiness, pleasure, and the avoidance of pain, pursued in the light of rational beliefs, are partly constitutive of our overall rationality as persons.

The broad conception of global rationality that has emerged, then, is this. Persons are rational, overall, when a suitable proportion of their beliefs, desires, and action tendencies—including those rooted in emotion—are individually rational and significantly connected with one another. When this is achieved, a suitable proportion of their other attitudes and of their emotions will, as a result, also be rational. The belief systems of rational persons adequately reflect their experience; their desires are appropriate to their experience and beliefs; their attitudes and emotions properly reflect their beliefs and desires; and their conduct is, sufficiently often, guided by these psychologically and normatively prior elements. They may differ greatly in what they believe, desire, and do, depending on their experience and what they build on it. But if they have sensory experience, as we all do, and if they reflect on certain obvious truths, as many of us do, then they must have a certain responsiveness to this experience taken in the context of these truths. This responsiveness yields beliefs, desires, and action tendencies appropriate to their experience in the ways described in this chapter. And if they have a good understanding of how others are like them in rationality, motivation, and sentience, then unless they lack the kinds of beliefs about others that, in the light of such an understanding, are normal for most of us, they tend to have some degree of altruistic desire. Rationality does not arise in a vacuum, and it comes in degrees, varying both with the well-groundedness of attitudes and actions and with their integration. But contrary to a well-entrenched view, rationality does not start with egoistic beliefs and desires, and as common and dominating as these can be, there are many conditions of human life in which rationality transcends them.

CONCLUSION

Human life as we know it begins with experience. We are born into a world of sensations, inner and outer; we are held, spoken to, and, if all goes well, cherished. As we develop, we discover more and more about our environment and, eventually, about the realm of abstract matters. We also bring something to experience, at least in the way of potentiality: a readiness to learn from it and even to be permanently shaped by it. Rationality is achieved when we attain the right kind of responsiveness to our experience and acquire a structure of attitudes and actions appropriate to it. Our actions and our attitudes, particularly our beliefs and desires, must adequately reflect our experience. The coherence of these elements with experience is a kind of external requirement for rationality. They must also be sufficiently integrated with one another. That integration is a kind of internal requirement for rationality.

Theoretical reason represents, in good part, our cognitive responses to experience, especially to sensory, intellectual, and emotional experiences, and it yields our map of the world. Practical reason represents, in good part, our conative responses to experience, and, in the light of our beliefs, it yields a kind of itinerary for our lives. A good map is correct, true to the territory it represents; a good itinerary takes us to worthwhile places. The cartographic analogy extends fully to theoretical and practical reason understood on externalist, realist assumptions. But even if we apply to belief and desire only the weak external requirement of coherence with our experience—which, as skeptics never tire of reminding us, can fail to correspond to a mind-independent reality—the analogy holds to this extent. A rational map must be appropriate to our experiential grounds for belief; and a rational itinerary must be appropriate to the features of experience, especially its rewarding and punishing aspects, that provide grounds for rational desire. There are objective standards both for adequate grounds and for the rationality of beliefs, desires, and actions based on those grounds. The standards are pliable and plural, but nonetheless enduring.

If we are to achieve a comprehensive understanding of rationality, it is best to begin with theoretical reason and to explore, as I have in Part I, the nature and grounds of rational belief. It is particularly appropriate to start with theoretical reason because it is generally better understood than practical reason and, in any case, if the latter can be seen to be like the former in major respects—and especially to be on a par with it in respect to certain skeptical problems—then the way is open for a better understanding of practical reason than can otherwise be achieved.

The rationality of beliefs is largely parallel to their justification, a concept central in epistemology. Understanding the nature and structure of justified belief requires considering both its basis and its ramifications once formed. Thus, Chapter 1 detailed experiential sources of non-inferential beliefs, the standard basic sources that provide both psychological and normative foundations of our belief systems; Chapter 2 examined their inferential development. In both realms there is not only the possibility of rationality for the elements in question—chiefly beliefs—and of the inferential extension of that rationality; there is also our persisting liability to defeat of our justification, or even our rationality, in holding one or another belief. The naturalness with which experience evokes rational belief carries no guarantee of invulnerability to erosion from below or overriding from above. But we have seen no good reason to doubt that there are rational beliefs.

Part II showed practical reason to be highly analogous to theoretical reason. Structurally, practical reason has both foundational and superstructure elements and cognitive links between the two. Substantively, it is responsive to experience in similar ways. But practical reason is not reducible to theoretical reason: practical rationality is not just a matter of having rational beliefs or other rational cognitions. Theoretical reason is less commonly thought to be reducible to practical reason, but reduction also fails in that direction. The analogy between them is, however, extensive and multidimensional. Part II developed it and, through it, provided an account of practical rationality: the rationality, above all, of actions and desires. In all of Part II, however, theoretical reason is more than an edifying analogue of practical reason. It is shown to supply, chiefly in the form of beliefs, much of the connective tissue of rationality. Without rational beliefs, we cannot make good inferences or find adequate means to our ends.

In a number of ways, action is like inferential belief. Its internal structure divides into basic elements and others grounded on them; intentional actions, like inferential beliefs, are based on the reasons that explain them; and intentional actions, like beliefs, are causally sustained by reasons. Both rational actions and rational beliefs, moreover, can be seen as grounded ultimately in experiential sources—sources of belief on the theoretical side and of desire on the practical side. Chapter 3 showed how this is so. It also developed a parallel between the structure of motivation, and correspondingly of our conduct, and that of belief. In each case there are inferential relations, the kind that figure centrally in theoretical and practical reasoning; there are rationality-conferring grounds of both inferentially sustained elements and more basic ones; and there are unifying elements, such as, on the theoretical side, framework beliefs like those that govern elementary inductive inferences and, on the practical side, master motives like the desire for a rich and happy life.

If experience is internal, how can it render rational our intrinsically wanting for *others* the same sorts of things that we want for ourselves? If rationality begins inside, why is it not confined there, as egoism has it? Chapter 4 showed that if we distinguish between wanting things for what they are—for instance, for their enjoyable qualities—and wanting them for oneself or for self-centered aspects of them, just as we should distinguish believing something on the basis of what we see and believing it on the basis of the self-ascriptive premise that *we* see it, then we can understand how the grounds of rationality can be internal without being egocentric. Encountering desirable qualities of experience in our own life does not require taking what is good about them to depend on their being ours. Even envy would be hard to understand if this were so. Why would I envy others the pleasures of my favorite activities if I did not take those pleasures to be much like my own enjoyment of the same kinds of things? The pleasure of hearing a fine sonata is no better because it is mine rather than someone else's.

This conception of the qualitative character of the sources of rational desire can be extended to understanding reasons for action and indeed for intention. It can also be confirmed by examining a number of ways in which theoretical reason, by revealing to us the desirable or undesirable features of various kinds of experience, can affect the rationality of our basic desires. Believing that a seaside walk would be delightful gives us good reason to want one; believing that a cold wind would chill us to the bone gives us good reason to avoid it. The normative power of theoretical reasons was explored in Chapter 5, which also critically compared my objectivist account of practical reason with the functionalist subjectivism of a broadly Humean instrumentalist conception. That conception was shown to be inadequate to account for our considered judgments about rational action, and objectivism emerges as the more plausible position to hold in view of what we reflectively take to be good reasons for action and what we regard as defeating would-be claims to provide a reason for action.

If practical reason is experientially and objectively grounded in the way I maintain, it is to be expected that altruism can be not only consonant with reason but, given certain kinds of experiences and rational beliefs, rationally demanded. This possibility was defended in Chapter 6. It suggests how a case can be made for the moderate rational requirement of some degree of altruistic desire on the part of normal persons, given certain experiences and certain common-sense rational beliefs. Its conclusion on this matter is that such desire is a demand of reason: more than a rational permission, yet less than a strict rational requirement. Failure to fulfill such a demand is not reasonable, even if not necessarily irrational.

Whether a rational person must be altruistic enough to be genuinely moral is a further question, and it appears that rationality is possible without the combination of experiences and beliefs in virtue of which moral deeds are rationally required. But to show that a rational person must be moral is more than a good theory of practical reason need do. It is enough to show that if we have an adequate understanding of others and are adequately rational in both our beliefs and our motivational responses to the prospect of others' experiences realizing the qualities we ourselves find rewarding, then we will tend to be altruistic in a way that supports a commitment to certain basic kinds of moral principles. These include principles of justice and moderate principles of beneficence. To say, however, that some degree of commitment to morality is natural in rational persons—and demanded in reasonable ones—with appropriate experience, beliefs, and desires is not to say that moral principles cannot be justified in any other way. They may still be epistemically autonomous. Principles that we would commit ourselves to, given practical rationality and sufficient information may also be seen to be sound from the point of view of theoretical reason alone. The justification of adhering to moral principles is in this way overdetermined.

In the light of the fallibilism, pluralism, and internalism of the theory of rationality set out and defended in Parts I and II, one might think that its objectivity is too highly qualified to avoid an ultimate commitment to a strong relativism. This is the prospect addressed by the opening chapter of Part III. The subject is difficult in part because there are so many kinds of relativism. I have distinguished relativism regarding grounds (relativity of normative status to grounds of the belief or other element in question), genetic relativism, contentual relativism, conceptual relativism, doxastic relativism, preferential relativism (a special case of relativity to grounds), and status relativism. Some of these views are surely true, others not.

Relativity to grounds and relativity of content are undeniable, and my theory of rationality accounts for them. Plainly, what is rational *in* us, at a given time, should vary with our grounds; what is rational *for* us, prospectively, should depend on what our grounds will sustain. In both cases there may be competing alternatives that are equally good, and rationality thus permits different preferences even in a single person: this is what preferential relativism affirms. Preferential relativity is to be expected given the complex organic way in which elements of intrinsic value combine with other elements to yield the overall value of the kind of multifarious experiences or prospects we must evaluate. In both theory and practice we are commonly confronted with equally good alternatives.

Genetic relativism, which above all asserts a developmental dependence of rationality on one's experience, seems sound construed as an empirical thesis but seems mistaken construed as the normative view that the *criteria* for the rationality of beliefs or other attitudes vary with, as opposed to taking into account, their differing origins. Conceptual relativity need not be accepted as a feature of judgments of either rationality or morality. The data of plurality and disagreement can be explained in terms of fallibilism, pluralism, and other notions that a good theory of rationality must in any case reflect. Doxastic relativism is implausibly subjectivist, status relativism needlessly skeptical. Diversity can leave room for unity, disagreement for objectivity, objectivity for internalism. An internalist objectivism provides room, in turn, for realism, though it does not entail it.

Theoretical and practical reason, then, each have an internal unity, and in a rational person they are in some measure unified with each other. Chapter 8 provides the major outlines of an account of this unity and proposes a conception of a globally rational person. If a realist view of the grounds of rationality is sound, we may add something to the notion of an internal unity as essential in rational persons: we may also say that their attitudes, particularly their beliefs and desires, mediate between them and the world. These attitudes are largely caused by our experience of the world, and they largely produce our interventions in it, which, in turn, enrich our experience. There is no way to give a brief summary of all the major elements in the theory of rationality developed in this book, but it may help to recall in broad terms the territory charted by the theory. I have examined both global and focal rationality: the rationality of persons and that of the specific elements essential in it, above all beliefs, desires and other attitudes, and emotions and actions. In both the global and the focal cases, rationality has two sides, the theoretical and the practical, and admits of degrees. Global rationality cannot be achieved in any degree apart from a measure of success on each side: particularly in an appropriate responsiveness to both theoretical and practical reasons. In structure, theoretical and practical reason are, in a moderate sense, each foundational. There are foundational elements, including as central cases direct beliefs and intrinsic desires; and there are superstructure elements, including as central cases the propositional attitudes based on such foundations. The two levels are connected by beliefs; and through those beliefs many elements are grounded in one or more others by theoretical or practical inferences. Rational foundational elements are not brutely or indefeasibly rational but rest on normative grounds. These, in turn are experiential. They represent a plurality of substantive categories but are neither restricted in content nor exhausted by any particular list of grounding elements, such as sensory experiences on the theoretical side or pleasure and pain on the practical side. Experience is basic in the structure of rationality and pervasive in determining its substance, but it leaves the content of rational beliefs and desires largely open. The theoretical grounds may be unified by the idea of counting toward truth, the practical ones by that of counting toward goodness. These ideas are not precise, but they do call attention to the different ways in which rationality can be conceived as well-groundedness: rational beliefs, for instance, are based on the kinds of experiential grounds that we take to be evidences of truth; rational desires are based on the kinds that we take to be evidences of goodness. Global rationality is reached when a person has a sufficiently integrated system of sufficiently well-grounded propositional attitudes, emotions, and actions. In meeting all of these standards, a rational person exhibits an adequate responsiveness to reasons.

Experience provides, as basis of rational cognition, grounds for the believability of propositions that appropriately reflect it; and experience contains, as a basis of rational desire, grounds for the desirability of the kinds of states of affairs we can realize. With its immensely rich sensory, cognitive, emotional, and conative dimensions, our experience reveals to us both good destinations to place on our itinerary and paths that lead to them. Our responses to experience are often automatic, as where we are immediately delighted by success or suddenly downcast by failure, but we need not be passive in responding to experience. As our experience and our reflections on it expand, we gain a basis for refining or criticizing the very beliefs, desires, and other elements previously rendered rational by that experience. Here the search for coherence often results in altering the foundations or digging beneath them in search of something firmer.

Insofar as we understand rationality in terms of this natural, causally structured engagement of our cognitive and motivational systems with the world, our conception of it may be said to be naturalistic. If rationality is not in a strong sense a natural property, it is firmly grounded in the world of experience. It is thus rooted in natural properties even if it turns out (as I suspect it may) to be ultimately irreducible to them. The same holds for justification, and, in both the theoretical and practical domains, for reasonableness.

Given this integration, in rational persons, between theoretical and practical reason, and given the far-reaching parallels between the two, there is a sense in which we may conclude that reason, conceived as a general human capacity, is, as Kant thought, unified. It is unified above all by its grounding, directly or through belief, in experience, sensory, introspective, memorial, and reflective. This experiential grounding accounts for two quite different and even ostensibly conflicting sides of rationality: its internalism and its objectivity. Its objectivity enables us to formulate some universally applicable standards. Its internalism enables us to account for the possibility of widely differing rational beliefs and desires. Its global application to persons enables us to account for the substantially holistic, integrative character of their rationality. Its defeasibility enables us to account for the changes in it that reflection and new experience can bring. If all this is so, then there is at least one sense in which value may be taken to be real. But it is not properly seen as "out there," independent of experience. It is realized *in* experience, in the pleasures of human relations at their best, the joys of aesthetic contemplation, the rewards of reflection.

The defeasibility of our reasons requires fallibilism about both the truth of our beliefs and the values of our ends. But if rationality will not tolerate dogmatism, it also rejects sheer anarchy. It gives us wide freedom in belief, desire, and action, but it also provides standards for assessing our uses of that freedom. Some of those uses may be, from the point of view of rationality, better than others, and we can be justified in believing that. Some may be, from that point of view, obligatory or prohibited, and we may be justified in believing that too. And many are neither obligatory nor prohibited. In that domain, we have great freedom. We may or may not succeed in making rational choices therein, but we can rationally assess how well we have done in our various pursuits, and we can try to be reasonable. There is firm ground to build on. There is an unlimited variety of raw material to shape into structures of our choosing. We can appraise these constructions as we build, reshape them from foundations to pinnacle, and extend them indefinitely in any direction. Reason gives us enduring standards for practice as well as theory, but it does not dictate our tastes. Its sovereignty in the structure of our lives is an essential foundation of our autonomy in living them.

NOTES

CHAPTER 1

1. For Aristotle's foundationalism see esp. the *Posterior Analytics*, bks. 1 and 2 (though this is not his only work in which the metaphor of foundations and super-structure seems appropriate). There is a large literature on foundationalism and the controversy between foundationalism and coherentism. I have stated both and given references to relevant literature, in "The Foundationalism-Coherentism Controversy: Hardened Stereotypes and Overlapping Theories," ch. 4 of my *The Structure of Justification* (Cambridge: Cambridge University Press, 1993).

2. This is defended in detail in my "Dispositional Beliefs and Dispositions to Believe," *Nous* 26 (1994), pp. 419–34. Since nothing major turns on the point here and it is independently plausible, I shall simply presuppose it.

3. William Alston and Panayot Butchvarov have both suggested that the notion of justification applies primarily to action (and perhaps applies to belief only in an extended sense). See, e.g., Alston's "Concepts of Justification," in his *Epistemic Justification* (Ithaca: Cornell University Press, 1989) and "Epistemic Desiderata," *Philosophy and Phenomenological Research* 53 (1993); and Butchvarov's *Skepticism about the External World* (Oxford: Oxford University Press, 1998).

4. For a brief account of how they are and are not different, particularly with respect to the sense in which they are "causal processes," see my *Epistemology* (London: Routledge, 1998), chs. 1 and 3.

5. This is not uncontroversial. See, e.g., Carl Ginet, *Knowledge, Perception, and Memory* (Dordrecht: D. Reidel, 1983). For a statement and brief defense of the preservative conception see my *Epistemology*, ch. 2. I should add that I am not assuming that memory must preserve knowledge in the *way* it preserves justification.

6. Some would say that experience is always conceptual, or even interpretive, in a way that implies using reason. Some such view may aid criticisms of

235

NOTES TO PAGES 17–18

foundationalism; see, e.g., Wilfrid Sellars, "Empiricism and the Philosophy of Mind," in his *Science, Perception, and Reality* (London: Routledge and Kegan Paul, 1963). But even if this view is sound and, in addition, the use of reason requires having an experience, say, considering some proposition, it does not follow (in part for reasons given later in discussing conceptual coherentism) that what justifies the belief arrived at through that use is that experience. Suppose a weaker thesis follows: that *some* experience is part of any justification grounded in the use of reason. There may remain a contrast (as noted in the text) between the way experience justifies here and the way it does in, say, perceptual cases.

7. In different terminology, to provide *situational justification*, justification, grounded in the relevant situation, for believing, and to confer *doxastic justification*, justification of an actual belief. The epistemic basis relation in question, which holds between a belief and a ground on which it is based (whether or not there is a process of inference from the latter to the former) is notoriously difficult to explicate. It has a causal component but is not merely a causal relation. For a detailed account of it (particularly in inferential cases) and references to other discussions of it, see my "Belief, Reason, and Inference," *Philosophical Topics* (1986), reprinted in *The Structure of Justification*.

8. See Wilfrid Sellars, *Science, Perception, and Reality*, on "the Myth of the Given." For a sympathetic but critical discussion of Sellars on this and related points see John McDowell, *Mind and World* (Cambridge, Mass.: Harvard University Press, 1994), esp. Lecture I, in which he discusses Donald Davidson's stronger view, on which "nothing can count as a reason for holding a belief except another belief." See Davidson's "A Coherence Theory of Truth and Knowledge," in Dieter Hendrich, ed., *Kant öder Hegel* (Stuttgart: Klett-Cotta, 1983). If Davidson's view is applied to reasons strictly conceived (in a way I describe in Chapter 2), my position can accommodate its most plausible version. It can surely accommodate McDowell's weaker claim that we can credit "experiences with rational relations to judgement and belief, but . . . only if we take it that experiences have conceptual content" (p. 162). I think, however, that one might also sustain the view McDowell ascribes to Gareth Evans: "that the non-conceptual content he attributes to experiences can afford 'not merely reasons but good reasons' for judgements and beliefs" (p. 162).

9. For a detailed discussion of the main issues and references to much relevant literature, see my "The Foundationalism-Coherentism Controversy: Hardened Stereotypes and Overlapping Theories" and *Epistemology*, ch. 7 (both cited earlier). See also William P. Alston's critical study of Sellars, "What's Wrong with Immediate Knowledge," *Synthese* 55 (1983); and Laurence BonJour, "Foundationalism and the External World," *Philosophical Perspectives* 13 (1999), pp. 229–49.

10. Sources of the temptation to assimilate justification as a status (property) with justification as a process, as well as indications of the assimilation in the literature, are noted in my "Foundationalism-Coherentism Controversy" and in *Epistemology*, ch. 7, and by Alston and other writers on the topic.

11. A central question in religious epistemology is whether there is an experiential source, other than ordinary perception, through which knowledge of God or of some spiritual reality can come. For a rigorous case that there can be a perceptual source of this kind, see William P. Alston, *Perceiving God* (Ithaca: Cornell University Press, 1991).

12. For a related argument, to the effect that seeing does not depend on the eyes, see *Epistemology*, ch. 1. If we alter the case so that what is different is on the experiential side, say, with a distinctive kind of phenomenal response, there seems to be room for a sixth sense.

13. It is difficult to describe the appropriate community. Native speakers of English who are at least moderately educated are the relevant group I know best; but my knowledge about, and experience with, other languages suggests that the points in question hold approximately as well for native speakers of other natural languages.

14. R. M. Chisholm is a case in point; see, e.g., his *Theory of Knowledge*, 3rd ed. (Englewood Cliffs: Prentice-Hall, 1989). Ginet, *Knowledge, Perception, and Memory*, is another epistemic deontologist (in taking justification to be a matter of what we may permissibly believe).

15. Alvin I. Goldman is a paradigm of a reliabilist. See his *Epistemology and Cognition* (Cambridge, Mass.: Harvard University Press, 1986) and the critical literature on reliabilism, e.g., by Richard Foley, *The Theory of Epistemic Rationality* (Cambridge, Mass.: Harvard University Press, 1987) and Paul K. Moser, *Knowledge and Evidence* (Cambridge: Cambridge University Press, 1989).

16. Ernest Sosa has developed such a view. See, e.g., "Knowledge and Intellectual Virtue," *The Monist* 68 (1985), in his *Knowledge in Perspective* (Cambridge: Cambridge University Press, 1991), which also contains later work on the topic. For other detailed treatments see Jonathan Kvanvig, *The Intellectual Virtues and the Life of the Mind* (Lanham, Md.: Rowman and Littlefield, 1992), James Montmarquet, *Epistemic Virtue and Doxastic Responsibility* (Lanham, Md.: Rowman and Littlefield, 1993), and Linda Zagzebski, *Virtues of the Mind* (Cambridge: Cambridge University Press, 1996).

17. In most cases that arise in this book, it is the grounding of justified *beliefs* (doxastic justification) or of other psychological elements that is in question; but a well-groundedness theory can also account for propositional justification, i.e., a proposition's being justified for a person, as where a conclusion I have not drawn, and do not yet believe, is justified by premises I have just arrived at. Here the justification I have for the conclusion is grounded in my justified premise beliefs, though, by contrast with the case in which, after I draw my conclusion, my belief is justified on the same basis, there is no causal relation between this justification and what it grounds. The premise beliefs *causally sustain* the belief justified on the basis of them; they do not causally but *evidentially sustain* the justification I have for forming that belief before I do so. Justification as such is not a term in causal relations, for reasons offered in my "Ethical Naturalism and the Explanatory Power of Moral Concepts," in my *Moral Knowledge and Ethical Character* (New York: Oxford University Press, 1997).

18. Prima facie justification may be fruitfully compared with prima facie duty as conceived, e.g., by W. D. Ross in *The Right and the Good* (Oxford: Oxford University Press, 1930), esp. ch. 2. Indeed, a Rossian duty surely is a case of prima facie (moral) justification.

19. This is not to imply that just *any* tactual belief is better justified than any conflicting visual one. Matters are far more complicated but need not be pursued in detail here.

20. This is not to deny that there may be justified beliefs of logical truths so luminous that the justification of these beliefs cannot be overridden. The point is that doxastic justification grounded in reflection can be overridden by factors that are at least not entirely a priori. That can be so even when the beliefs in question are true. For further discussion of this issue see Laurence BonJour, *In Defense of Pure Reason* (Cambridge: Cambridge University Press, 1997) and my "Self-Evidence," *Philosophical Perspectives* 13 (1999), pp. 203–28.

21. Another possibility is that there are other basic sources, arguably including some kind of coherence, that are comparatively weak, so, although they may add to the justification available through the standard sources, they are not sufficient to yield belief that is justified on balance (roughly, justified to a degree ordinarily sufficient to render a true belief knowledge). On the other hand, if they can add to justification from the standard sources, then they could render a belief that would not ordinarily defeat the justification of another belief able to do so. This would limit the self-sufficiency of the basic sources. We should surely be cautious about affirming even the de facto self-sufficiency of the sources, and I leave it open.

22. For two major accounts see Keith Lehrer, *Knowledge* (Oxford: Oxford University Press, 1974), and Laurence BonJour, *The Structure of Empirical Knowledge* (Cambridge, Mass.: Harvard University Press, 1985); and for instructive discussion see John Bender, ed., *The Current State of the Coherence Theory* (Dordrecht: Kluwer, 1989). Explanatory coherence is treated in detail by William Lycan; see, e.g., *Judgment and Justification* (Cambridge: Cambridge University Press, 1988). It should be noted that (in "Foundationalism and the External World," cited earlier) BonJour has since abandoned coherentism.

23. Here again I presuppose results from earlier work of mine and others. See, e.g., *Epistemology*, cited earlier, and, for some concessions to the view that justification implies the ability to justify, "Causalist Internalism," *American Philosophical Quarterly* 26 (1989), reprinted in *The Structure of Justification*. The metaphor of ice is good from another point of view: as skeptics would stress, thin ice can look thick. This is, however, consistent with the text.

24. If it is taken to be a relation internal to one's beliefs, their content does not matter, nor does their fit with one's experience. This sort of thing has been widely noted; see Moser, *Knowledge and Evidence*, and Bender, *Current State of Coherence Theory*, for some relevant points and many references.

25. There is far more to say about conceptual coherentism, but perhaps enough has been said to indicate how it enables a moderate foundationalism

position to take account of many plausible points made by Sellars, Quine, BonJour, McDowell, and others that have been taken (though not always by them) to imply that coherentism is a superior epistemological theory.

26. A detailed account of contextualism is given by Mark Timmons in *Morality Without Foundations* (New York: Oxford University Press, 1999), which, despite its title, indicates affinities between contextualist and foundationalist theories. Cf. David Henderson, "Epistemic Competence and Contextualist Epistemology," *Journal of Philosophy* (1994), pp. 627–49.

27. A detailed account of foundationalism and various misunderstandings of it is given in ch. 7 of my *Epistemology*.

28. In "Psychological Foundationalism," *The Monist* 62 (1978), reprinted in *The Structure of Justification,* I introduced the term 'psychological foundationalism' and explicated the thesis in detail.

29. This is of course controversial. I have argued for the point in "Justification, Truth, and Reliability," *Philosophy and Phenomenological Research* 49 (1988), reprinted in *The Structure of Justification.*

30. The qualification is intended to cover cases like this. One has a merely true memory belief, say, a somewhat hazy one for which one has too much conflicting evidence to qualify as knowing the proposition in question; then one comes to know it on the basis of new evidence, e.g., cogent testimony. One might say, on hearing the testimony, 'Yes, I remember'; but if this sense of 'remember' implies knowing, surely its implication of knowledge depends on the testimonial evidence just acquired. Memory has preserved the belief that becomes knowledge; but before getting that evidence, one only believes, and does not know, from memory.

CHAPTER 2

1. The anti-intellectualism I am sketching will put some in mind of connectionist models of the brain's sustenance of mental activity. I do not intend anything said here to require any specific neuropsychology; my effort is to keep the psychological commitments of my account of rationality minimal and to leave room for any plausible empirical results that may emerge. For wide-ranging discussion of connectionism as bearing on several topics in this and later chapters see Andy Clark and Peter Millican, eds., *Connectionism, Concepts, and Folk Psychology* (Oxford: Oxford University Press, 1996).

2. As the wording indicates, the notions of structurally and episodically inferential belief are not *historical:* a belief that is not arrived at by inference but now rests on one from premises just discovered is now episodically inferential. Thus, a belief initially formed by inference becomes structurally inferential when the premise belief(s) are no longer inferentially operative but remain equally a causal and evidential basis of that belief; it can cease to be inferential at all if all premise beliefs are forgotten; and it can become episodically inferential again, e.g., where one discovers new premises and infers the proposition from them.

3. Where a belief is not based on some further belief only because one has forgotten the relevant grounds, as where one is convinced of a point by an argument, yet forgets the premises, we can call it *historically inferential.* It is not the kind I have in mind as higher in the cognitive structure (than non-inferential beliefs), though in content it may be such that we would not accept it as justified by memory unless we took it to be memorially preserved from a time when it was inferentially justified. Inferential status is not the only basis for dividing cognitions into higher and lower, but it is a good one and it will serve here.

4. Neither seeing, e.g., nor the visual experience essential to it admits of justification. *Looking* does, but that is not equivalent to seeing. Where it yields seeing we have an action as well as the experience in which it issues, and the former is what admits of justification.

5. This would be a case of representation without a (substantive) representor: the structure and higher-order properties of the experiential properties would have the relevant correspondence with what is represented. Thus, while a sensedatum theory is not ruled out, my point is compatible with other theories of perception, including an adverbial one. Detailed discussion of these theories is provided in ch. 1 of my *Epistemology,* and the functional dependence of sensory qualities on the relevant objects is discussed in ch. 8.

6. Unlike justificatory power, the ability to ground *knowledge* (about the external world) is undermined by hallucination.

7. This seems to me to admit of exceptions and is the subject of a substantial literature. We need not go into the issue here; detailed discussion is given in my "Justification, Deductive Closure, and Reasons to Believe," *Dialogue* (1991), and in my "Deductive Closure, Defeasibility, and Skepticism," *Philosophical Quarterly* 45 (1995), pp. 494–99.

8. If, however, I do labor to make the connection and thereby understand the entailment in terms of self-evident steps I discovered in tracing it, my inferential justification is strengthened.

9. There are other cases; perhaps, e.g., something's being "intuitive" or its seeming right normally provides prima facie justification. A full classification is not needed here.

10. I have defended the implicit conception of rationalization and the basis requirement on justified belief, in "The Causal Structure of Indirect Justification," *Journal of Philosophy* 80 (1983) and in "Rationalization and Rationality," *Synthese* (1985), both in *The Structure of Justification.* Note that the example is of firmness, not strength: the strength of the porch is a matter of how much stress it *can* bear, and *potential* support is relevant to that. The cognitive analogue is not, however, justifiedness, which is at issue, but justifiability, which is not.

11. The rationalizing need not be consciously done as such. Such a case may be rare: there is a tendency, for rational persons, to "use" a "premise" they believe as an at least partial basis of conviction the moment they come to believe that it supports something they already believe. I use scare quotes because (1) we do not have direct voluntary control of the relations between our beliefs,

and (2) it is misleading to call the proposition a premise when, in the situation imagined, one has neither inferred anything from it nor seen it as one. The justification one merely has for a belief by virtue of possessing an unused (good) premise for it is a kind of *structural justification*, a notion explicated in my "Structural Justification," *Journal of Philosophical Research* 16 (1991), reprinted in *The Structure of Justification*.

12. That there are many ways to adjust to disconfirmation is a major lesson of the Quine-Duhem thesis; and that changes in the justificatory status of one belief may affect that of many others is a weaker version of Quine's holism, expressed in part as early as "Two Dogmas of Empiricism." For a short, lucid expression of some of his views on these issues see W. V. Quine and Joseph Ullian, *The Web of Belief*, 2nd ed. (New York: Random House, 1978), esp. ch. 8.

13. Richard Rorty's *Philosophy and the Mirror of Nature* (Princeton: Princeton University Press, 1979) illustrates this point and has influenced many philosophers, particularly those not highly conversant with contemporary epistemology. Cf. Michael Williams, *Groundless Belief* (Oxford: Blackwell, 1977).

14. On this interpretation of the Cartesian axiomatism requirement, even if we do not treat one's (first-person, indexical) belief that one exists as justified a priori, we can construe it as epistemically certain because, first, it is a priori and necessary that *if* one believes (or in any way) takes oneself to exist, then one does, and second, for this reason such a belief or taking cannot be false, even though the corresponding existential propositions can be, since none of us necessarily exists. The status of such *cogito* beliefs is discussed in some detail in my "Self-Evidence," cited earlier.

15. Two points of clarification. First, such an experience can occur even through hallucination, so one might more accurately speak of a perceptual *experience* principle. Second, having the impression that *x* is *F* entails not believing that it is but only being disposed to believe that it is (it is also not entailed by believing that *x* is *F*, since that is quite possible without having this impression); and in 'an impression of *x*'s being *F*' the position of '*x*' is not referential: there need be no such thing, even at the level of sense-data. There are problems about how the content of the impression is related to the belief, but these need not be settled here. It should be said, however, that if the impression is sensory, this restricts the range of '*F*'. At least the typical cases will be "observable" properties, such as color, shape, and texture. Nothing I say here turns on difficulties about just how we should explicate the notion of a sensory impression.

16. In "Justification, Truth, and Reliability," I discuss a set of such principles in detail. The epistemological works of Roderick M. Chisholm, William P. Alston, Fred Dretske (e.g., *Knowledge and the Flow of Information* [Cambridge, Mass.: MIT Press, 1981]), Alvin I. Goldman, Keith Lehrer, Laurence BonJour, Peter D. Klein (e.g., *Certainty: A Refutation of Skepticism* [Minneapolis: University of Minnesota Press, 1981]), Paul K. Moser, and Richard Foley, among others cited in this and the previous chapter, should also be consulted on this topic.

17. The accessibility qualification is required because lesser accessibility in one item will create an imbalance; e.g., if my inferential (or perceptual) grounds for *p* are quite clear to me, whereas I would have to reflect considerably on what I believe (or perceive) in order to acquire the same degree of justification in believing *q*, which is obviously incompatible with *p*, then my initial justification (for *p*) is not defeated. Roughly, merely structural justification for *q* does not defeat an equal degree of doxastic justification for *p*. One is not vanquished by an enemy still a good distance away; but if a superior enemy is around the corner and one might be expected to check that location, one may be as good as lost.

18. A general formulation of this kind of problem is given by Richard A. Fumerton in *Reason and Morality* (Ithaca: Cornell University Press, 1990): for any criterion of rationality, we must decide what happens when one justifiably but falsely believes that it is satisfied, or that it is not. He is not content to let any first-order criterion carry all the weight. The problem is not easily solved; for discussion see Richard Foley, "Fumerton's Puzzle," *Journal of Philosophical Research* 15 (1990). My suggestion, in outline, is that the theory of justification must attend to *both* basic sources and defeaters but must account for the power of defeaters in terms of their own grounding in those sources. Hence, the criterion of justification (or rationality) should deal with second-order epistemic beliefs largely through its accounts of transmission and defeasibility.

19. At least since Harry G. Frankfurt's "Freedom of the Will and the Concept of a Person," *Journal of Philosophy* 68 (1971), appeal to second-order attitudes, especially in relation to rationality and autonomy, has been fashionable. Fruitful theorizing has been done along these lines, but these appeals need restricted application and careful defense if we are to avoid a dogma of the superiority of the higher order.

20. The preface paradox suggests the overall set will not be for at least many who are self-critical. Suppose I believe that I have at least one false belief, as rational persons presumably should, just as it is rational for most writers of books to believe they have made at least one false statement therein, even if they continue to believe each statement individually. Then there would seem to be *some* kind of incoherence in the entire set of my beliefs. It is not of a kind that is damaging to any major thesis of this book.

21. In "The Foundationalism-Coherentism Controversy: Hardened Stereotypes and Overlapping Theories," ch. 4 of *The Structure of Justification*, I explore whether coherence could be a *conditionally basic source* of justification: a generator of some degree of justification beyond the initial justification owed to foundational elements. I am not foreclosing this possibility.

22. I do not deny that there can be "unconscious beliefs," at least in the sense of beliefs one cannot know or believe one has without special techniques or the help of someone else. But even here one might be aware of the belief, yet give what one is aware of a different description, e.g.. "an inclination to think of the proposition in question." Imagine, however, that one's brain is rigged so that if

one starts to become aware of a belief under any description, one ceases to have it. Here there is some question whether the belief can do justificatory work, in part because one could probably not even have an awareness of one's viewing the proposition as a good premise for one's beliefs, since this tends to imply believing it. Perhaps, however, the capacity for that awareness is only a condition for giving, as opposed to having, justification. If this example does show that justificatory beliefs need not be accessible to introspection, it constitutes a special exception—which we might call *dissociated justification*—and does not undermine the accessibility requirement for normal cases.

23. It is natural to take concepts to be abstract entities, but the points here do not require that they be so viewed.

24. There is a large literature on the controversy. See Chisholm, *Theory of Knowledge* (e.g., 2nd ed.); Alston, *Epistemic Justification;* Foley, *The Theory of Epistemic Rationality;* Moser, *Knowledge and Evidence;* and my *The Structure of Justification.*

25. William P. Alston has argued for this in *Epistemic Justification*, as I have in *Epistemology.* The latter also argues for internalism about justification side by side with externalism about knowledge; see esp. ch. 8. For detailed discussion of such a dual approach see James Sennett, "Toward a Compatibility Theory for Internalist and Externalist Epistemologies," *Philosophy and Phenomenological Research* 52 (1991).

26. Two clarifications may help here. First, among the capacities required for a justified belief are all the conceptual ones needed to understand its propositional object; these may be immensely complex for certain propositions. Second, my concern is not propositional justification, roughly the justification of a proposition for a person; but that notion may be adequately understandable in terms of doxastic justification: it is plausible to suppose that a proposition is justified for a person if and only if the person has grounds for it such that in virtue of believing it on the basis of them the person would be justified in so believing.

27. To be sure, there are *types* of things, such as actions, that are justified in the circumstances but can be *performed* irrationally, as where rejecting a solicitation is justified by reasons but carried out from foolish suspicions. But here it is different—if easily conflated—things that are appraised as justified and not rational.

28. If p is false, it isn't "there" to be a reason there is, i.e., a normative reason; and since a false proposition does not genuinely explain anything, p cannot be a reason *why* either. To be sure, *that p seems true* or is well evidenced can be true when p is not and can be a reason there is to believe p. But here we have an epistemic fact, not a falsehood, serving as a reason. In *this* case we might say of p itself that it is "an apparent reason" (a term suggested to me by Derek Parfit) for something else and that on the basis of it believing that can be rational. (The notion of a fact here carries no metaphysical baggage; we may perhaps let it be simply a truth, taking 'truth' in the ontologically thinnest sense that will serve.)

243

29. They only *tend* to create knowledge because there are cases in which the justification, whatever its degree, is the wrong kind to render a true belief knowledge. For instance, even if I justifiedly and truly believe my ticket will lose a sweepstakes with a million coupons and one winner, I get no closer to knowledge (or at best approach it asymptotically) if the number of coupons increases, even though my belief gains proportionately in probability.

30. For most people, it is both natural and rational to believe, on first considering the proposition, that for every condition, there is a class of entities that meet it. One need only reflect, however, to see that then there must be a class of all classes that meet the conditions of non-self-membership. This, however, would be a member of itself if and only if it is not!

31. As Aristotle said in characterizing the kinds of acts that are just, "acts are called just and self-controlled when they are the kind of acts which a just or self-controlled man would perform" (*Nicomachean Ethics* 1105b5f).

32. In "Justification, Truth, and Reliability" I argue for the integration of the property of justifiedness with the property of justification; and in "Faith, Belief, and Rationality," *Philosophical Perspectives* 5 (1991), I compare and contrast rationality and justification in the way just indicated. As to the contrast between rationalization and justification, the former term, so far as it is non-pejorative, applies mainly to belief *types*; thus, even if I give a good rationalization for my instantiating the *type, believing that p*, I do not necessarily show that my *token* of that type, *my* belief that *p*, is rational. It may, e.g., be based on superstition, which may be why I want to rationalize it. This last claim is defended in my "Rationalization and Rationality," in *The Structure of Justification*.

CHAPTER 3

1. Speech acts and other symbolic acts, such as gestures, are commonly exceptions to this point, but it may be more qua expressing intentional attitudes like belief than as actions that they have intentional objects. It should also be granted that some goal state with intentional content may *underlie* every action (and does if, as many action theorists hold, every action is intentional under some description); but whereas a belief cannot be the belief it is apart from its content, the dependency of an action on any particular goal that underlies it is not constitutive of the action in this way. Even if some actions, e.g., assisting someone, are conceived as *necessarily* goal-defined, say, as based on an other-regarding goal, there is at least no specific goal that is required, whereas one cannot believe that *p* unless the propositional content of *p* is precisely what one believes.

2. I have explicated action for one or more reasons in "Acting for Reasons," *Philosophical Review* 95 (1986), in my *Action, Intention, and Reason* (Ithaca: Cornell University Press, 1993), and there argue that with the possible exception of intrinsically motivated actions, actions for reasons are based on motivation—on wants, in the widest sense, in which they include desires—by virtue of connecting beliefs.

3. There is one exception to this: the ground of my (perfectly justified) belief that I believe a student of mine will succeed may be that very belief. It is as though I could just "see" it (or some manifestation of it).This second belief can certainly be rational. Here, however, its rationality has nothing to do with its role in justifying my second-order belief that I have it, nor have I inferred my having the belief that the student will succeed: this belief itself is my ground, not expressive of a premise I use to arrive at my second-order belief that I have the original one.

4. Three qualifications are needed here. First, a belief arising purely from wishful thinking may be non-inferential, yet not rest on a basic source, e.g., perception. A behavioral analogue might be an action we cannot do at will—basically—but are helped to do non-instrumentally by, say, brain stimulation: like many beliefs that arise from wishful thinking, it is the kind we would ordinarily do by doing something else or not at all. Second, the typical (but not the only) way in which one belief rests on another is inferential, but many actions performed by performing some other, e.g., making noise by turning a key, are not connected with it by a reason or any reasoning process. Third, for convenience I talk as if, e.g., stepping on the gas and accelerating were two actions rather than a single one under two descriptions. But nothing I say need deny the latter point; e.g., we can say that it is by instantiating the act-property, *stepping on the gas*, that we instantiate the act-property, *accelerating*, and that here one concrete action exemplifies both properties.

5. The directness here is not causal: what is ruled out is indirect—in the sense of inferential—belief. That is mediated by another belief with a special role. There may be causal intermediaries (even including beliefs, in a non-inferential role relative to the direct one).

6. In "Is Raising One's Arm a Basic Action?" and "Volition and Basic Action," in Hugh McCann, *The Works of Agency* (Ithaca: Cornell University Press, 1998), McCann provides an account of volition and how it serves as basic. Other recent informative discussions of this issue are found in John Searle, *Intentionality* (Cambridge: Cambridge University Press, 1983), Myles Brand, *Intending and Acting* (Cambridge, Mass: MIT, 1984), Michael Bratman, *Faces of Intention* (Cambridge: Cambridge University Press, 1999), Alfred Mele, *Springs of Action* (New York: Oxford University Press, 1992), and, esp., Carl Ginet, *On Action* (Cambridge: Cambridge University Press, 1990).

7. That there is a suitably broad sense of 'want' I have argued in "Intending," *Journal of Philosophy* 70 (1973), and I have tried to explicate wanting in the relevant sense in "The Concept of Wanting," *Philosophical Studies* 21 (1973), both in my *Action, Intention, and Reason*. In places I shall for stylistic purposes shift between 'want' and 'desire', though I do not take these terms to be equivalent. Nothing should turn on these shifts.

8. I have discussed both kinds of foundationalism in "The Structure of Motivation," *Pacific Philosophical Quarterly* 61 (1980). The grounding may be indirect and may involve many links in the motivational chain. As with belief, the relevant basis relation (expressed by—among other phrases—'in order to' in its main use)

is *non-transitive:* one can *A* in order to *B*, and *B* in order to *C*, say, to enjoy oneself, without *A*-ing in order to *C.* For one might not appropriately connect *A* with *C.* An important exception to the view that intentional actions are grounded in intrinsic desires is this. One might have forgotten why one was going into the kitchen, hence have a desire to do so that is merely non-intrinsic: neither intrinsic nor instrumental. Such a *residual desire* can still explain why one got up from one's chair. Residual desires are discussed again in Chapter 5.

9. More generally, the by-relation between actions need not be cognitively mediated. One can do one thing by doing another where the second *is* one's means but is not envisaged as such.

10. This does not imply that every intrinsic want has another want based on it: although foundations normally have something built on them, they need not. The superstructure may also crumble leaving the foundations intact. It is also possible (as described in note 8) for a kind of *motivational inertia* to keep a previously instrumental desire from extinguishing when one has ceased to believe its realization would contribute to that of any intrinsic desire one has. I also leave open the possibility of wants that *cannot* be (inferentially) based on others, as arguably some beliefs cannot be so based on others. It is an interesting question whether Aristotle so conceived the desire for one's own happiness. Hume apparently viewed the desire to avoid pain in this way; see the passage quoted in note 15.

11. One want may be causally grounded in a second without being inferentially based on it (there might, e.g., be only a wayward causal chain connecting them). I have in mind the practical inferential relation present when one wants *A* as a means to *B*, and in *that* sense wants it on the basis of wanting *B.*

12. I have argued that circular inferential chains of the relevant kind are apparently impossible for beliefs, in *Epistemology,* ch. 7; for desires, in "The Structure of Motivation"; and for valuations, in "Axiological Foundationalism," *Canadian Journal of Philosophy* 12 (1982), in *The Structure of Justification.* I have tried to show that causal chains are, however, crucial for justification and rationality, in "The Causal Structure of Indirect Justification," *Journal of Philosophy* 70 (1973) and "Rationalization and Rationality," *Synthese* 65 (1985), both in *The Structure of Justification.* Even if circular chains are possible, positing them would be bad epistemology and unrealistic psychology.

13. If, as I hold, intrinsic wanting is not merely wanting something other than as a means, then there can be wants that are neither intrinsic nor instrumental. I ignore this possibility here; surely no remotely normal person could have only non-intrinsic wants, but they are significant and will be discussed in Chapter 5.

14. A treatment of motivational foundationalism in general and Aristotle's version in particular is given in my "The Structure of Motivation."

15. In *An Enquiry Concerning the Principles of Morals,* Hume says, "Ask a man *why he uses exercise;* he will answer *because he desires to keep his health.* If you then enquire, *why he desires health,* he will readily reply, *because sickness is painful.* If you push your enquiries further, and desire a reason *why he hates pain,* it is impossible he can ever

give any. This is an ultimate end, and is never referred to any other object." See p. 134 of the reprint of the 1777 edition (La Salle, Ill.: Open Court, 1960).

16. Two qualifications are needed. (1) I am tentatively assuming something to be qualified later: that an *instrumental* want can be rational even if the want it subserves is not rational and perhaps is not even intrinsic, as it would not be if desire were infinitely regressive, in the sense that, for anything one wants, say, *A*, one wants it just for the sake of something else, say, *B*, and that just for the sake of *C*, etc. (2) Here as elsewhere I sometimes use phrases like 'believes it will realize' and 'wants to satisfy' schematically. What the agent actually believes is something like this: that if I get *x* (the thing instrumentally wanted) I will produce *y* (the thing intrinsically wanted). Any number of specific wants and beliefs can serve; and only careful examination of the particular case can yield a precise specification of what they are. Behavioral data alone can never yield it; this can be viewed as a special case of *underdetermination* of theory by data.

17. There is, to be sure, an analogue of psychological certainty, which is a matter of the way a belief is held and is not a normative property. The conative analogue would be something like the *entrenchment* of a desire, which is similarly a matter of how it is possessed and not a normative property.

18. As I construe foundationalism simpliciter, and as it is best construed if we are to see it, in historical perspective, as heavily bound to a plausible regress argument, it simply says that the structure of a body of justified beliefs (or other justified intentional elements) is foundational; it leaves to particular theorists how strong the foundations must be—beyond a capacity to stop the regress—what sorts of content they may have, how they uphold the superstructure, and other matters, such as the appropriate transmission principles. I am construing motivational foundationalism in the same way, and as allowing the same kind of latitude.

19. Some critics of foundationalism have not sufficiently appreciated this point about the independence of content from the justifiedness of beliefs having that content. See, e.g., Michael Williams, *Unnatural Doubts* (Oxford: Basil Blackwell, 1991). The issue here is foundational belief and desire, but the point holds for virtually any beliefs and desires. If there are qualifications, such as the apparent impossibility of unjustifiedly believing that if Shakespeare is identical with the author of *Hamlet*, then the author of *Hamlet* is identical with Shakespeare, they will not undermine the theory of rationality being developed.

20. I mean this to apply to human persons. I grant that, say, for religious reasons, one might try to cultivate indifference to one's suffering and happiness. This counts against a crude hedonistic notion of rational desire, but it seems intelligible only on the supposition that there is a kind of happiness, here presumably a spiritual kind, in one's sense of succeeding. Paradoxically, perhaps, the success seems incomplete unless there remains a residual, perhaps fleshly, desire to avoid pain, or some material desire to achieve happiness, which one feels one is *overcoming*. Similar points may apply to the possibility of, say, wanting *only* to create art. Surely one might intrinsically want a kind of aesthetic satisfaction that amounts to one's own version of happiness. If not, I doubt such a person would be *fully*

rational. For discussion of the naturalness and pervasiveness of considerations of pleasure and pain (among others) in persons it is intuitively plausible to consider rational, see Bernard Gert, *Morality: Its Nature and Justification* (New York: Oxford University Press, 1998).

21. For some reasons to think this see Gert's *Morality*. I am not here imagining a person with *only* selfish intrinsic desires but assume for the sake of argument that, given suitable beliefs, even such a person could be minimally rational. Much that bears on this question will emerge in the next two chapters.

22. This point is relevant to the much discussed problem of evil. The value of relief from certain pains may outweigh the disvalue of suffering them.

23. This dependence would not imply that rational desire is entirely a matter of rational belief. The case illustrates only defeasibility of a non-instrumental desire by a belief, not positive dependence of an intrinsic desire on the belief that its object has certain qualities. Moreover, my view is consistent with the thesis that practical and theoretical reason are two aspects of the same basic capacity, as Kant apparently held. He says, e.g., that "in the final analysis there can be but one and the same reason which must be differentiated only in application." See *Foundations of the Metaphysics of Morals*, trans. Lewis White Beck (New York: Liberal Arts Press, 1959), section 392.

24. I am assuming that if I merely have a faint hope, I do not intend; 'I intend' expresses too much confidence. For supporting argument see my "Intending, Intentional Action, and Desire," in Joel Marks, ed., *The Ways of Desire* (Chicago: Precedent Publishing Co. 1986). It may also be possible that a *non-actional* desire, e.g., simply to *have* an appraisal, is sufficient basis for an intention without independently issuing—though it does tend to issue—in a hope, want, *or* intention to act.

25. Indeed, motivational internalists insist that normative beliefs imply some degree of motivation quite apart from independent desires, and many of them hold—plausibly, in my view—that such beliefs are also capable of justifying desires to act in accord with the beliefs. There is a large literature on this kind of thesis. See, e.g., William K. Frankena, "Obligation and Motivation in Recent Moral Philosophy," in A. I. Melden, ed., *Essays in Moral Philosophy* (Seattle: University of Washington Press, 1958) and Bernard Williams, "Internal and External Reasons," in his *Moral Luck* (Cambridge: Cambridge University Press, 1981), an essay much discussed in later literature. Extensive critical discussions of the issues it raises are provided by Stephen L. Darwall, *Impartial Reason* (Ithaca: Cornell University Press, 1983), Derek Parfit, *Reasons and Persons* (Oxford: Oxford University Press, 1984), and "Reasons and Motivation," *Proceedings of the Aristotelian Society*, supplementary vol. 71 (1997), David Brink, *Moral Realism and the Foundations of Ethics* (Cambridge: Cambridge University Press, 1989), and Simon Blackburn, *Ruling Passions* (Oxford: Oxford University Press, 1998). I have discussed the issue in detail, and cited many other treatments, in "Moral Judgment and Reasons for Action," in my *Moral Knowledge and Ethical Character* (New York: Oxford University Press, 1997).

26. That intending is understandable in terms of wanting and believing is especially controversial, but a number of philosophers have argued for the view. I have done so in "Intending," and defended the account in "Intending and Its Place in the Theory of Action," in Ghita Holmstrom-Hintikka and Raimo Tuomela, eds., *Contemporary Action Theory*, vol. 1 (Dordrecht: Kluwer, 1997). See also Bratman, *Faces of Intention;* McCann, *The Works of Agency;* Wayne Davis, "A Causal Theory of Intending," *American Philosophical Quarterly* 26 (1989); and Mele, *Springs of Action.* I offer an account of the structure of valuation, and discuss axiological foundationalism in relation to epistemological foundationalism in detail, in "Axiological Foundationalism," reprinted in *The Structure of Justification.*

27. A *de dicto* belief would also serve, e.g., the belief that if the third ring was short and not followed by a fourth, then the phone was answered; and many *de re* beliefs would do. For discussion of this problem and a case for connecting beliefs in each instance, see my "Belief, Reason, and Inference," *Philosophical Topics* 14, 1 (1986), reprinted in *The Structure of Justification.*

28. I discuss the counterpart briefly in "An Epistemic Conception of Rationality," *Social Theory and Practice* 9 (1983), reprinted in *The Structure of Justification.* For valuable related discussion of a coherentist view of rational action, critical of the view on grounds overlapping mine, see Darwall, *Impartial Reason,* esp. ch. 4.

29. Hume might also have considered—as certainly an instrumentalist may— what agents ought to believe given their evidence, but I am not explicating Hume here and will ignore this complication. For a Humean view that incorporates this epistemic perspective on practical rationality see Richard A. Fumerton, *Reason and Morality* (Ithaca: Cornell University Press, 1990).

30. The notion of less satisfaction here is problematic. The notion is surely not additive, and it is not clear whether number of desires as well as their combined strength should count. Is the goal just total quantity of satisfaction or, say, the satisfaction of the most desires, other things equal? If number counts, we may have an impure instrumentalism; if it does not (and indeed even if it does), would it be instrumentally rational to cause oneself to have as one's only desire a terrifically intense one for a single thing if that were the easiest strong desire to satisfy? This or a similar strategy might be the best way of getting the maximum quantity of desire satisfaction.

31. The most common interpretation of appropriateness here is optimality, in the sense that the action is at least as good as any available alternative from the point of view of satisfying one's intrinsic desires. Satisfaction itself may be construed quantitatively or in some other way, e.g. (more plausibly), in terms of quantity taken in relation to beliefs, second-order desires (say, for primacy of some of my desires over others), and perhaps other factors. The rationality of extrinsic desires is understood similarly, in terms of the contribution their realization would make to satisfying intrinsic desires.

32. The classical decision-theoretic view of rational action seems a case in point. Indeed, it is arguable (though I cannot explore the issue here) that a pure instrumentalist must hold a maximization view, since otherwise rational actions

would not accord fully with intrinsic desires. I do not regard Hume as committed to pure instrumentalism, but a case can be made for this. I suggest some reasons to think Hume a more guarded instrumentalist, in ch. 2 of my *Practical Reasoning* (London: Routledge, 1989). A kind of Humean instrumentalism is defended in Fumerton, *Reason and Morality*, and helpful discussion of the decision-theoretic approach to rationality is given by Robert Nozick in *The Nature of Rationality* (Cambridge, Mass.: Harvard University Press, 1993). For a detailed treatment of some relevant aspects of decision theory see Mark Kaplan, *Decision Theory as Philosophy* (Cambridge: Cambridge University Press, 1996).

33. I am referring here to the "satisficing" conception of rational action, on which much has been written in the literature of ethical theory and, especially, decision theory.

34. It may be significant that Shakespeare presents this description as a self-criticism. Malcolm surely rejects a pure instrumentalist standard. By that standard, quantity of desire being equal, the scullery maid will do as well as Cleopatra.

35. For an indication of how such a foundationalism may be constructed, see Richard Foley, *Working without a Net* (Oxford: Oxford University Press, 1993).

36. R. B. Brandt holds a sophisticated theory of this sort. See *A Theory of the Good and the Right* (Oxford: Oxford University Press, 1979). An interesting foil is Foley, *Working without a Net*. Foley also proposes a kind of reflectivity test, but in denying a constitutive role to facts and logic, he is subjectivistic in a way Brandt is not. It is interesting to consider both views as first-person versions of ideal observer theories. For a more recent, more qualified defense of the informed-preference theory of rationality view, see Thomas L. Carson, *Value and the Good Life* (Notre Dame: University of Notre Dame Press, 2000). Carson contrasts his view with Brandt's full-information view and describes his own more moderate theory as "modeled on Crispin Wright's concept of 'superassertability'" (p. 7).

CHAPTER 4

1. Forms of instrumentalism are widely held and are defended in detail by both Fumerton, in *Reason and Morality*, and Allan Gibbard, in *Wise Choices, Apt Feelings* (Cambridge, Mass.: Harvard University Press, 1991). T. M. Scanlon says, of this kind of view (of which he is critical in a number of places), that "in recent years 'the (most) rational thing to do' has most commonly been taken to mean 'what most conduces to the fulfillment of the agent's aims'." See *What We Owe to Each Other* (Cambridge, Mass.: Harvard University Press, 1998), pp. 191–92. For some who hold instrumentalist or similar views, the notion of intrinsic goodness is even ultimately unintelligible. For a variety of objections to the notion as often understood see Tara Smith, "Intrinsic Value: Look-Say Ethics," *Journal of Value Inquiry* 32 (1998). Some of these are at least implicitly answered in my "The Axiology of Moral Experience," *Journal of Ethics* 2 (1998).

2. Some pleasures may in another way be *transexperiential*. Suppose I have a perfect hallucination of playing a sonata and the experience is pleasurable. It

would seem that if I am not playing the sonata then I am not enjoying playing it, though this is perhaps not self-evident. Cf. Robert Nozick's discussion of a pleasure machine, in *Anarchy, State, and Utopia* (New York: Basic Books, 1974), pp. 42–45. I may, however, have the pleasures *as of* playing it, and for hedonism that may be all that matters. I return to this issue later.

3. This raises the possibility of an *adverbial theory of pleasure* as an account of its ontology. I leave its ontology open; my concern here is more its logic and its phenomenology. I also lack space to pursue some of the immense literature on pleasure. For references to some of it and a critique of a widespread conception (not implicit in my view) see Fred Feldman, "On the Intrinsic Value of Pleasures," *Ethics* 107 (1997), pp. 448–66.

4. *Pace* Aristotle, perhaps, presumably even happiness can be wanted as a means, though this is probably not a way of instrumentally wanting it that his view required denying. The *ultimate* ground of the relevant want might still have to be happiness.

5. One could want a thing for some of its enjoyable qualities and actually enjoy it for other such qualities, but I ignore this complication here. I also ignore certain differences between pleasure and pain, e.g., in their phenomenology. There are related differences between hedonic desires and hedonic aversion. But I doubt that anything in my argument turns on these differences.

6. We could speak of an *intrinsic want* where the object is wanted for something the subject (in some sense) takes to be intrinsic to that object, and *wanting intrinsically* where the subject is correct in that taking. This is a distinction well worth observing, but in part because, typically, wanting something for its own sake meets the latter condition, and most intrinsic wants of interest to us are of this sort, I do not adopt the suggested terminological regimentation.

7. If one must in such cases have a self-concept in the content of the relevant desire, there is still no particular way in which one must conceive oneself. Deep difficulties beset explication of the relevant notion and the associated *de se* locutions, such as 'he himself'. For an extensive treatment of these problems see Hector-Neri Castañeda, e.g., "He*: On the Logic of Self-Consciousness," *Ratio* 8 (1966), and, for later statements, his contribution to James E. Tomberlin, ed., *Action, Language, and the Structure of the World* (Indianapolis: Hackett Publishing Co., 1983). If action-wants have objects embodying a self-concept, so does intending. Indeed, there is perhaps more reason to attribute such content to intending, since, for one thing, it may imply a more definite (often reflective) focus on the object.

8. Some of this may serve as a gloss on Jean-Paul Sartre's famous pronouncement that existence precedes essence. It may perhaps be implicit in the idea that, as I am suggesting here, our *experience* of ourselves is conceptually (and in other ways) prior to our developing a *concept* of ourselves, or of what we ought to be.

9. On analogy with the standard terminology for belief, substantival wants may be called *de re*, being "of the [relevant] thing"—I can want, of the pain, that it stop, just as I can believe, of the man in the mirror, that he has a stain on his coat—and propositional wants may be called *de dicto*, being "of the [relevant] proposi-

tion"—wanting that world peace prevail is (in this way) like believing that it will. The middle case (which may have no close cognitive analogue) we call *infinitival wanting*, since action-wants are always *to do* something. For discussion of the belief cases see John Perry, e.g., "Self-Notions," *Logos* 11 (1990). Cf. David Lewis, "Attitudes *De Dicto* and *De Se*," *Philosophical Review* 88 (1979), reprinted with a postscript in his *Philosophical Papers*, vol. 1 (Oxford: Oxford University Press, 1983).

10. Often, of course, we have only potential knowledge of the relevant properties; e.g., I am only disposed to believe, from what I remember, that the waters will be rough, but do not believe it and so do not know it. Here it is even less plausible to think that wanting to swim in those waters entails wanting to swim in them *as* rough.

11. What I say is very much in the spirit of Joseph Butler's view of desire in relation to selfishness. See esp. his Sermon IV, "Upon the Love of Our Neighbor," in Stephen L. Darwall, ed., *Five Sermons* (Indianapolis: Hackett Publishing Co., 1983). Butler says, e.g., "That all particular appetites and passions are toward *external things themselves*, distinct from the *pleasure arising from them*, is manifested from hence—that there could not be this pleasure were it not for that prior suitableness between the object and the passion; there could be no enjoyment or delight from one thing more than another, from eating food more than from swallowing a stone, if there were not an affection or appetite to one thing more than another" (p. 47). His thrust, however, does not concern the exact content of the desire in the way mine does—and indeed I would resist his inference from conditions for the existence of pleasure to conditions for the contents of conative attitudes. His main point is that even when the object is sought for pleasure, *it* is sought. It is consistent with what he holds that although, say, my passion for tennis is for *it* and not for my pleasure or even for an internal sense of the zesty athletic experience, *what* I want is that *I* play tennis (his example in the first quotation is in fact of an action). Nor does Butler emphasize the psychological or conceptual primitiveness of certain kinds of objects of desire. Still, what he says is compatible with, and I think well supports, the view I am proposing.

12. Hedonists are not always clear on this matter. In *Utilitarianism* (esp. ch. 2.) Mill maintains that happiness is pleasure and freedom from pain (as if this designated one thing of value), but he also says that many things can be desired as "parts" of happiness. Since I do not endorse hedonism, I will not try to sort out the main variants here. For related discussion of hedonism and of intrinsic value in general see E. J. Bond, *Reason and Value* (Cambridge: Cambridge University Press, 1983), and Noah Lemos, *Intrinsic Value* (Cambridge: Cambridge University Press, 1994). I ignore the wider hedonistic view that the good is the pleasant, the bad the unpleasant; this is more plausible than the more common hedonism but is still vulnerable to the kinds of objections I pose.

13. In ch. 11 of *Moral Knowledge*, where experientialism is treated in more detail, it is formulated as the position that only states of experience have intrinsic value (or intrinsic disvalue). In different language, these states are experience-

tokens, but one might call a type of experience (derivatively) intrinsically valuable provided all of its tokens are. The intuitive idea is that value is realized in the *lives* of conscious beings. This notion is intended broadly enough to extend to theology; it does not rule out the possibility of infinite intrinsic value being realized in the divine mind.

14. The debate over explanationist realism continues. Important aspects of this debate are found in the recent literature on moral realism. For a discussion of the issues and references to some major papers, see my "Ethical Naturalism and the Explanatory Power of Moral Concepts," in *Moral Knowledge*. This paper also discusses supervenience of normative properties on natural ones, whereas here I speak of grounding, in a way that leaves open what kind of supervenience it represents. Such supervenience would in any case not entail physicalism. Pertinent discussion of how common-sense psychology of a kind taken seriously in this book can avoid commitment to physicalism is found in Lynne Rudder Baker, *Saving Belief: A Critique of Physicalism* (Princeton: Princeton University Press, 1987). Notice, incidentally, that (as I argue in "Ethical Naturalism") there is some question whether, even as experienced, intrinsic value, say the goodness of pleasure— as opposed to the natural properties it is grounded in, such as the psychological processes that underlie the pleasure—explains anything (empirically). If not, then the imagined explanationist way of defending experientialism will lead to denying that there is anything of intrinsic value.

15. Indeed, as a disposition, the wanting does not by itself, apart from events that manifest it, even promote pleasure or serve as a means to it: acting on it (or some other event connected with it in the right way) does this causal work.

16. It might follow that the thing in question is *necessarily* good, but this is a different concept. Perhaps God could have created something that, in every possible world, is merely instrumentally good, in which case it would be necessarily but not intrinsically good.

17. This paragraph is a response in part to Franz Brentano's idea that pleasure in pleasure is intrinsically good because of its object, though there we do not have a counterexample to experientialism. For discussion see R. M. Chisholm, *Brentano on Intrinsic Value* (Cambridge: Cambridge University Press, 1986).

18. Experientialism is defended in detail, in part by distinguishing intrinsic from inherent value and in part by appeal to a version of Moore's principle of organic unity, in ch. 11 of *Moral Knowledge*. For critical discussion of that principle see Michael J. Zimmerman, "Virtual Intrinsic Value and the Principle of Organic Unities," *Philosophy and Phenomenological Research* 59 (1999).

19. The term 'inherently valuable' was C. I. Lewis's label for things whose (proper) contemplation is intrinsically valuable. See *An Analysis of Knowledge and Valuation* (LaSalle, Ill.: Open Court, 1946), p. 391. I take it that inherent value is possessed on the basis of intrinsic properties, and I leave open whether *every* instance of proper contemplation or appropriate experience of them for their own sake has intrinsic value or whether there is simply an appropriate kind of tendency for them to have it.

20. I assume that no candidate for inherent value is such that it cannot be contemplated, e.g., is such that on being contemplated it ceases to exist.

21. To be sure, a rational intrinsic desire can be *cognitively grounded*, i.e., (roughly), grounded in a justified belief that realizing it would be, say, rewarding. But (as indicated in more than one place in this book) the justification of such a belief will itself be experientially grounded, e.g., in one's having found a kind of experience enjoyable.

22. Here as elsewhere I presuppose a distinction between qualities in the abstract and their tokens. There is a similar distinction in the case of desires (and beliefs). In the light of it, we may plausibly say that whereas the rationality, *for* people of a certain sort, of the "property" *wanting to hear Beethoven's Appassionata*, is grounded in the enjoyable qualities of that experience (for such a person), the rationality of a particular intrinsic desire for continuation of a particular hearing of it is grounded in the tokens of those qualities in the person's experience.

23. I am conceiving the grounding relation, as I do supervenience, as a kind of asymmetric relation of determination, but cannot explicate it further here. For wide-ranging instructive discussion, see Jaegwon Kim, e.g., "Concepts of Supervenience," *Philosophy and Phenomenological Research* 45 (1984), "Supervenience as a Philosophical Concept," *Metaphilosophy* 21 (1990), and "The Non-Reductivist's Troubles with Mental Causation," in John Heil and Alfred Mele, eds., *Mental Causation* (Oxford: Oxford University Press, 1993). I leave open whether one can *know* that an intrinsic desire is rational other than through experience of its object (or of something similar), and whether there can be rational intrinsic wants for something not experienceable, such as the truth (as opposed to contemplating the truth) of a certain mathematical proposition.

24. Cf. G. E. Moore: "when I talk of a thing as 'my own good' all that I can mean is that something which will be exclusively mine, as my own pleasure is mine . . . is also *good absolutely*. The *good* of it can in no possible sense be 'private' or belong to me; any more than a thing can *exist* privately or *for* one person only. The only reason I can have for aiming at 'my own good' is that it is *good absolutely* that what I so call should belong to me. . . . But if it is *good absolutely* that I should have it, then everyone else has as much reason for aiming at *my* having it as I have myself." See *Principia Ethica* (Cambridge: Cambridge University Press, 1903), p. 99. Moore is talking mainly about the *value* of what one wants; I am more concerned with the content of what one wants. Even if the content of a want is essentially egoistic, its realization might be good absolutely. But my view of content is also compatible with Moore's view here and makes at least one implication of this view (one explored in detail in Chapter 6) seem not unnatural—that there is reason for each of us to promote the good of others.

25. For an important and influential view like both Moore's and mine in significant ways, see Thomas Nagel, *The Possibility of Altruism* (Princeton: Princeton University Press, 1970). But his emphasis, more than mine, is on how one conceives oneself and others; mine, more than his, is on the content of rational desires, and I include desires whose rationality seems prior to any comparative con-

ception of oneself in relation to others. (I also develop my position on rational desire, in Chapter 6 as well as here, in relation to its parallels to rational belief.) On his more recent view, which I also take to be supportive of the theory I am developing, the sufferer's "awareness of how bad it [pain] is doesn't essentially involve a thought of it as his. . . . If I lacked or lost the concept of myself as distinct from other possible or actual persons, I would still apprehend the badness of pain, immediately." See *The View from Nowhere* (New York: Oxford University Press, 1986), p. 161. Nagel's focus differs from mine, however, in being, like Moore's, on the *value* of *what* we desire as opposed to the *rationality* of the relevant desires, and correspondingly on the difference between apprehending goodness and, as in my examples, experiencing natural properties on which goodness supervenes. In my view, experiencing the grounds of rational desire is *prior* to apprehension of goodness and does not require even implicitly conceptualizing the object of desire *as* good, even when an intrinsic want is rational because it is a desire of something for properties of it in virtue of which it is in fact intrinsically good. His view may also rule out less than mine regarding the relation of the person to the object of intrinsic desire; it may leave open, e.g., that a *non-comparative* self-concept is required for intrinsic desire. I require no self-concept at all.

26. I have developed this distinction in "Dispositional Beliefs and Dispositions to Believe," *Nous* (1994), which constructs a theory to account for the second distinction, between primary and self-referential aspects of perceptual belief. Both distinctions are commonly neglected, and their neglect is serious, as I argue, regarding the first, in "The Foundationalism-Coherentism Controversy" (ch. 4 of *The Structure of Justification*). For detailed discussion of the second distinction (or one much like it), which supports my approach here, see Paul K. Moser, *Knowledge and Evidence*. Note that normally seeing precedes acquisition of a concept of seeing; hence, it is plainly possible to see without believing that one does.

27. Many would argue that to be justified in believing one *sees* something requires justification for believing (though not one's actually believing) such entailed propositions as that the circumstances are favorable, e.g., in lighting. I would not say this, since I deny the relevant principle of the transmission of justification; but so far as any such consequence is entailed by justification for believing one sees something, the case for such sense-specific perceptual beliefs being the primitive ones is even weaker.

28. Perhaps one must conceive it as, say, that green thing over there; but apparently no conceptualization is required beyond what is implicit in having the perceptual belief about it (this is not, of course, easy to specify). In the parallel case of desire, again nothing seems required beyond what is implicit in wanting the object *for* the relevant properties (or apparent properties).

29. It is interesting to compare with my view elements of Jean-Paul Sartre's in *The Transcendence of the Ego*, trans. Forest Williams and Robert Kirkpatrick (New York: Simon and Schuster, 1957). He says, e.g., "Reflection 'poisons' desire. On the unreflected level I bring Peter help because 'Peter is having to be helped'. But if my state is suddenly transformed into a reflected state, then I am watching

myself act . . . It is no longer Peter who attracts me, it is *my* consciousness which appears to me as having to be perpetuated" (p. 59).

30. Such an abnormal want may have to be artificially induced, but pure instrumentalism has no plausible way to block artificial induction of a desire from conferring instrumental rationality. This issue is treated in "Autonomy, Reason, and Desire," reprinted in *Moral Knowledge*. A pure instrumentalist may rule out desires objectionable on strictly logical grounds, e.g., having plainly inconsistent objects, but this will not eliminate the myriad anomalies that the view allows as conferring rationality.

CHAPTER 5

1. I say 'normally' because there are complications, such as temporarily forgetting something one wants more than one wants to do the thing in question, and as a result intending to do something else, which one believes incompatible with the first. This is discussed in some detail in my "Intending," cited earlier.

2. Two qualifications are needed here. First, granting that we speak of intentions *that*, e.g., that no one borrow a car, these seem roughly equivalent to intentions to do something, typically, something the agent thinks appropriate to bringing about the relevant state of affairs. Second, if one takes ability and opportunity broadly enough, one might say that the tendency will always be realized under the specified conditions. But such things as temporarily forgetting one's plan can result in not doing even something one intends to do and easily can do. Sometimes we say, 'Oh, I just remembered. . . . ' If nothing triggers one's memory, one could fail entirely in such a case and miss a good opportunity.

3. A partial account of the sorts of elements that can trigger intentions is given in my *Practical Reasoning*, ch. 5, on the dynamics of action.

4. Donald Davidson among others has been attracted to this line; see, e.g., his "Intending," in his *Essays on Actions and Events* (Oxford: Oxford University Press, 1985). For further development of the view, see David Velleman, *Practical Reflection* (Princeton: Princeton University Press, 1989). Motivational internalism in some forms goes part way toward this view, not by making intentions belief-like but by making certain beliefs intention-like. For assessment of the issue see my "Moral Judgment and Reasons for Action," in *Moral Knowledge*, and Brink, *Moral Realism and the Foundation of Ethics*.

5. A cognitive-motivational account of intending is defended in my "Intending" and later papers, esp. "Intending and Its Place in the Theory of Action," both cited earlier, but this account will not be presupposed here.

6. As will be evident later in this chapter, in speaking of wants as providing reasons to act, I am not suggesting that they need not be grounded. Just as a belief can express a premise that provides one with a reason to believe, only if the former belief is well-grounded, a want must be well-grounded if it is to give one a reason to act. If the belief is not well-grounded, holding the further belief on the

basis of it is not justified; if the desire is not well-grounded, an action (wholly) in its service is not rational.

7. If there are exceptions to this, they come from cases like that of the toxin, which one takes because one has good reason to *intend* to do something—being offered a large sum simply to intend it—yet no reason to *do* it. I have already suggested that this seems better conceived as a case in which one has a reason to *cause* oneself to intend something. A distinct possibility is to conceive such reasons as directed toward the attitude of intending, but not its content: they are reasons *for intending* to A but not *to A*. This line is suggested, in relation to belief, by Walter Sinnott-Armstrong, in "Moral Skepticism," in Walter Sinnott-Armstrong and Mark Timmons, eds., *Moral Knowledge?* (Oxford: Oxford University Press, 1996).

8. The phrase 'for its own sake' is not meant to express part of the *content* of the intention: just as wanting something for its own sake is not a kind of wanting of it but wanting it for a certain kind of reason, intending to do something for its own sake is (at least normally) intending to do it for a similar kind of (intrinsic) reason. If one thinks one has control over whether one does something for its own sake as opposed to doing it for a further end, one could then say one intends to do it for its own sake, meaning to imply that the content of one's intention is: to do it for the sake of doing so. But it is by no means clear that this is an act-description. One can certainly intend to *cause* oneself to do a deed for its own sake—as opposed to, say, for money—and this is what one might be best taken to mean in so speaking; but that is a different matter and does not conflate actions with the reasons for which they are performed.

9. I argue for this, with reference to Kant's *Foundations of the Metaphysics of Morals*, in ch. 3 of *Practical Reasoning*.

10. This paragraph is highly qualified in part because I do not rule out that beliefs and desires are interconnected in such a way that the isolation of one from the other imagined here is not possible. Note, however, that even if this is so, presumably a person could be neurally manipulated so as to be temporarily without beliefs or without desires. The points made in the paragraph could be relativized to this case.

11. In my "Structural Justification," reprinted in *The Structure of Justification*, I discuss various ways in which one may have evidence. The points there apply to having reasons for belief as well as for action.

12. In my "Dispositional Beliefs and Dispositions to Believe," I discuss whether a mere disposition *to* believe the relevant proposition would do here. I argue that it would not; some might think otherwise, but the standard view seems sufficiently reasonable not to need argument to serve in the way it does here.

13. See, e.g., Carl G. Hempel, "Rational Action," in his *Aspects of Scientific Explanation* (New York: Macmillan, 1965). But Fumerton (in *Reason and Morality*) apparently does require rationality here (see, e.g., p. 101), and certainly a maximization of expected utility view may do so. For an account of how a similar rationality requirement figures in Aristotle, see Alasdair MacIntyre, *Whose Justice? Which Rationality?* (Notre Dame: University of Notre Dame Press, 1988). He says that

"as Aristotle understands practical rationality . . . Such a person must first be moved by a belief about what good is best for him. . . . But for it to be rational to be moved by that belief, that belief itself must be rationally well-grounded" (p. 125).

14. "Rationalization and Rationality," cited earlier in connection with justification of belief, also argues for the explanatory connection in the action case. The connection with Kant is intended; Aristotle similarly insisted on actions being rooted in character if they are to express virtue. This is argued in my "Acting from Virtue," in *Moral Knowledge*.

15. These five kinds of reasons are introduced and discussed in my "Acting for Reasons," in *Action, Intention, and Reason*. I might add that since motivating reasons are operative in producing or sustaining action, one might also call them *activating* reasons; and since subjective reasons may or may not activate but are the appropriate kind to motivate, one could call them *motivational* as opposed to motiva*ting*. But for our purposes there is no need to complicate the terminology in the text. For a related and generally complementary treatment of reasons for action, see Derek Parfit, "Reasons and Motivation," *Proceedings of the Aristotelian Society,* Supplementary Volume 71 (1997), and T. M. Scanlon, *What We Owe to Each Other,* esp. ch. 1. Scanlon's account, however, requires beliefs *about* reasons in a number of places where mine would require (given certain dispositions) simply *having* the reasons in question.

16. As these qualifications suggest, there is some question just how "implicit" a reason for action (or belief) can be and still be possessed. I can have some reason to meet someone where I can easily see that I would enjoy it but do not now either see that or want to do it. A further question is whether, if the relevant belief is unjustified or the relevant desire(s) irrational, the person has a *reason* or just a *motive* (for which the term 'reason' is also used, particularly in the phrase 'reason why'. A plausible option is to say that a possessed reason need not be good, though there may be limits to how bad it can be and still qualify as a reason as opposed to motive.

17. This is not to propose an analysis of desirability, but I take it to be normative in a sense entailing that there are objective reasons to want what is desirable. Cf. the "internalist requirement," endorsed by Christine Korsgaard and others, to the effect that we must be capable of wanting what we have (normative) reason to do. See, e.g., her "Skepticism about Practical Reason," *Journal of Philosophy* 86 (1983), pp. 5–25, and the related discussions in her *Sources of Normativity* and "The Normativity of Instrumental Reason," in Garrett Cullity and Berys Gaut, eds., *Ethics and Practical Reason* (Oxford: Oxford University Press, 1997), pp. 215–54. This last work, drawing on her critical interpretation of Kant, supports the critique of instrumentalism given in this chapter. A different anti-instrumentalist position drawing on Kant is found in much work by Alan Gewirth. A short statement of his position is "Can Any Final Ends Be Rational?" *Ethics* 102 (1991), pp. 66–95; and for critical perspectives on instrumentalism usefully compared with both Korsgaard's and Gewirth's, see Jean Hampton, "On Instrumental Rationality," in Jerome B. Schneewind, ed., *Reason, Ethics, and Society: Themes from Kurt Baier, with*

His Responses (LaSalle: Open Court, 1996), and Berys Gaut, "The Structure of Practical Reason," in Cullity and Gaut, eds., *Ethics and Practical Reason*. Gaut's paper is also critical of Kantian constructivism. Baier's reply (pp. 249–62) defends his own version of instrumentalism. For some points for which instrumentalists and non-instrumentalists may vie, cf. Harry G. Frankfurt, "On the Usefulness of Final Ends," in his *Necessity, Volition, and Love* (Princeton: Princeton University Press, 1999), and Peter Railton, "On the Hypothetical and Non-Hypothetical in Reasoning about Belief and Action," in Cullity and Gaut, *Ethics and Practical Reason*.

18. I argue for this in "The Concept of Wanting," in my *Action, Intention, and Reason*.

19. Instrumentalists may argue that pain and pleasure *entail* positive and negative (aversive) desire, respectively, hence must supply reasons for action. I think there is no such entailment (in part because pain and pleasure are prior to the conceptualization needed for the relevant desires). In any case, the relevant desires by themselves need not confer reasons for action just *because* they are non-instrumental desires; as I argue shortly, the instrumentalist would still need an argument to show that it is not because of their content, e.g., being for something good, that they provide reasons.

20. Hume appears to do this, for reasons I have indicated in ch. 2 of *Practical Reasoning*. Certainly R. B. Brandt does it in *A Theory of the Good and the Right*.

21. There are other appropriate models, such as that of a compressed spring: release is natural, though it need never occur; and there is no specific direction it must take apart from belief, which is meant to guide it. Historically, the mechanical metaphors and models so influential in the seventeenth and eighteenth centuries may have played a role in making instrumentalism appealing. Baron d'Holbach is especially suggestive: "the soul is nothing more than the body considered relatively to some of its functions more concealed than others . . . it is subjected to the influences of those material and physical causes which give impulse to the body. . . . Man's life is a line that nature commands him to subscribe upon the surface of the earth. . . . ' See ch. 11 of *The System of Nature* (1770), trans. H. D. Robinson. Other suggestive metaphors and models can be found in Hobbes and Hume.

22. The problem can also be raised in relation to Buridan's ass: if, like that poor creature paralyzed by the equal and opposite attractions of food and water, I am caught between two obviously incompatible things that I want equally, say, to escape the fire by land and to escape it by sea, and I have no third want that provides a reason to break the tie, then I have no reason to break it, and unless nature comes to my aid by giving me, say, a desire to avoid the increasingly hot dilemma, I have no reason even to break the tie to save my life.

23. On this point Derek Parfit's *Reasons and Persons* and his paper cited in note 15 are instructive.

24. Granted, there are cases in which we apparently know something from memory even when we have forgotten our grounds; but I believe that knowledge

and justification are different in this respect, as I argue in "Memorial Justification," *Philosophical Topics* 23 (1995), pp. 31–45.

25. The implicit view of pleasure I take from Richard Brandt, who may have been influenced by John Stuart Mill on the point: "desiring a thing and finding it pleasant, aversion to it and thinking of it as painful . . . are two parts of the same phenomenon—in strictness of language, two different modes of naming the same psychological fact . . ." (*Utilitarianism*, ch. 4). I am not aware that the use I make here of this conception of pleasure has been proposed by anyone else. For a good survey of views on the nature of pleasure see William P. Alston's article on pleasure in *The Encyclopedia of Philosophy* (New York: Macmillan, 1967).

26. I say 'normally' because a belief can be induced by, say, brain manipulation. I should add that the relevant experience includes belief formation or contemplation of one's beliefs or their propositional objects: this can be crucial for inferential, as opposed to experiential, belief formation. For an account of how information can be received, especially through perception, without being encoded in beliefs, see Fred Dretske, *Knowledge and the Flow of Information*, cited in Chapter 2, note 16.

27. For a discussion bearing on this problem (but not, I think, on solving it), see Robert Nozick, *The Nature of Rationality*, esp. pp. 133–51.

28. For a case supporting this line, see Derek Parfit's attack on instrumentalism, and on the idea that desire alone can confer reasons for action, in his *Practical Realism* (in preparation). For a more sympathetic examination of the kind of instrumentalism in question with special reference to Bernard Williams as a major proponent of it, see Garrett Cullity, "Practical Theory," in Cullity and Gaut, *Ethics and Practical Reason*.

29. Here I ignore the possibility that there need be no connecting belief for a rational basic action. Even there, however, the agent will be disposed to believe that (say) the way to *A* is simply to do it (as opposed to doing it by doing something else).

30. This qualification may express the minimal truth in motivational internalism: the possibility of motivation, and of acting on the basis of it, may be implicit in there being a normative reason for action.

31. In "Doxastic Voluntarism and the Ethics of Belief," *Facta Philosophica* I, 1 (1999), I defend this point. See also Alston's *Epistemic Justification* for extensive criticism of voluntarism and Matthias Steup, "Epistemic Deontology and the Voluntariness of Belief" (in preparation), for a response that defends a version of voluntarism. For critical discussion of Alston's and, especially, John Locke's, treatment of voluntarism, see Nicholas P. Wolterstorff, *John Locke and the Ethics of Belief* (Cambridge: Cambridge University Press, 1996), e.g., pp. 101–18. Valuable recent discussions are contained in Anthonie Meijers, ed., *Belief, Cognition, and the Will* (Tilburg: Tilburg University Press, 1999). It is arguable that the case regarding *acceptance* differs from the one I make here concerning belief. My "Doxastic Voluntarism" bears directly on this; for different but broadly supporting views see Eric Olsson, "Doxastic Decision Theory, Voluntarism and the Primacy

of Practical Reason," and Raimo Tuomela, "Belief versus Acceptance," pp. 73–84 and 85–98 respectively in Meijers, *Belief, Cognition, and the Will*. Further discussion pertinent to the decision-theoretic approach is found in Kaplan's *Decision Theory as Philosophy*, Bas C. Van Fraassen, "Belief and the Will," *Journal of Philosophy* 81 (1984), and Isaac Levi, *The Fixation of Belief and Its Undoing* (Cambridge: Cambridge University Press, 1991).

32. Foley, in *The Theory of Epistemic Rationality*, takes this sort of line at times, though he never says that practical rationality is more fundamental than theoretical. It is surprising how infrequently it is noted that it is unclear what it means to talk of the *goal* of belief, if beliefs are not actions.

33. This is argued in detail in ch. 6 of my *Epistemology* (Routledge, 1998).

34. If one thinks of values, which surely do have motivating power, as beliefs, as E. J. Bond does in *Reason and Value*, the way is open for considerable movement on this path. But although beliefs can be excellent evidence of values, it there adequate reason to think the latter are *constituted* by the former?

35. Motivational internalism is assessed in detail, and shown to be implausible in any strong form, in "Moral Judgment and Reasons for Action," in *Moral Knowledge*, which also gives numerous references to relevant literature on the topic.

36. There is the possibility of having the knowledge "wired in," as it would be to one's clone. But even this kind of knowledge is in some sense experiential and would not constitute a problem for the point I am making.

CHAPTER 6

1. William K. Frankena maintains that egoism about the grounds of rationality was in fact dominant in Greek philosophy (especially Plato and Aristotle). See "The Concept of Rationality in the History of Ethics," *Social Theory and Practice* 9 (1983).

2. For a psychologically informed discussion of what empathy is and how it may figure in ethics see Alvin I. Goldman, "Empathy, Mind, and Morals," *Proceedings and Addresses of the American Philosophical Association* 66, 3 (1992). Also relevant is the position (discussed by Goldman) of Robert M. Gordon in "Folk Psychology as Simulation," *Mind and Language* 1 (1986).

3. This raises the question whether it can be more rational, or at any rate rationally preferable, to act on the basis of a (rational) want that is less rational than a competitor but motivationally stronger. I think so, though the matter may be left open here; but if so, it may be only because reason to satisfy one's rational desires grows with their strength as well as with their degree of rationality. That point, in turn, would have a basis in two points: the psychological truth that we tend to suffer more frustration from failure to satisfy stronger desires than weaker ones and the normative truth that frustration, as a discomfort, generates reasons for action.

4. The organicity of both value and reasons for action is discussed in some detail in chs. 3 and 4 of my *Intuition and Intrinsic Value* (in progress). See also

Lemos's *Intrinsic Value* and Zimmerman, "Virtual Intrinsic Value and the Principal of Organic Unities."

5. Granted, at least typically, if it is not rational to do something, then it is not rational to *intend* to do it; but even intrinsic wanting does not imply intending, and this thesis should not be confused with, or taken to imply, the counterpart one for wanting and acting.

6. A verse I have heard attributed to the Buddha portrays a mother who is watching her children play happily in the sand. When they come to her, she brushes the sand from their hair and pats their heads. The elemental image is ethically significant. It is not that the mother acts from a sense of obligation; she acts from the kind of natural altruistic feeling that makes others seem important, in the way they must if a sense of obligation is to take hold.

7. A number of my reasons for rejecting such skepticism (and a number of references to relevant literature) are given in ch. 9 of my *Epistemology*. In "Skepticism in Theory and Practice," ch. 3 in *Moral Knowledge*, I critically compare practical with epistemological skepticism and suggest how both may be resisted.

8. This integration characteristic of rational persons makes a restricted version of motivational internalism plausible for them, roughly the thesis that some degree of motivation to act on a self-addressed moral judgment is implied by a rational person's holding it; I explain why this is plausible in ch. 10 of *Moral Knowledge*.

9. My points here are also consistent with the possibility that one has better justification for believing the experience good, in one's own case, than for believing a similar one good, in another person's life. But that does not undermine the overall case I am making for the rationality of altruism.

10. See, e.g., p. 419 of P. H. Nidditch, ed., *A Treatise of Human Nature*.

11. My main concern here is normative, but insofar as evolutionary considerations are relevant to my view they appear to support it. Given, among other things, how much better our evidence tends to be regarding what conduces to our own survival as opposed to that of others, we are more likely to survive if we tend, at least in a wide range of cases, to prefer self-realization (roughly, pursuit of one's own good) and self-preservation over other-regarding behavior. On the other hand, for socially dependent beings like us, self-realization and self-preservation will fail if they are not tempered by a measure of something at least close to altruism—particularly toward children. If we have been selected for some such balance between self-realization and self-preservation and, on the other hand, altruism, this supports both my view that altruism is natural and my point that a measure of self-preference is sometimes excusable. First, rationality obviously has survival value, and there is thus some reason to think that what is natural for us in the way of basic desires that govern at least much of our behavior, if a product of selection, should be at least minimally rational. Second, if self-preference is "wired in," this is good reason to take it to be, if not rational, excusable. For related discussions of evolutionary considerations bearing on altruism, see Philip Kitcher, "The Evolution of Human Altruism," *Journal of Philosophy* 90 (1993), pp. 497–516, and

Elliott Sober and David Sloan Wilson, *Unto Others: The Evolution and Psychology of Unselfish Behavior* (Cambridge, Mass.: Harvard University Press, 1999).

12. The same holds for increases in the probability of success attributed to an instrumental action. But that is not my point; there need be no probability ascribed at all (and perhaps not even a disposition to assign any definite one). Strength of belief, by contrast, is a variable always instantiated by our beliefs. I have discussed this distinction in some detail in "Action Theory as a Resource for Decision Theory," *Theory and Decision* 20 (1986), pp. 207–21.

13. I have developed and defended this line on the reasonable limitation of the duty of beneficence in "A Kantian Intuitionism," in progress.

14. See, e.g., John Rawls, *A Theory of Justice* (Cambridge, Mass.: Harvard University Press, 1971), and *Political Liberalism* (New York: Columbia University Press, 1993), and Scanlon's *What We Owe to Each Other*, esp. pp. 191–97, for different perspectives on these two concepts. In *Political Liberalism*, esp. pp. 48–54, Rawls approvingly describes W. M. Sibley's "The Rational Versus the Reasonable," *Philosophical Review* 62 (1953) as pointing out that "Knowing people are rational we do not know the ends they will pursue, only that they will pursue them intelligently. Knowing that people are reasonable where others are concerned, we know that they are willing to govern their conduct by a principle from which they and others can reason in common" (p. 49n). My view of reasonableness helps to explain the plausibility of the second point, though it entails only something slightly weaker. The first claim seems to me too weak and is qualified in some detail by the treatment of global rationality in Chapter 8.

15. That in special cases weak-willed action may be rational, though it *tends* to count against rationality, is argued in detail in my "Weakness of Will and Rational Action," reprinted in *Action, Intention, and Reason.*

16. The question whether reasonableness is governed by substantive criteria, as opposed to being, say, subjectivist in the way rationality as conceived by instrumentalists is, may be fruitfully compared with the same question for autonomy (which I take to be a candidate for a requirement on reasonableness). The latter question is pursued in detail in my "Autonomy, Reason, and Desire," reprinted in *Moral Knowledge.* Cf. the complementary discussion of autonomy in Joseph Raz, *The Morality of Freedom* (Oxford: Oxford University Press, 1986), esp. pp. 369–90. For extensive historical analysis of autonomy and related notions see Jerome B. Schneewind, *The Invention of Autonomy* (Cambridge: Cambridge University Press, 1998).

17. For informative discussion of some of the connections between altruism and evolutionary considerations, see Kitcher, "The Evolution of Human Altruism," and Sober and Wilson, *Unto Others.*

18. Perhaps one tends to think of the matter thus: to satisfy a desire is to realize its content; to satisfy my desire to read a sonnet is for me to read it; hence, my reading it must be its content. I think there is an equivocation here, on 'content': in the first premise it is the *property* to be instantiated by me, here reading the sonnet; in the second it is the *satisfaction conditions* for that instantiation, here my

doing the reading. There *are* desires with the specific content: that I read the sonnet. But this need not be one of them; it is more like believing oneself *to be* reading than like believing the proposition *that* one is, where one figures in that proposition through some descriptive concept. One has a basic sense of oneself in the first case, but a self-concept does not essentially figure in the object—the 'content' of the belief—as some notion of oneself does in the second case.

19. W. D. Ross ably discusses these conflicts in *The Right and the Good*, esp. ch. 2. I explore his resolution and some aspects of the general issue in "Intuitionism, Pluralism, and the Foundations of Ethics" and in "A Kantian Intuitionism," both cited earlier. Another plausible resolution is given by Bernard Gert in *Morality*, Part I. A further problem is what counts as equality where it figures as a moral standard. This is a problem for any plausible ethical position. Some of what follows will clarify the notion, but there is no need to offer an account of it here.

20. Just what versions of the categorical imperative are supported by what I have been saying is a difficult matter. I provide some indications in ch. 3 of my *Intuition and Intrinsic Value*, in progress.

21. There is also a connection with the contractarian strain in Kant on which John Rawls, among others, has drawn. If rationality is understood as I propose, then it is to be expected that rational persons would choose, as guides for life in a shared world, the sorts of moral principles I have suggested might be central. Rawls's veil-of-ignorance framework might help to show this. I cannot establish this here, but the general point might be this: rational persons who regard themselves as fundamentally similar to others in rationality, motivation, and sentience would want principles that, first, protect them from harm and assure them of a certain kind of equal treatment, and second, within these limits, encourage positively good treatment of others (encourage rather than require, because making us behave beneficently is one way in which we can be treated merely as means).

22. I am assuming that *de dicto* propositional attitudes, roughly those whose full content is expressed in a 'that'-clause, are individuated propositionally; two ascriptions of (*de dicto*) belief, e.g., attribute the same belief only if the 'that'-clauses express the same proposition and not just necessarily equivalent propositions. With *de re* attitudes, such as a desire, regarding a pain, that it stop, the crucial question is how to individuate the properties apparently expressed by the 'that'-clause. It is an interesting question, which I here leave open, whether one could want the stopping of a pain in a sufficiently coarse way to enable us to ascribe the same want using a predicate that expresses a concept not logically equivalent to the notion of stopping.

23. I have tried to clarify what Kantian ethics is committed to regarding the kind of motivation appropriate to acting morally, in "Internalism and Externalism in Moral Epistemology," in *Moral Knowledge*. In "Acting from Virtue," *Mind* 104 (1995) (also in *Moral Knowledge*) I explicate that notion in a way applicable to both virtue and non-virtue theories. If, as seems likely, acting morally is quite similar to acting from (moral) virtue, then the conditions for doing so are permissive enough to permit the account of rationality developed here to apply to at least the standard cases of moral action.

24. The dominance view will also seem plausible to those who hold the strong motivational internalist thesis that if one judges that all things considered one ought to do something, then one has *overriding* motivation to act accordingly; for to them it will seem that failure, in practice, to give supremacy to the moral point of view would bespeak a kind of inconsistency between belief and action.

25. This has been widely discussed. See, e.g., William K. Frankena, *Ethics,* 2nd ed. (Englewood Cliffs, N.J.: Prentice-Hall, 1973), Brandt's *A Theory of the Good and the Right,* Thomas Nagel's *The View from Nowhere,* Gert's *Morality,* and Bruce Russell, "Two Forms of Ethical Skepticism," in Louis P. Pojman, ed., *Ethical Theory* (Belmont, Calif.: Wadsworth, 1989).

26. See Russell, "Two Forms of Ethical Skepticism," for a case against even this claim and Gert, *Morality,* for a defense of it.

27. The notion of self-evidence I am using (drawn from my "Self-Evidence," cited earlier) is roughly this: a proposition is self-evident provided that adequately understanding it is sufficient to ground justification for believing it (which does not entail that the understanding actually produces belief), and believing it on the basis of such an understanding of it is sufficient to ground knowing it. The understanding need not be temporally immediate; hence, not everything self-evident is luminous in the way simple logical truths are. Nor is it implied that what is self-evident cannot *also* be known inferentially.

28. See esp. Ross, *The Right and the Good,* ch. 2. It should be noted, however, that what Ross calls self-evident are propositions to the effect that there are prima facie duties, e.g., to keep one's promises, not to the effect that one has an actual duty, say, to keep a promise to return a weapon one borrowed. Moore's *Principia Ethica* is also highly relevant, as is Henry Sidgwick's *The Methods of Ethics,* 7th ed. (1907) (Chicago: University of Chicago Press, 1962), e.g., Book I, ch. 8, and Book III, ch. 1.

29. I have defended this view elsewhere, e.g., in "Moral Epistemology and the Supervenience of Ethical Concepts," *Southern Journal of Philosophy* (1991), pp. 1–24 (reprinted in *Moral Knowledge*), but it is not essential to the theory of rationality being developed. The unified, foundationalist, experiential conception is at least largely neutral between empiricism and rationalism.

30. This epistemic autonomy thesis regarding certain moral principles is argued in detail in my "Intuitionism, Pluralism, and the Foundations of Ethics," ch. 2 in *Moral Knowledge* and, in part, in chs. 3 and 10 as well. This notion of epistemic autonomy does not make empirical the truth of moral principles but is broadly rationalistic. One could frame an empiricist notion of epistemic autonomy, but I doubt that such a notion would do justice to the intuitive concept of epistemic autonomy in question.

31. These analogies are pursued, and their epistemic significance explored, in my paper "An Epistemic Conception of Rationality," in *The Structure of Justification.*

32. I assess such a realist view in ethics, and outline an alternative realism, in "Ethical Naturalism and the Explanatory Power of Moral Concepts," reprinted in *Moral Knowledge.*

CHAPTER 7

1. It is important to remember two points here: that 'experience' ranges over the kind of reflection through which a priori propositions are known; and that the pertinent notion of rationality here is consonance with reason, not mere absence of irrationality.

2. Even if these conditions cannot be satisfied in a normal human life, there is the logical possibility that a person may come into being as an adult who satisfies them for a time. It should also be remembered that I do not take even a strong disposition to believe a proposition to be an actual belief of it. This issue is discussed later.

3. That this can be so is suggested by the literature on religious experience. A classical source here is William James, *The Varieties of Religious Experience*. For a comprehensive treatment see Alston, *Perceiving God*.

4. Here and elsewhere in this book the relevant kind of taking does not require using (or even having) the relevant concept of rewardingness. It is enough that there be *some* rewardingness property, roughly a desirability-characteristic, that the person takes the desired thing to have. A similar conceptual latitude applies in comparable cases of cognitive grounding.

5. For justification, too, there is a counterpart of the distinction between an intrinsic desire that is rational and intrinsically rational desire: a justified intrinsic desire need not be intrinsically justified, and I do not claim that any desires are in the latter category. Similarly, although there are justified non-inferential beliefs, these need not be intrinsically justified. It is not obvious that any beliefs are intrinsically justified (or rational), but some examples suggest that in this matter theoretical reason is more closely tied to content than practical reason: believing certain simple self-evident truths, such as that if *A* is identical with *B* then *B* is identical with *A*, may be intrinsically rational and intrinsically justified because the understanding required for believing them at all is sufficient to render the beliefs in question well-grounded. Even here, however, the ground, and not the content alone, is what provides the rationality or justification.

6. This could be argued to be a special case of the point, stressed by Quine and others, that (experiential) data underdetermine theory. Notice also that even if one could not reason without believing some of a certain range of logical truths, there would be various equivalent propositions that could serve the purpose of, e.g., the logical principles underlying elementary forms of inference such as *modus ponens*.

7. I put the point this way because, in some cases in which one forgets one's grounds, one remains memorially justified in the original belief. Here, however, the thesis is not plausible taken in itself and is indeed such that first, one would not have held it if one lacked the grounds for it, and, second, one is puzzled by one's believing it now.

8. For discussion of agent-relative reasons see Thomas Nagel, *The View from Nowhere*, esp. pp. 152–53 and 158–59, and *The Last Word* (New York: Oxford Uni-

versity Press, 1997), e.g., pp. 5–7. Informative recent discussion, with many references to contemporary treatments, is also provided by David McNaughton and Piers Rawling in "Value and Agent-Relativity" and "Agent-Relativity and Terminological Inexactitudes," *Utilitas* 7, nos. 1 and 2 respectively, pp. 31–47 and 319–25.

9. Mainly rather than entirely because relativity of content *can* be exhibited in a case where one has good grounds for (say) believing *p* but does not believe on the basis of them. We can then say that *p* is rational for one in relation to one's grounds. The reference is still prospective, however, in the sense that we appropriately envisage one's coming to believe *p* on those grounds.

10. Gilbert Harman has argued that moral judgments exhibit relativity in a sense close to the one in question here. For a recent statement of his view see Gilbert Harman and Judith Jarvis Thomson, *Moral Relativism and Moral Objectivity* (Oxford: Blackwell, 1996), in which Thomson presents an opposing view and each criticizes the other. For further analysis of relativism see ch. 8 of T. M. Scanlon, *What We Owe to Each Other*. MacIntyre's *Whose Justice* is also pertinent here. Cf. Paul K. Moser, *Philosophy after Objectivity* (New York: Oxford University Press, 1993). Moser extensively discusses the related views of Richard Rorty and Hilary Putnam and develops a highly qualified version of relativism, "conceptual relativism." See, e.g., pp. 185–87.

11. The thesis suggested here is that of linguistic relativity (the Sapir-Whorf hypothesis, articulated by Edward Sapir and Benjamin Lee Whorf). Much of what I say about conceptual relativity can be applied to the linguistic case. A related discussion of relativism is found in Hilary Putnam, *The Many Faces of Realism*.

12. There has been much empirical work on the universality of moral and other normative concepts. Richard B. Brandt has both done and studied such work and is a valuable source on the topic. See esp. his *Ethical Theory* (Englewood Cliffs: Prentice-Hall, 1959) and *A Theory of the Good and the Right*. It is interesting to note that even Ruth Fulton Benedict, in her famous statement of cultural relativism, conceded that "it is quite possible that a modicum of what is considered right and what wrong could be disentangled that is shared by the whole human race." See "Anthropology and the Abnormal," *Journal of General Psychology* 10 (1934).

13. One way to put this is to say that the standards of rationality are, as internal, *intrasubjective* and, as universal, *intersubjective*.

14. A striking illustration of this point is provided by Gilbert Harman: "If he [Hitler] was willing to exterminate a whole people, there was no reason not to do so: that is just what is so terrible about him." See *The Nature of Morality* (New York: Oxford University Press, 1977). What there was reason (for him) to do is a matter of his desires; what there is reason for us to oppose in him is a matter of ours (which also partly determine why we find him so terrible); but *that* these are our reasons (and determine what actions are rational for us) is, on the instrumentalist view in question, an objective matter. The same holds for a constrained instrumentalism such as Brandt's in *A Theory of the Good and the Right*, though its application could yield different judgments about what reasons we have. For Harman's more re-

cent treatment of relativism, see Harman and Thomson, *Moral Relativism and Moral Objectivity*, and his *Reasoning, Meaning, and Mind* (Oxford: Oxford University Press, 1999), esp. Part I.

15. One might think that here the sources of practical reason may have the same kind of collective autonomy as the sources of theoretical reason; but this must be qualified by the point (in chapter 5) that theoretical reason has an authority over practical reason that the latter does not have over the former. It may yet be true that, say, when I have a belief defeating the rationality of a desire of mine, the defeat could not succeed unless based *partly* on my having practical reasons whose force it brings against that desire, as where the memory of the agony of being burned is crucial in defeating a desire not to help put out a fire.

16. This applies particularly in scientific and other cooperative enterprises. There is a sense, however, in which scientific rationality is *social*. This book does not consider social knowledge or justification, in part because individual knowledge and justification are in most respects more basic. For discussion of the relation between the two and a number of references to the relevant literature, see ch. 9 of *Epistemology* and my "The Place of Testimony in the Fabric of Knowledge and Justification," *American Philosophical Quarterly* 34, 4 (1997). A contrasting view is provided by Helen E. Longino, "The Fate of Knowledge in Social Science," in Frederick Schmitt, ed., *Socializing Epistemology: The Social Dimensions of Knowledge* (Lanham, Md.: Rowman and Littlefield, 1994). Cf. Elizabeth Anderson, "Feminist Epistemology: An Interpretation and Defense," *Hypatia* 10 (1995).

17. We could each do contrary things in different domains, e.g., lowering taxes in one state and raising them in another; but that is not comparable to beliefs of contrary propositions, only to beliefs of contrasting ones, say, that a tax increase would be good in Lincoln and that it would be bad in London or New York.

18. Critics of foundationalism have been especially inclined to deny that this applies in the case of beliefs. See, e.g., Michael Williams, *Unnatural Doubts* (Oxford: Basil Blackwell, 1991).

19. The intrinsic preferability need not be *hedonic*. One might argue, with Mill, that some pleasures are, as pleasures, higher than others; but since I take hedonism to be too narrow a theory of the grounds of rational desire, I would not take intrinsic preferability to have to rest on hedonic elements.

20. There may be elements in Wittgenstein that encourage this, such as his suggesting that there is a point in giving justifications at which we simply note that "this language game is played." But given that the game is playable in indefinitely many languages, this is more a linguistic formulation of foundationalism than an anchoring of basic justification in the linguistic practices of any single linguistic community. In any case, such anchoring may be only superficially linguistic: that language must be used in *giving* a basic justification does not imply that what *does* the basic justifying is itself linguistic. For a well developed practice conception drawing on Wittgenstein, Thomas Reid, and others,

see Alston's *Perceiving God*, and for related discussion of the notion of a practice see Alasdair MacIntyre, *After Virtue* (Notre Dame: University of Notre Dame Press, 1981).

21. William P. Alston speaks of our standard doxastic practices and takes the term to include our practice of taking perception as a source of non-inferential justification and knowledge. Here the actions central in the practice are not belief-formations (which he does not consider actions) but, especially, those that constitute our critical discourse. See esp. *The Reliability of Sense-Perception* (Ithaca: Cornell University Press, 1993), esp. chs. 1 and 2.

22. It is an interesting question how many of the insights of a contextualist theory of justification (or of normative notions generally) the points in this section can accommodate. Surely it is at least a number of them. For a short presentation of a contextualist view of justification, see Mark Timmons, "Outline of a Contextualist Moral Epistemology," in Walter Sinnott-Armstrong and Mark Timmons, eds., *Moral Knowledge?* A full statement of Timmons's view is given in his *Morality without Foundations* (New York: Oxford University Press, 1999).

23. In "Ethical Naturalism and the Explanatory Power of Moral Concepts," in *Moral Knowledge*, I argue that a plausible realism need not be causal or explanationist, but here I leave open the kind of realism that best fits an objectivist theory of rationality.

24. For one thing, if it can be true that an attitude is rational (or irrational) given certain facts about, say, its grounds, why not say that it can be true, in the light of certain facts and in a sense implying cognitivity, that an action is right? Irrationality in belief, e.g., seems to be implied by certain kinds of inconsistency. To avoid the asymmetry here in treating normative terms, one may decide to construe all of them noncognitively, something I would resist. For extensive discussion of this general issue see Allan Gibbard, *Wise Choices, Apt Feelings* (Cambridge, Mass.: Harvard University Press, 1990). Particularly pertinent to my points in this section is James Dreier's critical discussion of Gibbard's position in Dreier's "Transforming Expressivism," *Nous* 33, 4 (1999), esp. pp. 566–70.

25. I have argued for this in "Justification, Truth, and Reliability" and in "The Old Skepticism, the New Foundationalism, and Naturalistic Epistemology," both in *The Structure of Justification*.

CHAPTER 8

1. In speaking of beliefs and desires as elements in us I do not mean to prejudge the issue of whether the content of propositional attitudes is ultimately individual or, as Hilary Putnam, Tyler Burge, and many others have argued, partly external. The epistemological internalism of this book can be accommodated to a moderate semantic externalism about content. I have discussed this question in some detail in "Mental Causation: Sustaining and Dynamic," in Heil and Mele, *Mental Causation*, pp. 53–74. This volume contains several other papers bearing on the issue.

NOTES TO PAGES 196–99

2. Here I ignore the apparent possibility of a person's being neurologically manipulated so as to have no beliefs but only dispositions to form them.

3. Two points may help here. First, being "justified in believing" is construed (as in Chapter 2) as stronger than having *some* degree of justification (for which the point here does not hold). Second, obviousness is not easily characterized, but the most relevant notion is that of a proposition such that a rational person who understands and considers it strongly tends to believe it immediately thereupon. Further discussion of the notion is given in my "Self-Evidence," *Philosophical Perspectives* (1999).

4. I mean access to *what* grounds the rationality, not to *how* it does so. I bypass difficulties about precisely what access requires. For discussion of internalism and externalism, see William P. Alston, "Internalism and Externalism in Epistemology," *Philosophical Topics* 14 (1986), and my "Causalist Internalism," reprinted in *The Structure of Justification.*

5. I critically assess this aspect of virtue theory in "Acting from Virtue," reprinted in *Moral Knowledge,* and explore virtue epistemology in "Epistemic Virtue and Justified Belief," forthcoming in Abrol Fairweather and Linda Zagzebski, ed., *Virtue Epistemology: Essays on Epistemic Virtue and Responsibility* (New York: Oxford University Press). For a further analysis of aspects of virtue epistemology see Sosa's *Knowledge in Perspective.*

6. The causation need not, of course, be deterministic (and I leave open whether it is even nomic), nor is determinism regarding human actions or other events presupposed in this book.

7. Roderick Chisholm and Keith Lehrer represent, respectively, foundationalist and coherentist theorists who hold non-causal views here. See, e.g., Chisholm's *Theory of Knowledge,* 3rd ed. (Englewood Cliffs: Prentice-Hall, 1989), and Lehrer's *Knowledge.* In "Causalist Internalism," I argue that a plausible internalist view can accommodate as strong a causal requirement on justification as is appropriate to the concept of justification.

8. Keith Lehrer has held a view of this kind. See, e.g., his "Metaknowledge: Undefeated Justification," *Synthese* 74 (1988); and for much discussion of his overall theory, Bender, ed., *Current State of Coherence Theory.* Cf. Gilbert Harman, *Thought* (Princeton: Princeton University Press, 1973).

9. There is of course controversy over whether even scientific assessments of claims apparently about the world are "value-free." That they can be free of at least any inappropriate influence by *moral* values is argued in my "Scientific Objectivity and the Evaluation of Hypotheses," in Merrilee H. Salmon, ed., *The Philosophy of Logical Mechanism* (Dordrecht: Kluwer, 1989). (This volume also contains a reply to my essay by Arthur W. Burks.) Freedom from epistemic evaluation is another matter; that is not required for rational scientific judgment. The issue here turns on whether the notion of justified belief, or at least the notion of knowledge, is analyzable simply in terms agreed at the outset to be non-normative, e.g., observational, psychological, and causal terms.

10. I have argued indirectly for the importance of wants and beliefs, in understanding both actions and the other propositional attitudes, in "Intending" (reprinted in *Action, Intention, and Reason*); this paper explicates intending in terms of believing and wanting. In "A Cognitive-Motivational Theory of Attitudes," *Southwestern Journal of Philosophy* 5 (1974), I explicate attitudes by appeal to beliefs and wants. The importance of both for valuations is suggested in my "Axiological Foundationalism," *Canadian Journal of Philosophy* 12 (1982). They are also crucial in understanding traits. See, e.g., William P. Alston's "Toward a Logical Geography of Personality," in H. Kiefer and M. Munitz, eds., *Mind, Science, and History* (Albany: State University of New York Press, 1970); and R. B. Brandt, "Traits of Character: A Conceptual Analysis," *American Philosophical Quarterly* 7 (1970).

11. In the *Meditations*, e.g., Descartes's overall conception seems to be one on which the will may in certain cases directly bring about—or withhold—belief. In Meditation I, he says, "I ought no less carefully to withhold my assent from matters which are not entirely certain and indubitable than from those which appear to me manifestly to be false" and "I ought not the less carefully to refrain from giving credence to these opinions than to that which is manifestly false," where for him 'giving credence' seems roughly equivalent to 'assenting' (Haldane and Ross trans.) And later: "They [my errors] come from the sole fact that since the will is much wider in its range and compass than the understanding I do not restrain it within the same bounds . . ."; the apparent implication is that false beliefs, at least, arise only through some kind of willing. He also says that "if I abstain from giving my judgment on any thing when I do not perceive it with sufficient clearness and distinctness, it is plain that I act rightly and am not deceived" (Meditation IV). His overall emphasis here seems to be more on the possibility of *withholding* belief than on "enacting" it, but there is still at least a substantial voluntarist strain in his thinking.

12. Chapter 5 contains references to a number of relevant papers, including my "Doxastic Voluntarism and the Ethics of Belief."

13. My analysis of doxastic voluntarism in "Doxastic Voluntarism and the Ethics of Belief" supports these points.

14. I have defended this conception of attitudes in "A Cognitive-Motivational Theory of Attitudes," and, with respect to a wide range of psychological literature, in "On the Conception and Measurement of Attitudes in Contemporary Anglo-American Psychology," *Journal for the Theory of Social Behaviour* 2 (1972).

15. A plausible account is provided by Robert M. Gordon in *The Structure of Emotions* (Cambridge: Cambridge University Press, 1989). For other helpful discussions see Robert C. Solomon, *The Passions* (Notre Dame: University of Notre Dame Press, 1983), Patricia S. Greenspan, *Emotions and Reasons* (London: Routledge, 1988), and O. H. Green, *The Emotions* (Dordrecht: Kluwer, 1991).

16. What about emotions and feelings grounded in fictional or aesthetic experiences? These raise special problems. Some of what I have said is readily adaptable to fictional cases; e.g., one's indignation at the behavior of a character in a

play could be irrationally strong. Non-representational art poses further problems. Some of them are illuminated by reflection on the distinction between emotion and feeling and the point that emotion may be partly constituted by non-inferential belief or basic desire or both. For a more detailed discussion of how feelings and other experiential elements can play a role in justification of emotions, attitudes (including beliefs and desires), and moral judgments, see my "The Axiology of Moral Experience."

17. It should be noted that in taking the rationality of an emotion to be determined chiefly by its cognitive and motivational elements I do not imply that beliefs or desires constituent in it cannot be basic: take a non-inferential belief that an approaching animal is dangerous to one and an intrinsic aversion to someone's insensitivity. But it seems to be the rationality of these, and not their basic character, that is crucial for that of the emotion. One might argue that some rational emotions are "precognitive," embodying no beliefs, or non-motivational, having no behavioral direction. I believe the cases suggesting this are instances of feelings of the kind that form part of an emotion once the cognitive and motivational elements properly join them. But doubtless such feelings can play a (non-inferential) evidential role. If, however, some emotions can be precognitive or non-motivational, their rationality can be construed much as I earlier construed that of non-inferential belief and intrinsic desire. The overall theory of rational persons to emerge here would not be greatly changed.

18. Having allowed that a rational belief might fail to be justified, I should say that this point does not imply that a person can have rational beliefs without having *any* that are justified.

19. I argue for this in Part I of *Practical Reasoning*. To be sure, Kant might reject the applicability of the term 'want' to motivation as he conceives it.

20. Conceivably, dispositions to believe would serve here; but if so, their rationality would be assessed in a way similar to the assessment of the beliefs themselves, and in part for that reason I largely ignore this complication.

21. The kind of defect I am describing, at least in the cognitive sphere, is the sort Alvin Plantinga discusses in detail under the heading of "proper function." See *Warrant and Proper Function* (New York: Oxford University Press, 1993).

22. If one wonders why I do not reject this view as implying a vicious regress of the kind that Lewis Carroll (in "What Achilles Said to the Tortoise") showed for the view that the principle—or perhaps we should say *a* principle—that governs a valid inference is a premise in it, the answer is that believing such a principle does not require it to be a premise in the inference in question. What is wrong with the view is subtler than its plainly entailing a regress.

23. For extensive discussion of the extent to which normative notions (especially moral ones) are rule-governed, see Charles Larmore, *Patterns of Moral Complexity* (Cambridge: Cambridge University Press, 1987), esp. ch. 1.

24. Some detailed discussion of how belief-formation may be conceived as a discriminative response to experience is provided in my "Dispositional Beliefs and Dispositions to Believe."

25. I have developed this idea further, and distinguished between freedom and autonomy, in "Acting for Reasons," reprinted in *Action, Intention, and Reason.* A detailed account of autonomy is given in my "Autonomy, Reason, and Desire," *Pacific Philosophical Quarterly* 72 (1992), reprinted in *Moral Knowledge.*

26. There has been a tendency in recent literature on autonomy to give a major role to second-order desires. For an account of autonomy that seeks to keep that role within reasonable limits see my "Autonomy, Reason, and Desire." Limitations of the appeal to second-order elements are also discussed in Chapter 5 in relation to instrumentalism. Further critical examination of their role is provided by Mele, *Autonomous Agents* (New York: Oxford University Press, 1995), esp. ch. 4, sects. 2–4.

27. I am here leaving open the issue of the compatibility of freedom and determinism. For an indication of how this is possible given the causal elements I countenance in linking actions to their grounds, see ch. 10 in my *Action, Intention, and Reason.* Further discussion and alternative conceptions are provided by Alfred Mele in *Autonomous Agents,* John Martin Fischer and Mark Ravizza, S.J., in, *Responsibility and Control* (Cambridge: Cambridge University Press, 1998), which also has much discussion of responsiveness to reasons in a sense relevant to my account of rationality, and Robert Kane, *The Significance of Free Will* (New York: Oxford University Press, 1996). Kane's book is the topic of a symposium in *Philosophy and Phenomenological Research* 60 (2000), with Bernard Berofsky, John Fischer, Galen Strawson, and Kane responding.

28. *An Inquiry Concerning Human Understanding,* Section IV, Part II.

29. But although Aristotle says that happiness consists in contemplation, he also says that "the good of man [i.e., happiness] is an activity of the soul in conformity with excellence or virtue, and if there are several virtues, in conformity with the best and most complete" (*Nicomachean Ethics* 1098a16–18). He seems almost willing to say not that all happiness consists in contemplation, but that only the *highest* happiness does.

30. I have noted above that one might at least fail to want intrinsically to do something at the last moment one is enjoying it. A deeper point is that enjoyment is sufficiently experiential and occurrent to be distinct from wanting, which is basically a dispositional psychological property: this would explain how we can *come* to want something we are loath to try and initially dislike, *by* finding it enjoyable once we experience it.

31. This presupposes that action-wants can be directed toward present activity; if they are all future-directed, then at least at the last moment one is enjoying something it can be rational not to want to (continue to) do it.

32. I defend this and other points relevant to the eudaemonistic principle and others in this chapter, in chs. 3 and 11 of *Moral Knowledge,* concerning, respectively, the status of theoretical and practical reasons and the nature of intrinsic value and its relation to reasons for action.

33. If, from moment to moment, there should be massive *changes* in what a person remembers, there would be some question of whether the same person

continues to exist. It may be that although a given person can be rational at one time and not another, no rational person can be rational *merely* at a time and never for any extended period. I leave this open here, but my inclination is to think that a person could exist for just a short time and might in that case be properly called rational if all the appropriate synchronic criteria are met.

34. For a different view, emphasizing only the rational permissibility of altruistic and moral motivation, see Bernard Gert, *Morality*. His view also differs from mine in taking rationality to require, regarding pleasure, only *not* intrinsically wanting its loss (though to be sure he is taking what is rational to be simply what is not irrational, which would at least narrow the contrast here). Critical discussion of this point is provided in my "Reasons and Rationality in the Moral Philosophy of Bernard Gert," forthcoming.

35. The idea that the primary bearers of intrinsic (as opposed to inherent) value are experiential is explored in detail and given qualified support in ch. 11 of *Moral Knowledge*.

36. This is not to presuppose an intuitionist theory of our justification for normative principles. But when adequately developed such a theory has much to recommend it, as I argue in detail in *Intuition and Intrinsic Value*, in preparation.

37. Bernard Gert, in *Morality*, contends that rationality is just the absence of irrationality, but combines this with a list theory of rationality. I find most of his list plausible; but insofar as I am proposing a list of what might be called rationally demanded ends, I am building in elements of defeasibility he does not note, citing some other ends, and leaving the "list" open-ended.

38. For an account of the relation between moral judgment (and other moral cognitions) and motivation, with numerous references to the literature on the topic, see my "Moral Judgment and Reasons for Action," ch. 10 in *Moral Knowledge* and reprinted in Cullity and Gaut, *Ethics and Practical Reason*.

39. There may be limits to the *kind* of irrationality possible. For discussion of how the very notion of belief implies some minimal rationality, see Jaegwon Kim, "What Is 'Naturalized Epistemology'?" *Philosophical Perspectives* 2 (1988), which to some degree follows Donald Davidson's work on this topic.

40. See, e.g., my "Self-Deception and Rationality," in Mike W. Martin, ed., *Self-Deception and Self-Understanding* (Lawrence: University Press of Kansas, 1985), and "Weakness of Will and Rational Action," reprinted in *Action, Intention, and Reason*.

41. Donald Davidson makes a good case for the presupposition of rationality involved in the attribution of beliefs. See his "A Coherence Theory of Truth and Knowledge," in D. Hendrich, ed., *Kant öder Hegel* (Stuttgart, 1981). He imposes stronger rationality constraints on belief attribution than I would, however.

42. The relevant sense of counting toward seems broadly teleological. I have elaborated this view in "Justification, Truth, and Reliability," reprinted in *The Structure of Justification*. Cf. Chisholm, *Theory of Knowledge* (all three editions), Foley, *Working without a Net*, and Alvin Plantinga, e.g., "Positive Epistemic Status and Proper Function," *Philosophical Perspectives* 2 (1988).

43. This is not meant to be a precise formulation; it does not, e.g., take account of justified beliefs about the future. Even these, however, are produced by real elements that affect the future, as when knowledge of one's own future actions are grounded in one's intentions to perform them: here both the belief and the event it depicts are roughly common effects of the same causes, and, as with perceptual belief, what makes it knowledge is an appropriate connection with the relevant aspect of the world.

INDEX

acceptance, 201, 260n31
accessibility, 38, 48–9, 242n17
action
  basic, 63–65, 116. *See also* volition
  grounds of, 63, 66
  hierarchical view of, 63–65
  individuation of, 245n4
  intentional, 66–67, 244n1
  joint, 187
  moral, 159–60
  non-intentional, 130
  rational. *See* belief; desire;
    instrumentalism; intention;
    rationality; reasons; well-
    groundedness
  reasoned, 129, 258n15
  See also reasonableness; reasons;
    reasons-responsiveness;
    response tendencies
Adams, Robert M., x
Alston, William P., x, 235n3, 236n9,
  237n11, 241n16, 243nn24,25,
  260nn25,31, 266n3, 270n4,
  271n10
altruism, 139–44, 168, 218–19, 262n11
  as a virtue, 139
altruistic principle, 219
Anderson, Elizabeth, 268n16
Aquinas, St. Thomas, 210

Aristotle, 13, 68, 71, 205, 215, 216,
  235 n1, 244n31, 246n10,
  246n13, 251n4, 258nn13,14,
  261n1, 273n29
assent, 132. *See also* belief
attitudes, 74, 202, 204, 264n22
  causal sustenance of, 177
  intentional, 159
  practical, 110
  propositional, 75, 76, 172, 202, 204,
    205, 207, 224
  See also belief; desire; grounding;
    intention
autonomy, 242n19, 263n16
  behavioral, 212
  epistemic, 21–24, 121, 165, 230
    265n30
  of ethics, 165–66, 230, 265n30
  of practical reason, 133–34
  structural, 75
axiological experientialism, 98–100,
  252n13
axiological foundationalism, 75,
  249n26
axiomatism, Cartesian, 41–42,
  241n14. *See also* Descartes

Baier, Kurt, 259n17
Baker, Lynne Rudder, x, 253n14

basic action. *See* action, basic
basic source, 18, 172, 238n21. *See also*
　　sources of justification
basis relation
　　causal, 38–39, 236n7. *See also*
　　　　grounding; justification
　　direct, 205
　　epistemic, 236n7
　　indirect, 205
　　practical, 245n8
belief, 241n14
　　as causal sustainer, 237n17
　　as evidential sustainer, 237n17
　　basic, 5, 65
　　choosing, 201
　　cogito, 63–65, 241n14
　　connectedness of, 208
　　connecting, 76, 117, 220, 244n2
　　contrasted with disposition to form,
　　　　25, 76, 174, 207
　　de dicto, 251n9, 264n22
　　de re, 251n9, 264n22
　　de se, 251n7, 252n9
　　direct, 135, 145n5
　　entrenchment of, 208
　　foundational, 65
　　framework, 206
　　goal of, 132
　　inferential, 32–35, 198, 239n2,
　　　　240n3
　　　　episodically, 35
　　　　historically, 240n3
　　　　structurally, 35
　　instrumental, 61
　　motivating power of, 132–33
　　perceptual, 224
　　rational, 206. *See also* justification;
　　　　rationality; reasonableness;
　　　　well-groundedness
　　reasons for, 52–54, 112
　　scope, 208
　　second-order, 45–46, 163–64
　　sources of, 16
　　strength of, 208, 263n12
　　unconscious, 242n22
　　unity in. *See* integration
　　valuational, 224

　　withholding of, 271n11
　　See also desire; doxastic voluntarism;
　　　　reasons; response tendencies
Bender, John, x, 238n22, 238n24
Benedict, Ruth Fulton, 267n12
beneficence, 137, 146, 153
Berofsky, Bernard, 273n27
Blackburn, Simon, 248n25
Bok, Hilary, x
Bok, Sissela, x
Bond, E. J., 252n12, 261n34
BonJour, Laurence, x, 236n9, 238n20,
　　238n22, 239n25, 241n16
Brand, Myles, 245n6
Brandt, R. B., 250n36, 259n20,
　　260n25, 265n25, 267nn12,14,
　　271n10
Bratman, Michael A., x, 245n6,
　　249n26
Brentano, Franz, 253n17
Brink, David, 248n25
Buddha, 262n6
Burge, Tyler, 269n1
Buridan's ass, 259n22
Burks, Arthur W., 270n9
Butchvarov, Panayot, x, xi, 235n3
Butler, Joseph, 252n11

Camus, Albert, 142
caring, 137, 168, 220
Carroll, Lewis, 272n22
Carson, Thomas L., 250n36
Castañeda, Hector-Neri, 251n7
certainty
　　epistemic, 241n14
　　psychological, 247n17
Chang, Ruth, x
Chisholm, R. M., 237n14, 241n16,
　　243n24, 253n17, 270n7,
　　274n42
Clark, Andy, 239n1
closure, 43–44, 240n7
cognitive commitment, 109, 111
cognitivism. *See* noncognitivism
coherence, 18, 24–28, 46–48, 130,
　　210, 227, 238n24
　　motivational, 71

coherentism, 24–28, 132, 210, 235n1
    conceptual, 27, 47
    practical, 76–79
    See also justification, coherence
        theory of
commitment, motivational. *See*
    motivational commitment
commitment, practical. *See* practical
    commitment
commitment, theoretical. *See*
    cognitive commitment
compatibilism, 273n27
composition principles, 208
compulsion, 211–12
conative theory of pleasure. *See*
    pleasure, conative theory of
conceptual dependence, 23
conditionally basic source, 130,
    242n21
Conee, Earl, x
connecting belief. *See* belief,
    connecting
connectionist models, 239n1
constitutive means, 84–85
contextualism, 28, 191, 239n26,
    269n22
Copp, David, x
Crawford, Dan, x
Crisp, Roger, x
Cullity, Garrett, 260n28

Dancy, Jonathan, x
Darwall, Stephen L., x, 248n25,
    249n28
Davidson, Donald, 236n8, 256n4,
    274nn39,41
Davis, Wayne A., x, 249n26
decision theory, 117, 239n32, 250n32
defeasibility, 8, 20–21, 40–43, 45–46,
    74, 114, 126, 139, 175, 248n23
dependence, conceptual. *See*
    conceptual dependence
dependence, epistemic. *See* epistemic
    dependence
d'Holbach, Baron, 259n21
Deigh, John, x
DePaul, Michael, x

Descartes, René, 20, 200, 201, 271n11
desirability, 94, 121, 138, 158, 193,
    214, 218, 224, 232, 258n17
desire, 108–111, 260n25, 273n30
    altruistic, 139–44
    basic, 5, 7, 112
    behavioral, 91
    de dicto, 251n9
    de re, 251n9, 264n22
    experiential, 90–91
    foundational, 112
    hypothetical, 124, 125
    instrumentally rational, 69
    intrinsic, 63, 81–83
    intrinsically rational, 68
    non-instrumental, 82, 125
    objectual, 91
    overcoming of, 247n20
    propositional, 91
    rational, 68–74, 136–37
    reasons for, 86, 89, 100, 114
    residual, 246n8
    satisfaction of, 249nn30,31, 263n18
    second-order, 126, 212, 249n31,
        273n26
    strength of, 147, 217
    whimsical, 150
    See also belief; grounding;
        intention; reasons; wanting
dispositions to believe, 14, 25, 113,
    114, 174, 272n20
doxastic practice, 269n21
doxastic voluntarism, 200–02
Dreier, James, 269n24
Dretske, Fred, x, 241n16, 260n26
Driver, Julia, x
duty, prima facie, 238n18

egocentrism. *See* egoism
egoism, 7, 71, 105, 136, 138, 153, 216.
    See also epistemic egocentrism
emotion, 173, 202–04, 226, 271n16,
    275n17
empathy, 137–38, 146, 168
empiricism, ix, 265n29
enjoyment. *See* happiness; pleasure
envy, 229

epistemic autonomy. *See* autonomy, epistemic
epistemic basis relation. *See* basis relation, epistemic
epistemic dependence, 25–26, 174–75
epistemic egocentrism, 103, 105. *See also* egoism
epistemic principles, 41–46, 192, 209
ethics, autonomy of. *See* autonomy
eudaemonism, 71, 215–16
Evans, Gareth, 236n8
evidence
  divided, 21, 196
  having, 105, 257n11
  of the senses, 185
evil, problem of. *See* problem of evil
excusability, 146, 151, 152, 164, 207
experientialism, axiological. *See* axiological experientialism
externalism, 243n25
  applied to desire, 199–200
  semantic, 269n1
  See also internalism; reliabilism

fallibilism, 230, 231, 233
feelings, 203–04, 271n16, 272n17
Feldman, Fred, 251n3
Fischer, John Martin, 273n27
Fogelin, Robert, x
Foley, Richard, x, 237n15, 241n16, 242n18, 243n24, 250nn35,36, 261n32
foundationalism, ix, 235n1, 247n18
  axiological, 75, 249n26
  Cartesian, 41–43, 70
  epistemological, 30–31, 249n26
  moderate, viii-ix, 30, 79
  motivational, 68
  procedural, 79
  psychological, 29–30
  second-order, 42–43
  structural, 70, 232
  subjective, 78, 79
  substantive, 80
Frankena, William K., 248n25, 261n1, 265n25
Frankfurt, Harry G., 242n19, 259n17

freedom, 200, 211–12, 233
Fricker, Elizabeth, x
Fumerton, Richard A., 242n18, 249n29, 250n32, 257n13

Gaut, Berys, x, 259n17
Geivett, Douglas, x
Gert, Bernard, x, xi, 248n20,21, 264n19, 265n25, 274nn34,37
Gert, Joshua, x
Gewirth, Alan, 258n17
Gibbard, Allan, 250n1, 269n24
Ginet, Carl, 235n5, 237n14, 245n6
global rationality. *See* rationality, global
Goldman, Alvin I., 237n15, 241n16, 261n2
Goldstein, Irwin, x
Gordon, Robert M., 261n2, 271n15
Greco, John, xi
Green, O. H., 271n15
Greenspan, Patricia S., 271n15
Griffin, James, x
grounding, 2–3, 14, 112, 143, 171, 177, 197, 237n17, 254n23
  causal, 166–77, 246n11
  cognitive, 254n21
  conative, 66–67
  discriminative, 103, 167, 168
  direct, 19, 135, 205
    inferentially, 33
    normatively, 135
    psychologically, 135
  experiential, 193, 232
  indirect, 19, 205, 207, 245n8
  motivational, 62–63. *See also* grounding, causal
  psychologically compelling, 187
  See also well-groundedness

Hampton, Jean, 258n17
happiness, 72, 215–17, 247n20
  in one's life, 215
  with one's life, 215
  See also pleasure; rewardingness
Harman, Gilbert, x, 267n10, 267n14, 270n8
hedonic principle, 217

hedonism, 83, 94–98, 247n20, 252n12, 268n19
Heil, John, x
Hempel, Carl G., 257n13
Henderson, David, 239n26
Hobbes, Thomas, 184, 259n21
holism, 241n12
Hooker, Brad, x
hope, 106, 117, 248n24
Horgan, Terence, x
Hubin, Donald, x
Hume, 5, 68, 145, 205, 213, 246n10, 249n29, 250n32, 259nn20,21

ideal observer theories, 250n36
incoherence, 24, 218, 219, 242n20
indeterminacy, 182
indexicality, 93, 103, 241n14
inference, 32–35, 42. See also belief; grounding; justification
inferentialism, viii, 134
inherent value. See value, inherent
instrumentalism, 76–80, 122–28, 147, 249n30, 260n28
  as a functionalism, 77
  Humean, 249n32
  procedural, 79–80
  See also rationality, instrumental
integration, 147, 209–10, 227, 262n8
intellect, 111, 112, 131
intellectualism, 103, 186, 207, 225
  anti-, 205, 239n1
intention, 66, 108–11, 248n24, 249n26, 256n2, 256n4, 257n7, 262n5
intentional action, 244n1
internalism
  applied to desire, 199–200
  epistemic, 48–49, 65, 223
  motivational, 133, 248n25, 256n4, 260n30, 261n35, 262n8, 265n24
  normative, 131, 231, 267n13
intrinsic desire. See desire, intrinsic
intrinsic value. See value, intrinsic
introspection, 15, 48
intuitionism, 165, 166, 274n36
irrationality, 9, 52, 63, 118, 164, 222

James, William, 266n3
Johnson, David Alan, xi
justifiability, 38–39, 240n10. See also justification; justifiedness
justification, 14, 17–18, 266n5
  a priori, 48, 238n20
  causal sustenance requirement for, 39
  coherence theory of, 17, 46–48
  compared with justifiedness. See justifiedness
  compared with rationality, 49–52
  conferral of, 16–17, 37
  contrasted with justifiability, 38–39
  degree of, 2, 38, 42, 51, 157, 270n3
  direct, 265
  dissociated, 243n22,
  doxastic, 236n7, 237n17, 242n17, 243n26
  experiential, 16
  first-order, 25
  generation of. See epistemic principles; grounding; reasons; well-groundedness
  grounds of, 17
  having, 207. See also justification, propositional
  indefeasible, 20
  inferential, 165
  intrinsic, 266n5
  moral, 238n18
  prima facie, 20–21, 238n18
  on balance, 44
  practice of, 244n32, 268n20
  prima facie, 20–21
  process of, 18, 236n10, 244n32, 268n20
  property of, 236n10, 244n32
  propositional, 237n17, 243n26
  regress of, 247n18
  the role of coherence in, 24–26
  second-order, 25
  self-sufficiency of, 23
  sources of, 13–31
    autonomy of, 22–24, 268n1
    basic, 18
    conditionally basic, 242n21
  structural, 241n11

justification (*continued*)
transmission of, 37, 38–40
See also justifiedness; rationality;
reasonableness; well-
groundedness
justifiedness, 14, 18, 171. *See also*
justification; justifiability

Kain, Philip, x
Kane, Robert, x, 273n27
Kant, Immanuel, 111, 158, 205, 215,
232, 248n23, 258n14, 258n17,
264n21, 272n19
Kantian ethics, 160, 162, 264n23
Kapitan, Tomis, x
Kaplan, Mark, 261n31
Kim, Jaegwon, x, 254n23, 274n39
Kitcher, Philip, 262n11, 263n17
Klein, Peter D., 241n16
knowledge, 6, 15–16, 30, 55, 113, 187,
223, 244n29, 270n9
Kornblith, Hilary, x
Korsgaard, Christine M., x, 258n17
Kulp, Christopher, x
Kvanvig, Jonathan L., x, 237n16

Lamore, Charles, 272n23
Lehrer, Keith, x, 238n22, 241n16,
270nn7,8
Lemos, Noah, x, 252n12, 262n4
Levi, Isaac, 261n31
Lewis, David, 252n9, 253n19
list theory of rationality, 189, 274n37
See also pluralism
Locke, John, 36
logical truth, 174, 193
Longino, Helen E., 268n16
love, 8, 160
Lycan, William, 238n22

MacIntyre, Alasdair, x, 257n13,
269n20
masochism, 193
maximization, 147, 187, 249n30,
249n32
McCann, Hugh J., x, xi, 245n6,
249n26
McDowell, John, x, 236n8, 239n25

McLaughlin, Brian P., x
McNaughton, David, 267n8
Mele, Alfred R., x, xi, 245n6, 249n26,
273n26
memory, 15, 21, 138, 205, 216–17,
235n5
Mendola, Joseph, x
Meyer, Michael, xi
Mill, John Stuart, 96, 161, 172,
260n25
Miller, Richard W., x
Millgram, Elijah, x
Millican, Peter, 239n1
Montmarquet, James A., x, 237n16
Moor, James, x
Moore, G. E., 253n18, 254n24,
265n28
moral justification, 179, 238n18
moral knowledge, 165
moral motivation. *See* motivation,
moral
moral obligation, 179, 181
moral paramountcy, 163
moral persons, 221
moral priority, 162, 163–64
moral properties, 161, 166–67
moral reasons. *See* reasons, moral
moral rules, 221
moral supremacy, 162, 221
moral value. *See* value, moral
moral virtue. *See* virtue, moral
Moser, Paul K., x, 237n15, 238n24,
241n16, 243n24, 255n26,
267n10
motivation, 61, 66, 265n24
Humean view of, 118
intrinsic, 116
moral, 161. *See also* motivational
internalism
motivational coherentism. *See*
coherentism, motivational
motivational commitment, 109, 111
motivational grounding. *See*
grounding, motivational
motivational internalism, 166,
248n25, 256n4, 260n30, 262n8,
265n24
Murphy, James Bernard, x

Nagel, Thomas, x, 254n25, 266n8
noncognitivism, 7, 107, 192, 269n24
normative reason. *See* reasons,
    normative
Nozick, Robert, 250n32, 251n2, 260n27

objectivity, 54, 105, 119, 166, 184,
    191–92, 231
obligation, moral. *See* moral
    obligation
Olsson, Eric, 260n31
O'Neill, Onora, x
optimality, 249n31
overdetermination, 14, 230

pain, 71, 72–73, 85, 93, 95, 193,
    259n19, 264n22
Pappas, George, x
Parfit, Derek, x, xi, 243n28, 248n25,
    258n15, 259n23, 260n28
perception, 13–15, 18, 43, 192
    extrasensory, 19
    theistic, 237n11
Perry, John R., x, 252n9
physicalism, 253n14
Pines, Paul, x
Plantinga, Alvin, 272n21, 274n42
Plato, 261n1
Platonism, 225
pleasure, 83–86, 146, 273n30
    adverbial theory of, 251n3
    conative theory of, 127–28
pluralism, 70, 95, 188, 193. *See also*
    value, intrinsic
Pojman, Louis, x
Post, John, x
practical argument, 129, 134
practical basis relation, 245n8
practical commitment, 111. *See also*
    motivational commitment
practical reason. *See* instrumentalism;
    justification; rationality;
    reasonableness; reasons;
    rewardingness; well-
    groundedness
practical reasoning, 129, 134
practical reasons. *See* reasons,
    practical

practical skepticism, 104–105
practice of justification, 244n32
preface paradox, 242n20
Prior, William, x
problem of evil, 248n22
propositional justification, 237n17,
    243n26
prudence, 154, 217
Putnam, Hilary, 267nn10,11, 269n1

qualities of experience, 17–18, 82–85,
    88, 92–93, 136–38, 147, 158,
    254n22
Quine, W. V., 239n25, 241n12, 266n6
Quine–Duhem thesis, 241n12

Radcliffe, Elizabeth, x
Railton, Peter, x, 259n17
rationalism, ix, 23, 265n29. *See also*
    Descartes
rationality
    basic sources of, 172–73
    compared with justification, 49–52
    compared with reasonableness,
        149–53
    compared with virtue, 55–56
    conceived as rule-governed, 208
    conceived holistically, 222, 225–26
    conceived naturalistically, 232–33
    conceived structurally, 179
    defeasible, 71
    degree of, 186, 220, 261n3
    direct, 71–72
    global, 55–56, 175, 195–226, 232
    indefeasible, 79, 232
    instrumental, 69, 154–55
    intrinsic, 68, 70, 175, 266n5
    of persons. *See* rationality, global
    prima facie, 185
    in a practice, 190
    of a practice, 190
    practice conception of, 188–91
    transmission of, 205, 213
    See also grounding; justification;
        reasonableness; reasons; well-
        groundedness
rationalization, 39, 240n10, 240n11,
    244n32

rational requiredness, 50
Ravizza S. J., Mark, 273n27
Rawling, Piers, 267n8
Rawls, John, 263n14, 264n21
Raz, Joseph, 263n16
realism, 105, 167, 191–92, 214, 227,
    231 253n14, 269n23
  explanationist, 98
  normative, 166–67
reason
  consonance with, 52, 74, 103, 216
  demands of, 153
  interpersonal character of, 155–57
  unity of, 231–33
  See also justification; rationality;
      reasonableness; reasons; well-
      groundedness
reasonableness, 149–53, 171, 191,
    223, 263n16
  conceived as a virtue, 152
  demands of, 144
  focal, 151
  global, 151
  social aspects of, 151
  See also justification; rationality;
      reasons; well-groundedness
reasoning, 33, 198, 212–13
reasons
  activating, 258n15
  agent-relative, 176, 184
  as abstract, 54–55
  best, 130
  to cause, vs. reasons for, 85
  cognitive, 53–55
  cognitively grounded, 113, 173
  contrasted with causes, 54
  defeasibility of, 233. See also
      defeasibility
  experiential, 173
  explanatory, 4, 53, 119, 120
  external, 53
  having, 112–13
  implicit, 115, 258n16
  to intend, 110
  justificatory, 4, 36, 37
  minor, 53
  moral, 162–66, 221–22
  motivating, 53, 119

normative, 4, 53, 119, 121, 243n28
  overall, 138, 162–64
  possessed, 53–54 , 119, 120
  practical, 47, 108, 119, 164
  psychologically unrealized, 114
  responsiveness to, 74, 149–150, 151,
      216, 232
  as states, 54
  status of moral, 162–64
  strength of, 145, 146. See also
      defeasibility
  theoretical, 4
  undefeated, 130. See also
      defeasibility
  See also grounding; justification;
      reasonableness; reason states;
      response tendencies; well-
      groundedness
reason states, 119. See also reasons,
    normative
reflection, 16, 48, 238n20
Reid, Thomas, 268n20
relativism, 171–94
  causal genetic, 177
  conceptual, 178, 180
  doxastic, 181–82
  instrumentalist, 184
  normative genetic, 177
  status, 182–83
relativity, 173–85
reliabilism, 48, 199, 237n15
representation, 240n5
response tendencies, 56, 74, 103, 128,
    136, 175, 206, 209, 216, 226. See
    also grounding; justification;
    reasons, responsiveness to
rewardingness, 96–97, 141, 166, 188,
    193, 266n4
Rorty, Amelie, x
Rorty, Richard, 241n13, 267n10
Ross, W. D., 165, 264n19, 265n28
Ruben, David-Hillel, x
Russell, Bertrand, 55
Russell, Bruce, x, xi, 265n25, 265n26

Sapir-Whorf hypothesis, 267n11
Sartre, Jean-Paul, 251n8, 255n29
satisfaction. See desire, satisfaction of

satisficing, 250n33
Sayre-McCord, Geoffrey, x
Scanlon, T. M., x, 250n1, 258n15,
    263n14, 267n10
Schneewind, Jerome B., 263n16
Searle, John, R., 245n6
self-concepts, 92–93, 102, 155–56,
    251n7, 254n25, 264n18
self-deception, 222
self-evidence, 140, 165, 172, 265n28,
    266n5
self-interest, 96, 155, 216, 218
self-knowledge, 20. *See also* belief;
    cogito; introspection
self-preservation, 262n11
self-realization, 167
Sellars, Wilfrid, 17–18, 236n6, 236n8,
    236n9, 239n25
Sencerz, Stefan, x
Sennett, James, 243n25
Senor, Thomas, x
sense-data, 36,
sense-datum theory, 240n5
Sibley, W. M., 263n14
Sidgwick, Henry, 265n28
Sinnott-Armstrong, Walter, x, 257n7
situational justification. *See*
    justification, situational
skepticism, 25, 49–50, 143–44, 187.
    See also practical skepticism
Smith, Michael, x
Smith, Tara, 250n1
Sober, Elliott, 263n11, 263n17
Socratic teaching, 34, 41
Solomon, Robert C., 271n15
Sosa, David, x
Sosa, Ernest, x, 237n16, 270n5
sources of justification. *See* basic
    source; justification, sources of
speech acts, 244n1
Steup, Matthias, x, 260n31
Strawson, Galen, 273n27
structural justification. *See*
    justification, structural
Stump, Eleonore, x
Sturgeon, Nicholas, x
subjectivity, 182, 184, 224. *See also*
    objectivity

supervenience, 253n14, 254n23
Swinburne, Richard, x

theoretical commitment. *See* cognitive
    commitment
theoretical reason. *See*
    foundationalism; justification;
    rationality; reason;
    reasonableness; well-
    groundedness
Thomson, Judith Jarvis, x, 267n10
Throop, William, x
Timmons, Mark C., x, xi, 239n26,
    269n22
Tolhurst, William, xi
truth, 224, 243n28
Tuomela, Raimo, x, 261n31

Ullian, Joseph, 241n12
unconscious belief. *See* belief,
    unconscious
underdetermination, 14, 92, 266n6
utilitarianism, 147, 160

valuation, 75, 106, 220
valuational principle, 220
value, 73, 214, 253n13, 253n14,
    254n24
  inherent, 100, 253n19
  intrinsic, 74, 95, 99–101, 183,
    253n14, 254n24, 261n34
  moral, 96, 270n9
  overall, 138–39
  See also reasons; rewardingness;
    well-groundedness
van Fraassen, Bas C., 261n31
van Roojen, Mark, x
Velleman, David, 256n4
virtue, 152, 163, 208, 258n14, 264n23,
    270n5, 273n29
  epistemic, 19, 237n16
  moral, 163
  second-order, 152
Vogel, Jonathan, xi
volition, 65, 245n6
voluntariness, 190, 203, 211
voluntarism, doxastic. *See* doxastic
    voluntarism

Wallace, Jay, xi
wanting, 61, 62, 66, 245n7, 272n19.
    See also desire
weakness of will, 150, 222
Wedgwood, Ralph, xi
well-groundedness, 19, 28, 78, 88,
    129, 131, 134, 171–72, 180,
    216, 232, 255n6. *See also*
    grounding; justification;
    rationality; reasons
will, 64–65, 111, 112, 131, 271n11

Williams, Bernard, 248n25, 260n28
Williams, Michael, 241n13, 268n18
Wilson, David Sloan, 263n11, 263n17
wishful thinking, 27, 47, 185, 245n4
Wittgenstein, Ludwig, 268n20
Wolterstorff, Nicholas, 260n31
Wright, Crispin, 250n36

Zagzebski, Linda, x, 237n16
Zimmerman, Michael A., xi, 253n18,
    262n4